Re-Reading the Prophets
through Corporate Globalization

CENTER AND LIBRARY FOR THE BIBLE AND SOCIAL JUSTICE SERIES

Laurel Dykstra and Ched Myers, editors
Liberating Biblical Study
Scholarship, Art, and Action in Honor of the Center and Library for the Bible and Social Justice

Norman K. Gottwald
Social Justice and the Hebrew Bible
3 volumes

Elaine Enns and Ched Myers
Healing Haunted Histories
A Settler Discipleship of Decolonization

Richard A. Horsley
Jesus and the Politics of Roman Palestine

Matthew J. M. Coomber
Re-Reading the Prophets through Corporate Globalization
A Cultural-Evolutionary Approach to Economic Injustice
in the Hebrew Bible

Re-Reading the Prophets through Corporate Globalization

A Cultural-Evolutionary Approach to Economic Injustice in the Hebrew Bible

Matthew J. M. Coomber

CASCADE *Books* · Eugene, Oregon

RE-READING THE PROPHETS THROUGH CORPORATE
GLOBALIZATION
A Cultural-Evolutionary Approach to Economic Injustice in the
Hebrew Bible

Center and Library for the Bible and Social Justice

Original hardback edition (2010) published by Gorgias Press, Pisca-
taway, New Jersey.

Cascade Books
An Imprint of Wipf and Stock Publishers
199 W. 8th Ave., Suite 3
Eugene, OR 97401

www.wipfandstock.com

Paperback ISBN: 978-1-6667-0075-6

Cataloging-in Publication Data:

Names: Coomber, Matthew J. M., author.
Title: Re-reading the prophets through corporate globalization : a cul-
    tural-evolutionary approach to economic injustice in the Hebrew
    Bible / Matthew J. M. Coomber.
Description: Eugene, OR: Cascade Books, 2022. | Center and Library
    for the Bible and Social Justice Series. | Includes bibliographical
    references and index.
Identifiers: ISBN: 978-1-6667-0075-6 (paperback).
Subjects: Bible. Prophets—Criticism, interpretation, etc. | Social jus-
    tice—Religious aspects—Judaism. | Economics—Moral and ethi-
    cal aspects. | Globalization—Economic aspects.
Classification: HM671 .C645 2022 (print).

For my wife, Sarah

CONTENTS

PREFACE TO THE CASCADE BOOKS PAPERBACK EDITION

THE ACCIDENTAL BEGINNINGS OF RE-READING THE PROPHETS THROUGH CORPORATE GLOBALIZATION

As a seminary student aspiring towards priestly ordination in the U.S. Episcopal Church, I spent sleepless nights working to discern whether my call was to parish ministry or a vocation in the academy. Eventually, the pull toward doctoral studies grew greater, and I promised both God and myself that any future academic career would set its focus beyond the walls of the academy. A few years later, as a newly ordained priest starting a doctoral program at the University of Sheffield, I was ready to delve into prophetic texts against economic exploitation, set in the context of late eighth-century Judah. This was to be my starting point for exploring whether or not biblical literature could effectively confront modern economic injustices.

Early into my studies at Sheffield it became apparent that a sizable obstacle stood between me and my research: the biblical texts with which I was working offered very few contextual clues. Hidden are the identities of those who would "join house to house, field to field" (Isa 5:8), the methods employed to seize the land rights of others, and any indication as to who suffered as a result. This body of prophetic literature also neglects to list which Judean laws, if any, had been broken by these actions. And to make matters yet more difficult, most of these writings—or at least the versions that had been handed down—were penned centuries after the period to which they were attributed. In short, any contextual markers that may have been apparent to the oracles' ancient audiences are a mystery to modern readers.

One can imagine the zero-gravity feeling I experienced when I realized the difficulty I faced in discerning the relevance of these prophetic texts to the modern world, when their own ancient contexts are unclear. It was apparent that my research required reorientation, leading my doctoral studies to shift from exploring whether or not prophetic texts can effectively confront modern systemic-poverty to a study on how modern circumstances might shed light on the hidden contexts behind this area of literature. Through an interdisciplinary approach that drew upon economic anthropology, I developed a heuristic tool for exploring the hidden economic contexts that rural Judean producers faced during the massive demographic shifts that took place in the late eighth century. It was my hope that by engaging this new line of research, I might also make progress on my original question pertaining to the relevancy of prophetic texts to modern justice concerns.

The interpretive tool presented in this book draws upon cyclical patterns of land consolidation that are found around the world and across time, in which societies abandon producer-focused subsistence strategies in favor of political-economic schemes that favor administrators. Due to evidence of this pattern unfolding as Judah was absorbed into Assyria's imperial economy in the late eighth century, and the fact that there are several instances of this pattern taking place in living memory, I found a basis for comparative study. Through examining the effects of this same land-consolidation pattern on farming communities in mid-twentieth century ce Tunisia, new insights were gained into the economic contexts surrounding prophetic complaints against usufruct abuse[1] and other concerns, including religious corruption and the weakening of community bonds among rural producers. Research I have conducted and published since *Re-Reading the Prophets through Corporate Globalization* has used these discoveries to explore my original question of whether or not Hebrew prophetic texts might effectively address injustice in the modern world.

---

[1] "Usufruct" refers to the right to access the productive capabilities of a plot of arable land (i.e. the right to farm that land and reap the benefits).

INSIGHTS GAINED SINCE FIRST PUBLICATION

Upon revisiting earlier publications, I inevitably consider what I would have done differently were I to have had the knowledge I have gained since. While the body of this paperback edition remains in its original form, I will use this section to offer some insights that I have gained which are relevant and might prove useful while reading this book.

Biblical ethoi are as complex and diverse as the biblical texts from which they originate. The Hebrew Bible's laws, stories, and sayings pertaining to right economic-conduct represent theologies and cultures that span centuries. Therefore, to superimpose any single economic ethos upon the entirety of the Hebrew Bible would be as foolhardy as imposing a single economic ethos on second-millennium Christianity. For example, whereas Genesis 41 champions centralized control of production and distribution, Micah 2 reflects a desire for local control without intervention. While Proverbs 18 proclaims what modern readers might call *self-determination* as the path out of impoverishment, Deuteronomy 15 acknowledges systemic poverty and demands relief for the afflicted. But despite the Hebrew Bible's diversity of viewpoints, a recurring thread runs throughout its texts, surfacing and resurfacing among laws, stories, oracles, and proverbs that are separated by culture, geography, and time: the biblical ethos of community responsibility for the wellbeing of the individual.

While I had recognized a biblical spirit of concern for those who had fallen between society's cracks, I first encountered this overarching ethos of community responsibility through Richard Horsley. Over the past several years, this recurring biblical ethos—which the biblical authors borrowed from yet earlier cultures—has become a primary area of my research, and one which I see as connected to my work in this book.

A prime example of the ethos of community responsibility for the wellbeing of the individual is found in YHWH's charge to ensure the care of the needy (*'evyon*) in the Deuteronomic Code. Written in the context of sabbatical laws that sought to take the *bite*[2] out of debt, this ethos is embodied in a radical declaration:

> There will, however, be no one in need among you, because the LORD is sure to bless you in the land that the LORD your God is giving you as a possession to occupy, if only you will obey the LORD your God by diligently observing this entire commandment that I command you today. (Deut 15:4–5)

In a sign that the authors of Deuteronomy 15 were not naïve about the prospects of God's people adhering to the aforementioned commandment, verse 11 acknowledges that "there will never cease to be some in need on the earth." Norman Gottwald laments that readers often "pervert" this verse by treating it as defeatist, claiming that poverty is unavoidable and not much can be done about it. Rather, Gottwald argues, "Far from justifying poverty as a natural phenomenon, the text is clearly saying that there will always be people who fall into poverty, but they must be cared for by an open-handed and open-hearted community," referencing verses 7–10.[3] Gottwald's argument is bolstered by the Deuteronomic Code's warning that not only should people be willing to help a neighbor in need, but that the help must be given willingly and with a positive attitude:

> You should rather open your hand, willingly lending enough to meet the need, whatever it may be. Be careful that you do not entertain a mean thought, thinking, "The seventh year, the year of remission, is near," and therefore view your needy neighbor with hostility and give nothing; your neighbor might cry to the LORD against you, and you would incur guilt. (Deut 15:8–9)

Such a command was particularly pertinent to those for whom the passage was first written down: elites who were able to access written texts. This ethos of community responsibility is also present in the jubilee laws of the Holiness Code, which relate more directly to the interpretive model being presented in this book.

---

[2] The Hebrew word *nashekh*, or "bite," is also a word used for collecting interest on a debt.
[3] Gottwald, "Early Israel," 7.

In agrarian societies around the world and throughout time, from Bronze-Age Nuzi to twentieth century CE Tunisia and Vietnam, access to arable land has ensured access to livelihood, shelter, and the dietary sustenance of those who farm. A cornerstone to safeguarding this access has been to make any permanent transfer of usufruct illegal, religiously taboo, or both.[4] Drawing upon YHWH's voice, the authors of Lev 25:23–24 sought to convey the importance of such protections by writing:

> But the land must not be sold beyond reclaim, for the land is mine [YHWH's]; you are but strangers resident with me. Throughout the land that you hold, you must provide for the redemption of the land.

Similar to Deuteronomy 15, this passage may be idealistic but it also contains pragmatic elements. A complete ban on usufruct-transfer could prove fatal for families suffering successive crop failures, which were not uncommon due to the erratic meteorological conditions of the Southern Levant. During times when food-stuffs were desperately needed, usufruct could be used as a means of exchange; a total ban on usufruct exchange would have left desperate families with few options for recourse. Therefore, the Jubilee authors worked to ensure that no transfer of usufruct could be permanent, thus lessening the potential for abuse. This was facilitated through a series of safety nets.

Jubilee's first safety net demanded, "If your kinsman is in crisis and has to sell part of his holding, his nearest redeemer shall come and redeem what his kinsman has sold" (Lev 25:25). In other words, if a struggling farmer had to sell a portion of his[5] usufruct, it was the duty of the farmer's nearest kin to spend what was required to restore the struggling farmer's access to his landed inheritance. It should be noted that no stipulations were included in this command; whether the farmer struggled due to poor luck or poor decision-making, his kin were responsible for restoring the family's usufruct, if able.

---

[4] This matter is addressed on pages 180–83 of this volume.
[5] These masculine pronouns reflect the fact that only men could own land.

The second safety net stipulated that if the struggling farmer became able to repurchase the land, himself, he was to do so right away (Lev 25:26–27). The purchase price was, however, to reflect the remaining value of the contract. If a farmer had sold the usufruct of ten units of land for ten years in exchange for ten units of grain, and was able to repurchase the usufruct after five years, only five units of grain was to be owed to the creditor: the creditor had benefited from those five years of access to the land's productive capabilities and, therefore, that portion was not owed. Unlike economic systems driven by profit, this system's priority was weighted toward mutual benefit.[6]

If the first two safety nets failed to restore the struggling farmer's usufruct, a final line of defense was provided in Lev 25:28: the year of jubilee. Having deemed the land as the property of YHWH, and mortals as the deity's tenants (v. 23), no Israelite had the right to sell any part of the land; only the land's usufruct could be sold, and for a maximum of forty-nine years. In the final year of the cycle, all usufruct was to be returned to its original family. A struggling farmer might not live to see the land returned, but the law would help protect his family from inter-generational poverty. Simultaneously, it would have helped to keep families in positions of advantage from compounding their wealth through acquiring the lands of desperate farmers, and gaining control over them.

Like so much pertaining to the ancient world, it is impossible to determine the motivations behind the jubilee laws in the Holiness Code. Whether they were to protect producers from losing their families' usufruct, to reclaim land for elites upon return from the Babylonian Exile, to fulfil cultic functions, or as an ancient form of *virtue signaling*, these laws were included in Hebrew sacred texts, and the pre-biblical ethos they represent are referenced time and again. The ethos surfaces in laws against tampering with boundary markers (Deut 19:14 and 27:17; Prov 22:28 and 23:10), stories that condemn the abuse of neighbors of lower status (1 Kings 21; 2 Kings 12; Nehemiah 5), and of particular importance to this book, it is reflected in the prophetic oracles that attacked

---

[6] Roland Boer describes the differences between debt and credit systems in *Sacred Economy*, 156–63.

those who violated their neighbor's access to usufruct, as found in Isa 5:8–10 and Mic 2:1–4.

Had I written this book in 2022, I would have connected the prophetic condemnations against usurping a neighbor's usufruct in Isa 5:8–10 and Mic 2:1–4 to the ethos of community responsibility for the wellbeing of the individual. While including this ethos would not have altered the book's trajectory or conclusions in any significant way, it would have effectively highlighted how these texts—and the concerns they appear to express—connect with numerous other passages throughout the Hebrew Bible. Whether Isa 5:8–10 and Mic 2:1–4 were written out of concern for those who lost access to usufruct in eighth-century Judah or a later time, out of prophetic authors' self-interest in the face of reforms that adversely affected religious elites, or a combination of these factors,[7] connecting Isa 5:8–10 and Mic 2:1–4 to an overarching biblical ethos would have been an interesting exploration. For the time being, such a survey will have to wait for a future publication.

IN GRATITUDE FOR THOSE WHO MADE THIS PAPERBACK EDITION POSSIBLE

It was not long after finishing my doctoral studies that Gorgias Press and I signed a contract to publish *Re-Reading the Prophets through Corporate Globalization*. I was grateful for their willingness to take on a new scholar, and I am deeply thankful for their generosity in releasing the paperback rights to Cascade Books. It was K. C. Hanson who invited me to publish this paperback edition with Cascade, and I offer him my heartfelt thanks; he has been a fantastic partner throughout the process. I would also like to extend my gratitude to Crystal L. Hall for taking the time to proofread this introduction and for sharing her expert insights and advice. And last, but surely not least, I am ever grateful to my loving parents, James and Eleanor, who have proofread every piece of academic work I have ever written, including this one.

Matthew J. M. Coomber, March 2022

---

[7] Coomber, "Caught in the Crossfire?"

WORKS CITED

Boer, Roland. *The Sacred Economy of Ancient Israel.* Library of Ancient Israel. Louisville: Westminster John Knox, 2015.

Coomber, Matthew J.M. "Caught in the Crossfire? Economic Injustice and Prophetic Motivation in Eighth-Century Judah." *Biblical Interpretation* 19 (2011) 396–432.

Gottwald, Norman K. "Early Israel as an Anti-Imperial Community." In *Social Justice and the Hebrew Bible*, 2:3–19. Center and Library for the Bible and Social Justice Series. Eugene, OR: Cascade Books, 2016.

PREFACE

This book is a revised version of the Ph.D. thesis that I completed in October 2009 at the University of Sheffield, "The Song Remains the Same? Corporate Globalization as a Model for Interpreting Prophetic Complaints Against Landownership Abuse."

I arrived in Sheffield in the autumn of 2005, ready to explore the similarities between ancient prophetic complaints against injustice and the injustices that have been carried out through corporate globalization during the past sixty years, or so I had thought. As is often the case with research, several obstacles to achieving my initial goal quickly appeared, placing the course of my research on a very necessary detour.

The most obvious obstacle to comparing ancient and modern instances of economic injustice against farmers was a lack of evidence pertaining to the ancient context. Modern examples of the oppression of farmers as a result of neoliberalism are abundant, but finding convincing evidence for the injustices referred to in the writings of the Hebrew Prophets proved to be a far more difficult task. Faced with only half of a comparative structure, which makes for a poor contrast, I set out to see if an ancient context could be found.

Prophetic complaints against landownership abuse in the Hebrew Bible rarely disclose the identities of perpetrators, victims, or the socio-economic circumstances surrounding the injustices that they decry; this was the root of my comparative dilemma. In searching for answers or clues, I turned to biblical commentaries for direction. Several commentaries *did* provide a context for Judean landownership abuse, often blaming a group of amoral merchants who stole land from defenseless farmers. I could have used this scenario as a basis for my research, but found this interpretation to be unsatisfactory. While the *evil merchant versus the poor farmer* appeared to be the prevalent consensus amongst several scholars, any justification for this conclusion was rarely offered. With the notable exceptions of Joseph Blenkinsopp and Ehud Ben Zvi, many of the commentaries that I encountered appeared to reiterate a common view that lacked either a discernable or accountable origin. It was upon the discovery of Marvin Chaney and D.N. Premnath's use of societal patterns in addressing prophetic complaints against injustice that I found a foothold.

In no way do I consider the interpretive approach offered in this book as a model for providing definite historical answers to the many contextual questions that surround prophetic complaints against economic injustice. Rather, it is my hope that the cultural-evolutionary theory proposed here can serve as a heuristic tool to allow new questions to be asked and new life to be breathed into a body of biblical literature that addresses a variety of important justice issues, from political and religious corruption to the mistreatment of vulnerable members of society. I also hope to demonstrate that the challenges that these ancient authors faced may not have been so dissimilar from those that we face today, despite the vast differences between their social worlds and ours.

Matthew J.M. Coomber
March 20, 2010

ACKNOWLEDGMENTS

The research that comes out of a Ph.D. dissertation may be credited to a single individual, but it is achieved through the help, advice, and generosity of many. I would like to take this opportunity to thank some of the many people who have made this book possible.

There are many, many people who influenced me in a variety of ways before I arrived at the Ph.D. phase of my education. Some of my early influences include Kathy Dane, Ken Grant, Larry Alderink, James Aageson, Ernest Simmons, Roy Hammerling, Steven Paulson, Kyle Pasewark, Shawn Carruth, Dzogchen Ponlop Rinpoche, Judith Simmer-Brown, Brian Irwin, John McLaughlin, W. Derek Suderman, and David Neelands. I would also like to offer my special thanks to the late Brian Peckham, SJ. Brian was both a mentor and a dear friend who helped me to approach and appreciate of the Hebrew Bible and the richness of its languages from a variety of perspectives.

The help, advice, and time given by my doctoral supervisor at Sheffield, Hugh Pyper, were both generous and invaluable. Hugh was instrumental in helping me to clarify my ideas and to "get all of the horses running in the same direction." He was an absolute joy to work with and I am immeasurably thankful for the time that he spent going over my work and for all of his helpful comments. I would also like to give special thanks to Keith Whitelam, who made a significant contribution to this study. Keith not only helped me to find the answers that I sought, but how to frame the question.

James Crossley was a great source of support throughout my Ph.D. studies and an astute internal examiner. I am thankful for his support and encouragement, and all the advice that he provided both during my oral defense and after. He is a great asset to both the Biblical Studies Department in Sheffield and the field. I would like to thank my external examiner, David Chalcraft, whose sociological insights and continuing encouragement have been invaluable. His ability to approach biblical texts from such a wide variety of perspectives is a great gift to the field of biblical studies.

There are so many more whose influence and encouragement deserve mention, but to keep this section of the book within a reasonable size, I must abbreviate. I would like to acknowledge the significant contributions of all of those in the Department of Biblical Studies, both faculty and staff, who took an interest in my research and were quick to offer advice and support. In particular I would like to thank Philip Davies, Diana Edelman, Will Lamb, Barry Matlock, John Rogerson, Loveday Alexander, David Clines, Alison Bygrave, and Gillian Fogg. I would also like to thank my fellow students, both within and outside the field: Richard Hawes, Il-Seung Chung, Dohyung Kim, Michelle Krejci, Sehyun Kim, Cynthia Shafer-Elliott, Stephen Woolen, Gillian Heald, Emmanuel Twum-Baah, and Pawel Wolinski, Eleanor Macdonald, Jamie Hilton, Isabelle Charmantier, Brian Clarke, Kathleen Noss Van Buren, Tyler Van Buren, Mania Mokhtarzadeh, Ebrahim Gharaee, Sean Devlin, and Cynthia Yip, who helped to make the experience so enjoyable.

My heartfelt thanks go out to all of the other academics that answered my questions, responded to my emails, and offered their encouragement. Among these are Paul Joyce, Mary Mills, George Brooke, Diana Lipton, Walter Houston, Gerald West, Francesca Stavrakopolou, John Barton, Bernard Jackson, Joseph Blenkinsopp, Stanley Hauerwas, Noam Chomsky, Ariel Buira, Israel Finkelstein, Stephen J. King, Mario Liverani, Margaret Barker, Philip Esler, and Indranil Dutta. Thank you to Katie Stott at Gorgias Press for all of her help with the publication of this book, from start to finish.

I would like to acknowledge the invaluable contribution that my family has made. I am so very thankful for my parents, Jim and Eleanor, who spent countless hours proofreading my work, sending plenty of books and care packages, and made a number of trips to visit us in England. They were a wonderful source of support, as they have always been. Thanks to my sister Sarah and her husband Jon, who came to England to visit us and were always quick to offer their encouragement. I am thankful for the great support, and encouragement of Sue and Steven Kading, who raised my wife to be a wonderful person. I am very thankful for all of the support and help that I received from Matt and Sam Kading, Liz Kading, and Ben Scully. I want offer a special thanks to thank my son, Alistair Matthew, who came into our lives while in Sheffield. His love of lights, puppies, trains, trees and his contagious excitement for the world around him always keep me laughing and serve as a constant reminder of what really matters in life. Finally, I want to thank my wife, Sarah, for whom this book is dedicated. She put food on the table, a roof over our heads, and helped me to keep things in perspective by making me take breaks to enjoy the beautiful nature that surrounds Sheffield. Without her and her support, none of the following could have been done.

ABBREVIATIONS

AH	*anno Hegirae* 'In the year of Muhammad's flight from Mecca to Medina' (from 622CE)
BCE	Before the Common Era
CE	Common Era
EB	Early Bronze Age
EEC	European Economic Community
G24	Group of Twenty-Four (Nations)
G7	Group of Seven (Nations)
GDP	Gross Domestic Product
HIPC	Highly Indebted Poor Countries
IA	Iron Age
IBRD	International Bank for Reconstruction and Development
IFI	International Financial Institution
IMF	International Monetary Fund
JPS	Jewish Publication Society
JSOT	Journal for the Study of the Old Testament
MB	Middle Bronze Age
NGO	Non-Governmental Organization
OPEC	Organization of Petroleum Exporting Countries
SAP	Structural Adjustment Program
UGTT	Union Générale des Travailleurs Tunisiens
UNCHR	United Nations Commission on Human Rights
UNICEF	United Nations Children's Fund

1 INTRODUCTION: THE LOST CONTEXTS OF EIGHTH-CENTURY PROPHECY

The prophetic books of the Hebrew Bible offer a wealth of material that addresses a variety of forms of economic injustice. From decrying the vanity of the cows of Bashan who were accused of oppressing the poor and crushing the needy[1] to lamenting against those who exploited their workers to serve their own interests on days of fasting,[2] the prophetic writers did not shy away from confrontation or pull any punches with those whom they believed had unjustly denied the needs of others for personal gain. However, while texts within Amos, Micah, and Isaiah that are attributed to the eighth century BCE offer examples of economic injustice in ancient Palestine, they present a cumbersome obstacle: the ambiguity that surrounds their socio-historical contexts. Take Isa. 5.8, for example:

הוי מגיעי בית בבית   שדה בשדה יקריבו

עד אפס מקום   והושבתם לבדכם בקרב הארץ:

The only contextual information provided by this verse against landownership abuse is that one generic group displaced another generic group by joining houses and fields together. Although the missing contextual factors, such as the identities of the perpetrators and the victims of this injustice, the motivations behind these land acquisitions, and their overall effects on Judean society, would have

---

[1] Amos 4.1–3

[2] Isa. 53.3

[3] "Ah, you who join house to house, who add field to field, until there is room for no one but you, and you are left to live alone in the midst of the land!"

3

been apparent to the authors' original audiences,[4] they remain hidden from the twenty-first century reader.

As is so often the case when dealing with the ancient world, attempts to interpret biblical accounts of landownership abuse in eighth-century Judah have been frustrated by both a lack of extra-biblical evidence and confusion as to how to interpret what little evidence is available. Rather than presenting a detailed account of the socio-economic realities that Judeans faced during this transformative period, in which population levels appear to have surged and economic activity flourished,[5] limited archaeological and literary data pertaining to land tenure in Judah provides a picture that is unclear at best and virtually undecipherable at worst. Baruch Levine notes that in addition to a biblical record that is devoid of any actual documents of land conveyance or deeds of land ownership in Palestine, "we do not possess court records, official correspondence or royal edicts from the kingdoms of northern Israel or Judah."[6] Due to such deficiencies, it is not likely that the effects of the economic and societal changes that took place in eighth-century Judah will ever be known with certainty. The only clues that are available to those who would attempt to decipher the socio-economic contexts behind landownership abuse in eighth-century Judah are the remains of significant urban and rural building projects, which indicate a period of increased economic activity, and the rather vague protests of a segment of the religious elite that are attributed to this time, but cannot be dated with certainty.[7] Just

---

[4] "Authors'" and "audiences" are in the plural to reflect the years of redaction that took place prior to canonization.

[5] Finkelstein and Silberman, "Temple and Dynasty: Hezekiah, the Remaking of Judah and the Rise of the Pan-Israelite Ideology," *JSOT* 30, no. 3 (2006).

[6] Levine. "Farewell to the Ancient Near East: Evaluating Biblical References of Ownership of Land in Comparative Perspective," in *Privatization in the Ancient Near East and Classical World* eds. Hudson and Levine; Cambridge: Peabody Museum of Archaeology and Ethnology, 1996), 224.

[7] Much debate has surrounded the dating of prophetic literature in the past few decades. This debate with only play a peripheral role in this book, as the actual dating of these complaints against landownership

as the effect that this period of heightened economic growth had on the inhabitants of Judah will remain somewhat of a mystery, so too will the socio-economic contexts that lie beneath the prophetic texts that address infringements on land rights.[8]

Despite a lack of evidence pertaining to the societal contexts behind these prophetic complaints, several biblical scholars have sought to understand the circumstances that are believed to have resulted in a loss of land, home, and inheritance for at least a segment of the Judean population in the eighth century. Alongside the importance that these texts hold for three of the world's major religions,[9] they are of particular interest because they address a type of injustice that has been a part of the human experience for millennia. From the warnings of the Egyptian teacher Ptah-Hotep in third millennium BCE to the protests of *Subcomandante Insurgente* Marcos in the modern-day Mexican state of Chiapas, the threat that the unjust seizure of land poses for farmers and social stability has inspired condemnation from religious and political leaders alike. The desire to understand the socio-economic contexts behind prophetic complaints against injustice have not only raised questions about the abuses themselves, but several peripheral questions as well, such as who wrote these texts, what their motivations were, and whether any larger societal issues might be hidden within the complaints.

While some biblical scholars have produced a socio-economic context for their interpretations of these texts by only using what little information is available within the biblical record, other scholars have looked for clues outside the field of biblical studies. Both Marvin Chaney and D.N. Premnath, for example, have applied the recurring patterns of abuse that cultural-evolutionary theorists as-

---

abuse is not as significant to the overall thesis as the fact that they are attributed to the eighth-century.

[8] It is not even likely that the final redactors of Isa. 5.8–10 and Mic. 2.1–2 were completely aware of these contexts since they were likely compiled centuries after these events took place.

[9] The book of Isaiah is found in both the Hebrew Bible and the Christian Old Testament, while Islam reveres the writings attributed to the prophet Isaiah.

sociate with rapid economic development in agrarian societies, which often results in heightened trade activity and a centralization of production and landownership. Through considering these cultural-evolutionary patterns alongside the significant demographic and economic developments that took place in late eighth-century Judah, Chaney's and Premnath's findings have produced valuable results that offer new avenues through which to interpret prophetic complaints against injustice.

Although Chaney and Premnath have each made important contributions by shedding new light on the missing contexts behind prophetic complaints against injustice, their research has thus far been limited to applying abstract theories to the ancient past. This book will argue, with all necessary caveats, that the use of cultural-evolutionary theory in biblical studies can be augmented by considering the tangible effects of cultural evolution on modern-day agrarian societies as they are absorbed into our current economic world-system: corporate globalization. To accomplish this exercise, two passages that address the problem of landownership abuse in Judah, Isa. 5.8–10 and Mic. 2.1–2, will be considered alongside 1) evidence of a major societal shift in Judah during the period to which these passages are attributed and 2) the effects of cultural evolution on a modern-day agrarian society that has been thrust into social, economic, and cultural changes by the neoliberal ideals and policies of corporate globalization: the north African country of Tunisia. Before delving into the potential value of using a modern context to evaluate the abuses found in such passages as Isa. 5.8–10 and Mic. 2.1–2, a look at previous interpretations of these texts is needed.

A. TRADITIONAL INTERPRETATIONS OF LANDOWNERSHIP ABUSE IN EIGHTH-CENTURY JUDAH

Although there is no extra-biblical literature to support the righteous indignation that is expressed in Isa. 5.8–10 and Mic. 2.1–2, the evidential merit of these texts is no less valuable than a single dinosaur bone upon which a paleontologist will reconstruct an entire species. While these passages only provide a vague account of a perceived crime, as described by a single segment of Judah's literate elite, Isa. 5.8–10 and Mic. 2.1–2 offer a set of clues upon which biblical scholars have worked to reconstruct a socio-economic context for eighth-century Judah. Some scholars have attempted to reveal these contexts by considering either Isa. 5.8–10 or Mic. 2.1–2 on their own, while others have engaged in comparative analysis with other texts of the Hebrew Bible to gain a clearer understanding of the circumstances behind these protests against unjust land-acquisitions. Approaches such as these were used by several biblical commentators in the early to mid-twentieth century and, ultimately, led to a degree of repetition and stagnation within the field.

Biblical Commentary on Mic. 2.1–2 and Isa. 5.8–10

Before exploring various commentators' interpretations of the socio-economic context behind land ownership abuse in eighth-century Judah, it is important to address the subjective nature of biblical commentary. The medieval historian Norman Cantor claims that every history is an autobiography,[1] and the same holds true for biblical commentary. Although attempts may be made to view the world through the biblical authors' eyes, a person can never be entirely divorced from their own experiences and what they bring to the text.[2] Even when taking a mindful approach,

---

[1] Cantor, *Inventing the Middle Ages: The Lives, Works, and Ideas of the Great Medievalists of the Twentieth Century* (Cambridge: Lutterworth Press, 1992).

[2] In conversations with Hugh Pyper, he has rightly pointed out that it is difficult enough to discern the meanings of biblical texts from one's

commentators are unable to escape from the religious, political, and other societal biases and presumptions that ultimately find their way into their work. As the examples that are offered in this section reveal, biblical commentaries can often divulge more about the socio-economic world of the commentator than the period of the biblical text in question. Since this inability to remove oneself from his or her own paradigm works as a great equalizer, all that can be expected from commentators and historians is that they employ a wide periphery of perspective and work diligently to recognize and acknowledge the biases that they will ultimately bring to their interpretations.

While the inability of an individual to step outside of one's own place in time and culture presents one challenge to the biblical commentator, David Clines notes that the inability of some commentators to separate their interpretations from the ideologies found within biblical texts offers another.[3] Lamenting that such care is seldom taken, Clines writes that "it is a rare scholar who will step outside the ideology of the text and notice how severely traditional commentary has been constrained by the outlook of the text."[4] In many cases, a commentator's failure to distance him or herself from the ideology of the text can lead to a perpetual reiteration or reconfirmation of what previous commentators have already offered, adding little new to the conversation. Such failures can also lead to, what are hopefully, disingenuous statements. For example, in Juan Alfaro's commentary on Mic. 6.13–14 he flatly supports the text's claim that the total destruction of a nation is a righteous means of punishing a wealthy minority who have acted unjustly.[5] Such a bold statement that blindly backing the Iron Age principles reflected in the text is on par with supporting a call for

---

own perspective, let along trying to do so from the perspective of a person from the ancient Near East.

[3] These two problems can easily become confused as one projects their beliefs and notions about the biblical world onto that world, and then defends that perspective through the biblical author's voice.

[4] Clines, *Interested Parties: The Ideology and Readers of the Hebrew Bible* (ed. Exum; Sheffield: Sheffield Academic Press, 1995), 77.

[5] Alfaro, *Justice and Loyalty: A Commentary on the Book of Micah.* (Grand Rapids: Eerdmans, 1989),72.

the total destruction of Zimbabwe and its inhabitants as a response
to President Mugabe's oppressive policies towards his people. By
most modern standards, such a collective approach to punishment
appears outrageous. Nevertheless, such assertions are frequently
found in biblical commentary. While some commentators are careful to recognize the biases they bring to biblical texts, maintain an
degree of distance, and recognize that a picture-perfect image of
eighth-century Judah cannot be reconstructed, others are quick to
take sides with the ancient authors and draw definitive conclusions
with a level of certainty that would suggest that they had either
been first-hand witnesses or participants in the biblical events.

Mic. 2.1–2

2.1 הוי חשבי־און   ופעלי רע על־משכבותם

באור הבקר יעשוה   כי יש־לאל ידם:

2 וחמדו שדות וגזלו   ובתים ונשאו

ועשקו גבר וביתו   ואיש ונחלתו:6

Of the two passages addressed in this chapter, Mic. 2.1–2 offers the
most scathing indictment against those who oppressed their fellow
Judeans through the use of land seizures. Both the level of disdain
that these prophetic writers held for the perpetrators and the seriousness with which they addressed the offence of land ownership
abuse is found in the authors' use of the adjective רע,7 the noun
און,8 and the verb עשק9 to describe the people and the actions of
those who took the real property of others. It is through the rage
and passion with which this passage condemns the actions of those

---

6 "Woe to them who plan wickedness and make evil on their beds; at
morning light they do it because the power is in their hands. They desire
fields and they rob them, and houses, and they take them away. They oppress a man and his house, a man and his inheritance."

7 *Evil, wicked.* Brown, et al., *The Brown-Driver-Briggs Hebrew and English
Lexicon: With an Appendix Containing the Biblical Aramaic: Coded with Strong's
Concordance Numbers*: 948.

8 *Harm* or *injustice*, Brown, et al.:20.

9 To *oppress* or *extort* Brown, et al.:799.

who seized land that Joseph Blenkinsopp bases his view of Micah as a fierce defender of the rights of small-scale farmers.[10] A number of commentators, as shown below, interpret Mic. 2.1–2 as YHWH's interjection in a confrontation between wealthy elites and poor farmers.

A Common Interpretation

Despite the level of outrage that is expressed in Mic. 2.1–2, the authors of the passage did not offer their audience very much information as to the socio-economic context behind the land acquisitions that they were protesting. As in the example of Isa. 5.8 above, although contextual concerns may have been apparent to those whom they were addressing, such as the identities of perpetrators and victims, these factors remain hidden from the modern reader. All that can be extracted from a quick reading of Mic. 2.1–2 is that a group within the religious establishment accused one generic group of oppressing another generic group through coveting and seizing their land. Although the open set of questions that such a vague account allows could lead modern commentators in any number of interpretive directions, many of the commentaries that were produced in the past fifty years have been rather limited in their interpretations, varying only slightly from a consensus view that had developed by the mid-twentieth century.

Commentators James Mays and Ralph Smith have interpreted the tension being expressed within Mic. 2.1–2 as of an entirely economic nature, making the issue of landownership one that pit the wealthy against the poor. Mays and Smith each claim that it was *businessmen* who had been responsible for the suffering of those who lost their land. Mays interprets the offences carried out in Mic. 2.2 to be a product of economic prosperity, writing of vast "economic development which, supported by the policies of the royal court, had reached its climax in the eighth century."[11] According to Mays' assessment, as affluence increased, the government became more prone to corruption, allowing merchants to extend their

---

[10] Blenkinsopp, *A History of Prophecy in Israel: Revised and Enlarged* (Louisville: Westminster John Knox Press, 1996), 93.

[11] Mays, *Micah: A Commentary* (London: SCM Press LTD, 1976). 64.

wealth through land acquisition. Mays presents a group of oppor-
tunist merchants who, in his traditional view of Judean society, disregarded the land rights that had been established in the Torah, and
Lev. 25 in particular, to pursue prosperity at the expense of small-
scale farmers, who were vulnerable to corrupt judges.

Echoing Mays' interpretations of Mic. 2.1–2, Smith finds economic power and the involvement of a greedy merchant class to be
central to this passage. He suggests that the chief offenders in Mic.
2.1–2 were "a relatively small group of greedy, powerful businessmen who spent their nights devising schemes to take control over
the lands of the small farmers."[12] According to Smith, it was
through the businessmen's ability to pervert Judah's legal channels
that economic elites were able to expand their fiscal power and take
their neighbors' homes and land. Both Mays' and Smith's interpretations of the passage are based upon the existence of a long-
established Judean policy toward land tenure for these corruptible
judges and hypothetical businessmen to pervert. However, recent
interpretations of the archaeological record, published after Mays'
and Smith's commentaries were written, suggest that there is a lack
of evidence to support the existence of such an administrative body
that could uphold such a pan-Judean code under a YHWHist ideology prior to the eighth century. Mays' and Smith's assessment of
the passage works better with the more traditional interpretations
of Judean history, to which they subscribe.

As opposed to the *ruthless businessman* motif that Mays and
Smith propose, Juan Alfaro offers an alternative scenario that
maintains the notion that the protagonists of Mic. 2.1–2 were
members of the economic elite. Rather than placing merchants as
the culprits behind the land seizures, Alfaro argues that the economic elites in the passage were members of an organized criminal
cartel of "professional land-grabbers."[13] Alfaro explains that "the
rich are to constitute a 'family' [referring to the word מִשְׁפָּחָה in
verse three], a group of gangsters similar to a mafia family."[14] Al-

---

[12] Smith, *Micah - Malachi* (eds. Hubbard, Barker, Watts and Martin; 58
vols.; vol. 32; Waco: Word Books, 1984), 24.

[13] Alfaro, *Justice and Loyalty: A Commentary on the Book of Micah.*, 22.

[14] Alfaro, *Justice and Loyalty: A Commentary on the Book of Micah.*, 25.

faro's translation of the Hebrew is intriguing, but he fails to provide any justification of his interpretation of מִשְׁפָּחָה as a Gambino-like crime syndicate.[15] The word מִשְׁפָּחָה is traditionally translated as *clan* or *family*,[16] rather than a *mafia-style organization*.[17] Alfaro's rendering of the passage, which suggests the presence of an ancient racketeering ring that specialized in land acquisition, appears to be forced, inserting modern concepts of organized crime into the ancient past without providing any detailed justification for his assumptions.

In each of Mays', Smith's, and Alfaro's commentaries, we find Mic. 2.1–2 to represent a struggle between wealth and poverty. Whether businessmen or mobsters, the perpetrators within the passage use their wealth to gain power over the impoverished, even though there is no mention of merchants or the poor anywhere in the passage. It is likely that the victims of these land seizures became financially crippled after losing their property, but there is no textual reason to believe that the oppressed had been impoverished before they lost their land. Perhaps these traditional interpretations are correct, but no justification for their contextual hypotheses is offered in their commentaries. Perhaps Mays' and Smith's interpretations are rooted in the socio-economic environment in which their commentaries were written. During the 1970s and the 1980s in the United States it was common for large corporations and banks to increase their profits by foreclosing and consolidating the lands of struggling farms;[18] such a real-world understanding of land acquisition could easily find its way into these commentators' work. However, not all interpretations of Mic. 2.1–2 find economic elites to be behind the Judean land seizures.

---

[15] The Gambino family is a prominent New York-based organized crime cartel, of which the famed John Gotti, was the head in the late 1980s and early 1990s.

[16] Brown, et al.:1046-47.

[17] I have not been able to find this interpretation anywhere outside of Alfaro's commentary.

[18] Dorsey, "Free Enterprise vs. The Entrepreneur: Redefining the Entities Subject to the Antitrust Laws," *University of Pennsylvania Law Review* 125, no. 6 (1977). Humphries, "U.S. Small Farm Policy Scenarios for the Eighties," *American Journal of Agricultural Economics* 62, no. 5 (1980): 882-88.

Political Power

While Mays, Smith, and Alfaro appear to have only used clues within Mic. 2.2 to draw their contextual conclusions, other commentators' interpretations of the land seizures referred to in Mic. 2.2 are based on information given in the previous verse. Information that is provided by Mic. 2.1 has led some to consider that the protagonists of the passage were not necessarily merchants, but people with significant political or legal influence. This theory is based on the suggestion that Judean land seizures were not executed spontaneously, but through premeditation and the use of an undefined power.

Ludwig Köhler interpreted the warning in Mic. 2.1 against those whom do evil on their beds and perform it in the morning as an indication that the land seizures in Mic. 2.2 were not carried out on a whim, but were the result of careful forethought and planning.[19] Whereas the criminal acts of those who wish to remain discreet tend to be planned during the daytime and carried out at night, Mic. 2.1 presents the reverse order. This reversal of how one might expect a crime to be committed may highlight the hubris with which the antagonists carried out their oppressive acts, perhaps suggesting that, although these land seizures had offended the religious sensibilities of the passage's authors, they were either lawful or condoned by local authorities.[20] If this were the case, such complacency could have been a point of contention among some members of the religious elite.

In addition to the idea that these land acquisitions were premeditated, other commentators have considered the final words of

---

[19] Köhler, *Hebrew Man* (trans. Ackroyd; London: SCM Press, 1956), 151. Ehud Ben Zvi notes that "do evil upon their beds" should not be taken literally. Ben Zvi argues that to do so is misleading as it fails to "recognize the metathetic parallelism in this line, namely, the implied transposition of verbs. In other words, the evildoers do their scheming, not their wrong deeds, while in bed." Ben Zvi, *Micah* (ed. Rolf P. Knierim; vol. XXIB; Grand Rapids: Eerdmans, 2000), 43.

[20] Or at the very least, condoned. "Local authorities" could refer to any degree of complexity from an advanced state legal system to a council of elders.

Mic. 2.1, כִּי יֶשׁ־לְאֵל יָדָם,[21] to further indicate that the injustices
carried out in verse two were committed by people in positions of
political power. Both Ben Zvi and John Dearman claim that the
phrase כִּי יֶשׁ־לְאֵל יָדָם supports the idea that these Judean land
seizures were carried out by those who could use their influence to
take land from their subordinates.[22] Through connecting the phrase
כִּי יֶשׁ־לְאֵל יָדָם to the ability to influence legal courts, Dearman
writes that "'because god/power is in their hand' seems to have a
legal connotation implying a right or prerogative and thus is com-
patible with a social setting of legal procedure in the gate of the
village."[23] Engaging in a less detailed analysis, Ben Zvi simply states
that the land seizures referred to in Mic. 2.2 were associated with
"worldly power."[24] Taking into account that worldly power had
enabled the perpetrators to take the land and inheritance rights of
others, Ben Zvi argues that Mic. 2.1–2 addresses "the concentration of property through land foreclosure, which may be accompanied by eviction and similar actions."[25] Whether this power was
political or economic in nature, since such power could also have
been rooted in a merchant's ability to bribe judges, Dearman and
Ben Zvi find that Mic. 2.1–2 addresses a tension between power
and subjugation rather than simply one of wealth and poverty.

Whereas Mays, Smith, Alfaro, and other scholars have made
the identification of the perpetrators of these land acquisitions a
priority, it is interesting to note that Ben Zvi finds value in the passage's ambiguity. Ben Zvi contends that the choice to leave out the
identity of those who took the land of others allows the passage to
take on a general form that is "devoid of unequivocal markers
pointing to a specific historical situation…these wrongdoers are

---

[21] "…for it is in the power of their hand."

[22] Dearman and Ben Zvi both note that this is the formula used in
Gen. 31.29, יֶשׁ־לְאֵל יָדִי לַעֲשׂוֹת עִמָּכֶם רָע, "It is in my power to do
you harm…" See Dearman, *Property Rights in the Eighth-Century Prophets: The
Conflict and its Background* (eds. Roberts and Talbert; vol. 106; Scholars
Press: Atlanta, 1988), 46. Ben Zvi, *Micah*, 43.

[23] Dearman, *Property Rights in the Eighth-Century Prophets: The Conflict and
its Background*, 46.

[24] Ben Zvi, *Micah*, 43.

[25] Ben Zvi, *Micah*, 44.

presented as a timeless type of 'land-grabber'"[26]: one that could be taken up by different referents depending on the reader's circumstances. While this characteristic can be of value in relating ancient injustices to the present, for the purposes of exploring the socio-economic contexts behind the text, the possible identity of these individuals will be pursued.

Isa. 5.8–10

5.8 הוֹי מַגִּיעֵי בַיִת בְּבַיִת שָׂדֶה בְשָׂדֶה יַקְרִיבוּ

עַד אֶפֶס מָקוֹם וְהוּשַׁבְתֶּם לְבַדְּכֶם בְּקֶרֶב הָאָרֶץ:

9 בְּאָזְנָי יְהוָה צְבָאוֹת אִם־לֹא בָּתִּים רַבִּים לְשַׁמָּה יִהְיוּ

גְּדֹלִים וְטוֹבִים מֵאֵין יוֹשֵׁב:

10 כִּי עֲשֶׂרֶת צִמְדֵּי־כֶרֶם יַעֲשׂוּ בַּת אֶחָת

וְזֶרַע חֹמֶר יַעֲשֶׂה אֵיפָה:[27]

The complaints found in Mic. 2.1–2 and Isa. 5.8–10 share similarities that are often cross-referenced by commentators.[28] As in Mic. 2.2, and mentioned above, the authors of Isa. 5.8 condemn one anonymous group for taking the homes and land of another anonymous group of victims. It may be due to these similarities, and the fact that these two passages are attributed to the same period, that several commentators' interpretations of Isa. 5.8–10's socio-economic context dovetail with those that have been attached to Mic. 2.1–2: presenting the economic elite as the culprits who took land from Judah's most vulnerable farmers.

---

[26] Ben Zvi, *Micah*, 44.

[27] "Woe to you who touch house to house, join field to field, until there ceases to be room and you dwell alone in the midst of the land. In my ears (said) the LORD of hosts surely many houses will lay desolate, great and pleasant ones without inhabitant. For ten acres of vineyard will produce one bath and a homer of seed will produce a ephah."

[28] A useful example of this can be found in von Rad, *Old Testament Theology* (eds. Mays, Newsom and Petersen; trans. Stalker; 2 vols.; vol. 1; Louisville: Westminster John Knox Press, 1962), 150, n.5.

The Businessman Motif

The common notion of wealthy businessmen seizing land from poor Judean farmers, as found in Mays' and Smith's interpretations of Mic. 2.1–2, is commonly found in commentaries on Isa. 5.8–10. Edward Kissane, Otto Kaiser, and A.S. Herbert have each argued that Isa. 5.8–10 reflects a time in which wealthy individuals oppressed the poor by working to bypass their rights in order to accumulate greater land wealth. The section heading of Kissane's analysis of Isa. 5.8–10, "The Rapacity of the Rich, and Jahweh's Threat of Requital," points to such a socio-economic context.[29] Kissane offers a scenario in which *wealthy* Judeans employed an extensive scheme to displace *the poor* so that they could build up large estates for themselves.[30] As a consequence of the plot, Kissane writes, "…the poor were reduced to the position of slaves and hirelings."[31] Through his traditional view of a well-established Judean state that followed a set of laws that had been built upon the commands of YHWH,[32] Kissane concludes that Isa. 5.8–10 addressed a rebellion amongst the rich against Judah's YHWHist-based legal system, which had previously ensured special protections for the poor, as found in Lev. 25.[33] Although the socio-economic context that Kissane deduces from Isa. 5.8–10 is rooted in early twentieth-century scholarship, several subsequent commentaries written in the mid to late-twentieth century do not deviate very far from his interpretations.

Herbert and Kaiser follow Kissane's vision of Isa 5.8–10's socio-economic context, also interpreting the passage as a condemna-

---

[29] Kissane, *The Book of Isaiah: Translated from a Critically Revised Hebrew Text with Commentary* (2vols.; vol. 1; Dublin: Browne and Nolan Limited, 1941). 57.

[30] Kissane, *The Book of Isaiah: Translated from a Critically Revised Hebrew Text with Commentary*, xl.

[31] Kissane, *The Book of Isaiah: Translated from a Critically Revised Hebrew Text with Commentary*, 57.

[32] It should be highlighted that Kissane's commentary was written in 1941, before recent interpretations of Judah's archaeological record were proposed.

[33] Kissane, *The Book of Isaiah: Translated from a Critically Revised Hebrew Text with Commentary*, 57.

tion against wealthy individuals who had seized land and destroyed the livelihood of poor farmers. Whereas Herbert envisions greedy merchants who "sought to buy up houses in the city and peasant holdings in the country,"[34] Kaiser's commentary offers a more elaborate account. Placing the passage into his understanding of eighth-century Judean society, which envisions a powerful Judean state that had dominated the region by the late Iron Age, Kaiser claimed that the "success of [King] Uzziah's foreign policy, the tributes of neighbouring countries, and the latifundia economy practiced by the king [brought] ready money" into the country.[35] Increased wealth among businessmen and Judah's "rising monetary economy," Kaiser continues, "led to a crisis among small house owners and land owners… who became totally dependent upon the large capitalists."[36] Subsequent archaeological interpretations that have become commonly accepted in biblical scholarship render a lot of Kaiser's interpretation moot, such as a lack of evidence for a monetary system in eighth-century Judah and a state that would have been in a position to impose tributes upon its much more powerful neighbors.[37] Nevertheless, the socio-economic contexts that Kaiser and Herbert present dovetail with Kissane's early twentieth-century interpretation of Isa. 5.8–10, as well as the above interpretations of land ownership abuse in Mic. 2.1–2.

Common Contexts

Several of the above commentators offer a socio-economic context in which a just economic and judicial system was corrupted by the ambitions of individual members of Judah's wealthy elite. In their bid to increase property wealth by creating vast estates, these corrupt individuals have been traditionally portrayed as infringing

---

[34] Herbert, *The Book of the Prophet Isaiah: Chapters 1-39* (eds. Ackroyd, Leaney and Packer; Cambridge: Cambridge University Press, 1973). 51.

[35] Kaiser, *Isaiah 1-12: A Commentary* (London: SCM Press LTD, 1972), 65.

[36] Kaiser, *Isaiah 1-12: A Commentary*, 65.

[37] Furthermore, "large capitalists" imposes modern economic concepts on the ancient texts, which does not only force modern assumptions on the past, but confuses the intent of the author.

upon the rights of Judean farmers, who were defenseless to resist the will of those who took their land for personal gain.

The lack of variation that is offered in many of these commentators' accounts might be attributed to their failure to, as Clines suggests, remove themselves from the authority of the biblical authors' accounts, and the overall biblical narrative in which they are set.[38] The above commentaries tend to assume the existence of a powerful Judean monarchy that oversaw a pan-Judean legal system that had been founded upon YHWHist law and developed with the best interests of the poor in mind. Considering that the concerted international efforts of the IMF and the World Bank to ensure protection for those most vulnerable to economic development in the twentieth-century CE have failed,[39] the presence of such a disciplined economic utopia in the eighth-century BCE is unlikely. Furthermore, alternative interpretations of archaeological evidence, which developed after most of these commentaries were published, suggest that no such dominant Judean state, or pan-Judah devotion to YHWH, existed prior to the late eighth century, if then.[40] Whether or not a Judean state had existed before the late eighth century, it is highly unlikely that the golden age of justice to which some of these commentators refer was ever a reality.

In contrast to the commentaries of Mays, Smith, and Kissane, Joseph Blenkinsopp's and John Hayes and Stuart Irvine's commentaries on Isa. 5.8 offer a more nuanced socio-economic approach,

---

[38] Rather, taking sides with the prophetic voice as they understood it through their own worldview. Mays and Alfaro, for example, both published their books in the 1980s: a decade known for a decrease in financial regulation under the Regan Administration in the United States. A biblical commentator who had lived through the Bolshevik Revolution in Russia may have interpreted this passage as pertaining to government land-seizure, either by the former establishment or by the Red Army, depending on political perspective.

[39] Kuhn, "United Nations Monetary Conference and the Immunity of International Agencies," *The American Journal of International Law* 38, no. 4 (1944): 663. Grey, "The Monetary Conference and China," *Far Eastern Survey* 13, no. 18 (1944): 165.

[40] Finkelstein and Silberman, "Temple and Dynasty: Hezekiah, the Remaking of Judah and the Rise of the Pan-Israelite Ideology."

taking injustices that are addressed elsewhere in Isaiah into consideration. Through cross-referencing Isa. 5.8–10 with complaints against injustice that are found in Isa. 10.1–2, in which the authors accuse those in positions of political power of drafting decrees and regulations to rob the poor of their rights, Blenkinsopp argues that the indictment in Isa. 5.8 was aimed toward the Judean political establishment, rather than wealthy individuals.[41] Blenkinsopp concludes that "[Isa.] 10:1–4a leads on naturally into 5:8–10, the theme of which is the manipulation of the legal system in order to confiscate houses and land."[42] Through cross-referencing Isa. 5.8 with Isa. 3.14, Hayes and Irvine's commentary also finds that political forces had been at work. Taking into account the authors of Isa. 3.14's condemnation of elders and princes for devouring the vineyard and keeping the spoils of the poor in their houses, Hayes and Irvine conclude that

> …if the people being condemned [in Isa. 5.8–10] are the same as those in 3.14–15, then Isaiah is denouncing the government officials and social leaders who, through money lending, land foreclosures, and their status as political administrators, are amassing enormous wealth from the peasant and small landowning classes.[43]

These interpretations, and those given by Ben Zvi and Dearman, which place the ruling elite at fault for eighth-century Judean land seizures, are in line with Marvin Chaney's and D.N. Premnath's interpretations of Isa. 5.8–10 and Mic. 2.1–2. However, unlike the traditional interpretations addressed above, Chaney and Premnath each view the problem of landownership abuse as having been much more widespread, affecting the whole of Judean society.

---

[41] Blenkinsopp, *Isaiah 1-39* (19; eds. Albright and Freedman; New York: Doubleday, 2000), 211.

[42] Blenkinsopp, *Isaiah 1-39*, 211.

[43] Hayes and Irvine, *Isaiah, the Eighth-Century Prophet: His Times and Preaching* (Nashville: Abingdon, 1987), 103.

B. CHANEY'S AND PREMNATH'S INTERPRETATIONS

Chaney's and Premnath's interpretations of the land seizures that are referred to in Isa. 5.8–10 and Mic. 2.1–2 are not completely divorced from the consensus view that many traditional commentators have prescribed to these texts. However, rather than relying solely on the scarce contextual evidence that is provided by these passages and the historical narratives that the biblical account provides, Chaney's and Premnath's interpretations are rooted in the radical societal changes that appear to have taken place in Judah during the late eighth century BCE, including unprecedented levels of economic development and population growth.[1] Unlike Mays, Smith, and Kissane's assessments of land seizures in Isaiah and Micah, Chaney and Premnath do not consider the land ownership abuses found in Isa. 5.8–10 and Mic. 2.1–2 to be the work of a few wicked individuals who broke from the norms of Judean society, but part of a transformative period in the eighth century, which reshaped previous approaches to land management.[2] Noting the work of other commentators on the subject, Chaney highlights this key point at which his contextual interpretations break from traditional commentary, writing,

> ...many modern readers of the prophetic books assume that these texts excoriate a few venal individuals who deviated from norms otherwise observed in what was a healthy and just economic system... little could be farther from the realities of an-

---

[1] Finkelstein and Silberman, "Temple and Dynasty: Hezekiah, the Remaking of Judah and the Rise of the Pan-Israelite Ideology." Finkelstein and Na'aman, "The Judahite Shephelah in the Late 8th and Early 7th Centuries BCE," *Tel Aviv* 31, no. 1 (2004). Blakely and Hardin, "Southwestern Judah in the Late Eighth Century B.C.E.," *Bulletin of the American Schools of Oriental Research* no. 326 (2002). Eitam, "Tel Miqne-Ekron: Survey of Oil Presses: 1985," *Excavations and Surveys in Israel* 5: 1986, (1987).

[2] Chaney, "Bitter Bounty: The Dynamics of Political Economy Critiqued by the Eighth-Century Prophets," in *Reformed Faith and Economics* (ed. Stivers; Lanham: University Press of America, 1989). Premnath, *Eighth Century Prophets: A Social Analysis* (St. Louis: Chalice, 2003).

cient Israel and Judah. As a careful reading of the oracles concerning economic dynamics makes clear, the prophets critique
certain changes in the political economy as an integrated
whole.[3]

Chaney explains that the commonly held view of a few venal individuals corrupting a just system stems from the cultural context in
which many of these commentators worked. He writes that their
interpretations of the socio-economic context behind the passage
reflect "the extreme individualism of American culture," rather
than any evidence found within the text.[4] Rather than having been
the work of a few amoral merchants who had amassed enough
wealth to subvert the pillars of land tenure in eighth-century Judah,
Chaney and Premnath both suggest that the region's approach toward land ownership, as a whole, experienced an evolutionary
transformation during the eighth century. A major component of
this transformation, according to both Chaney and Premnath, involved a policy of latifundialization, or the consolidation of smaller
plots of land into large estates, which placed Judah's arable lands
under the control of wealthy landlords.[5]

Through employing a social-scientific approach that considers
the sorts of economic developments that would likely have moved
Judean agriculturalists away from subsistence strategies towards the
specialized cultivation of exportable crops to be precursors of
abuse, Chaney and Premnath have moved away from traditional
interpretations to add something new to the conversation. They
propose a scenario in which Judean society, as a whole, had

---

[3] Chaney, "Bitter Bounty," 16.
[4] Chaney, "Bitter Bounty," 16.
[5] Chaney, "'Coveting Your Neighbor's House' in Social Context,' in
The Ten Commandments: The Reciprocity of Faithfulness (ed. Brown; *Library of
Theological Ethics*, eds. Lovin, Ottati and Schweiker; Louisville, Kentucky:
Westminster John Knox Press, 2004), 308. Premnath, "Latifundialization
in Isaiah 5.8-10," in *Social-Scientific Old Testament Criticism* (ed. Chalcraft;
Sheffield: Sheffield Academic Press, 1997), 305-06.

adopted a new and transformative economic model.[6] It is upon this premise that they build their socio-economic context for land ownership abuse in Isa. 5.8–10 and Mic. 2.1–2.

Chaney's and Premnath's Approach

The interpretive method that Chaney and Premnath have adopted in their approach to prophetic complaints against landownership, which considers recurring societal patterns that often accompany heightened economic activity, has breathed new life into the conversation surrounding prophetic complaints against injustice. Through their method, they present an eighth-century context in which a cabal of Judean political elites worked to centralize the region's agrarian production through a process of latifundialization.[7] Chaney and Premnath claim that, through pressuring small-scale farmers into the specialized cultivation of exportable crops like grapes and olives, these farmers were left prone to crop failure and debt. As debts mounted, struggling farmers were forced into foreclosure, allowing Judean elites to gain control of their land and maximize the production of exportable commodities like wine and olive oil.[8] According to Chaney and Premnath, the social cost of this economic paradigm-shift was a loss of the traditional livelihood and inheritance rights of Judah's subsistence communities.

Chaney's and Premnath's hypotheses that farmers became prone to crop failure due to a shift away from subsistence agriculture and its risk-reducing strategies is plausible, considering that

---

[6] Chaney, "Micah - Models Matter: Political Economy and Micah 6:9-15," in *Ancient Israel: The Old Testament in its Social Context* (ed. Esler; London: SCM Press, 2005), 146-49.

[7] Chaney, "'Coveting Your Neighbor's House' in Social Context," 307-17. Premnath, "Latifundialization in Isaiah 5.8-10."

[8] Chaney, "Whose Sour Grapes? The Addressees of Isaiah 5:1-7 in the Light of Political Economy," in *The Social World of the Hebrew Bible: Twenty-Five Years of the Social Sciences in the Academy* eds. Simkins and Cook; *Semeia*, ed. Brenner; (Atlanta: Society of Biblical Literature, 1999), 106-09. Premnath, "Loan Practices in the Hebrew Bible," in *To Break Every Yoke: Essays in Honour of Marvin L. Chaney* eds. Coote and Gottwald, eds. Whitelam and Crossley; (Sheffield: Sheffield Phoenix Press, 2007). Premnath, "Latifundialization in Isaiah 5.8-10."

ancient Palestinian farmers were forced to contend with highly unfavorable meteorological conditions. Because of Palestine's geographical location at a crossroads between subtropical and temper-
ate atmospheric patterns, the highlands experience two distinct
seasons: a winter rainy season and a summer dry season. It is in the
balance between these varying times of precipitation that Judean
farmers had to calculate their farming strategies. A factor that made
such strategizing particularly difficult in Judah was that the winter
season does not follow a uniform pattern of precipitation, but can
rather play itself out in a variety of different ways, each of which
demand different planting and harvesting strategies. In the end,
farmers can expect total crop failure in three out of ten years due to
insufficient rainfall if risk-reducing measures are not employed to
hedge their bets.[9] Premnath claims that as specialized farming led
to crop failure, rulers and creditors were ready to offer high-interest
survival loans that destitute farmers would have had little choice
but to accept.[10] According to Chaney, as interest accrued and these
debts became unsustainable, indebted farmers would lose their an-
cestral land and homes to foreclosure.[11] Without subsistence
strategies to fall back on, farmers would have been especially vulnerable to this process. Chaney explains,

> Attenuation of risk-spreading measures rendered peasants ever
> more vulnerable to the vicissitudes of an erratic climate. When
> natural disaster struck, they were left no alternative to survival
> loans at *de facto* interest rates usurious by any standards. Fore-
> closure on family land and/or the indentured labor of family

---

[9] Karmon, *Israel: A Regional Geography* (London: Wiley-Interscience,
1971), 27. Hopkins, *The Highlands of Canaan: Agricultural Life in the Early
Iron Age* (ed. Flanagan; vol. 3; Sheffield: Almond, 1985), 87-89, 215.
Ashbel, "Israel, Land of (Geographical Survey): Climate," *Encyclopaedia
Judaica* 9:185. Borowski, *Agriculture in Iron Age Israel* (Boston: American
School of Oriental Research, 2002), 47.
[10] Premnath, *Eighth Century Prophets: A Social Analysis*, 95-96.
[11] Chaney, "Micah—Models Matter," Chaney, "Whose Sour Grapes?"
107.

members pledged as collateral was often at the discretion of
the wealthy urban creditors.[12]

For those reluctant to switch to specialized farming, Chaney suggests that rulers would simply "levy a heavy tax upon grain produced 'inefficiently' by the subsistence farmers of the hill country,"[13] to pave yet another way to survival loans and foreclosure.
Chaney adds, "The injustice of [the farmers'] loss of hereditary
lands and livelihood was aggravated by a cruel irony – many now
worked land that had been in their families for generations, but
they worked it as landless day laborers."[14] Chaney notes that while
elites benefited from the new economy, the traditional priorities of
"villagers" for the long-term sufficiency of mixed, subsistence agriculture and its penchant for risk spreading were overwhelmed by
these pressures, and land consolidation proceeded apace."[15] It was
against such a predicament for Judah's subsistence farmers that
Chaney and Premnath believe that the authors of Isa. 5.8–10 and
Mic. 2.1–2 protested.[16]

Through incorporating evidence that Judah experienced large-
scale development in the late eighth century into their interpretations, Chaney and Premnath point to ruling elites as targets of the
prophetic accusations found in Isa. 5.8–10 and Mic. 2.1–2.[17] Beyond sociological theories and archaeological evidence, however,
Chaney and Premnath find evidence of such an elite-based plot in
the texts themselves. Chaney and Premnath believe that the Hebrew words that were used by the authors of Isa. 5.8–10 and Mic.
2.1–2 support their interpretation of this socio-economic context,
involving an overhaul of Judah's land management systems, in the
eighth century.

---

[12] Chaney, "Micah - Models Matter: Political Economy and Micah
6:9-15," 148.

[13] Chaney, "Whose Sour Grapes?," 107.

[14] Chaney, "Whose Sour Grapes?," 109.

[15] Chaney, "Whose Sour Grapes?," 107.

[16] Chaney, "Whose Sour Grapes?," 107-09. Chaney, "Bitter Bounty,"
24-26. Premnath, *Eighth Century Prophets: A Social Analysis*, 100-07.

[17] Chaney, "Whose Sour Grapes?," 107-08. Premnath, *Eighth Century
Prophets: A Social Analysis*, 76-78.

Chaney's and Premnath's Word Analyses

Chaney and Premnath find that several of the Hebrew words that were used by the authors of Isa. 5.8 and Mic. 2.1–2 can take on additional meanings when used in an economic context. Based upon the work of William Moran, Chaney assigns a more complex meaning to the word בַּיִת[18] in Isa. 5.8 and Mic. 2.2 than *house*, as it is often translated in English-language bibles.[19] Moran discovered that the Akkadian word *bitu* did not simply refer to a domicile in second-millennium real-estate documents from Ugarit, but rather a field or a conjoined house and field.[20] Considering that the literary formula found in these documents is copied nearly verbatim in both the Ex. 20.17 and Deut. 5.21 versions of the command not to covet one's neighbor's בַּיִת, Moran concluded that the Hebrew word בַּיִת could also carry the same economic meaning as the Akkadian *bitu*.[21] Chaney contends that this is further supported in the fact that the same literary formula is also found in Deut. 6.10–11, Jos. 24.13, and Neh. 9.24–25.[22] Through employing Moran's discovery, Chaney argues that this same formula, and therefore this expanded meaning of בַּיִת, is present in both Isa. 5.8 and Mic. 2.2.[23] Chaney argues,

> When combined with Moran's evidence from Ugarit for the formulaic use of "house and field" and even "house" alone to mean first and foremost a plot of arable land, these data from the Hebrew Bible point to the same meaning for *bayit* in the tenth commandment, at least when interpreted in Micah's con-

---

[18] Commonly translated as "house," "temple," or "dwelling." See Brown, et al.: 108-10.

[19] Such as in the NRSV, JPS, KJV, and NIV

[20] Moran, "The Conclusion of the Decalogue: Ex 20:17-Dt 5:21," *Catholic Biblical Quarterly* 29, no. 4 (1967): 549-52.

[21] Moran, "The Conclusion of the Decalogue: Ex 20:17-Dt 5:21": 549-52.

[22] Moran, "The Conclusion of the Decalogue: Ex 20:17-Dt 5:21": 548, 551-52.

[23] Chaney, "'Coveting Your Neighbor's House' in Social Context," 308-09.

text… [to] excoriate the actions of powerful figures who illic-
itly "coveted" and "ripped off" agricultural real estate.[24]

Employing this interpretation of בַּיִת in the prophetic complaints
against land ownership abuse would imply that the protagonists of
these passages had not only robbed their victims of shelter, but had
reshaped the economic foundations of life in rural Judah. Chaney
does not elaborate why this would make a stronger argument for a
reference to the seizure of arable land or latifundialization when the
verse already addresses the seizure of שָׂדוֹת.[25] It could be that the
authors mentioned this twice for emphasis or that the use of בַּיִת
in the context of an estate would have made the accusation more
specific. Regardless, if Chaney is correct in his translation of בַּיִת
as house *and* arable land, it would further support the view that
these land seizures were not simply the work of a few "venal individuals" who sought to collect houses in the countryside, but a
concerted effort to seize Judah's arable lands and centralize the
region's productive capabilities.[26] Premnath subscribes to Chaney's
work on the use of בַּיִת, and further suggest that other Hebrew
words within Isa. 5.8 may also indicate a policy of latifundialization
that had been orchestrated by Judah's political elite.[27]

Another word that Premnath finds to be of particular interest
in reconstructing the socio-economic context behind Isa. 5.8–10 is
מָקוֹם, which is commonly translated as *room*, *space*, or *place*, in the
context of Isa. 5.8.[28] Offering an alternative interpretation to support his theory of a widespread policy of latifundialization in
eighth-century Judah, Premnath turned to the works of G.R.
Driver and William Johnstone, who have each concluded that

---

[24] Chaney, "'Coveting Your Neighbor's House' in Social Context,"
309.

[25] *Fields*

[26] Chaney, "Bitter Bounty," 16.

[27] Premnath, *Eighth Century Prophets: A Social Analysis*, 100-01.

[28] For example, מָקוֹם is translated as "room" in the NRSV and the
JPS Bibles, "space" in the NIV, and "place" in the KJV.

מקום contains a technical meaning when referring to real estate.[29] Premnath writes, "According to Johnstone, *maqom* in a technical sense refers to estate or property in addition to its general meaning of locality, place, or spot."[30] Although Johnstone did not apply this technical meaning to Isa. 5.8, himself, Premnath argues that this translation should apply on the basis that verse eight addresses the transference of real estate, leading Premnath to argue that מקום refers "to the landholding of a small peasant."[31] If Premnath's interpretation is correct, then עד אפס מקום could be translated as "until there is no small landholding," supporting the idea that the authors of Isa. 5.8–10 had addressed a disappearance of smaller farms that were suitable for subsistence agriculture.[32]

Premnath further turns his attention to the use of the word ישב in Isa. 5.8, which he views as an indication that the verse addresses abuses that were carried out by Judah's political elite. Although ישב is commonly translated as *to sit, to remain*, or *to dwell*,[33] Albrecht Alt proposed a different translation for when ישב is used in the context of real property.[34] In his study on Jud. 5.23, Alt found that ישב could refer to the possession or ownership of land by members of the aristocratic class, when used in the context of real estate.[35] Following this argument, Alt concluded that in Jud. 5.23 ישב designated the upper echelons of the Canaanite political structure: "...*die Besitzer und Herren des aristokratisch verfassten Ka-*

---

[29] Driver, *Canaanite Myths and Legends* (Edinburgh: T&T Clark, 1956), 30. Johnstone, "Old Testament Expressions in Property Holding," 6, (1969): 314-15.

[30] Premnath, *Eighth Century Prophets: A Social Analysis*, 101. Driver and Johnstone found this use of מקום in Gen. 23.20; Jud. 9.55, 19.28; 1 Sam 2.20, 27.5, 29.3; and 2 Sam 19.39. Johnstone, "Old Testament Expressions in Property Holding," *Uraritica* 6 (1969): 314.

[31] Premnath, *Eighth Century Prophets: A Social Analysis*, 101.

[32] The word אפס can also take on the meaning *only*, which in this context would suggest that there were only small properties, but this doesn't seem to fit, although may deserve exploration elsewhere.

[33] Brown, et al.:442-43.

[34] Premnath, *Eighth Century Prophets: A Social Analysis*, 101.

[35] Alt. "Meros," in *Kleine Schriften Zur Geschichte des Volkes Israel* (ed. Alt; München: C.H. Beck'She Verlagsbuchhandlung, 1953), 276.

naanäischen Gemeinwesens."[36] Applying this interpretation of יֵשֵׁב to Isa. 5.8, Premnath concludes that "it is these members of the ruling elite class who owned large estates. In Isaiah 5:8-9, the verbal and nominal forms of *yashav* should be seen in the context of the process of land accumulation."[37] Premnath points out that Norman Gottwald has also adopted this interpretation of יֵשֵׁב in Isa. 5.8, referring to the passage's perpetrators as "leaders in the imperial feudal statist system."[38] If correct, Premnath's interpretation would support Blenkinsopp's, Dearman's, and Hayes and Irvine's theories that it was the politically powerful, rather than economic elite, who instigated latifundialization and land ownership abuses in eighth-century Judah.

Premnath and Chaney's theories on word usage in Isa. 5.8 and Mic. 2.2 offer some additional insights. Through adopting the meanings that Moran, Johnstone, and Alt find for these words in other areas of the Hebrew Bible, Isa. 5.8 could be translated, "Woe to you who join estate to estate and field to field until there is no small landholding and you [aristocrats] have become landowners all by yourselves in the midst of the land." If the authors did indeed intend to ascribe each of these meanings to each of these words, as Premnath suggests, this translation would imply that the authors of Isa. 5.8 had condemned a process of institutionalized latifundialization that had been organized by the ruling elite for the benefit of the ruling elite. Considering the developments that took place in the late eighth-century BCE, precedents for increased social stratification and urban-based economic activity during periods of increased trade, and examples of institutionalized latifundialization in the ancient Near East,[39] such a rendering of Isa. 5.8 is not far-fetched.

---

[36] Alt. "Meros," 276. "…were written by the aristocratic owners and gentlemen of the Canaanite community."

[37] Premnath, *Eighth Century Prophets: A Social Analysis*, 102.

[38] Gottwald, *The Tribes of Yahweh: A Sociology of the Religion of Liberated Israel 1250-1050 B.C.E.* (London: SCM Press, 1979), 532.

[39] Kramer, *The Sumerians: Their History, Culture, and Character* (Chicago: The University of Chicago Press, 1963), 75. Matthews and Benjamin, *Old Testament Parallels: Laws and Stories from the Ancient Near East* (Mahwah, New Jersey: Paulist Press, 1997), 268-69, 77. Sparks, *Ancient Texts for the*

Although it is impossible to know with any certainty the actual intent behind the prophetic authors' and their redactors' use of בית, מקום, and ישב in their complaints against landownership abuse, Chaney's and Premnath's theories illustrate how using societal patterns of cultural evolution can challenge previous interpretations and open up new ways of approaching biblical texts. It should be noted that while Premnath's theories have provided valuable insights, they are often presented with a degree of certainty that fails to inform the reader of the significant amount of speculation that he has to use in his approach. His introduction of groups such as *poor peasants* into these passages, which do not exist in either Isa. 5.8–10 or Mic. 2.1–2, is an example of how Premnath sometimes inserts his ideas into the text without acknowledging that they are his own. This is not to claim that his assumptions are incorrect, but to emphasize that when employing sociological theory in biblical studies, scholars must be cautious not to make definitive historical claims on the basis of social-scientific theories. The social sciences cannot offer definitive pictures of the ancient world; they can only facilitate new ways of approaching a text and analyzing previous interpretations.

Chaney's and Premnath's Socio-Economic Context for Isa. 5.8–10 and Mic. 2.1–2

At the heart of the socio-economic context that Chaney and Premnath assign to the accusations against land seizures found in Isa. 5.8–10 and Mic. 2.1–2 is a desire for greater economic efficiency held by Judah's political elite. Turning to evidence of increased wine and olive oil production in eighth-century Palestine, including the Samaria ostraca, tax receipts, an increase in presses, advances in press technology, and the free-standing vats and jars that appear to be from private estates, Premnath argues that such demands for the efficient cultivation of grapes and olives would be expected in

---

Study of the Hebrew Bible: A Guide to the Background Literature (Peabody: Hendrickson Publishers, 2005), 422. Although it cannot be known whether there was a direct historical basis to the story of Naboth's vineyard in 1 Kgs. 21.1-16, the existence of the story suggests that such problems existed in ancient Palestine.

eighth-century Judah.[40] Chaney and Premnath each conclude that foreign demand for wine, olive oil, and wheat led to a shift in economic strategy that incited Judah's leaders to cultivate "commercial crops for earning maximum economic gain"[41] at the expense of the land rights of Judean peasants.[42] Prior to this time, Chaney argues, Judean farmers had enjoyed the benefits of mix-subsistence agriculture, which offers greater security against crop failure and, quite arguably, less labor input.[43] If this was indeed the case, it is not difficult to understand how these changes would have upset Judah's agrarian producers as they saw their way of life uprooted to accommodate the desires of the powerful.

Chaney and Premnath find that this shift did not represent a complete turnaround of Judean agrarian strategy but an intensification of the more lucrative aspects of previous strategies. Chaney notes that viticulture was not introduced during the economic developments that took place in the eighth century, but that the cultivation of olive trees had been a part of Judean agrarian practice for centuries. [44] Chaney explains that "tree and vine crops would have rounded out the repertoire of village agriculture in the hills... [and] their processed fruit could be stored stably for extended periods, making them valuable contributors to the goal of spreading risk."[45]

---

[40] Premnath, *Eighth Century Prophets: A Social Analysis*, 58-66.

[41] Premnath, *Eighth Century Prophets: A Social Analysis*, 94.

[42] Premnath, *Eighth Century Prophets: A Social Analysis*, 94. Premnath, "Latifundialization in Isaiah 5.8-10," 302-03. Chaney, "Whose Sour Grapes?," 107.

[43] Chaney, "Whose Sour Grapes?," 107. Societies that do not concentrate on the generation and protection of large surpluses often have fewer labor duties to contend with. As agriculture intensifies, so does a farmer's workload. Boserup, *The Conditions of Agricultural Growth: The Economics of Agrarian Change under Population Pressure* (New York: Aldine Publishing Company, 1965), 44-55. David Hopkins gives a detailed explanation of the benefits of subsistence farming in Iron Age Palestine in Chapter Nine of Hopkins, *The Highlands of Canaan: Agricultural Life in the Early Iron Age.*

[44] Chaney, "Bitter Bounty," 22-23.

[45] Chaney, "Bitter Bounty," 23. According to the biblical narrative, the Israelites were commanded to plant fruit trees upon coming into the land (Lev. 19.23). David Hopkins also notes that "tree and vine crops contribute to the diversity of the Highlands' subsistence means in a way

However, as elites worked to maximize their profits through the export of these goods, new land management strategies had to be employed to increase production.

With the rise of a more advanced political economy in Judah, traditional means of production became antiquated. Chaney and Premnath argue that as opportunities to profit from interregional trade increased, Judah's ruling elite made olive and grape cultivation a priority rather than a means to supplement subsistence needs.[46] Such a shift in prioritization would have had far-reaching consequences for Judah's farming communities. As opposed to subsistence strategies, which work to ensure the wellbeing of farmers and their families, an increase in the cultivation of goods for export tends to have the reverse effect: creating an environment in which farmers do not receive a proportionate amount of benefit in return for their labor. Premnath explains,

> Commercial crops require extensive plantations and thus have to occupy large expanses of land in response to market pressures. Growing cash crops for export and local consumption adversely affects the production of staple crops. Here again the peasants are the hardest hit. The need to buy their own staple foods forces them into an unfamiliar market system where they can be cheated by false measures and rigged scales.[47]

According to Premnath, it was out of selfishness and greed that Judah's ruling and economic elites traded traditional priorities of risk reduction and self-sufficiency for the ability to increase their lucrative exports of wheat, olive oil, and wine. In line with Ben Zvi's theory, Chaney and Premnath believe that through creating a risky agrarian environment, creditors and administrators drove sub-

---

that does not sharply compete with but rather complements the other foci of agriculture energies." Hopkins, *The Highlands of Canaan: Agricultural Life in the Early Iron Age*, 227.

[46] Premnath, *Eighth Century Prophets: A Social Analysis*, 56-66. Premnath, "Latifundialization in Isaiah 5.8-10," 303. Chaney, "Micah - Models Matter," 146-47.

[47] Premnath, "Latifundialization in Isaiah 5.8-10," 303. Premnath appears to make reference to prophetic complaints against false scales, as found in Mic. 6.11.

sistence farmers into debt and eventual foreclosure.[48] With debt as their weapon, Chaney and Premnath believe that Judah's most powerful inhabitants were able to overtake the land of Judah's weakest citizens.[49]

To summarize, according to Chaney's and Premnath's assessments of the socio-economic events of eighth-century Judah, Judean subsistence farmers' "inefficient" strategies were replaced to facilitate an increase in specialized cultivation, allowing elites to produce the revenue required to import luxury items, military goods, and architectural supplies, all at the expense of Judah's farming communities.[50] As the desire for the efficient production of export goods intensified, so did an elite-based policy of latifundialization that brought Judean farms under the control of a few powerful landlords. Chaney and Premnath suggest that it was the consequences of these events that the authors of Isa. 5.8–10 and Mic. 2.1–2 addressed.

C. CONCLUSION

Through considering potential economic motivations associated with the economic developments that appear to have taken place in eighth-century Judah and employing detailed word studies in their interpretations of Isa. 5.8–10 and Mic. 2.1–2, Chaney and Premnath have offered an alternative perspective to the predominate

---

[48] Ben Zvi, *Micah*, 44., Chaney, "Whose Sour Grapes?," 107. Premnath, *Eighth Century Prophets: A Social Analysis*, 105. This theory is also supported by Hoppe. See Hoppe, *There Shall Be No Poor Among You* (Nashville: Abingdon Press, 2004), 77.

[49] Chaney finds that the placement of Isa. 5. 8–10 within Chapter Five further suggests that the passage addresses a widespread policy of latifundialization, rather than isolated instances of land acquisition. The poem that makes up Isa. 5.1-7, commonly known as *The Song of the Vineyard*, imagines Judah as a vineyard that has fallen into disrepair despite YHWH's care. Due to its failure to produce, YHWH promises its destruction. In relation to the rapid agricultural intensification that occurred in the eighth century, Chaney finds that this poem to address the hardships that were placed upon farmers during a rising political economy. See Chaney, "Whose Sour Grapes?."

[50] Chaney, 'Whose Sour Grapes?," 107.

consensus view on land ownership abuse in ancient Judah that had developed by the mid-twentieth century. Through interpreting literary and archaeological evidence through the lens of societal development, Chaney and Premnath place responsibility for these landownership abuses at the feet of political elites who had restructured Judean land management, rather than with a few isolated instance of corruption.[51] This alternative perspective presents a more widespread consolidation process, which would have had repercussions throughout Judean society. Through employing a methodology that lay outside of the biblical narrative and traditional biblical scholarship, Chaney and Premnath have been able to bring new insights to their interpretations of these two texts. They argue that the wide-ranging consequences of the societal transformations that took place in the eighth-century would have included a reorganization of Judah's land management and labor strategy, capital production, and the region's systems of exchange, distribution, and consumption.[52] Through using evidence of societal change in eighth-century Judah, Chaney and Premnath have been able to offer new insights and raise new questions to help address the ambiguity that surrounds the socio-economic context behind Isa. 5.8–10 and Mic. 2.1–2.

One question that Premnath's interpretation raises is whether or not the abuses referred to in the prophetic literature would have only been inflicted upon the poorest of Judah's inhabitants. Was it really only the "landholding of a small peasant"[53] that would have been sacrificed to facilitate economic change in Judah, or is it possible that the not so "small" could have also suffered as a result of these societal changes? Another question that needs to be addressed in light of views of Judah's history that do not assume a pan-Judean YHWHist state existing prior to the late eighth century, is how these circumstances would have altered relations between members of Judah's political elite and religious leaders. Were Isa. 5.8–10 and Mic. 2.1–2 written and preserved solely out of selfless

---

[51] Chaney, "Bitter Bounty," 16. Premnath, *Eighth Century Prophets: A Social Analysis*, 44-93.

[52] Premnath, "Latifundialization in Isaiah 5.8-10," 302-06.

[53] Premnath, *Eighth Century Prophets: A Social Analysis*, 101.

compassion for struggling farmers, or was there another motive that is hidden in the text? Before such questions can be addressed and a potential augmentation of cultural-evolutionary approaches can be explored, two matters need to be considered: the social-scientific patterns upon which Chaney and Premnath base their works and the archaeological evidence for the presence of these patterns in Judah during the eighth century BCE. The following chapter will consider the economic motivations behind cultural-evolutionary patterns and the potential value of these recurring patterns as interpretive tools before exploring the evidence of such patterns in the ancient Near East.

2 CULTURAL-EVOLUTIONARY THEORY AND ECONOMIC MOTIVATION

Although very little is known about the authors and redactors of the Hebrew prophetic texts that are attributed to the eighth-century BCE, it is apparent that they wrote from an ideological perspective. Those who composed these texts against various forms of injustice were driven by their religious, social, political, and economic motivations, or at least by those of the people who had commissioned them to write. Although the precise nature of their motivations cannot be fully known, these ancient writings are the product of the societal conditions in which their authors and redactors lived. As Paula McNutt argues, whether they contain accurate historical information or not, the biblical narratives

> ...must be understood first and foremost as representing notions, beliefs, and myths constructed to serve some purpose in the social and historical contexts in which they were written, edited, and arranged in their present form.[1]

Those who employ social-scientific criticism in biblical research find value in considering the societal contexts in which biblical texts were formed, and subsequently reshaped, in order to better understand the motivations and meanings behind these writings. Taking this as a starting point for understanding these ancient texts, biblical scholars and social scientists alike, from Max Weber and Gerhard Lenski to Norman Gottwald and Thomas Overholt, have

---

[1] McNutt, *Reconstructing the Society of Ancient Israel* (Louisville: Westminster John Knox Press, 1999), 4.

either directly or indirectly used sociological patterns as a means of interpreting the texts of the Hebrew Bible.[2]

Deciphering the societal contexts that lay behind Hebrew prophetic literature is a complicated and tedious endeavor; this is especially true of the complaints against landownership abuse that are attributed to eighth-century Judah. Faced with a very limited body of textual and archaeological evidence, scholars find it necessary to deal with varying degrees of speculation, a less than preferred avenue of academic practice.[3] As addressed in Chapter One, Marvin Chaney and D.N. Premnath have employed the concept of cultural evolution in their interpretations of prophetic complaints against injustice, reading the prophetic account alongside evidence of massive societal development in eighth-century Judah.[4] By engaging in this process, they have attempted to piece together a picture of what life may have been like in eighth-century Judah and to gain greater insights into the socio-economic context that lay be-

---

[2] Weber, *Ancient Judaism* (trans. Gerth and Martindale; London: The Free Press, 1952). Lenski, *Ecological-Evolutionary Theory: Principles and Applications* (Boulder: Paradigm Publishers, 2005). In the eighth chapter of his book Lenski uses his ecological-evolutionary approach to deconstruct the monarchy in the biblical narrative. Gottwald, *The Tribes of Yahweh: A Sociology of the Religion of Liberated Israel 1250-1050 B.C.E.* (London: SCM Press, 1979). Overholt. "Prophecy: The Problem of Cross-Cultural Comparison," in *Anthropological Perspective on Old Testament Prophecy* eds. Culley and Overholt; Chico, CA: Society of Biblical Literature, 1982).

[3] Baruch Levine addresses this dilemma and various approaches that have been taken to cope with it in Levine. "Farewell to the Ancient Near East: Evaluating Biblical References of Ownership of Land in Comparative Perspective," in *Privatization in the Ancient Near East and Classical World* eds. Hudson and Levine; Cambridge: Peabody Museum of Archaeology and Ethnology, 1996), 224-29.

[4] Chaney, "Bitter Bounty: The Dynamics of Political Economy Critiqued by the Eighth-Century Prophets," in *Reformed Faith and Economics* (ed. Stivers; Lanham: University Press of America, 1989). Chaney, "Micah - Models Matter: Political Economy and Micah 6:9-15," in *Ancient Israel: The Old Testament in its Social Context* (ed. Esler; London: SCM Press, 2005). Premnath, *Eighth Century Prophets: A Social Analysis* (St. Louis: Chalice, 2003), 43-98.

hind such passages as Isa. 5.8–10 and Mic. 2.1–4.[5] The fruition of Chaney's and Premnath's work has made significant contributions to the field by providing new models for interpreting these passages.

Naturally, an approach that combines archaeological evidence and social-scientific theory with a social-scientific method that demands the use of analogy and speculation creates a minefield in which those who use cultural-evolutionary theory must tread. No one can claim to have a full understanding of the societal contexts of the prophetic texts attributed to eighth-century Judah or even to know with certainty the periods in which they were written and modified.[6] Furthermore, there is a temptation, to which Premnath sometimes yields, to rely upon social-scientific models to supplement the lack of extra-biblical evidence pertaining to prophetic accounts of economic exploitation. As Lester Grabbe points out, theories derived from the social sciences are not facts, but interpretations to be critically examined against the data that does exist and then modified or discarded as necessary.[7] Rather than providing historical evidence, societal patterns can only indicate an expected societal reaction to a given stimulus. To use these models as mines from which to gather new data for the interpretation of biblical texts would risk a fall into circular reasoning. As Philip Davies warns, scholars often end up prescribing a cultural and historical context for a text and then proceed to evaluate that text against their own reconstructed background.[8] Rather than considering social-scientific methods as sources for evidence, Philip Esler argues

---

[5] Premnath has also used the tenets of cultural-evolutionary theory in his approaches to Isa. 1.21–26; 2.12–17 ; Hos. 5.10; 8.14; Amos 3.9–11; 6.1-3; Mic. 1.5b–6 , 9–10 [Heb.]; 6.9–16.

[6] van Seters, *In Search of History: Historiography in the Ancient World* (New Haven: Yale University Press, 1983). Davies, *In Search of Ancient Israel* (148; eds. Clines, Davies and Jarick; Sheffield: Sheffield Academic Press, 1995). Whitelam, *The Invention of Ancient Israel: The Silencing of Palestinian History* (London: Routledge, 2001). Halpern, "Erasing History: The Minimalist Assault on Ancient Israel," December 1995, no. 11 (1995).

[7] Grabbe, *Ancient Israel: What Do We Know and How Do We Know It?* (London: T&T Clark, 2007), 5.

[8] Davies, *In Search of Ancient Israel*.

that social-scientific interpretation should be used as a heuristic tool that "fires the social-scientific imagination to ask new questions of data, to which only the data [itself] can provide the answers."[9] The best defense against either creating a false history or falling into a trap of circular reasoning is to understand and appreciate both the advantages and limitations of social-scientific models. A key component to such a defense is an understanding of the origins and mechanisms of a given model.

Before the potential value of integrating the abuses associated with corporate globalization into a social-scientific model for biblical interpretation can be assessed, it is necessary to have a fundamental understanding of the social-scientific schools upon which cultural-evolutionary theory is based, and *ipso facto* the works of biblical scholars who have based their interpretations upon cultural-evolutionary theory. Such an understanding will make it easier to reveal the benefits and deficiencies of previous scholars' use of cultural-evolutionary theory, as well as the benefits and drawbacks of employing modern manifestations of recurring societal patterns as a new interpretive tool.

---

[9] Esler. "Social-Scientific Models in Biblical Interpretation," in *Ancient Israel: The Old Testament in its Social Context* (ed. Esler; London SCM Press, 2005), 3.

A. FOUNDATIONS AND DEVELOPMENT OF CULTURAL-EVOLUTIONARY THEORY

Chaney's and Premnath's work on landownership abuse in eighth-century Judah is grounded, in part, in the idea of cross-cultural evolutionary theory. Cultural-evolutionary theory, which finds commonality in the ways that societies develop in response to various types of stimuli, became a significant focus of anthropologists and sociologists in the late nineteenth-century. Early theorists such as Lewis Morgan and Henry Maine found that societies undergo a series of evolutionary processes in their development, not far removed from Charles Darwin's theory of biological evolution.[1] Morgan and Henry argued that as societies face new challenges, successful societies tend to evolve into a more perfect and ordered organism. This process of evolution was initially believed to unfold in a linear progression that worked as a liberating force, freeing people from an animalistic or inferior existence through bringing them into an ordered and 'civilized' state.[2] This sentiment is made clear in the title of Morgan's 1877 publication, *Ancient Society: Or, Researches in the Lines of Human Progress From Savagery Through Barbarism to Civilization*. As more enlightened views on race and ethnicity developed within the academy, Morgan's and Maine's early, and blatantly racist, view of cultural-evolutionary theory became so controversial that it was eventually discarded from the field of anthropology for an entire generation.

As with any theoretical work, social-scientific or other, Morgan's and Maine's findings reflected the social and cultural norms of their time. The pious nature of upper-class society in Victorian Britain and the United States in the late nineteenth-century, as well as the racial and cultural attitudes that fuelled European colonialism, are found in the theory that societies evolved to tame

---

[1] Morgan, *Ancient Society: Or, Researches in the Lines of Human Progress from Savagery through Barbarism to Civilization* (New York: H. Holt and Company, 1907). Maine, *Ancient Law: Its Connection with Early History of Society and its Relation to Modern Ideas* (London: Murray, 1905).

[2] Morgan, *Ancient Society: Or, Researches in the Lines of Human Progress from Savagery through Barbarism to Civilization*, 5-6.

base desires and bring humanity under control. Such sentiments are clearly reflected in Morgan and White's progressive view of the evolution of societies. The transference of their world-view's xeno-phobic attitudes to their scholarly work is illustrated in Morgan's comparisons between Caucasian and non-Caucasian cultural development. Morgan writes,

> The remote ancestors of the Aryan nations presumptively passed through an experience similar to that of existing barba-rous and savage tribes. Though the experience of these nations embodies all the information necessary to illustrate the periods of civilization, both ancient and modern, together with a part of that in the later period of barbarism, their anterior experi-ence must be deduced, in the main, from the traceable connec-tion between the elements of their existing institutions and in-ventions, and similar elements still preserved in those of savage and barbarous tribes.[3]

Morgan's assessment reveals prejudices and ethnocentric attitudes that would be considered to be unacceptable by modern scholarly standards.

Due to the highly ethnocentric sentiments of the first cultural evolutionists, who based their criteria for progress upon the ad-vances of western civilization, Europe and the United States were considered to be the pinnacle of societal development. Allen John-son and Timothy Earle note that in its infancy, cultural-evolutionary theorists concluded that African, Indian, and aborigi-nal societies had not advanced to the technological level of western societies because of their racial inferiority. It was assumed that the *stunted* societies found in the rest of the world, particularly those in Africa and among the North and South American indigenous peo-ples, were the result of racial inferiority.[4] Caucasians, it was thought, were the only race capable of attaining such high levels of achievement.[5]

---

[3] Morgan, *Ancient Society*, 8.

[4] Morgan, *Ancient Society*, 5-6.

[5] Johnson and Earle, *The Evolution of Human Societies: From Foraging Group to Agrarian State* (Stanford: Stanford University Press, 2001), 3.

Beyond nineteenth-century societal influences, the idea that societies evolved from chaos into order also appears to have been rooted in the legal background that several of the early cultural-evolutionary theorists shared. Morgan and Maine were both legal professionals, and their work was inspired by their studies on the evolution of law, which dealt with notions of a progression from lawlessness toward social order. Morton Fried notes that among these early theorists, "...the close connections between jurisprudence and anthropology led to equal closeness in the development of their views of the evolution of law and political society."[6] A perspective rooted in the legal profession may have led these theorists to view cultural-evolutionary theory through the linear perspective that they proposed.

Despite the racism and xenophobia that rested at the foundations of cultural-evolutionary theory in the nineteenth century, Morgan's work put forth the idea that similar patterns of societal progression exist throughout history and across cultures. Although the idea of a linear progression of a single societal pattern has since been largely discredited, as described below, Morgan's thesis was valuable in promoting the concept that societal development is not simply the result of random occurrences and responses to various events, but of societies' similar reactions to common stimuli across culture and time. The racism that was inherent in the early stages of cultural-evolutionary theory, which reflected a predominant nineteenth-century western world-view, serves as an important reminder that it is very difficult, if not impossible, to separate a scholar's work from the world view in which it is produced. Biblical scholars who use social models like cultural-evolutionary theory must not only strive to be conscious of the cultural contexts and assumption of those who authored and revised the biblical texts

---

[6] Fried, *The Evolution of Political Society* (New York: Random House, 1967), 16. A useful example of how Maine's legal work led to cross-cultural and cross-chronological discoveries can be found in Walter Neale's treatment of Maine's study of Hindu village economics: Neale. "Reciprocity and Redistribution in the Indian Village: Sequel to Some Notable Discussions," in *Trade and Market in the Early Empires* (ed. Karl Polanyi; Chicago: Henry Regnery Company, 1957), 219-22.

over millennia past, but also their own cultural contexts and assumptions.

Reactions to Xenophobia in Early Cultural-Evolutionary Theory

Both the racist direction and the progressive-linear view of societal development that early cultural-evolutionary theorists proposed, which failed to recognize the negative effects that progress can have on societies, provoked a backlash that rendered the theory as practically taboo for an entire generation.[7] In the early to mid-twentieth century Franz Boas, a prominent sociologist and an ardent campaigner against racism, protested against the xenophobic attitudes that had been propagated by early cultural-evolutionists like Morgan and Main. But Boas went beyond addressing the racist elements that these theorists had brought to the field; he discredited the entire pursuit of cultural-evolutionary theory on the basis that it was inherently racist.[8]

The Relativist School

Contrary to the idea that similar cross-cultural patterns of evolution recur as societies evolve, Boas and his students propagated the notion that although relationships between historical cultures could be found in a few exceptional cases, many such explorations demanded too much reliance on "imagination" and "assumption" to be of any scholarly value.[9] Rather than viewing societal evolution as a product of racial ability, Boas believed that societies evolve as a result of the unique challenges that they, and their sub-societies,

---

[7] Karl Marx and Friedrich Engels would be exempt from this second criticism, as their late nineteenth-century work tackled the negative outcomes of cultural evolution head-on.

[8] Liss, et al., "Diasporic Identities: The Science and Politics of Race in the Work of Franz Boas and W.E.B. DuBois, 1894-1919," *Cultural Anthropology* 13, no. 2 (1998): 138-40.

[9] Boas, "Psychological Problems in Anthropology," *The American Journal of Psychology* 21, no. 3 (1910). Boas, "History and Science in Anthropology: A Reply," *American Anthropologist* 38, no. 1 (1936): 138-39.

encounter.[10] Although he did concede that similarities might exist in a few isolated cases, Boas argued that because of the unique nature of the challenges that individual societies face, the pursuit to find common links between societies was unlikely to produce any valuable results.[11] This perspective on societal development came to be known as *relativism*.

Although the relativist perspective addressed a variety of important considerations regarding the limitations of cultural-evolutionary theory, it failed to acknowledge the potential value in considering the cross-cultural similarities that do exist in societal development. Unwilling to distil the notion of common societal development from the racist implications that early cultural-evolution theorists attached to the discipline, Boas argued that the field should be abandoned altogether. Arguing that cultural-evolutionary theory was a waste of time, he wrote,

> Anthropological research that compares similar cultural phenomena from various parts of the world, in order to discover the uniform history of their development, makes the assumption that the same ethnological phenomenon has everywhere developed in the same manner. Here lies the flaw…no such proof can be given.[12]

The flaw in Boas' argument was that it demanded too much from cultural-evolutionary theory, failing to consider its value as a sociological model rather than a source for historical data. As with all models, cultural-evolutionary theory cannot be expected to produce perfectly identical or accurate results across the expansive spectrum of time and space. To set the expectations that Boas placed upon a social-scientific theory is to expect a level of mathematical precision, which simply does not exist in the social sciences.

---

[10] By sub-societies I refer to Boas' view that various groups within a given society will react differently to a variety of stimuli, such as the differences between the way peasants and aristocrats will act in a given society. For more on this see Boas, "Psychological Problems in Anthropology": 372.

[11] Boas, "History and Science in Anthropology: A Reply."

[12] Boas, *Race, Language, and Culture* (New York: The Free Press, 1966), 273.

As Lenski notes, more recent concepts of cultural-evolutionary theory take into account that evolutionary theory, whether related to "chemistry, biology, or the social sciences, is destined to remain an inexact science, since exact sciences require that processes have deterministic outcomes."[13] Mainstream cultural-evolutionary theorists today do not delude themselves into believing that such deterministic outcomes are possible within the field. In the relativists' reaction to the racist assumptions of early cultural-evolutionary theorists and through setting too high a standard, Boas and his students dismissed potentially valuable data and effectively removed cultural-evolutionary theory from American anthropological discourse for an entire generation.[14]

Despite an overreaction to the use of race in early cultural-evolutionary theory, the relativist school made some important contributions to theories of cultural evolution and raised a few important points for biblical scholars to consider. The relativist response to the ethnocentrism that was inherent in early cultural-evolutionary theory highlights the limitations of using social-scientific models in biblical interpretation. Boas was correct to argue that cultural-evolutionary theory cannot provide a template through which to understand all ethnological phenomena, such as population growth, because such events do not always unfold in the same manner.[15] Due to variations that do indeed exist, biblical scholars should not attempt to employ these theories in order to produce a definitive picture of the ancient societies of the biblical world, and several biblical scholars have realized this in their approaches. As Lester Grabbe stresses, "Theories derived from the social sciences are simply models to be tested against the biblical

---

[13] Lenski, *Ecological-Evolutionary Theory: Principles and Applications*, 6. Of course even the deterministic outcomes found in sciences like medicine are continually disproved as knowledge within the field expands.

[14] Johnson and Earle, *The Evolution of Human Societies*, 3. For more on the work of Boas' students, see Lowie, *Are We Civilized?* (New York: Harcourt, Brace, and Company, 1929). Kroeber, *Anthropology: Culture Patterns & Processes* (New York: Harcourt, Brace, & World, 1963). Mead, *Continuities in Cultural Evolution* (New Haven: Yale University Press, 1964).

[15] Boas, *Race, Language, and Culture*, 273.

and other data, not conclusions to be imposed on the sources."[16] Although the relativist view neglects the heuristic value of cultural-evolutionary theory, allowing scholars of various academic disciplines to approach a variety of questions from new angles, the relativists highlighted cultural-evolutionary theory's inability to produce a historical framework for a given society's development. However, to silence the use of cultural-evolutionary theory in biblical scholarship, as Boas would have suggested, would be to throw away a valuable interpretive tool.

The Theory of Multilinear Evolution

Despite the relativists' insistence that the pursuit of cultural-evolutionary theory was useless, an accumulation of archaeological and ethnographic evidence that supported the general ideas of cultural-evolutionary theory eventually became too great for social scientists to ignore. In the 1950s anthropologists began to revisit the idea that societies with little or no contact tend to evolve in similar ways, leading a number of social scientists to resurrect the theory of cultural evolution in the mid to late-twentieth century. Influential scholars such as Leslie White and Julian Steward improved upon Morgan's and Maine's foundational ideas while discarding the racial elements that had been attached to them.[17] For example, Steward argued that just because Maine's insights concerning kin-based societies were racially limited in their scope did not mean that parallels between development forms found in Western Europe and other areas of the world did not exist in the Americas and the eastern Mediterranean.[18] Although Steward was sympathetic to Boas' concerns regarding xenophobia and racism, he understood that these aspects of late nineteenth century cul-

---

[16] Grabbe, *Ancient Israel: What Do We Know and How Do We Know It?* , 5.

[17] White, *The Evolution of Culture: The Development of Civilization to the Fall of Rome* (New York: McGraw-Hill, 1959). Steward, *Theory of Culture Change: The Methodology of Multilinear Evolution* (London: University of Illinois Press, 1955).

[18] Steward, *Theory of Culture Change*, 15-16.

tural-evolutionary theory were a product of their time.[19] Through
acknowledging that the theory did not have to rely on notions of
racial supremacy, Steward and his colleagues were able to resume
research in cultural-evolutionary theory, minus the blatantly xeno-
phobic views that were so prevalent during the initial development
of the field.

Beyond Steward's contention with cultural-evolutionary theory's racist foundations, he also found the idea of a universal pattern of societal evolution to be unsound. Unlike Boas, who used
the notion of universal evolutionary progression to dismiss cultural-evolutionary theory, Steward abandoned a strict adherence to
universalism and put forth the idea that societies evolve in ways
that reflect their particular environment, but that similarities exist
between like types.[20] The idea that societies progress in similar yet
unique ways came to be known as *multilinear evolution*. Steward recognized that a society based in a rain forest, for example, would
face different challenges and therefore evolve differently from a
society based in an arid region, as dictated by their specific societal
needs. Able to move past universal views of cultural evolution,
Steward opened the debate to a multilinear approach that considered various paths that societies might take in their evolutionary
process.[21] Such a proposal simultaneously took into account Boas'
observation that different societies face unique challenges, while
allowing for the fact that some societies face parallel challenges due
to similarities in their environments.

The notion that environmental factors, such as climate, food
availability, and distribution needs, influence a society's evolutionary process sparked an ecological approach to cultural-evolutionary
theory.[22] Johnson and Earle write that Steward's multilinear approach, based upon ecological influences, helped ethnographers
such as Rappaport and Netting "to understand how specific as-

---

[19] Steward, "Problems of Cultural Evolution," 12, no. 2 (1958): 209.

[20] Steward, *Theory of Culture Change*, 18-19.

[21] Steward, *Theory of Culture Change*, 28-29.

[22] This has played an especially predominate role in some biblical
scholars interpretations of prophetic complaints against injustice attributed to eighth-century Judah, as will be detailed below.

pects of culture from subsistence practices to social organization to complex ritual cycles, served to solve critical problems of group and individual survival."[23] The ecological approach of multilinear development has important implications for this thesis as it can help to narrow the focus of research. In considering whether or not corporate globalization can provide a useful tool with which to address questions surrounding land ownership abuse in Judah, it is beneficial to focus on modern agrarian societies that share common environmental features with ancient Palestine. Societies that have developed in arid, hilly regions with similar types of crops are likely to produce more valuable comparisons and less irrelevant data. However, it is important to remember that even if an absolutely identical environmental location could be found, a modern society cannot necessarily be expected to develop in exactly the same ways as ancient Judah; religious and other cultural factors that can affect a society's developmental trajectory have to be considered and brought into the equation. Therefore, highlighting the differences between data pertaining to eighth-century Judah and the modern example is just as important as highlighting their similarities, so as to avoid tailoring a socio-economic context that fits the thesis' central argument. The researcher must resist the temptation to pick and choose data that fits a preconceived notion and ignore variables that do not connect.

Not all anthropologists who subscribe to multilinear evolution agree with Steward's theory that ecological concerns drive the economic behaviors of societies and individuals. Scholars such as Jonathan Friedman and Dominique Legros argue that economic motivations are what lead to cultural change and evolution, rather than biological need.[24] Like the ecological view, this perspective also

---

[23] Johnson and Earle, *The Evolution of Human Societies: From Foraging Group to Agrarian State* (Stanford: Stanford University Press, 1987), 3. See also Rappaport, *Pigs for the Ancestors* (New Haven: Yale University Press, 1967). Netting, *Hill Farmers of Nigeria: Cultural Ecology of the Kofyar of the Jos Plateau* (Seattle: University of Washington Press, 1968). Netting, *Cultural Ecology* (Menlo Park, CA: Cummings, 1977).

[24] Friedman, "Marxism, Structuralism and Vulgar Materialism," *Man* 9, no. 3 (1977). Legros, "Chance, Necessity, and Mode of Production: A

plays a significant role in influencing the interpretations of biblical scholars who consider the Assyrian conquest of Palestine and increased social stratification in their assessments of land-ownership abuse in passages such as Isa. 5.8–10 and Mic. 2.1–2.[25]

Marxist Critique of Cultural Evolutionism," *American Anthropologist* 79, no. 1 (1977).

[25] Chaney, "Micah - Models Matter: Political Economy and Micah 6:9-15." Premnath, "Latifundialization in Isaiah 5.8-10," in *Social-Scientific Old Testament Criticism* (ed. Chalcraft; Sheffield: Sheffield Academic Press, 1997). Gottwald, *The Tribes of Yahweh: A Sociology of the Religion of Liberated Israel 1250-1050 B.C.E.* (London: SCM Press, 1979), 532. Ben Zvi, *Micah* (ed. Rolf P. Knierim; vol. XXIB; Grand Rapids: Eerdmans, 2000), 44. Blenkinsopp, *Isaiah 1-39* (19; eds. Albright and Freedman; New York: Doubleday, 2000), 211.

B. MOTIVATIONS FOR ECONOMIC BEHAVIOR

The multilinear approach to cultural evolution has not created a unified theory as to how societies evolve, but has ignited an ongoing debate over the economic motivations that drive societies to change, out of which various schools and sub-schools have been born. Due to the number and complexity of these schools, and in the interest of staying within the parameters of the subject at hand, this section will limit itself to the development of those schools that are most relevant to the use of cultural-evolutionary theory in interpretations of Isa. 5.8–10 and Mic. 2.1–2: the *substantivist/structuralist* and the *formalist/ecological* schools.[1] Beyond providing a variety of perspectives as to how cultures develop, these two schools of thought can work together to effectively keep each other in balance. Since cultures do not follow a single evolutionary progression, as had been originally proposed by Morgan and Maine, and since cultures can evolve in ways that are contrary to what a given theoretical school might expect, cross-referencing data through *substantivism/structuralism* and *formalism/ecological* theories can be a beneficial practice. Although such an approach does not create a "foolproof" system for evaluating societal change, it provides a useful tool for approaching ancient cultures, such as those found in Judah, which have left behind only very limited literary evidence.

The debate between substantivist/structuralist and formalist/ecological schools has played an important role in the development of modern cultural-evolutionary theory. Theorists such as Johnson and Earle, who have studied the evolutionary changes that occur as political economies develop within subsistence communities, have used aspects of both of these schools in their work. Through understanding the catalysts behind people's economic

---

[1] One particular school that will not be addressed here is the evolutionary biology approach. This theory claims that economic activity, in short, is driven by our desire to reproduce. For more information on this theory see Boyd and Richerson, *Culture and the Evolutionary Process* (London: University of Chicago Press, 1985). Wright, *The Moral Animal: Evolutionary Psychology and Everyday Life* (London: Abacus, 1996).

activities, any existing cross-cultural connections, discrepancies, and analogies can be illuminated more effectively.

The Substantivist/Structuralist Schools

From deciding on a make of car to who pays for the bill at the end of a night out, societal pressures have a powerful effect on the economic decisions that individuals make, and the nature of these pressures are often unique to the culture to which they belong. A westerner partaking in a Japanese business dinner at a restaurant will probably notice that each employee will choose the exact same meal that the highest-ranking official orders. Should the western guest break protocol and order something else off of the menu, a level of discomfort among the hosts will be noticeable, as he or she inadvertently implies that their superior had made an error in his or her choice of meal. It is culturally manufactured pressures such as these that form the basis of the substantivist school's understanding of economic motivation.

At the heart of substantivist economic theory that was developed by Karl Polanyi in the 1950s[2] is the notion that people's economic motivations are governed by societal rules and norms.[3] The substantivist theory went against the idea that economic motivations were governed by the biological needs of individuals or the societies in which they live, as was commonly held at the time.[4] According to substantivist theorists such as Polanyi, George Dalton, and Marshall Sahlins, economic motivations are derived from people's dependence for living upon nature and each other, based upon the societal rules set up by institutions, even if those decisions go against what is in the best interest of the individual.[5]

---

[2] The substantivist theory would eventually come to be known as the structuralist theory in the 1970s, as explained below.

[3] Polanyi. "The Economy as an Instituted Process," in *Trade & Market in the Early Empires* (ed. Polanyi; Chicago: Henery Regnery Company, 1957).

[4] Johnson and Earle, *The Evolution of Human Societies*, 17.

[5] Polanyi. "The Economy as an Instituted Process," 243. Polanyi, *The Livelihood of Man* (ed. Pearson; London: Academic Press, 1977). Dalton, "Economic Theory and Primitive Society," 63, no. 1 (1961). For example, if the Japanese boss ordered a dish that an employee was allergic to, that

Polanyi argued that, throughout history, market systems of various degrees of complexity had been governed by political, social, and moral norms.[6] From the cultivation of crops to the shipment of goods, Polanyi believed that that these societal pressures had removed the biologically-based economic decision-making power from the individual.[7] Complementary to Polanyi's theory, Dalton claimed that anthropologists who had taken a biological view of economic incentive had confused biological motivations for social orientation, claiming that "hunger is natural in the sense of biological, but it is not synonymous with an incentive to produce."[8] The substantivists took note that factors such as honor, greed, shame, and fear can have a very powerful influence on an individual's or group's economic decisions, taking precedent even over the most vital of needs, such as food, shelter, and the avoidance of violence.

The substantivist perspective's mechanical view of societal structures was partially due to a difference in the definition of *scarcity of means*, which both the substantivist and traditional economic schools saw as a catalyst for change. Whereas traditional anthropologists thought of scarcity of means in terms of food, shelter, and safety, Stuart Plattner observes that the substantivists "defined the scarcity of *means* in primitive society as a scarcity of *wealth*, a particular condition caused by the 'penetration' of Western capitalism into native societies."[9] This viewpoint, which leads one to wonder whether substantivists did not believe that societal pressures and economic exploitation existed before the advent of Western capitalism, is reflected in Dalton's work. He argues that economic systems are based upon "definite institutional arrangements — structured rules of the game — to assure continuity of sup-

---

employee would be more likely to order the dish and go hungry than to choose another item from the menu.

[6] Polanyi. "The Economy as Instituted Process," in *Economic Anthropology: Reading in Theory and Analysis* eds. LeClair and Schneider; New York: Holt, Rinehart, and Winston, INC., 1968), 124-27.

[7] Polanyi. "The Economy as Instituted Process," 124-27.

[8] Dalton, "Economic Theory and Primitive Society": *American Anthropologist* 5, 22n.

[9] Plattner. "Introduction," in *Economic Anthropology* (ed. Plattner; Stanford: Stanford University Press, 2002), 13.

ply, that is, to assure repetition of performance."[10] Such a perspective gives credence to the idea that decision-making is dominated by societal rules, while leaving biological considerations as secondary, at best.

An example of the substantivist view of economic decision-making is found in the choices that have been made by the Boa Venture sharecroppers of Brazil. As opportunities for foreign trade arose in the twentieth century, the sharecroppers' traditional subsistence-based economy was intensified to facilitate market-oriented production.[11] Throughout this transitional process the sharecroppers consented to a variety of seemingly counter-productive economic demands as a result of the societal norms to which they were subject. Despite enduring levels of land rent that consumed between twenty-five to thirty percent of their productive income, the Boa Ventura sharecroppers adhered to a patronage system that left them at the edge of starvation.[12] While some landlords treated their tenants better than others, Allen Johnson finds that a psychological dependence between the landlords and their sharecroppers kept the system in check, making it very difficult for contracted norms to be broken.[13] A substantivist perspective would point out that, rather than refuse the oppressive demands of the minority elite to pursue what is best for the sharecropper community, cultural norms trapped these Brazilian farmers into an exploitative relationship that was the product of abusive cultural institutions.

In the 1970s the substantivist school enjoyed a resurgence of thought with a new generation of theorists and came to be known as the *structuralist* school. Structural Marxists such as Friedman, Maurice Godelier, and Legros focused their work on the questions of how societal structures determine the economic activities of individuals, proposing that the control of economic resources is cen-

---

[10] Dalton. "Economic Theory and Primitive Society," in *Economic Anthropology: Reading in Theory and Analysis* eds. LeClair and Schneider; New York: Holt, Rinehart, and Winston, INC., 1968), 149.

[11] Johnson and Earle, *The Evolution of Human Societies*, 335.

[12] Johnson and Earle, *The Evolution of Human Societies*, 335.

[13] Johnson, "The Psychology of Dependence Between Landlord and Sharecropper in Northeastern Brazil," 18, no. 2 (1997): 425-27.

tral to maintaining a society and the internal structures of stratification therein.[14] According to Godelier, the ability of a society to survive is determined by a combination of its ability to decide on and
allocate its members' access to resources, to control the means of
production, to allocate a labor force from among a society's members, and to establish the correct social form of redistribution.[15]
Ignoring the presence of biological motivations behind individual's
economic decisions, this new body of structuralists, like their
predecessors, focused entirely on the role of social institutions as
the prime factor behind economic motivation.

Although structuralism has proven valuable in its ability to
highlight the role that societal norms play in the decision-making
processes of individuals and societies, it often views economic activity within a very narrow framework. By concentrating entirely on
the role of social stratification and the importance of societal
norms, structural arguments neglect some rather important biological aspects of social motivation. In opposition to the structuralist
school, Stephen Sanderson claims,

> Structuralism has shown itself to be concerned with an ex-
> tremely narrow range of social reality, mostly myth and other
> symbolic systems. It has had almost no concern at all with
> most of the major issues taken up by many of the greatest so-
> cial scientists from the middle of the nineteenth century until
> the present.[16]

Cultural evolutionists of the ecological persuasion find that this
neglect has led to an incomplete picture of the evolutionary process. Johnson and Earle argue that the problem with using social
structures as the starting point for understanding societal develop-

---

[14] Friedman, "Marxism, Structuralism and Vulgar Materialism," 9, no.
3 (1974). Godelier, *Perspectives in Marxist Anthropology* (Cambridge: Cambridge University Press, 1977). Legros, "Chance, Necessity, and Mode of
Production." Johnson and Earle, *The Evolution of Human Societies: From
Foraging Group to Agrarian State*, 9.

[15] Godelier, "Infrastructures, Societies, and History," *Current Anthropology* 19, no. 4 (1978): 763.

[16] Sanderson, *The Evolution of Human Sociality: A Darwinian Conflict Perspective* (Lanham, Maryland: Rowman & Littlefield Publishers, 2001), 42.

ment is that it leaves "the nagging question of where [these struc-
tures] came from in the first place."[17] In the end, the structuralists
are left with a chicken-and-egg dilemma that cannot be answered
without considering biological motivators in economic activity: why
would people have adhered to the development of oppressive
structures in the first place if there had been no motivation, like
biological needs, to do so?

Substantivist/structuralist models play an important part in
various biblical scholars' interpretations of prophetic complaints
against economic exploitation. Chaney, Premnath, Dearman and
David Hopkins all envision a patronage system in eighth-century
Judah that left small-scale farmers dependent upon systems of reciprocity, debt, and coercion. As a result, those in power were able
to centralize Judah's agrarian sector and abandon the region's subsistence strategies, even though these moves would have been converse to many farmers' own best interests.[18] The scenario that these
scholars produce from reading prophetic texts through evidence of
heightened economic activity in the eighth-century BCE is not unlike that of the Boa Ventura sharecroppers in several ways: heightened trade and market-oriented agriculture led to increased social
stratification and a waning of the precedence of subsistence strategies. Premnath claims that "the primary producers were in no way

---

[17] Johnson and Earle, *The Evolution of Human Societies*, 9.

[18] Chaney, "Bitter Bounty," 25-27. Dearman, *Property Rights in the
Eighth-Century Prophets: The Conflict and its Background* (eds. Roberts and Tal-
bert; vol. 106; Scholars Press: Atlanta, 1988), 78-83. Hopkins. "Bare
Bones: Putting Flesh on the Economics of Ancient Israel," in *The Origins
of the Ancient Israelite States* eds. Clines, Davies and Jarick; vol. 228 of *JSOT*;
Sheffield: Sheffield Academic Press, 1996), 132-39. Premnath, "Loan
Practices in the Hebrew Bible," in *To Break Every Yoke: Essays in Honour of
Marvin L. Chaney* eds. Coote and Gottwald, eds. Whitelam and Crossley;
Sheffield: Sheffield Phoenix Press, 2007). Switching from the safety of
subsistence farming, which offers effective risk-reduction strategies in
Palestine's unpredictable agricultural environment, to the specialized
farming of revenue-producing goods is not in the best interest of a small-
scale agriculturalist. In the absence of a biological motivation, we are left
to conclude that institutional motivations were behind the subsistence
farmers' decision to switch to specialized farming.

benefited by the fruits of their labor."[19] Dearman, Premnath, and Hopkins claim that the catalyst for change involved a shift from what they believe to have been traditional reciprocal methods of exchange toward a redistributive system run by an emboldened political economy.[20] In line with the substantivist view of economic motivation, these biblical scholars' interpretations of economic activity in eighth-century Judah presents a class of farmers forgoing their best self-interests for the economic benefit of an oppressive ruling elite. Data viewed through the substantivist/structuralist viewpoint will be used in determining whether or not structural changes that occur as modern agrarian societies evolve to engage trade can provide new ways of looking at prophetic complaints attributed to eighth-century Judah.

The ecological schools of economic theory provide another useful way of understanding societal evolution. Unlike the structuralist perspective, ecological theorists do not rely so much on how societal structures shape cultural evolution, but on issues of scarcity and starvation. Like structuralist ideas, ecological notions of development are also found in Chaney's and Premnath's reconstructions of eighth-century Judah, as will be detailed below.[21]

The Formalist/Ecological Schools

Until the development of the substantivism in the 1950s, the principal view of societal development was *formalism*; substantivists such as Polanyi and Sahlins viewed their school as its antithesis.[22] Formalist theorists such as Cyril Belshaw, Scott Cook, and D.M.

---

[19] Premnath, "Latifundialization in Isaiah 5.8-10," 308.

[20] Dearman, *Property Rights in the Eighth-Century Prophets: The Conflict and its Background* (eds. Roberts and Talbert; Scholars Press: Atlanta, 1988), 142-49. Premnath, *Eighth Century Prophets: A Social Analysis*, 78-98. Hopkins. "The Dynamics of Agriculture in Monarchical Israel," in *Society of Biblical Literature 1983 Seminar Papers* (ed. Richards; Chico, California: Scholars Press, 1983), 201.

[21] Chaney, "Bitter Bounty." Lang. "The Social Organization of Peasant Poverty in Biblical Israel," in *Anthropological Approaches to the Old Testament* (ed. Lang; London: SPCK, 1985), 85-89.

[22] Polanyi. "The Economy as an Instituted Process," 243. Sahlins, *Stone Age Economics* (Chicago: Aldine-Atherton, 1972), xi-xii.

Goodfellow proposed that individuals make rational economic decisions for themselves, based upon their individual needs and desires.[23] Goodfellow believed that, whether in the case of modern or ancient societies, it was only logical for people to make choices that mirrored either their immediate or long-term needs. Goodfellow wrote,

> Economic choice is constantly exercised by the individual both in disposing of resources for consumption and in the disposal of resources for further production. An individual who disposes unsuccessfully of his supplies will enjoy less satisfactions [sic.] than his neighbors; a household which ineffectively applies its resources to the creation of further commodities will likewise see its members less well supplied with consumable produce than appears to work.[24]

Although formalism acknowledges that societal factors play a role in a farmer's decision-making process, ultimately, if that farmer makes favorable choices in regard to the use of resources, he or she will be rewarded. Conversely, if that same farmer should make errors in his or her decision-making, a less satisfactory outcome will result, thus shaping his or her economic strategy and the decision-making process. An example of the subjective nature of choice can be found in the same example of the Boa Ventura sharecroppers given above.

To a person outside the Boa Ventura sharecroppers' culture, their decision to pay expensive rates for rent and to adhere to an abusive patronage system may appear to be an entirely negative situation that is based on societal pressures. However, Johnson found that from within the system, although the sharecroppers'

---

[23] Belshaw, *Traditional Exchange and Modern Markets* (Englewood Cliffs, N.J.: Prentice-Hall, 1965). Cook, "The Obsolete 'Anti-Market' Mentality: A Critique of the Substantive Approach to Economic Anthropology," *American Anthropologist* 68, no. 2 (1966). Goodfellow, "The Applicability of Economic Theory to So-Called Primitive Communities," in *Economic Anthropology: Readings in Theory and Analysis* (eds. LeClair and Schneider; New York: Holt, Rinehard, and Winston, 1968).

[24] Goodfellow, "The Applicability of Economic Theory to So-Called Primitive Communities," 61.

decisions involved a high level of submission, they were also deliberate and based on biological self-interest. Johnson explains that in the late 1960s these Brazilian sharecroppers received little to no governmental support, such as food aid or medical care.[25] Highly susceptible to drought and famine during times of crisis, "tenant farmers viewed patrons as more than a necessary evil: they were beneficial and strengthening."[26] Although the nature of the relationship between the landowner and the sharecropper may have been exploitative on one level, the decision made by Boa Ventura sharecroppers to comply with abusive societal structures was a rational choice that fulfilled the biological needs of their immediate socio-political situation. This example illustrates that substantivism and formalism are not necessarily exclusive approaches to understanding economic motivation, but can exist simultaneously. Economic players, from administrator to laborer, exercise choice within the rules and norms of a society, even when those choices may be limited by societal constraints.[27]

---

[25] Johnson, "The Psychology of Dependence Between Landlord and Sharecropper in Northeastern Brazil": 426.

[26] Johnson, "The Psychology of Dependence Between Landlord and Sharecropper in Northeastern Brazil": 426.

[27] Ideas about "choice" and "standard of comparison" are detailed in Heimann, *History of Economic Doctrines* (New York: Oxford Press, 1945), 4–5. "Self-interest" is as variable as the individual in question, and depends on one's standard for comparison. Saving money and planning for retirement may serve the self-interests of a professional. A student's self-interests may be fulfilled through incurring debt to pay for an education that will ensure future benefits. For a peasant, self-interest may be served by submitting to corvée labor projects, which will gain the favor of a patron who will, in turn, assist the peasant at a later time. On the other hand, that same peasant could chose to refuse corvée labor demands and reap whatever consequences may follow. Either decision has the potential to produce various outcomes that may be of advantage to the peasant. For more on the debate between these two schools see Polanyi, "The Economy as an Instituted Process," 243. Cook, "The Obsolete 'Anti-Market' Mentality: A Critique of the Substantive Approach to Economic Anthropology": 330-333. Sanderson, *The Evolution of Human Sociality*, 42. Sahlins, *Stone Age Economics*, xi-xii. Belshaw, "Reviewed Work(s): Stone Age Economics by Marshall Sahlins," *American Anthropologist* 75, no. 4

In response to the revival of the substantivist school in the 1970s came a surge of new material from the formalist school, which eventually came to be referred to as the *ecological school.* While proponents of the ecological view of cultural evolution, such as Roy Rappaport and Donald Hardesty, maintained the formalist position that the demand to meet the basic requirements of survival and propagation play a direct role in the economic aspects of cultural evolution, they clarified that social norms also play a significant role.[28] Adding to Steward's work, Hardesty proposed that while societies do evolve as they adapt to their ecological circumstances, this did not occur independently of societal norms. Hardesty observed,

> External processes affect a population's relationship with food, water, weather, and other organisms, among other things. By contrast, internal processes include such things as behavioral, physiological, and genetic responses to population density.[29]

This statement exemplifies how the ecological school is able to acknowledge the importance of both biological and societal influences on cultural evolution.

Anthropologists who adhere to the ecological perspective take issue with structuralist attempts to neglect the biological element in cultural evolution. Ecological-evolutionary theorist Lenski, whose work is used in both Chaney's and Premnath's interpretations of Hebrew prophecy attributed to the eighth-century BCE and who himself has done a cultural-evolutionary study on the development of the Israelite monarchy,[30] claims that "any satisfactory theory of human societies must be both ecological and evolutionary in nature. Human societies do not stand outside the evolving global eco-

---

(1973): 959. Friedman, "Marxism, Structuralism and Vulgar Materialism": 456-57.

[28] Murphy, "Basin Ethnography and Ecological Theory," in *Languages and Cultures of Western North America* (ed. Swanson; Pocatello: Idaho State University Press, 1970). Hardesty, *Ecological Anthropology* (New York: Wiley, 1977).

[29] Hardesty, *Ecological Anthropology*, 11.

[30] Lenski, *Ecological-Evolutionary Theory.*

system; on the contrary, they are an integral part of it."[31] Ecological theory claims that not only are societies directly influenced by their ecological surroundings, but that changes to that environment will result in societal change. Beyond ecological factors, Lenski claims that social and cultural components such as language, technology, morality, ideology, kinship, economy, polity, and religion are a response to a variety of genetically based needs, which the human genome cannot provide for itself.[32] This view addresses the chicken-and-egg scenario that structuralism creates by not considering the origins of societal structures; Lenski claims that societal structures are originally rooted in the biological needs of a society, such as food, shelter, and protection from violence.

Structuralism and the Ecological in the Context of Biblical Interpretation

The interplay between the structuralist and ecological schools of economic thought has significant implications for the use of cultural-evolutionary theory as an interpretive tool in biblical studies. One case in which this exchange proves useful is in addressing the several interpretations of Mic. 2.1–2 and Isa. 5.8 that appear to take for granted that the victims of these instances of land ownership abuse were the hapless prey of greater financial or societal interests.[33] Although the protagonists of these passages likely held positions of power, as will be addressed below, the interplay between structural and ecological theories highlight that a degree of caution must be exercised in absolving small-scale farmers from any responsibility in the matter.

---

[31] Lenski, *Ecological-Evolutionary Theory*, 45.

[32] Lenski, *Ecological-Evolutionary Theory*, 55.

[33] Blenkinsopp, *Isaiah 1-39*, 211. Weber, *Ancient Judaism*, 56-57. Chaney, "Whose Sour Grapes? The Addressees of Isaiah 5:1-7 in the Light of Political Economy," in *The Social World of the Hebrew Bible: Twenty-Five Years of the Social Sciences in the Academy* eds. Simkins and Cook; *Semeia*, ed. Brenner; Atlanta: Society of Biblical Literature, 1999), 107. Dearman, *Property Rights in the Eighth-Century Prophets: The Conflict and its Background*, 42-44.

Premnath's claim that rural producers "benefited in no way"[34] from the increased trade activity in eighth-century Judah is a bold assertion, considering the lack of available evidence that he has to work with; this is a good example of using a social-scientific approach as a source for historical data, rather than as an interpretive tool. From a structuralist perspective, Premnath's view, which reflects a common assumption in commentaries on Isa. 5.8 and Mic. 2.2, dovetails with the structuralists' emphasis on the influence that societal structures have over economic decision-making: that the Judean farmers, as an imagined class,[35] would have been powerless to resist the will of the elite. However, through combining both structural and ecological concerns, some of the complex factors that arise during radical economic transitions become better illuminated. A blossoming wine and olive oil market in the eighth century, to which Israel Finkelstein and Neil Asher Silberman refer,[36] could very well have tempted some small-scale Judean farmers to abandon their subsistence strategies in favor of specialized production. From an ecological perspective, it may have appeared to be in the farmers' best interest to concentrate on olive and grape cultivation so as to profit from new trade opportunities, despite risks such as crop failure and dependence on creditors' loans. In modern Afghanistan, for example, opium-poppy farmers, as a whole, have not needed a lot of coercion to abandon subsistence strategies in order to grow poppies. In recent years these farmers have refused calls by the Afghan government to resume the cultivation of subsistence crops, even through they were promised economic aid in return.[37]

---

[34] Premnath, *Eighth Century Prophets: A Social Analysis*, 102.

[35] It is very rare for farmers to constitute a separate class in agrarian societies, where people of many levels of income and influence participate in farming in one way or another.

[36] Finkelstein and Silberman, "Temple and Dynasty: Hezekiah, the Remaking of Judah and the Rise of the Pan-Israelite Ideology," *JSOTS* 30, no. 3 (2006): 264.

[37] Özerdem, "Disarmament, Demobilisation, and Reintegration of Former Combatants in Afghanistan: Lessons Learned from a Cross-Cultural Perspective," *Third World Quarterly* 23, no. 5 (2002): 970. It should be acknowledged that some of the refusals might not represent an unwill-

Rather than accept such incentives, poppy farmers have blocked roads, burned government vehicles, and fired upon Afghan officials in order to protect their lucrative business interests.[38] Although it cannot be known for certain, it is possible that eighth-century Judean farmers would have also wanted to take advantage of new lucrative trade opportunities as their land was absorbed into the Assyrian economy. Those who took the risk and failed may have been driven into debt and subsequent foreclosure while others prospered and sought to expand their riches by increasing their land wealth. Such a scenario may depend on a capitalist world-view, but is worth contemplating. Through considering both ecological and structural motivations in tandem, new possibilities emerge that present a more complex scenario than Premnath's suggestion of universal suffering among Judean farmers.[39]

Chaney and Premnath both use elements of the structural and ecological schools in their interpretations of prophetic complaints against economic injustice. Although they do not explicitly identify their work with either school, their acknowledgment of both biological and societal pressures in their reconstructions of the socio-economic contexts behind Isa. 5.8–10 and Mic. 2.1–2 reflects the

---

ingness to change their agrarian direction, but a distrust of the current Afghan government.

[38] Özerdem, "Disarmament, Demobilisation, and Reintegration of Former Combatants in Afghanistan: Lessons Learned from a Cross-Cultural Perspective": 970.

[39] Deciphering even the complex motivations of modern farmers, whom a researcher can interview and study first hand, is a difficult task. To uncover the motives behind the economic actions of eighth-century Judean subsistence farmers is a challenge that raises a number of important questions, some of which might not be apparent to many twenty-first-century Western intellectuals. Perhaps the choice to leave subsistence farming for specialized crop production appeared foolish to eighth-century Judean farmers, but the biological and societal factors that may have inspired their decisions are not known. Premnath's theory that these subsistence farmers did not benefit from the changes that took place in the eighth century BCE is an important point to consider, but the certainty that he exhibits is difficult to either evidence or defend.

wide focus that is taken by proponents of the ecological school.[40] While strong structuralist themes can be found in Chaney's and Premnath's theory that Judean courts and systems of patronage played a significant role in the eviction of farmers from their lands, both scholars also consider the potential biological need to centralize agrarian production in order to facilitate the massive levels of population growth that occurred in the late eighth century.[41] Additionally, Chaney's and Premnath's emphases on the importance of subsistence strategies in ancient Judah also recognize the ecological significance of farmers' economic motivations.[42] The issues that have been raised in the debate between structuralist and ecological economic views are essential in exploring how Chaney's and Premnath's interpretations can be evaluated and, perhaps, expanded through examining the effects of corporate globalization on modern agrarian societies.

The material given above provides a general understanding of the theories behind economic motivation and cultural-evolutionary perspectives. Before these theories can be used to employ modern examples for the interpretation of prophetic complaints, an understanding of how the recurring societal patterns found in the cultural evolution of agrarian societies is required. The following section will explain how subsistence economies function and how small-scale farmers are often adversely affected as new trade opportunities or periods of population growth lead to greater dependence on agrarian intensification.

---

[40] Chaney, "Bitter Bounty." Premnath, *Eighth Century Prophets: A Social Analysis*, 5, n.1.

[41] Chaney, "Bitter Bounty." Lang. "The Social Organization of Peasant Poverty in Biblical Israel," 85-89. Chaney, "Micah - Models Matter," 147. Another issue that acknowledges both biological and structural concerns is Premnath's consideration of the Assyrian threat and a potential migration of Samarian refugees from the North, which would have demanded greater systems of organization. Premnath, *Eighth Century Prophets: A Social Analysis*, 16-17.

[42] Chaney, "Whose Sour Grapes?," 106-9. Premnath, *Eighth Century Prophets: A Social Analysis*, 56-57.

C. THE DEVELOPMENT OF POLITICAL ECONOMIES IN SUBSISTENCE COMMUNITIES

Economic Strategy in Subsistence Agriculture

Biblical scholars such as David Hopkins, Paula McNutt, and Finkelstein and Silberman address the importance of *subsistence-based strategies* and *subsistence economies* when commenting on agricultural activity in eighth-century Judah, a period in which subsistence farming is thought to have been diminished to make room for state-controlled trade strategies.[1] Subsistence economies are those in which producers generate goods, whether through hunting and gathering, crop cultivation, animal husbandry, or a combination of these, to meet the basic needs of the household or its immediate community. As Johnson and Earle explain, the overriding goal of a subsistence strategy "is to fulfill the population's needs at the lowest possible cost that affords security."[2] Unfettered with large economic goals that involve external human-made variables like trade networks or the accumulation of capital, a subsistence economy's strength is found in its simplicity.[3]

In line with the multilinear approach to cultural evolution, a variety of strategies may be employed to create an effective subsistence system, each one catering to the particular climatic and resource conditions of a given society's environment. In the erratic precipitation patterns of the southern Levant, various water conservation and crop-mixing strategies have been important safeguards that were designed to increase the likelihood of a successful

---

[1] Hopkins, "Life on the Land: The Subsistence Struggles of Early Israel," *The Biblical Archaeologist* 50, no. 3 (1987). Hopkins, "Bare Bones," 133-34. Premnath, *Eighth Century Prophets: A Social Analysis*, 8-14, 133-34. McNutt, *Reconstructing the Society of Ancient Israel*, 54-55. Finkelstein and Silberman, "Temple and Dynasty": 264, 268-69. Liverani, *Israel's History and the History of Israel* (London: Equinox, 2007, 154-57. Blenkinsopp, *Sage, Priest, Prophet: Religious and Intellectual Leadership in Ancient Israel* (ed. Knight; Louisville: Westminster John Knox Press, 1995), 161.

[2] Johnson and Earle, *The Evolution of Human Societies*, 23.

[3] Invasion or annexation by a foreign power is one variable that is, at times, impossible to avoid.

harvest and, thus, a community's survival.[4] Just as farmers from this region learned to adapt to their environments through crop diversification and focusing their efforts on the cultivation of hardy cereals and grains, agrarian societies around the world have developed and relied upon strategies that cater to their own environmental conditions.

An important aspect of subsistence strategies is a consist approach to cultivation that reflects the community's environment. Anthropologist Robert Dewar notes that the food-production strategies of subsistence farmers in Southeast Asian agrarian societies are extremely diverse, adapting to their various climatic conditions. While farmers who live in areas that experience plentiful rainfall tend to grow a wide variety of grains and rice, farmers from regions that experience unpredictable or scarce levels of rainfall, such as New Guinea and Australia, avoid grain cultivation in favor of hardier root and tree crops.[5] When economic or societal conditions are disrupted, overturning a region's traditional subsistence strategies, crop failure often results, as was the case when European settlers came to Australia. Rather than adapting to their new environment, the settlers who came to Australia chose to cultivate familiar European crops rather than focus on those that had sustained the aboriginal peoples for millennia. As a result of their decision to introduce foreign crops and agrarian strategies instead of following the subsistence strategies used by the indigenous population, the settlers watched their crops wither in Australia's arid climate.[6] As a consequence of their failure to employ native subsistence strategies, they suffered from severe food shortages.

When left undisturbed, subsistence-based societies tend to be fairly stable since levels of production dictate the numbers that the

---

[4] David Hopkins and Oded Borowski have both written extensively on these strategies. See Hopkins, *The Highlands of Canaan: Agricultural Life in the Early Iron Age* (ed. Flanagan; vol. 3; Sheffield: Almond, 1985), 235-45. Borowski, *Agriculture in Iron Age Israel* (Boston: American School of Oriental Research, 2002), 18-20.

[5] Dewar, "Rainfall Variability and Subsistence Systems in Southeast Asia and the Western Pacific," *Current Anthropology* 44, no. 3 (2003), 376-77.

[6] Dewar, "Rainfall Variability and Subsistence Systems," 376.

land can sustain. As James Acheson writes, "Small populations operating with a low level of technology and local markets will rarely overexploit resources" since subsistence societies only need to meet sustainable levels of production and do not demand the large amounts of resources that are required for engaging in interregional trade.[7] However, when populations began to exceed their regions' carrying capacities in the ancient Near East, Robert Coote and Keith Whitelam note, controlling factors such as disease, famine, and conflict often brought numbers back down to manageable levels.[8] For a society to successfully navigate these controlling factors and enable further population growth, major societal changes need to take place.

Causes and Consequences of Adaptation

Whether stimulated by migratory movements, colonization, changes in the environment, or technological advances, a variety of challenges emerge as societies that rely upon mixed-subsistence strategies experience a rapid increase in population growth. As the balance between the land's carrying capacity and its finite quantity of resources is disrupted, traditional subsistence strategies that were previously able to sustain the local population become inadequate. When a society's top-tier food stores become scarce, people are forced to turn to less desirable foods that had once served as buffers in times of shortage. As these second-tier foods become a part of the population's staple diet, the society is left without insurance against crop failure, leading to an increased risk of starvation.[9] Johnson and Earle note that it is during these dangerous times, as new challenges and pressures such as production risk, resource competition, a need for capital investment in technology, and the need for trade arise, that family-based production strategies are

---

[7] Acheson. "Management of Common-Property Resources," in *Economic Anthropology* (ed. Plattner; Stanford: Stanford University Press, 2002), 372.

[8] Coote and Whitelam, *The Emergence of Early Israel: In Historical Perspective* (SWBA 5; ed. Flanagan; Sheffield: Almond Press, 1987), 50-52.

[9] Johnson and Earle, *The Evolution of Human Societies*, 16.

abandoned.[10] The choice to abandon family-focused subsistence strategies is an example of biologically-based economic decision-making leading to cultural evolution.

As the carrying capacity of a region is strained, the production and distribution of goods requires a greater degree of management. Anthropologist George Cowgill claims that although this problem is a significant obstacle for societies that experience continued growth, it is often a self-correcting predicament. In agreement with Coote and Whitelam's theory on self-regulating factors in ancient Palestine,[11] Cowgill writes,

> Sudden shortage crisis, such as crop failures and ensuing famine, usually has led to hoarding, exhaustion of reserves, a sharp rise in food prices, and death by starvation and disease on a large scale, rather than to developmental innovations to avert the crisis. If for no other reason the stress occurs too suddenly and too unpredictably for much to be done about it.[12]

Cowgill is correct to highlight the fact that population growth does not necessarily precipitate long-term societal change, but increases in population can serve as a catalyst for cultural evolution when societies successfully overcome these problems. Nolan and Lenski note that innovative responses to such challenges can facilitate yet further increases in sustainable population size.[13] Although such a cycle cannot persist indefinitely, societies can continue to grow and evolve through the introduction of increased collaborative organization, centralized political-economic strategies, and, ultimately, increased societal differentiation.

When the strain on the land's carrying capacity renders traditional subsistence strategies insufficient, two classic forms of production-risk management tend to be implemented: 1) the development of community food storage centers and 2) the creation of

---

[10] Johnson and Earle, *The Evolution of Human Societies*, 30-32.

[11] Coote and Whitelam, *The Emergence of Early Israel*, 51.

[12] Cowgill, "On Causes and Consequences of Ancient and Modern Population Changes," *American Anthropologist* 77, no. 3 (1975): 507.

[13] Nolan and Lenski, *Human Societies: An Introduction to Macrosociology* (Boulder: Paradigm Publishers, 2004), 53-54.

reciprocal arrangements among different communities.[14] Risk can be reduced through managing the production and consumption of foodstuffs while expanding cultivation efforts in areas that were not previously tilled.[15] By successfully following these strategies, which have been employed by various cultures from prehistoric France and ancient Nevada to modern-day Java, communities have increased the likelihood of successful harvests, kept waste to a minimum, and effectively managed rapid increases in population growth.[16] Although such efforts can increase a community's chance of survival, they come at a significant cost: subsistence farmers are forced to abandon family-centered production strategies and accept outside forms of control. In the end, families trade the independence that is associated with subsistence-based production and become an integral part of a society's cultural values and norms for intercommunity-based strategies that can protect against famine.

Another common means of coping with depleted resources, which is often practiced in congruence with the development of systems of central management, is increased involvement in trade. Johnson and Earle note that trade with other communities can effectively compensate for agrarian challenges such as seasonal or annual shortfalls.[17] Not only can stores be supplemented through importing foodstuffs in times of scarcity, but technologies can also be imported to help increase the efficiency of domestic production. Johnson and Earle write, "…trade in specialized goods increases the overall efficiency with which a population can be provisioned from limited resources, and thus the capacity to sustain a larger population on the same resource base."[18] But as with organized

---

[14] Johnson and Earle, *The Evolution of Human Societies*, 16.
[15] These strategies appear to have been implemented in eighth-century Judah, as addressed in Chapter Three.
[16] Mellars, "The Ecological Basis of Social Complexity in the Upper Paleolithic of Southwestern France," in *Prehistoric Hunter-Gatherers: The Emergence of Cultural Complexity* eds. Price and Brown; London: Academic Press, 1985). Larson, "Population Growth, Agricultural Intensification, and Cultural Change among the Virgin Branch Anasazi, Nevada," *Journal of Field Archaeology* 23, no. 1 (1996): 69-70.
[17] Johnson and Earle, *The Evolution of Human Societies*, 31.
[18] Johnson and Earle, *The Evolution of Human Societies*, 31.

surplus and inter-communal reciprocity strategies, trade comes at a cultural cost to subsistence farmers; to make an efficient enough use of trade to make it worthwhile, a group of people has to take control of production and oversee the exchange of goods. The development or strengthening of such a management class will, ultimately, further erode family-based decision-making powers and independence. Families that had been accustomed to using their own judgment in the cultivation of crops and the production of goods to benefit their immediate communities are made to produce for people whom they may never meet. Enduring both management from and also labor for people outside of the immediate community is a foreign concept for a subsistence farmer that, culturally, is not often easy to accept.

The idea of population growth as a catalyst for cultural change may relate to the changes that took place in Judah during the late eighth century. Although the cause behind the apparent boom in population at that time cannot be known for certain, several biblical scholars and archaeologists, including Finkelstein and Silberman and Larry Herr, have suggested that the Assyrian destruction of the Northern Kingdom around 720 BCE led to a massive migration of refugees into Judah.[19] Regardless of the reason for this growth, a significant and sudden population increase would have placed a greater burden on the land that would likely have led to such measures as an increased centralization of agrarian production help protect against starvation. However, it is unlikely that population growth was the only instigator of the societal changes that occurred in Judah. Finkelstein and Silberman note that a variety of factors are likely to have led to agricultural centralization and cultural change in late eighth-century Judah, highlighting that "in a few decades, Judahite demography, economy, and society were totally revolutionized. Judah was transformed from an isolated formative tribal state into a developed state, fully incorporated into the

---

[19] Finkelstein and Silberman, "Temple and Dynasty": 265-69. Herr, "Archaeological Sources for the History of Palestine: The Iron Age II Period: Emerging Nations," 60, no. 3 (1997): 157. Davies and Rogerson, *The Old Testament World* (Louisville: Westminster John Knox Press, 2005), 81. McNutt, *Reconstructing the Society of Ancient Israel*, 151.

Assyrian global economy."[20] From massive population growth in rural and urban areas to Judah's entrance into the Assyrian global economy and the wider world system in which it participated, Judah experienced a radical demographic shift that would have had major implications for the daily lives of the region's farmers. To facilitate such levels of growth, a strong political economy would have been required.

Negative Consequences of a Strengthened Political Economy

The largest benefits and debits of a political economy, namely the ability to efficiently orchestrate the production, storage, and distribution of food at the cost of self-sufficiency, have been addressed above. With the development of the administrative bureaucracies that oversee this management come increased opportunities for exploitation. Unlike the family-focused strategies of the subsistence economy, the interests of the political economy reach far beyond the immediate household as goods and services produced by individual families are exchanged throughout networks of interconnected communities, for what Mancur Olsen referred to as the "collective good."[21] Although a share of the surplus goes to benefit the interests of individual producers, eventually, the best of the *collective good* is directed toward an emerging ruling class. The development of this new ruling elite, who become responsible for the collection, storage, protection, trade, and distribution of the community's goods, leads to the development of class divisions and social stratification. Sanderson notes that "at some point, some people get themselves into a position by means of which they can compel other people to work for them and produce substantial quantities of storable food."[22] As a result, systems of exploitation

---

[20] Finkelstein and Silberman, "Temple and Dynasty": 266.

[21] Olson, *The Logic of Collective Action: Public Goods and the Theory of Groups* (Cambridge, Mass: Harvard University Press, 1965), 15. Johnson and Earle, *The Evolution of Human Societies*, 364. Polanyi claimed that at the heart of the political economy is the creation and distribution of surplus. Polanyi. "The Economy as Instituted Process," 262-63.

[22] Sanderson, *The Evolution of Human Sociality*, 300-01.

develop, and the economic activities to which structuralists refer
begin to shape economic decision-making.

Increased Exploitation

The development of exploitative systems begins as a small segment
of the population that had previously farmed or hunted to produce
foodstuffs is released from its laborious duties to specialize in essential administrative responsibilities that ensure that the political
economy functions efficiently and staves off starvation.[23] As a result, this new class is rendered agriculturally non-productive and
dependent upon the community's surplus for its sustenance.[24]
These developments lead to the creation of power structures that
had been unnecessary in a subsistence economy, placing an administrative minority within a society above the producing majority.

As new societal roles emerge, such as that of an administrator,
tax collector, or religious leader, interaction between community
members begins to change. The total dependence of the elite upon
the labor of the rest of the community is an alien concept to a society accustomed to self-sufficiency, challenging traditional norms
surrounding labor, landownership, and social interaction. Fried
notes that "by differentially distributing access to basic means of
livelihood and by simultaneously making possible the exploitation
of human labor in the conventional Marxist sense, stratified societies create pressures unknown in egalitarian and rank societies."[25]
The conflict between societal norms and biological need is found
in this situation. While the community decides to employ higher
levels of organization for survival, the norms that develop out of
this organization lead to the exploitation of the majority of that

---

[23] Economic anthropologist Francis Berdan states that this extra time
allows the emerging ruling elite to participate in political and economic
activities, craft production, trading enterprises, as well as in religious of-
fices. Berdan, "Trade and Markets in Precapitalist States," in *Economic Anthropology* (ed. Plattner; Stanford: Stanford University Press, 2002), 80.

[24] Berdan, "Trade and Markets in Precapitalist States," 80. Deist, *The
Material Culture of the Bible: An Introduction* (70; ed. Carroll; Sheffield: Sheffield Academic Press, 2000), 169.

[25] Fried, *The Evolution of Political Society*, 186.

community's population. As traditional methods of production and conservation are overturned to facilitate new strategies, tensions begin to rise.

During these periods of transition the external demands placed on farmers who have been accustomed to working for their own benefit, as well as keeping their labor efforts to a minimum, create significant tensions between producers and managers, sometimes leading to revolt.[26] In order to maintain their positions of power, elites need to ensure that participation in the political economy continues to be to the advantage of farming families. The building of irrigation systems, community defenses, or other public works that cannot be easily achieved by individual families helps to ensure that farmers find it more costly not to participate in the political economy than to accept its demands.[27] However, sometimes populations cannot be convinced to accept the demands of a political economy through these means. As Lenski, Lenski, and Nolan observe, "An ideology that [motivates] farmers to produce more than they needed to stay alive and productive, and convinces them to turn that surplus over to someone else" may be required to ensure compliance.[28] The creation of fictive kinships to simulate an artificial sense of historical community between peoples has been a common method through which families have been convinced to work together for the benefit of a larger community.[29] The reinterpretation of religious beliefs or doctrines is another method that will be discussed at length below.

---

[26] Lenski, et al., *Human Societies: An Introduction to Macrosociology* (New York: McGraw-Hill, 1991), 162. Kautsky, *The Politics of Aristocratic Empires* (New Brunswick: Transaction Publishers, 1997), 278-92.

[27] Johnson and Earle, *The Evolution of Human Societies*, 27-29.

[28] Lenski, et al., *Human Societies*, 162.

[29] Nolan and Lenski, *Human Societies*, 149. Johnson and Earle, *The Evolution of Human Societies*, 25. Lee, *The !Kung San: Men, Women, and World in a Foraging Society* (Cambridge: Cambridge University Press, 1979), 334-36.

Sustenance Concerns Become Overshadowed by Market Considerations

Although a political economy may be strengthened by the demands of population growth, agricultural centralization eventually leads to strategies based on cultivation-for-profit. Both Friend and Sanderson note that the goals of a political economy do not continue to focus on sustaining the needs of the community, but become refocused on fulfilling the desires of the ruling elite.[30] According to sociologists and economic anthropologists like Lenski, Plattner, and Johnson and Earle, a set of reoccurring patterns have tended to manifest themselves throughout time and across cultures, as agrarian societies have undergone rapid economic growth.[31] According to economic anthropologists and sociologists like Stewart Plattner, Lenski, Johnson, and Earle, patterns that transcend time or culture recur as agrarian societies have undergone rapid economic growth, which has be seen as far back as the early Bronze Age and as recently as modern-day Mexico and Vietnam.[32] During these periods of development administrators coerce farmers into abandoning traditional subsistence strategies and the socio-religious norms that had traditionally supported these practices, productive

---

[30] Fried, *The Evolution of Political Society*, 186. Sanderson, *The Evolution of Human Sociality*, 300-01.

[31] Plattner. "Markets and Marketplaces," in *Economic Anthropology* (ed. Plattner; Stanford: Stanford University Press, 2002), 180-81. Johnson and Earle, *The Evolution of Human Societies* (Stanford: Stanford University Press, 1987), 255. Nolan and Lenski, *Human Societies*, 159-60.

[32] Richard, "The Early Bonze Age: The Rise and Collapse of Urbanism," *The Biblical Archaeologist* 50, no. 1 (1987). Dever, "Archaeological Sources for the History of Palestine: The Middle Bronze Age: The Zenith or the Urban Canaanite Era," *The Biblical Archaeologist* 50, no. 3 (1987): 152. Hernández Castillo and Nigh, "Global Processes and Local Identity Among Mayan Coffee Growers in Chiapas, Mexico," *American Anthropology* 100, no. 1 (1998): 140. Chossudovsky, *The Globalization of Poverty* (Pincourt, Québec Global Research, 2003), 180-83. Hilton, "Peasant Movement In England Before 1381," 2, second series, no. 2 (1931): 122. There is also evidence for these patterns in thirteenth-century England and sixteenth-century Japan. Plattner. "Markets and Marketplaces," 180-81. Johnson and Earle, *The Evolution of Human Societies*, 255. Nolan and Lenski, *Human Societies: An Introduction to Macrosociology*, 159-60.

capabilities are consolidated to enable the mass production of exportable goods through the consolidation of small farmsteads into large estates, or *latifundia*, as elites hoard the benefits of these developments within their own class through systems of patronage and exclusion.[33]

According to Lenski, ruling elites employ a wide range of strategies to seize their subjects' lands… from driving farmers into debt through taxation or loans to using threats of physical violence.[34] As the land becomes consolidated into large landholdings, or *latifundia*, rulers tend to use systems of favoritism and exclusion to grant these estates to loyal members of their own class, ensuring that the lands are used to further elite interests.[35] As the land becomes more concentrated and the political economy strengthens, farmers are forced to abandon risk-reducing subsistence strategies to facilitate the cultivation of revenue-producing crops. As the needs of the producer become secondary, farmers are forced to endure hardships, such as limited access to arable land, food, and specialized goods.[36] Johnson and Earle describe the end result as a shattering of "whatever remained of the self-sufficiency of the [subsistence farming] household."[37] Such scenarios are common throughout the modern developing world.[38]

It is the recurring nature of this pattern of exploitation that has drawn biblical scholars to use cultural-evolutionary theory as a means to understand societal change in eighth-century Judah, and offers the possibility that modern manifestations of these changes may be able to inspire new interpretations of the data presented in

---

[33] Plattner. "Markets and Marketplaces," 180-81. Johnson and Earle, *The Evolution of Human Societies*, 255. Nolan and Lenski, *Human Societies*, 159-60.

[34] Lenski, *Power and Privilege: A Theory of Social Stratification* (New York: McGraw-Hill Book Company, 1966), 220.

[35] Lenski, *Power and Privilege*, 220.

[36] Fried, *The Evolution of Political Society*, 186. Sanderson, *The Evolution of Human Sociality*, 300-01.

[37] Johnson and Earle, *The Evolution of Human Societies*, 273.

[38] Hernández Castillo and Nigh, "Global Processes and Local Identity Among Mayan Coffee Growers in Chiapas, Mexico": 140. Chossudovsky, *The Globalization of Poverty*, 180-83, 221-22.

the prophetic literature and the archaeological record. As Lenski warns, however, any such patterns rarely reoccur without variation and cannot create a perfect picture of what might happen in another time and place.[39] Nevertheless, the possibility of such a pattern occurring in eighth-century Judah has offered a model through which biblical scholars have interpreted prophetic texts attributed to that time, and through which an opportunity is created for examining the negative effects of corporate globalization as an interpretive tool.

---

[39] Lenski, *Ecological-Evolutionary Theory*, 6.

D. THE INTERPRETIVE VALUE OF CULTURAL-EVOLUTIONARY THEORY IN BIBLICAL STUDIES

Not all scholars agree that the use of cultural-evolutionary theory, or any other social-scientific theory for that matter, can play a constructive role in the field of biblical studies, and the questions that they raise must be considered and addressed before engaging in the present study. As evident in this chapter, many social scientists adamantly believe that cultural-evolutionary theory can help to develop an understanding of how ancient societies functioned and responded to factors such as population growth, foreign dominance, and economic opportunity. Goodfellow, for one, claims that modern economic theory is applicable to "primitive societies."[1] He argued that the fact that such divergent peoples can live within a single culture is a key to understanding how similarities can exist not only between contemporary cultures, but also between cultures that existed in different periods of time. Addressing the question as to whether modern economic theory can provide insight into primitive cultures, Goodfellow wrote,

> ...if [a social scientific model] does not apply to the whole of humanity then it is meaningless. For there is no gulf between the civilized and the primitive; one cultural level shades imperceptibly into another and more than one level is frequently found within a single community.[2]

While a sizeable gulf may be absent, the differences between ancient and modern are many and deserve our respect and attention.

Even though the instruments of production, trade, and the economic philosophies that drive cultural evolution in various societies may be significantly different, the hardships that producers face as political economic interests overpower subsistence concerns appear similar, regardless of time or culture. During periods of agricultural centralization and political development in both early and

---

[1] Goodfellow. "The Applicability of Economic Theory to So-Called Primitive Communities."

[2] Goodfellow. "The Applicability of Economic Theory to So-Called Primitive Communities," 57.

modern states, including fourth century BCE Athens, thirteenth century CE England, sixteenth century CE Japan, and twentieth century CE Tunisia, farmers have suffered under increased exploitation and land poverty as a minority of elites have enjoyed the economic benefits that can be gained from latifundialization and increased social stratification.[3]

Despite Goodfellow's insistence that the present can help us to understand the past, scholars like Malina, Grabbe, and Esler have justifiably raised concerns as to how the social sciences have been used in biblical Studies.[4] The social sciences can be easily misused if they are treated as a natural science like chemistry or medicine, as the early nineteenth century French philosopher Auguste Comte did with his theories on "social laws."[5] Definitive laws of behavior and development do not exist in societies, as they tend to work and evolve in dynamic ways. Changing political and social climates and external factors can create varied responses to a given stimulus even within the single society, such as the differing public reactions to the United States' involvement in the Korean and Vietnam wars. Attempts to use the social sciences in this way produce false results that are counterproductive to the field. Rather than employ such a rigid approach, Esler suggests an approach akin to that of Weber, who defined sociology as "a science which attempts the interpretive understanding of social action in order

---

[3] Berdan, "Trade and Markets in Precapitalist States," in *Economic Anthropology* (ed. Plattner; Stanford: Stanford University Press, 1989), 80. Asheri, "Laws of Inheritance, Distribution of Land and Political Constitutions in Ancient Greece," *Historia* 12, (1963): 4. Johnson and Earle, *The Evolution of Human Societies*, 254-55. Hilton, "Peasant Movement In England Before 1381": 122. United Nations Children's Fund, *The State of the World's Children* (New York: Oxford University Press, 1989).

[4] Malina, "The Social Sciences and Biblical Interpretation," in *The Bible and Liberation: Political and Social Hermeneutics* (ed. Gottwald; Maryknoll, New York: Orbis Books, 1983), 12-13. Grabbe, *Ancient Israel*, 5. Houston, *Contending for Justice: Ideologies and Theologies of Social Justice in the Old Testament* (London: T&T Clark, 2006), 6-7. Esler. "Social-Scientific Models in Biblical Interpretation."

[5] Comte, *Introduction to Positive Philosophy* (ed. Ferré; Indianapolis: Bobbs-Merrill, 1970).

thereby to arrive at a causal explanation of its course and effects."[6] Through using social-scientific theories for interpretive purposes, rather than as a source for definitive historical answers, new avenues through which to approach the biblical texts can be discovered. It is through this realization that the tenets of cultural-evolutionary theory can be a benefit, rather than a hindrance, to the field of biblical studies.

Chaney's and Premnath's use Cultural-Evolutionary Theory

Chaney's and Premnath's approach to the social sciences in their research on the socio-economic context behind prophetic literature attributed to eighth-century Judah appears to appreciate the complex nature of cultural evolution. Rather than adhering to a single school of thought, both Chaney and Premnath take a combined approach, making it difficult to pin down their methodologies in a concise manner. Chaney states that he finds value in the ecologically-based evolutionary approaches used by Gerhard and Jean Lenski, the Marx and Malthus-based cultural materialist ideas of Marvin Harris, and the structural functionalist philosophy of Talcott Parsons, each of which are reflected in his work.[7] In the introduction of Premnath's book, *Eighth Century Prophets: A Social Analysis*, he explains that a twin focus of systemic sociological approach is employed, which combines both comparative and historical approaches.[8] Premnath appears to pattern his work after Chaney's

---

[6] Quoted by Esler from Weber, *The Theory of Social and Economic Organization* (ed. Parsons; trans. Henderson and Parsons; New York: The Free Press and Collier Macmillian Publishers, 1964). in Esler. "Social-Scientific Models in Biblical Interpretation," 5.

[7] Chaney, "Systemic Study of the Israelite Monarchy," in *Social Scientific Criticism of the Hebrew Bible and Its Social World: The Israelite Monarchy* (ed. Gottwald; vol. 37 of *Semeia: An Experimental Journal for Biblical Criticism*; Decatur, Georgia: The Society of Biblical Literature, 1986), 51.

[8] Premnath, *Eighth Century Prophets: A Social Analysis*, 3. The comparative dimension looks at eighth-century Palestine in relation to other societies, while the historical considers major events that modified the society as a whole.

approach, combining the works of the Lenski and Lenski, Harris, and Parsons in his research.[9]

Although Chaney's and Premnath's diverse approaches can invite the danger of cherry-picking those sociological and anthropological theories that support their work, there is significant value to be found in combining various approaches. Johnson and Earle believe that a multi-angular approach can reflect the complex nature of societies, giving credence to the variety of potential factors that cause societies to change.[10] Considering that no single methodology can address all of the nuances that make up a culture and lead to its evolution, there is an advantage in considering cultural evolutionary processes through a variety of lenses, with all necessary caveats. Following this reasoning, and in line with the ecological school of cultural-evolutionary theory, both the societal pressures and the biological motivations that have shaped the formation of agrarian societies in both the modern and ancient worlds will be considered.

As mentioned above, the evolutionary changes that took place in Tunisia in the twentieth-century CE, as the country was absorbed into the world-system of corporate globalization, will be used to augment the interpretive value of cultural-evolutionary theory. However, before such a study can commence, material evidence of transformative periods of economic development in the ancient Near East, and eighth-century Judah in particular, must be explored. The following chapter will use archaeological evidence and cultural-evolutionary theory to examine the economic cycles that appear to have taken place in Palestine as early as the Bronze Age and continued on to Judah's incorporation into a major world system in the late eighth and early seventh centuries BCE.

---

[9] Premnath, *Eighth Century Prophets: A Social Analysis*, 5, 1n.
[10] Johnson and Earle, *The Evolution of Human Societies*, 19-20.

3 TRADE AND TRANSFORMATION IN THE ANCIENT WORLD

Since the beginning of Early Bronze Age (EB) interregional trade has led to the exchange of both goods and cultural ideas throughout Palestine and the Near East.[1] Naturally, Sumerian merchants were unable to transport their merchandise around the globe as multi-national corporations do today, but they did transport goods throughout the world that was accessible to them. As a result, administrating officials and rural producers alike experienced the beneficial and harmful consequences of trade.[2] Sometimes the changes caused by increased economic activity were fleeting, lasting only a short time and with little long-term effect on the societies involved, while other instances created significant changes that led societies to evolve both economically and culturally.

Ancient examples of interregional trade systems, such as the world system that expanded across the Mediterranean and southern Europe during the rise of the Neo-Assyrian Empire in Iron Age II, are not divorced from the current world system of corporate globalization, but are its precursors. Joachim Rennstich, George Modelski, and William Thompson argue that modern economic-globalization is not a product of the twentieth century but the latest manifestation of an evolutionary process that has gone through

---

[1] Edens, "Dynamics of Trade in the Ancient Mesopotamian 'World System,'" *American Anthropologist* 94, no. 1 (1992): 132.

[2] Hudson, "The Dynamics of Privatization: From the Bronze Age to the Present," in *Privatization in the Ancient Near East and Classical World* eds. Hudson and Levine; Cambridge, MA: Harvard University, 1996), 43-46.

various cycles since the fourth millennium BCE.[3] Rennstich argues that

> ...whereas the driving logic (human agency) of this process remains the same, its context changes, constituting a 'social learning algorithm' of evolutionary change that is at work at all levels of the global system process (from the individual to the change of the global system as a whole).[4]

Although technological advances and the lessons learned from previous systems create differing contexts as trade develops and becomes more efficient, the key goals that drive the process remain unchanged. Complex systems of interregional trade, with similar outcomes for agrarian producers, have existed for millennia in various forms.

Evidence for such developments in ancient Palestine are found in archaeological and extra-biblical literary remains pertaining not only to Judah in the eighth and seventh centuries, but dating back to EB I. Although this evidence cannot give a clear picture as to how fluctuations in economic activity affected Judean society, many of the findings have been interpreted as having created significant societal changes that dovetail with the socio-economic context that Chaney and Premnath draw from Isa. 5.8–10 and Mic. 2.1–2. In order to get an idea of how developing world systems and their economic ramifications may have affected the lives of subsistence farmers in eighth-century Judah, this study will begin with the cycles of development that occurred throughout the Bronze Age. It is these cycles that can help to reveal the societal transforming potential that trade has on agrarian societies.

---

[3] Rennstich. "Three Steps in Globalization: Global Networks from 1000 BCE to 2050 CE," in *Globalization and Global History* eds. Gills and Thompson; vol. 2 of *Rethinking Globalizations,* ed. Gills; London: Routledge, 2006), 204-8. Modelski. "World System Evolution," in *World System History: The Social Science of Long-Term Change* eds. Denemark, Friedman, Gills and Moldeski; London: Routledge, 2000), 35-37. Modelski and Thompson, *Leading Sectors and World Powers: The Coevolution of Global Politics and Economics* (Columbia, SC: University of South Carolina Press, 1996).

[4] Rennstich. "Three Steps in Globalization: Global Networks from 1000 BCE to 2050 CE," 205.

A. EFFECTS OF INTERREGIONAL TRADE IN THE BRONZE AGE

Interregional trade during the Bronze Age is often evidenced through urban centers and their cycles of expansion and contraction. As shall be discussed in this section, both the waxing and the waning of these communities give evidence of the transformative power of economic development in agrarian societies. Before exploring the economic dealings of ancient communities, it is important to note that the words *urban* and *trade* can be misleading when used in the ancient context. For the modern individual, who lives in a world of powerful international organizations and alliances that reshaped much of the world in twentieth century CE, urbanism and trade in the ancient Near East can appear quaint by comparison. Unlike the massive metropolitan administrative centers of today, like New York City, which as of 2008 had an estimated population of over 8.3 million people[1] and covered an area of more than three-hundred square miles,[2] urban centers in the Early Bronze Age often ranged between ten and twenty acres in size.[3]

Although these ancient sites appear miniscule and scattered when compared to their modern counterparts, it would be a mistake to slight their relative importance. These ancient centers may not have been designed to produce or trade a volume of goods that would be noteworthy by twenty-first century standards, but as Martin Silver suggests, the extent of early industrialization "should be measured not in absolute terms, but in terms relative to the size of the economy."[4] Since no period in ancient Palestine's history would

---

[1] New York City, *New York City Department of City Planning* (New York City Department of City Planning, 2008 [February, 24 2010]); available from http://www.nyc.gov/html/dcp/html/census/popcur.shtml.

[2] U.S. Census Bureau: *State and County Quick Facts: New York (City), New York* (U.S. Census Bureau, 2000 [February, 24 2010]); available from http://quickfacts.census.gov/qfd/states/36/3651000.html.

[3] Richard, "The Early Bonze Age: The Rise and Collapse of Urbanism," 50, no. 1 (1987): 25.

[4] Silver, *Prophets and Markets: The Political Economy of Ancient Israel* (Boston: Klwer-Nijhoff Publishing, 1983), 15.

have had near the population levels of modern Israel, around 10.5 million,[5] current levels of production and distribution should not be held as a standard when considering ancient contexts.

Just as the word *urban* takes on a different meaning in the ancient Near Eastern context, so too does the word *trade*. In much of the early twenty-first-century CE world, the, trade is commonly associated with privately-owned businesses or corporations exchanging goods, services, or knowledge in an international marketplace. Before addressing trade in the ancient Near east, it must be acknowledged that superimposing this modern concept of trade on the Bronze and Iron ages is misleading. Moses Finley notes that unlike the privately managed trade that takes place today, ancient Near Eastern economies

...were dominated by large palace or temple-complexes, who owned the greater part of the arable [and] virtually monopolized anything that can be called 'industrial production' as well as foreign trade (which includes inter-city trade, not merely trade with foreign parts).[6]

Trade was not the result of individual or corporate efforts of private individuals, but was run by a single governing authority. A large reason for the government-domination of trade in the ancient world was due to the immense expenses that were involved in transporting goods and materials over long distances; individual merchants could not make small-scale trade profitable at such costs. This does not mean, however, that individuals did not partake in peripheral roles, such as cultivating crops that were in demand and selling goods alongside trade routes.

Finley finds that because this discrepancy between modern and ancient trade is often overlooked, those who attempt to wrestle with economic issues in the ancient world often draw false conclusions; they imagine trade to be executed through wide-reaching conglomerations of interdependent markets rather than ancient

---

[5] This number includes the inhabitants of Gaza and the West Bank.

[6] Finley, *The Ancient Economy* (2nd ed; Berkeley: University of California Press, 1985), 28.

states.[7] Failing to recognize these differences between modern and ancient economic practice can lead to problems of definition. For example, words like *economy* and *trade* will likely produce images in most modern minds that are not congruent what the realities of the ancient world. While I strongly argue that it is beneficial to use recent understandings of economic processes to ask questions of economic processes in the ancient world,[8] Finley contends that the ancients would not have thought of intellectualized their activities in these terms.[9]

While Finley's work primarily focuses on the politics and economic activities of ancient Greece and Rome, his warning is pertinent to the subject at hand. The center of landownership and trade in the ancient Near East was not private individuals or independent economic bodies but temples.[10] While terms like *political economy* and *economic strategies* and words like *trade* will be used throughout the rest of this chapter and book, it is important to remember their ancient contexts, which were largely centered in state activity.

Cycles of Urbanism and Trade in the Early Bronze Age

Palestine did not commit to long-term urban economic strategies to the same degree that other ancient Near Eastern societies had in the Early Bronze Age. Even in the Middle Bronze Age (MB), Palestinian urbanism was unexceptional. Steven Falconer notes that in

> ...comparison with Mesopotamian settlement patterns suggests Levantine urbanism was modest in scale and centralization. Middle Bronze Age urbanism may be profitably reassessed as a patchwork of settlement systems in which towns

---

[7] Finley, The Ancient Economy, 22-23.

[8] Such interaction between modern scientific-understanding and ancient realities, such as medical knowledge, is often used to determine ancient events, such as the recent conclusions on the death of Tutankhamen. See Wilford, "Malaria is Likely Killer in King Tut's Post-Mortem," (New York Times, February 16, 2010 [February 24, 2010]); available from http://www.nytimes.com/2010/02/17/science/17tut.html.

[9] Finley, The Ancient Economy, 23.

[10] Stevens, *Temples, Tithes, and Taxes: The Temple and the Economic Life of Ancient Israel* (Peabody, Massachusetts: Hendrickson Publishing, 2006).

and cities were concentrated on or near the Mediterranean coast.[11]

There is evidence that Palestine engaged in trade with its neighbors as early as the Neolithic period, but its inhabitants did not exchange their reliance on subsistence strategies for urban development as quickly as some of their neighbors.[12] From the sixth to the fourth millennia BCE, Suzanne Richard writes, Palestine was a land of "small regional village and pastoral societies, at a time when major advances toward the development of the city-state system in Mesopotamia was well underway."[13] It was not until EB I-III that Palestine's dispersed village culture began to transform into a system of larger settlements and engage in interregional trade, as evidenced by Egyptian materials found in Palestine and Canaanite pottery found in Egypt dating to EB I.[14] Richard claims that it was due to this development in EB I that the inhabitants of Palestine experienced significant changes in social and economic strategy, transforming a group of egalitarian tribal communities into a hierarchical pre-state society.[15] However, the changes that were brought about through political and economic interaction with

---

[11] Falconer, "Rural Responses to Early Urbanism: Bronze Age Household and Village Economy at Tell el-Hayyat, Jordan," 22, no. 4 (1995): 401.

[12] Richards, "Local Strategies for Coping with Hunger: Central Sierra Leone and Northern Nigeria Compared," *African Affairs* 89, no. 355 (1990): 22.

[13] Richard, "The Early Bonze Age: The Rise and Collapse of Urbanism": 22.

[14] Harrison, "Shifting Patterns of Settlement in the Highlands of Central Jordan during the Early Bronze Age," *Bulletin of the American Schools of Oriental Research* no. 306 (1997): 11-13. Harrison, "Economics with an Entrepreneurial Spirit: Early Bronze Trade with Late Predynastic Egypt," *The Biblical Archaeologist* 56, no. 2 (1993). Falconer, "Rural Responses to Early Urbanism." Ben-Tor, "New Light on the Relations Between Egypt and Southern Palestine During the Early Bronze Age," *Bulletin of the American Schools of Oriental Research* no. 281 (1991). Ward, "Early Contacts Between Egypt, Canaan, and Sinai: Remarks on the Paper by Amon Ben-Tor," *Bulletin of the American Schools of Oriental Research* no. 281 (1991).

[15] Richard, "The Early Bonze Age," 27.

neighboring civilizations did not eradicate Palestine's agrarian and pastoral traditions, but created a cyclical pattern that affected the degree of influence that subsistence farming had in the region.

As in much of the ancient Near East, the rise of urban development in Palestine did not follow a linear progression, but went through cycles of increasing and decreasing economic activity.[16] It is these cycles that offer potential evidence of cultural evolution and their common effects on subsistence communities in the ancient Near East, as will be discussed below.

Importance of Palestine's Geographic Location

Palestine's position between Asia and Egypt made it a focus of political and economic strategy for neighboring empires.[17] Due to the geographic value of Palestine's location, the region experienced reoccurring cycles of trade and population growth, followed by periods of decreased economic inactivity and lowered population levels in correlation with the rise and fall of these empires. While Palestine was able to benefit economically from its geographical position, it was also vulnerable to the political fluctuations of foreign powers. As a result, Falconer notes, the economic conditions of surrounding nations could either bring prosperity to the inhabitants of Palestine or cause a return to the self-reliant strategies of subsistence practices.[18] Although Palestine's geographical position may have worked as a double-edged sword in this way, the responses that the inhabitants of Palestine made to these cycles attest to the adaptability of decentralized agrarian communities. When trade enabled a favorable means of livelihood, the Palestinians participated. Conversely, when trade no longer provided a viable means of support, farmers and pastoralists reverted to the self-

---

[16] Mendenhall writes extensively on in his 'tenth generation' theory. Mendenhall, *The Tenth Generation: The Origins of the Biblical Tradition* (Baltimore: Johns Hopkins University Press, 1973).

[17] Richard, "The Early Bonze Age," 22.

[18] Falconer, "Rural Responses to Early Urbanism," 401.

sufficient subsistence strategies that had been practiced prior to development.[19]

The cyclical urban activity that took place in Early Bronze Age Palestine was characteristic of Near Eastern societies that did not fully develop their own political economies, but rather functioned as peripheral economies that revolved around core states, like Egypt or Babylon.[20] Referring to trade activity in the Early Bronze Age, world-systems theorist Andre Frank explains, "Expansion and contraction seem to begin in one part of the world system, usually in its core, and then to diffuse from there to other parts, including core competitors and periphery."[21] Palestine's situation was not unique. When expansion created a positive opportunity for other peripheral communities, these more remote rural areas would modify their economic strategies to benefit from their neighbors' economic growth. As opportunities to benefit from trade waned and urban activity became a burden, these rural areas would revert to subsistence strategies.[22] One such period of economic decline occurred at the end of the Early Bronze Age.

As with periods of increased trade activity, periods of dormancy had a significant effect on Palestinian communities. In contrast to the urban growth evidenced in EB I-III, a major economic lull occurred in EB IV/MB I, apparently as the result of unfavorable environmental factors and the sudden decline of Egyptian power.[23] Richard explains that as Egypt entered into the "dark age"

---

[19] For a useful description of these cycles please refer to Coote and Whitelam, *The Emergence of Early Israel: In Historical Perspective* (SWBA 5; ed. Flanagan; Sheffield: Almond Press, 1987), 72-80.

[20] Edens, "Dynamics of Trade in the Ancient Mesopotamian 'World System.'" Coote and Whitelam, *The Emergence of Early Israel*, 63-64.

[21] Frank, "Bronze Age World System Cycles," *Current Anthropology* 34, no. 4 (1993): 389.

[22] Frank, "Bronze Age World System Cycles," 389. If unable to generate wealth or food, urban centers placed an undue burden on societies, such as non-productive administrative workers that have to be supported by the greater community, as described in Chapter Two.

[23] Harrison, "Shifting Patterns of Settlement in the Highlands of Central Jordan during the Early Bronze Age," 19. Richard, "Toward a Consensus of Opinion on the End of the Early Bronze Age in Palestine-

of the seventh through the eleventh dynasties, interregional trade in the Near East came to a near standstill, disrupting economic activity in Palestine.[24] During this period all but a small number of the urban settlements that had grown out of EB I-III disappeared from the Palestinian lowlands as people reverted to an agricultural-pastoral economy. Following Frank's description of ancient Near Eastern core-periphery relations, the organization required to maintain trade activity became burdensome and was subsequently abandoned as the inhabitants of Palestine fell back on subsistence practices. Coote and Whitelam, who employed aspects of Lenski and Lenski's theories of cultural evolution in their approach to interpreting material evidence from ancient Palestine,[25] note that the abandonment of urban sites during periods of reduced trade activity is evidence of a migration to

> ...the more marginal and arid areas of Palestine [suggesting] a
> wish to avoid the more vulnerable lowlands, despite their rela-
> tive fertility, in order to develop a subsistence economy in re-
> sponse to the collapse of the urban economy based on trade.[26]

Such migrations suggest that interregional trade, whether in its ascendancy or decline, had a significant impact on the lives of Palestinian farmers.

Middle Bronze Age Cycles

It appears that Palestine experienced further societal transformations when interregional trade returned as a predominant economic force during MB II. When Egypt's return to power under the Twelfth Dynasty reopened Egyptian trade routes, communities in Palestine shifted their economic strategies once again to benefit

---

Transjordan," *Bulletin of the American Schools of Oriental Research* no. 237 (1980): 24.

[24] Richard, "The Early Bonze Age," 35.

[25] Coote and Whitelam, *The Emergence of Early Israel*, 21-22.

[26] Coote and Whitelam, *The Emergence of Early Israel*, 73. This phenomenon is also addressed in Dever, "Archaeological Sources for the History of Palestine: The Middle Bronze Age: The Zenith or the Urban Canaanite Era," 50, no. 3 (1987): 159.

from new trade opportunities.[27] The region began to rely less on
subsistence-centered economic strategies and focused itself more
on trade activity, revitalizing Palestine's abandoned urban centers.[28]
William Dever notes that as a result of increased Egyptian economic power, Palestine experienced a massive societal transformation around 2000 BCE, during which time "nearly all the old urban
Early Bronze tell-sites, many of them abandoned for centuries,
were reoccupied."[29] As trade became a profitable venture once
again, the inhabitants of Palestine experienced the societal effects
as people came back down from the highlands to reopen these
lowland centers.

An example of this societal shifting between greater and lesser
reliance on subsistence strategies is evidenced in shifting land use
patterns in the rural community of el-Hayyat. Between MB IIA and
IIB, the farmers of el-Hayyat appear to have concentrated more
effort on the specialized cultivation of fruit crops, indicating com-
mercially orientated agricultural activity. Falconer notes that between these two periods a marked shift in agrarian strategy is evidenced by a floral change in which "the frequency of fruit macrofossils rises and that of cultivated cereals drops."[30] During the same
period, domestic macrofossils show higher rates of cereal grain
deposition and insignificant changes in the mix of annual and per-
ennial crops, suggesting that an increase in fruit cultivation was not
carried out as a response to population growth.[31] Falconer writes,

> ...these ratios distinguish communal display behavior involv-
> ing highly valued, marketable fruit products in temple com-
> pounds from household plant consumption, which empha-
> sized grain and legume subsistence crops... implying greater
> participation in regional economies.[32]

---

[27] Coote and Whitelam, *The Emergence of Early Israel*, 73-74. Richard,
"The Early Bonze Age," 40. Dever, "Archaeological Sources for the History of Palestine," 152-54.

[28] Dever, "Archaeological Sources for the History of Palestine."

[29] Dever, "Archaeological Sources for the History of Palestine," 152.

[30] Falconer, "Rural Responses to Early Urbanism," 410.

[31] Falconer, "Rural Responses to Early Urbanism," 410-11.

[32] Falconer, "Rural Responses to Early Urbanism," 411.

While subsistence farming was not completely abandoned during this transition, land use was shifted to facilitate the cultivation of revenue-producing crops that were consumed outside of the family unit during a period of increased trade activity.

As in the Early Bronze Age, it appears that increased trade opportunities in the Middle Bronze Age led subsistence communities to supplement their subsistence strategies with the cultivation of crops that could be exported. Coote and Whitelam make this connection, writing, "…the division of settlement between small rural villages and large urban centers was reminiscent of the pattern of settlement during the Early Bronze II-III period."[33] Along with a resurgence of trade came a return to previous settlement patterns and economic strategies. Although the suspected development of maritime trade during this period would have likely introduced new elements to this phase of trade, the motives behind the migration to the lowlands and engagement in trade appear to have been the same.[34] Cycles of trade expansion followed by returns to subsistence-dominated economic activity would continue on into Iron Age II and, with each turn of the cycle, interregional trade brought societal change to the people of Palestine.

Evidence of Societal Transformation in the Bronze Age

As with social-scientific theories, archaeological evidence does not provide simple and direct answers, but requires an interpretive process. The waxing and waning of settlements in the lowlands may indicate that EB Palestinian communities worked to take advantage of foreign trade opportunities, but that does not necessarily mean that these activities triggered negative societal effects. However, some archaeologists and biblical scholars have interpreted the material remains attributed to this time to indicate the presence of the cultural-evolutionary patterns that tend to lead to abuse and exploitation. While it is not in the interest of this chapter to make

---

[33] Coote and Whitelam make this connection, writing that "the division of settlement between small rural villages and large urban centers was reminiscent of the pattern of settlement during the Early Bronze II-III period." Coote and Whitelam, *The Emergence of Early Israel*, 35.

[34] Coote and Whitelam, *The Emergence of Early Israel*, 35, 73-74.

an attempt to prove that Early and Middle Bronze communities experienced latifundialization or heightened social divisions, when considering evidence from communities like el-Hayyat that indicate subsistence techniques had made way for commercial interests, the possibility of such events should be considered. Several archaeologists and biblical scholars conclude that material evidence from the Bronze Age indicates that these cycles of trade caused societies in the ancient Near East to evolve and become more stratified. Additionally, the above material presents interpretations of evidence which suggest that the economic activities of neighbouring empires had an influence on the subsistence practices of EB and MB Palestinian communities. Through considering these interpretations of the archaeological record, the possibility that the rise and fall of empires may also have affected the way ancient Near Eastern peoples interacted and managed land will now be explored.

Social Stratification and a Concentration of Wealth

The extent to which wealth was hoarded among elites in the Bronze Age cannot be determined with certainty. However, the remains of some buildings attributed to periods of economic prosperity may indicate increases in social stratification that go hand-in-hand with uneven wealth distribution. One indication of such hierarchy in Palestine and surrounding regions during EB I is the adoption of a two-tiered settlement model, which was composed of a larger primary site and a smaller secondary community. Timothy Harrison explains that primary sites in neighbouring Jordan carried out administrative duties and were usually large communities that covered ten to twenty acres of land or medium communities that covered around 2.5 acres.[35] The associated satellite community, which measured less than 2.5 acres, functioned as a feeder community to support the economic activities of the primary site.[36] Dever and Richard find a parallel two-tiered system with roughly the same scale in size to the west of the Jordan River that dates

---

[35] Harrison, "Shifting Patterns of Settlement in the Highlands of Central Jordan during the Early Bronze Age," 19.

[36] Harrison, "Shifting Patterns of Settlement in the Highlands of Central Jordan during the Early Bronze Age," 19.

back to as early as EB I.[37] According to Richard, the twenty-two-acre community of Arad and the nearby two-acre site of Malhata represent such a system of community organization and ranked social ordering.[38] These sorts of ranked communities suggest that social hierarchies were deemed necessary on a macro-community level, suggesting the presence of hierarchical systems within individual communities.

Another indicator of the development of social stratification in the Early Bronze Age is found in the so-called "temple towns." Communities like Megiddo and Tel Gath, which had temple centers, display the interesting characteristic of inner-city walls, which Richard interprets as an indication of social hierarchies in EB I.[39] Writing of Megiddo, Richard explains that "a 'twinned' temple at Megiddo (stratum 19) was separated from a residential area by a walled courtyard" and that "differentiation of public and residential areas attests [to] a growing social stratification."[40] Whether the separation of a temple from the greater community was to preserve the sacredness of the temple or to protect surpluses or other valuables kept inside the temple, such physical divisions *suggest* systems of hierarchy.[41] Although it cannot be known for certain whether or not these separations represented increased social hierarchy due to cultural evolution, this interpretation is plausible considering that they seem to have been developed during a period of heightened urban development and trade. The need to keep one group of people separate from the general population suggests an unbalanced allocation of resources.

Increases in hierarchical positioning would not be surprising, considering that such activity commonly occurs as societies begin to gain more complex economic strategies. Economic anthropolo-

---

[37] Dever, "Archaeological Sources for the History of Palestine," 153-59. Richard, "The Early Bonze Age," 25-27.

[38] Richard, "The Early Bonze Age," 25, 27.

[39] Richard, "The Early Bonze Age," 26.

[40] Richard, "The Early Bonze Age," 26.

[41] "Suggest" has been emphasized because it cannot be known for certain that these walls symbolized systems of hierarchy. One must consider the possibility that the wall may have been built because someone thought it would look nice or to fulfill some type of symbolic function.

gist Francis Berdan argues the development of hierarchical structures is to be expected as agrarian societies open themselves to increased trade activity.[42] Coote, Whitelam, and Richard all find that
the material evidence from the Bronze Age indicates cycles of such
development in the ancient Near East.[43] From the development of
administrative centers in the lowlands for the management of trade
to the development of temple complexes that separated themselves
from the general public, the increased stratification that appears to
have taken place in the Bronze Age has been linked with cultural-
evolutionary patterns of exploitation. Whether in the case of twentieth-century globalization or interregional trade in fourth millennium BCE Palestine, there is evidence for this common characteristic of societal development.

Latifundialization in Bronze Age Palestine?

Unfortunately, available evidence pertaining to societal change during the Bronze Age does not reveal much about the impact that
these transformations had on the daily lives of Palestinian farmers,
at least directly. Documentation concerning land management or
practices of usury is absent, making it difficult to determine how
shifts toward trade activity and urban settlement affected those
who produced goods to support more complex economic strategies. It is even conceivable that farmers, themselves, could have
benefited from migration to the lowlands, where the soil is more
fertile and growing conditions are better. However, such a scenario,
although possible, would go against the norm since primary producers are more likely to suffer as a result of increased trade activity
and an entrance into world systems than to enjoy the benefits that
these developments can offer.[44]

---

[42] Berdan, "Trade and Markets in Precapitalist States," in *Economic
Anthropology* (ed. Plattner; Stanford: Stanford University Press, 1989), 78-
80.

[43] Coote and Whitelam, *The Emergence of Early Israel*, 70-80. Richard,
"The Early Bonze Age," 27.

[44] Chase-Dunn, et al. "Growth/Decline Phases and Semi-Peripheral
Development in the Ancient Mesopotamian and Egyptian World-
Systems," in *Globalization and Global History* eds. Gills and Thompson; *Re-*

As described above, administrative institutions and projects that are common to political economies are evidenced during various periods of the Bronze Age in Palestine. Although there is evidence that some rural communities, such as el-Hayyat, were engaged in trade on their own volition, Richard suggests that sophisticated systems of redistribution, with organized processing and distribution centers, were present in Palestine as early as EB II.[45] Richard claims that these centers indicate the presence of "an economy based on intensive agriculture and an international network of trade."[46] Such intensive agricultural systems and economic strategies that exceed familial goals require a centralized organization of land management to function efficiently, typically undermining a farmer's ability to execute his or her own judgment in making strategic decisions.[47] The ability to decide on what to cultivate and how to spread the risk of crop failure is eventually taken away from primary producers by a central authority.[48] In the end, the farmers who grow the raw materials that are processed into goods for export almost always lose. A notable exception to this rule would be the opium-poppy farmers of Afghanistan, as described in Chapter Two, serving as an important reminder that there will always be exceptions to more common societal patterns.[49]

---

thinking Globalization; London: Routledge, 2006). Bell. "The Social Relations of Property and Efficiency," in *Property in Economic Context* eds. Hunt and Gilman; Oxford: University Press of America, Inc., 1998), 39-40.

[45] Richard, "The Early Bonze Age."

[46] Richard, "The Early Bonze Age."

[47] Johnson and Earle, *The Evolution of Human Societies: From Foraging Group to Agrarian State* (Stanford: Stanford University Press, 2001), 27-37. Lenski, *Power and Privilege: A Theory of Social Stratification* (New York: McGraw-Hill Book Company, 1966), 220.

[48] Johnson and Earle, *The Evolution of Human Societies*, 26-27. It is the inability to select risk-reducing strategies that Hopkins finds of significant importance in Palestine. Hopkins, *The Highlands of Canaan: Agricultural Life in the Early Iron Age* (ed. Flanagan; vol. 3; Sheffield: Almond, 1985), 232.

[49] Özerdem, "Disarmament, Demobilisation, and Reintegration of Former Combatants in Afghanistan: Lessons Learned from a Cross-Cultural Perspective," *Third World Quarterly* 23, no. 5 (2002): 970.

Land management or ownership is often centralized to ensure that the land is used to maximize its revenue-producing potential for a society's administrative classes. Although subsistence crops continue to be cultivated and stored for distribution, agricultural production is streamlined to focus on the efficient growth of exportable goods. Duran Bell notes that plans implemented to increase the economic efficiency of a society during periods of agrarian intensification are directed at benefiting those at the top of the social hierarchy while those at the bottom gain little.[50] Bell explains, "...the immediate consequence of abandoning traditional forms [of agriculture] has been to reduce the share of the social product allocated to the direct producer."[51] Considering Richard's and Dever's view that Palestinian communities experienced cycles of increased social stratification as a result of heightened trade activity throughout the Bronze Age, the consolidation of land management during these periods would fit the pattern that Bell and other economic anthropologists address, and appears to have occurred elsewhere in the ancient Near East.

Latifundialization in the Wider Ancient Near Eastern Context

An important indicator of land seizure in the Bronze Age, and its potential negative effects on society, is found in admonitions against the practice. Two prominent Egyptian figures, for example, wrote on the importance of respecting the land rights of others. During the prosperous period of the Old Kingdom, between the late twenty-fifth and the early twenty-sixth centuries BCE, the Egyptian administrator and educator Ptah-Hotep proclaimed,

> If you inherit land, take only your own portion of the land, do not covet the land of others. Those who respect the land of others earn respect; those who defraud others lose their own land. To covet even a small thing is to transform the peaceful into warriors.[52]

---

[50] Bell, "The Social Relations of Property and Efficiency," 39-40.

[51] Bell, "The Social Relations of Property and Efficiency," 40.

[52] Matthews and Benjamin, *Old Testament Parallels: Laws and Stories from the Ancient Near East* (Mahwah, New Jersey: Paulist Press, 1997), 268-69.

Three important points can be drawn from Ptah-Hotep's proclamation. First, this ancient proclamation in and of itself suggests
that land seizures were common and problematic enough that
Ptah-Hotep felt obligated to address the issue, and scribes believed
it worthy to preserve. Second, the phrase "those who *respect* the
land of others earn *respect*"[53] suggests that depriving others of land
was not only a legal concern, which is indicated by the reference to
inheritance rights, but was also considered a moral offence. Third,
the final line of his statement, "To covet even a small thing is to
transform the peaceful into warriors," indicates that land seizures
had created significant enough tension within Egyptian communities that they threatened social stability, at least in isolated instances. This third millennium BCE condemnation of land seizures
does not reveal whether or not lands were being consolidated into
large latifundia, but it does suggest that lands were being taken
from their owners.

The proclamation given by Ptah-Hotep's, as may be expected,
did not put an end to land seizures in Egypt. Amen-em-ope, whose
teachings are attributed to the prosperous Nineteenth Dynasty,
between 1250 and 1000 BCE,[54] addressed the issue of land-tenure
abuse. Two millennia after the time of Ptah-Hotep, Amen-em-ope
referred to landownership abuse, writing,

> Do not move a surveyor's stone to steal a field, do not move
> the surveyor's line to take a farm. Do not covet another's land,
> do not poach on the widow's field. To forge a claim to the
> public path through a field, cries out to Thoth, divine patron
> of the moon, for justice. Those who seize public lands are
> enemies of the poor.[55]

Like Ptah-Hotep, Amen-em-ope appears to have viewed the issue
of land seizure as a matter of moral concern, as evidenced though
his reference to divine punishment. The invocation of the god

---

[53] Italics added

[54] This period includes the reign of Ramses the II, between 1279-
1213.

[55] Matthews and Benjamin, *Old Testament Parallels: Laws and Stories from
the Ancient Near East*, 277.

Thoth is significant since he was not only one of the most powerful gods in the Egyptian pantheon but played a key role in the judgment of an individual's soul after death.[56] Amen-em-ope's use of this particular god's name may attest to the seriousness with which the issue was addressed, indicating that to infringe on the land rights of others could have a negative bearing on an individual's final judgment.

Victor Matthews and Don Benjamin note that the writings associated with Ptah-Hotep and Amen-em-ope "demonstrate the consistency of Egypt's world-view over the 2000 years separating one tradition from another," from observations on wisdom to materialism.[57] The ongoing, or at least recurring, nature of the problem of land acquisitions is attested to by the fact that Amen-em-ope addressed this issue so long after Ptah-Hotep. It is not known to what degree officials or creditors may have heeded the words of these two influential Egyptians, but it appears that land acquisitions had a negative impact on certain sectors of Egyptian society during the Bronze Age. Other ancient writings make it apparent that not only the Egyptians suffered from these problems, as the harmful effects of land seizures are also evidenced in Sumerian texts.

As early as the mid-third millennium BCE, Sumerian rulers made proclamations against the abuse of their subjects' rights to access land. A twenty-fourth-century tablet discovered at Lagash reveals that even royalty, at least in theory, were subject to the land-rights laws that protected their people, and could be held liable for acquiring the real properties of their subjects without adhering to certain established protocols.[58] Noel Kramer explains that if a ruler wanted to acquire land from a subject, appropriate compensation had to be offered, as evidenced in a proclamation made by King Urukagina. In response to what King Urukagina considered to be an increasingly disproportionate partitioning of land, he proclaimed,

---

[56] Griffiths, "Eight Funerary Paintings with Judgment Scenes in Swansea Wellcome Museum" 68, (1982): 238.

[57] Matthews and Benjamin, *Old Testament Parallels*, 274.

[58] Kramer, *The Sumerians: Their History, Culture, and Character* (Chicago: The University of Chicago Press, 1963), 75.

When the house of a king's retainer was next to the house of a "big man" (and) that "big man" says to him, 'I want to buy it from you,' and if when he (the "big man") is about to buy it from him, he (the king's retainer) says, 'Pay as much as I think fair,' or 'Pay me in barley equivalent to my house,' then when he refuses to sell it, that "big man" must not coerce him to do so.[59]

Beyond demanding that compensation be given in return for land, Urukagina's terms insist that the conditions of payment had to be accepted as agreeable by the owner. According to Reuven Yaron, this provision served two purposes. First, it ensured that small-scale landowners could reserve the right to refuse the sale of their property, and second, if the land were sold, that the farmer would receive a fair price.[60] Yaron's assessment might be a bit more optimistic than the realities that stemmed from Urukagina's proclamation: rulers are often quite capable of finding ways to make their wealthy subjects, let alone the poor, accept their terms. If international organizations and charters that have been set up by economists who actually shaped policy around a concept of human rights in the twentieth century CE cannot protect the interests of the vulnerable, it is difficult to imagine that such Bronze Age proclamations would not have been subject to failure as well. Regardless of how much justice actually came from Urukagina's demands, the king's statement evidences that those in positions of power had used their influence to seize the lands of others. Such provisions to protect the land of farming families are also found in Nuzi and Mari, indicating that land seizures were a problematic part of life for the people of those societies as well.[61]

---

[59] Kramer, *The Sumerians*, 319.

[60] Yaron. "Social Problems and Policies in the Ancient Near East," in *Law, Politics, and Society in the Ancient Mediterranean World* eds. Halpern and Hobson; Sheffield: Sheffield Academic Press, 1993), 22.

[61] Purves, "Commentary on Nuzi Real Property in the Light of Recent Studies," 4, no. 2 (1945): 69. Zaccagnini, "The Price of Fields at Nuzi," *Journal of Near Eastern Studies* 22, no. 1 (1979): 15. Malamat, "Mari and the Bible: Some Patterns of Tribal Organizations and Institutions," *Journal for the American Oriental Society* no. 82 (1962): 148. Strict inheritance

Another proclamation attributed to King Urukagina appears to address the effects of latifundialization directly, and is of particular interest to this study as a whole; Urukagina's grievance against the consolidation of arable lands contains some interesting similarities to the complaint found in Isa. 5.8. Lamenting the consolidation of arable lands, Urukagina complained,

> The houses of the *ensi* [ruler] and the fields of the *ensi*, the houses of the (palace) harem and the fields of the (palace) harem, the houses of the (palace) nursery (and) the fields of the (palace) nursery crowded each other side by side.[62]

The authors of Isa. 5.8 also address the problem of estates crowding together as property is consolidated, writing,

הוי מגיעי בית בבית שדה בשדה יקריבו עד אפס

מקום והושבתם לבדכם בקרב הארץ:[63]

Both the king of Lagash and the authors of Isa. 5.8 appear to present a situation in which estate owners had expanded the size of their properties to the point that all others had been crowded out of the countryside.

Although these possible instances of landownership abuse, and potential latifundialization, amongst Sumerian and Egyptian societies do not provide evidence of latifundialization in Bronze Age Palestine, they illustrate the timeless nature of the problem of land seizure and indicate that it was a phenomenon not unknown in the ancient Near East. King Urukagina's second proclamation is of particular interest as it addresses an activity that is typical of agrarian societies undergoing increased trade. A precise correlation between these events and periods of societal transformation cannot

---

codes were set up in both Mari and Nuzi to prevent land from being transferred to people outside the family. As we can see in each of the above studies, people were able to work around the system by creating false adoptions that allowed the land to be transferred despite a lack of familial relation.

[62] Kramer, *The Sumerians*, 318.

[63] "Woe to you who touch house to house, join field to field, until there ceases to be room and you dwell alone in the midst of the land."

be proven, but it is interesting to note that the proclamations of Ptah-Hotep, Amen-em-ope, and Urukagina are all attributed to eras of significant economic power in Egypt and Mesopotamia: periods of active trade in which subsistence-based farmers are likely to have been most vulnerable. Although definitive proof is difficult, if not impossible, to establish when pertaining to almost any aspect of the ancient world, this section has presented some of the existing evidence of a connection between interregional trade and societal change in rural communities dating back to the Early Bronze Age.

It is important to state that in no way should it be assumed that Palestinian farmers enjoyed a utopian existence in the absence of interregional trade. However, considering the recurring nature of cultural-evolutionary patterns that introduce hierarchical systems that divide wealth unevenly and take land management out of the hands of subsistence farmers, it is likely that producers had to work harder for equal or reduced personal benefit during these periods of economic expansion. These cyclical patterns witnessed in the Early Bronze Age would continue to affect Palestinian communities on into Iron Age II, when the expanding Neo-Assyrian Empire had a significant impact on Palestinian economies as it brought them into an emerging trans-Mediterranean world system.[64] The next section of this chapter will address the effects of this pattern as it manifested itself in the eighth century BCE, and on which Chaney and Premnath base their interpretations of Isa. 5.8–10 and Mic. 2.1–2.

---

[64] It is important to note that these periods of ebbing power strengthen the notion of multilateral evolution and weaken the arguments of the earliest cultural evolutionary theorists, who believed that cultural evolution was a linear process from savagery to civilization, as discussed in the chapter on cultural evolutionary theory.

B. Eighth-Century Palestine and Neo-Assyrian Expansion

The influence that neighbouring empires had over agrarian life and economic strategy in Bronze Age Palestine continued on into the Iron Age. Andrew and Susan Sherratt explain that the eighth century BCE witnessed a period of heightened trade with "imperial expansion in the Levant, and economic expansion leading to state formation in the Aegean," as both of these regions "tapped into the resources of the central Mediterranean."[1] Due to this expansion of interregional trade and the development of new trading partners, Palestine experienced profound societal change as a rising Neo-Assyrian Empire destroyed kingdoms and accumulated vassals in the late eighth and early seventh centuries.

For the Assyrian Empire to continue its expansion, maintain political control over conquered regions, and generate wealth for the elite through increased trade opportunity and tribute, revenue had to be raised.[2] New developments in metallurgy, transportation, and agricultural production allowed the Assyrians and their trading partners to build upon ancient trade strategies with greater efficiency as trade routes opened throughout the Mediterranean.[3] To meet the demands of this new world system, the Philistine cities of Ekron and Ashkelon, both situated in close proximity to Judah, grew to become important centers of production and exchange. The development of these two cities highlights the scale of economic expansion that took place in the late eighth and early seventh centuries BCE. Furthermore, the impressive degree of their growth indicates the level of demand that Assyria's trade nexus would have placed upon nearby Judean agriculturalists.

---

[1] Sherratt and Sherratt, "The Growth of the Mediterranean Economy in the Early First Millennium BC," *World Archaeology* 24, no. 3 (1993): 369.

[2] Andrew and Sharon Sherratt give a useful overview of these needs, and the distinctive changes that they brought in the early first millennium BCE. Sherratt and Sherratt, "The Growth of the Mediterranean Economy in the Early First Millennium BC," 361-63.

[3] Sherratt and Sherratt, "The Growth of the Mediterranean Economy in the Early First Millennium BC," 369.

The Revitalization of Ekron

Although the area immediately surrounding Ekron was not known for its rich agrarian potential, the city itself was a highly valued center for the production of secondary goods, such as olive oil and dyed cloth. The growth that Ekron experienced in the early seventh century attests to the intense demands that trade had placed on the city and its surrounding region in the late eighth and early seventh centuries BCE. Having covered over fifty acres of land during this period, the modern archaeological site of Ekron, Tel-Miqne, is a testament to the important role that both this urban centre and the surrounding region played in Assyria's trade nexus.[4] As early as the eleventh century Ekron had been a hub for the production of olive oil, fine dyed cloth, and perfumed oil.[5] During an economic slowdown that occurred in the ninth century BCE, however, Ekron receded to a shadow of its former self and entered into a period of dormancy.[6] Although a portion of the city remained occupied, the once influential centre of production diminished from a sizable fifty acres to cover an area of only ten.[7] As throughout the ancient Near East, the influence of urban economic activity in Ekron waxed and waned in tandem with the rise and fall of foreign powers, transforming into a vibrant industrial centre in times of prosperity.

---

[4] Gitin and Dothan, "The Rise and Fall of Ekron of the Philistines: Recent Excavations at an Urban Border Site," *The Biblical Archaeologist* 50, no. 4 (1987): 198.

[5] Sherratt and Sherratt, "The Growth of the Mediterranean Economy in the Early First Millennium BC": 364.

[6] Gilboa. "Iron Age I-IIA Pottery Evolution at Dor-Regional Contexts and the Cypriot Connection," in *Mediterranean Peoples in Transition: Thirteenth to Early Tenth Centuries BCE* eds. Gitin, Mazar and Stern; Jerusalem: Israel Exploration Society, 1998), 423. Sherratt. "'Sea Peoples' and the Economic Structure of the Late Second Millennium in teh Eastern Mediterranean," in *Mediterranean Peoples in Transition: Thirteenth to Early Tenth Centuries BCE* eds. Gitin, Mazar and Stern; Jerusalem: Israel Exploration Society, 1998). Gitin and Dothan, "The Rise and Fall of Ekron of the Philistines": 205.

[7] Gitin and Dothan, 'The Rise and Fall of Ekron of the Philistines": 206.

The Scale of Ekron's Production Capacity

The rise of the Neo-Assyrian Empire and its incursion into the southern Levant brought new opportunities for prosperity, once again transforming Ekron into an industrial centre and resuming its role as a key producer of exportable goods. Na'aman writes that as Ekron was reawakened from a lengthy period of inactivity, "the city (Strata IC-IB) grew in the seventh century to about eight times the size of the earlier city (Stratum II)."[8] It appears that the motivation behind this expansion was to increase the production of the city's most valuable asset, its olive oil industry.[9] The scale of the findings at Tel-Miqne suggests that the city's oil-producing capabilities were unprecedented for its time. Twenty percent of strata I B-C sites, which date to the seventh century, were occupied by industrial zones; one of these zones alone contained 102 olive-oil installations.[10] Gitin and Dever note that of these 102 oil installations, 88 of them were of the more technologically advanced "Ekron" type, indicating that new ethnology had been employed to increase production.[11]

The scale of development and addition of new technological advances made Ekron a major centre of oil production in Iron Age II. Eitam explains that the magnitude of the olive-pressing facilities dating to seventh-century Ekron made this city's capabilities not only impressive for its time, but the largest olive-oil-producing centre of the ancient Near East.[12] Gitin and Dever calculate that when running at full capacity these instillations were capable of producing up to a thousand tons, or 1.1 million liters, of olive oil in a

---

[8] Na'aman, "Ekron Under the Assyrian and Egyptian Empires," *Bulletin of the American Schools of Oriental Research* no. 332 (2003): 81.

[9] Gitin and Dothan, "The Rise and Fall of Ekron of the Philistines": 218.

[10] Gitin and Dever, "Recent Excavations in Israel: Studies in Iron Age Archaeology," 48-49.

[11] Gitin and Dever, "Recent Excavations in Israel: Studies in Iron Age Archaeology": 48. These facilities housed large presses and storage vats.

[12] Eitam, "Tel Miqne-Ekron: Survey of Oil Presses: 1985," *Excavations and Surveys in Israel* 5: 1986, (1987): 72-74.

good harvest year.[13] Na'aman rightly contests Gitin and Dever's assumption on the basis that it cannot be verified that all of these instillations were simultaneously active. But regardless of whether or not all of these instillations were producing oil at the same time, the fact that Ekron had facilities capable of producing such quantities reveals that the city's administrators thought it necessary to accommodate the manufacture of unprecedented volumes of olive oil during a time in which trade routes were opening up, both inland and throughout the Aegean and Mediterranean seas.[14] The scale of Ekron's operation attests to the level of trade taking place during Assyria's expansion. The benefits to be gained from such economic activity, through either private or public channels, must have been worth the cost of creating and maintaining such a sizable production centre.[15]

---

[13] Gitin and Dever, "Recent Excavations in Israel: Studies in Iron Age Archaeology": 49.

[14] Sherratt and Sherratt, "The Growth of the Mediterranean Economy in the Early First Millennium BC": 369. Ballard, et al., "Iron Age Shipwrecks in Deep Water off Ashkelon, Israel," *American Journal of Archaeology* 106, no. 2 (2002): 161. There has been some debate surrounding the activity of these instillations. Lawrence Stager argues that the bulk of the industrial instillations mentioned above were not active until the last quarter of the seventeenth century BCE. Rather than a result of Assyrian influence, Stager believed that these instillations were constructed between 650 and 640 BCE, after Assyrian power had waned in the West (Stager, "Ashkelon and the Archaeology of Destruction: Kislev 604 BCE," 25 (Joseph Aviram Volume), no. 61*-74* [1996]). However, the inscription of Akhayush, which was discovered shortly after Stager published his conclusions, supports the activity of these instillations in the early seventh century. Na'aman writes that this inscription indicates "that the construction of the elite zone at Ekron, including the large temple, took place under the Assyrians in the first half of the seventh Century BCE. Hence, the great flourishing of Ekron had already begun at this time" (Na'aman, "The Distribution of Messages in the Kingdom of Judah in Light of the Lachish Ostraca" *Vetus Testamentum*, 53, no. 2 [2003]: 86). For a more detailed study of Stager's argument, see Stager, "Ashkelon and the Archaeology of Destruction: Kislev 604 BCE."

[15] "Private" is included here because while political institutions were the primary agents of trade, they did not control all trade. Diana Edelman points out that although the crown had "right of first selection" of im-

In order to justify the production capacity of Ekron in the seventh century BCE, a massive increase in olive cultivation would have been required, placing pressure on nearby farming communities. Na'aman, Finkelstein, Silberman, Gitin, Dever, and Alexander Fantalkin believe that such demands would have turned Ekron's attention to the fertile lands of Judah, whose olives would have been pressed at Ekron before their oil was exported throughout the Assyrian Empire and its trade network.[16] Fantalkin argues that the establishment of the massive olive oil operations at Ekron "doubtless demanded access to Judahite olive-orchards in the hill country," and that the temptation for cooperation between Judah and Ekron may have been "overwhelming at a time when both sides were forced to cooperate under the umbrella of their Assyrian masters."[17] Such evidence of such cooperation is found in an increase in specialized farming in Judah,[18] which will be addressed in greater detail below. Ekron's rapid growth, and the influence that the city had on surrounding agrarian communities, like those in Judah, did not develop on its own accord; it was the Assyrians who made the city's resurgence possible as a centre of interregional trade.

---

ported goods, private traders played a significant role in eighth and seventh century trade. For more information see Edelman, "Tyrian Trade in Yehud Under Artaxerxes I: Real or Fictional? Independent or Crown Endorsed?," in *Judah and the Judeans in the Persian Period* eds. Lipschits and Oeming; Winona Lake, Indiana: Eisenbrauns (2006), 221.

[16] Na'aman, "Ekron Under the Assyrian and Egyptian Empires": 81. Finkelstein and Silberman, "Temple and Dynasty: Hezekiah, the Remaking of Judah and the Rise of the Pan-Israelite Ideology," *JSOT* 30, no. 3 (2006): 265. Gitin and Dever, "Recent Excavations in Israel": 50-51. Avraham Faust and Ehud Weiss note that while olive oil would have been the primary good to come out of the Shephelah, grapes and grains were also grown in surplus for export throughout the Mediterranean and Mesopotamia. See Faust and Weiss, "Judah, Philistia, and the Mediterranean World: Reconstructing the Economic System of the Seventh Century B.C.E.," no. 338 (2005): 76, 80-83.

[17] Fantalkin, "The Final Destruction of Beth Shemesh and the *Pax Assyriaca* in the Judahite Shephelah: An Alternative View," *Tel Aviv* 31, no. 2 (2004).

[18] Finkelstein and Silberman, "Temple and Dynasty": 263.

It should be noted here that some scholars, such as J. David Schloen, argue for the possibility that the goods produced in Ekron were destined for regional markets rather than for far-away destinations. Schloen contends that the Spanish silver found on the site could have been the result of gifting among elites rather than large-scale economic exchange.[19] Although Philistine merchant wrecks found off the coast of Spain that are attributed to the seventh century and contain jars unique to Ekron could have been simply delivering tributes, the fact that they were sailing so far from Palestinian shores would suggest that trade was occurring throughout the Mediterranean.[20] Considering the massive volumes of olive oil being produce in Ekron, as explained above, it would make sense that this city's facilities were used to produce goods for long-distance trade, even if a significant portion of that oil was used within Assyria itself. In the end, however, whether the production of this oil was for foreign sale or for use within the Assyrian Empire, the societal changes that would be expected to accompany the growth of a major oil industry are likely to have been the same.

It appears that Ekron's economy did not only benefit from an increase in demand for processed goods, but that the city also enjoyed a favored status by the expanding Assyrian Empire. For a community in the path of Assyrian expansion to have had positive relations with their invaders was highly uncommon, attesting to the economic value that this city held as the Assyrian Empire engaged in a thriving world system.

The Significance of Surviving the Assyrian Threat

Archaeological evidence suggests that Assyrian expansion had a profound effect on Ekron, but what does Ekron's development reveal about the importance of trade to the Neo-Assyrian Empire? In short, the very fact that Ekron was able to benefit from Assyrian expansion, rather than suffer from its destructive power, attests to

---

[19] Schloen, *The House of the Father as Fact and Symbol: Patrimonialism in Ugarit and the Ancient Near East* (2; ed. Schloen; Winona Lake, IN: Eisenbrauns, 2001), 141-42.

[20] Master, "Trade and Politics: Ashkelon's Balancing Act in the Seventh Century BCE," no. 330 (2003): 59.

the value that Assyria placed on Ekron's ability to produce vast quantities of exportable goods. In referring to the unique position Ekron enjoyed under Assyrian control, John Holladay writes that the Assyrian statecraft employed a system of "terror psychology" to subdue its subordinates during its campaigns into the Levant.[21] Rather than build up the lands that they conquered, the Assyrians took pride in the punishments that they inflicted upon those who fell to their might. Evidence of Assyria's desire to terrorize is found in the punishments that are depicted on the reliefs that decorate the audience chambers of Assyrian kings,[22] and by Sennacherib boasting in that he had taken more than two hundred thousand captives while depopulating the Judean countryside.[23]

The destruction of conquered lands was not simply confined to remote areas that had not been developed. Albert Grayson points out that even places of strategic economic value were laid to ruin by the invading Assyrian armies, as revealed in texts that celebrate the destruction of agrarian sites of comparable economic potential to Ekron.[24] J. Schloen writes that such tales of conquest were "not simply propaganda without basis in fact, as indicated by archaeological evidence of the scale and savagery of Assyrian destructions at sites like Lachish."[25] Unlike in nineteenth-century CE European colonialism, the Assyrians had little interest in the economic development of the regions that they conquered, preferring

[21] Holladay, "Assyrian Statecraft and the Prophets of Israel," *The Harvard Theological Review* 63, no. 1 (2002): 37.

[22] Holladay, "Assyrian Statecraft and the Prophets of Israel": 37.

[23] Oppenheim. "Babylonian and Assyrian Historical Texts," in *Ancient Near Eastern Texts Relating to the Old Testament* (ed. Pritchard; Princeton: Princeton University Press, 1969), 287.

[24] Grayson, *Assyrian Rulers of the Early First Millennium BC. II, (858-745 BC)* (vol. 3; Toronto: University of Toronto Press, 1996), 60, 163, 187.

[25] Schloen, *The House of the Father as Fact and Symbol: Patrimonialism in Ugarit and the Ancient Near East*, 147, n.18. Sites in northern Syria also display such a fate, having been left in total economic ruin. See Diakonoff. "Main Features of the Economy in the Monarchies of Ancient Western Asia," in *Troisème Conference Internationale D'histoire Économique* (ed. Finley; Paris: Mouton, 1969), 29.

to simply exact taxes and confiscate wealth.[26] The best outcome that conquered peoples could hope for, Master explains, was that the Assyrians would take a hands-off approach and allow their communities to continue their previous economic activities.[27] Ekron's fate was remarkably different from the norm.

Ekron's escape from destruction at the hands of the Assyrians not only allowed the city to survive; it was a major catalyst for the city's growth. While nearby lands and chief rivals were laid to ruin by the invading Assyrian military, Ekron was increasingly able to enjoy a nearly competition-free economic environment.[28] Subsequently, Na'aman writes, Ekron could "take the place of its stronger neighbor to the east in the northern Shephelah, to exploit some of its agricultural territories, to expand its area and population, and to develop its economy."[29] Through expanding the area from which it could acquire raw materials, which Na'aman gauges to have been as far to the South as Beth-Shemesh,[30] Ekron was able to increase its output of secondary goods like olive oil and wine. This would have been a boon to Ekron for, as Susan and Andrew Sherratt note, these commodities were in high demand for the Assyrian Empire as it sought to develop trade networks in the Aegean and North Africa during the late eighth and early seventh centuries.[31]

For Ekron not only to have been spared militarily, but also to have been assisted economically by the Assyrians, appears to be the antithesis of Assyrian foreign policy at the time. Gitin and Na'aman claim that Ekron's good fortune was a testament to its economic potential,[32] but this explanation does not address the question as to

---

[26] Schloen, *The House of the Father as Fact and Symbol: Patrimonialism in Ugarit and the Ancient Near East*, 146.

[27] Master, "Trade and Politics: Ashkelon's Balancing Act in the Seventh Century BCE": 50.

[28] Na'aman, "Ekron Under the Assyrian and Egyptian Empires": 81.

[29] Na'aman, "Ekron Under the Assyrian and Egyptian Empires": 81.

[30] Na'aman, "Ekron Under the Assyrian and Egyptian Empires": 81.

[31] Sherratt and Sherratt, "The Growth of the Mediterranean Economy in the Early First Millennium BC": 366-71.

[32] Gitin, "Tel-Miqne - Ekron in the 7th Century B.C.E.: The Impact of Economic Innovation and Foreign Cultural Influences on a Neo-

why Ekron grew while other potential economic centers were destroyed. A possible explanation, relating to the increased importance of maritime trade and the development of new economies in the Aegean and southern Europe, may have to do with Ekron's close proximity to the valuable port city of Ashkelon.

Ekron's growth evidences a period of heightened economic activity in which an increased market for agricultural exports would have created a demand for the specialized cultivation of revenue-producing crops, such as grapes and olives. As detailed in the following section, such pressures would have created significant societal changes for subsistence farmers in neighbouring regions, such as Samaria and Judah. Whereas Ekron facilitated the production of secondary products, the Philistine city of Ashkelon enabled the exportation of these goods throughout the Mediterranean and Aegean.

Ashkelon in the Assyrian Trade Nexus

Ashkelon's maritime history extends back to the mid-fourth millennium BCE in the Early Bronze Age, when Egypt's desire for luxury goods from the southern Levant, like oil and wine, made the city a major centre of trade.[33] Beyond its maritime activities, Ash-

---

Assyrian Vassal City-State," in *Recent Excavations in Israel: A View to the West* (ed. Gitin; Dubuque: Kendall/Hunt, 1995), 50. Na'aman, "Population Changes in Palestine Following Assyrian Deportations," *Tel Aviv* 20, (1993): 106.

[33] King, "The Eighth, the Greatest of Centuries?," 108, no. 1 (1989): 8. Stager. "The Periodization of Palestine from Neolithic through Early Bronze Times," in *Chronologies in Old World Archaeology* (ed. Ehrich; Chicago: University of Chicago, 1992), 40. Master, "Trade and Politics": 47. Brody, "From the Hills of Adonis through the Pillars of Hercules: Recent Advances in the Archaeology of Canaan and Phoenicia," *Near Eastern Archaeology* 65, no. 1 (2002): 71. The earliest literary mention of Ashkelon dates to 1850 BCE in the Execration Texts: a series of Egyptian magical texts that were used to ensure control over various areas, using incantations and curses. Miller. "Palestine During the Bronze Age," in *The Biblical World* (ed. Barton; New York: Routledge, 2002), 378. King, *Amos, Hosea, Micah: An Archaeological Commentary* (Philadelphia: The Westminster Press, 1988), 53.

kelon also played a vital role in inland economics, as evidenced by as many as seven different land routes that radiated out of the port city during the Iron Age.[34] Ashkelon's importance as an eastern Mediterranean seaport during this time was made all the more important by a lack of natural harbors along the Palestinian coast. The city's role as a port was no less important in the Mediterranean world system that developed in Iron Age II, and is indicative of the importance and intensity of interregional trade during the rise of the Neo-Assyrian Empire.

In what would have been considered a great strategic victory for the Assyrian Empire, King Tiglath-Pileser III seized Ashkelon and placed the port city under Assyrian control during a campaign into Philistine between 734 and 732 BCE.[35] After Ashkelon was taken, it was absorbed into the Assyrian world system as a vassal city, as is evidenced in an Assyrian list of the empire's vassals.[36] The ability to readily access the resurging maritime trade networks of the eighth and seventh centuries through Ashkelon's port would have been of great economic and strategic value to the Assyrians, fulfilling their desire to increase revenue and acquire luxury goods from the West.

The Extent and Importance of Maritime Trade to the Assyrian Empire

Ashkelon's trade activity appears to have expanded far to into the Mediterranean to bring goods and revenue into the city, reaching civilizations along southern European and northern African coasts. An example of how systems of interregional trade evolve over time, the trade that was conducted through Ashkelon did not rep-

---

[34] Dorsey, *The Roads and Highways of Ancient Israel* (Baltimore: Johns Hopkins University, 1991), 59-60, 65-66, 189-96. These are the Ashkelon-Gaza Road, the Ashkelon-Yasur-el Mughar Road, the Ashkelon-Ekron-Kh. Sufin Road, Jerusalem-Elah Valley-Ashkelon Road, the Gedor-T. Goded-Ashkelon Road, the Lachish-Ashdod/Ashkelon Road, and the Ashkelon-T. Sheria-Beersheba Road.

[35] Blakely and Hardin, "Southwestern Judah in the Late Eighth Century B.C.E.," no. 326 (2002): 41-42.

[36] Oppenheim. "Babylonian and Assyrian Historical Texts," 291.

resent an entirely new system but an improvement on previous systems of trade. Sherratt and Sherratt note that the maritime network that had been established in the tenth and ninth centuries BCE grew in importance in the eighth century as the region was increasingly drawn into the trade nexus. Sherratt and Sherratt write that

> ...the continuing growth of Assyria drew trade and tribute from the Levantine cities, intensifying their quest for high-value materials further west; the emergence of city-states in the Aegean added new centres of production and demand for raw materials; indigenous foci in Villanovan Italy and southern Spain developed under strong external contacts.[37]

Although the extent of these routes attests to the size of this re-emerging world system and the distances that the trade ships could reach, control of Ashkelon was also of considerable economic and political importance on a more regional level. Moshe Elat notes that the acquisition of Ashkelon, along with Gaza, gave "Tiglath-Pileser III control over both the major power and the sea links upon which economic relations between Egypt and Philistia depended."[38] With Ashkelon under his control, the Assyrians were in a position to access and control a variety of trade routes and increase the power and wealth of their empire.

The remains found in shipwrecks dating to the eighth and seventh centuries BCE reveal the distances travelled by goods coming out of Ashkelon and other Eastern Mediterranean ports. A Phoenician shipwreck discovered off the coast of Spain in 1988 contained Phoenician red-slipped platters and bowls, as well as the ovoid store-jars that were typical of Ashkelon and Ekron.[39] Ivan Negueruela notes that out of all the items found in the wreck, it

---

[37] Sherratt and Sherratt, "The Growth of the Mediterranean Economy in the Early First Millennium BC": 366.

[38] Elat, "The Economic Relations of the Neo-Assyrian Empire with Egypt," *Journal of the American Oriental Society* 98, no. 1 (1978): 32.

[39] Master, "Trade and Politics: Ashkelon's Balancing Act in the Seventh Century BCE": 59.

was the ovoid store-jars that were the most predominant.[40] It should be noted that the presence of these jars does not prove that this ill-fated ship was bringing oil and wine to the coastal regions of modern-day Spain for trade. The ship may have been engaged in another type of mission, such as transporting gifts or tribute, and the stone jars could have simply contained supplies for the crew's long journey. However, considering the extent of trade that occurred in the eighth and seventh centuries, to which Sherratt and Sherratt refer, it is certainly plausible that this ship had been carrying goods from Ekron and Ashkelon. As Master notes, these jars were typically used by the Phoenicians to transport and sell olive oil from Ekron, as well as wine from Ashkelon, throughout the entire Mediterranean.[41] Whether this particular ship was sent out for trade or tribute, the distance it went from its homeland attests to the interconnected nature of Mediterranean societies during this period of heightened trade activity.

Ashkelon As a Centre of Trade

Further evidence of the demand for trade goods in the eighth century is found in two shipwrecks that were discovered off the Palestinian coast in 1997 by the U.S. Navy. The remains of two eighth-century ships, referred to as the *Tanit* and the *Elisa*, were found to contain a large number of amphorae, or tall narrow-mouthed jars: 385 and 396 respectively.[42] An impressive feature of these amphorae, Robert Ballard *et al.* note, was the precision of their construction.[43] The amphorae on both of these ships, which were able to hold approximately seventeen liters of liquid, deviated less than two centimeters in height and one centimeter in width from one an-

---

[40] Negueruela, et al., "Seventh-century BC Phoenician Vessel Discovered at Playa de la Isla, Mazarron, Spain," *The International Journal of Nautical Archaeology* 24, no. 3 (1995): 192-93.

[41] Master, "Trade and Politics: Ashkelon's Balancing Act in the Seventh Century BCE": 59.

[42] Ballard, et al., "Iron Age Shipwrecks in Deep Water off Ashkelon, Israel": 151.

[43] Ballard, et al., "Iron Age Shipwrecks in Deep Water off Ashkelon, Israel": 158-59.

other.[44] This level of skilled manufacturing on such a large scale suggests that a great degree of care was placed on providing accurate measurements, attesting to the seriousness with which trade goods and tribute items were exchanged. Although neither the origin nor the destination of these two ships can be known, the amphorae that they contained demonstrate a high level of sophistication in eighth-century trade.

Aside from exporting goods throughout the Mediterranean and Aegean, the Assyrians relied upon Ashkelon for the importation of luxury items. J.B. Pritchard explains that Ashkelon was one of the favored cities to be called upon by King Esarhaddon to provide materials for the construction of his new palace at Nineveh.[45] Additionally, Master notes that tribute lists from Ashkelon describe the city as "a plentiful source for highly prized Egyptian imports."[46] Ashkelon's favored status and value for importing high volumes of desired goods suggests the port city's prominence in Assyria's maritime trade activities.

Another indication of Ashkelon's economic value to the Assyrian Empire is found in the forgiving nature that the Assyrians had toward the city, which had a reputation for rebellion. The standard Assyrian practice for dealing with rebellious communities was to deport the people to somewhere else in the empire and repopulate the region with other conquered peoples, as occurred in Yamani in 712 and the Judean countryside in 701 BCE.[47] In stark contrast with this policy, when King Mitinti of Ashkelon rebelled against Tiglath Pileser III, the Assyrians simply replaced him with a puppet king, sparing the city's population and economy from rep-

---

[44] Ballard, et al., "Iron Age Shipwrecks in Deep Water off Ashkelon, Israel": 158-59.

[45] Pritchard, *Ancient Near Eastern Texts Relating to the Old Testament* (ed. Pritchard; Princeton: Princeton University Press, 1969), 291.

[46] Master, "Trade and Politics: Ashkelon's Balancing Act in the Seventh Century BCE": 50.

[47] Na'aman, "Population Changes in Palestine Following Assyrian Deportations": 107. Oppenheim, "Babylonian and Assyrian Historical Texts," 287. Master, "Trade and Politics: Ashkelon's Balancing Act in the Seventh Century BCE": 49.

rimand.[48] Despite the fact that Ashkelon rebelled against every subsequent Assyrian king, there is no evidence that the city was ever
razed or depopulated.[49] Assyrian tolerance for Ashkelon's rebellious nature attests to both the city's prominence as an economic
center and Assyria's dependence on interregional trade.

The distances travelled by Phoenician sailors, the demands for
the secondary goods that entered and left Ashkelon, and Assyria's
tolerance of Ashkelon's repeated rebellions further attest to the
extent and import of interregional trade in the eighth and seventh-
centuries BCE. Such economic demands, stemming from both
Ashkelon and Ekron's trade activities, would have placed increased
pressure on the neighbouring agrarian regions that were expected
to supply raw materials for the production of secondary goods. The
economic growth and vibrancy of Ekron and Ashkelon attest to
both the active trade climate of the eighth and seventh centuries
and, in and of themselves, facilitated a trade environment that
would transform the lives of the inhabitants of Judah.

[48] Tadmore, *The Inscriptions of Tiglath-Pileser III, King of Assyria* (Jerusalem: Israel Academy of Sciences and Humanities, 1994), 84. Assyria's forgiving nature toward Ashkelon had a secondary advantage for the city. As
in the case of Ekron, the Assyrian destruction of neighbouring communities ended nearly all in-land economic competition, such as wine and pottery production. Master writes that 'Ashkelon was economically successful
first and foremost because the Assyrians left it alone' (Master, "Trade and
Politics: Ashkelon's Balancing Act in the Seventh Century BCE": 60).
Faust and Weiss, "Judah, Philistia, and the Mediterranean World": 73.

[49] Elat, "The Economic Relations of the Neo-Assyrian Empire with
Egypt": 33.

C. Judah's Entrance Into an Eighth-Century World System

As in the Bronze Age, the degree to which Judah engaged in urban-based economic activity in Iron Age II was directly connected to the economic activities of neighbouring empires. Unlike the Bronze Age cycles, however, the rise of the Neo-Assyrian Empire in the eighth century produced a more direct and transformative relationship between the communities of Palestine and the system's core society than had previously been experienced. With the fall of Samaria to the North and Judah's entrance into vassalage under the Assyrians, economic adaptations, like settling along trade routes to benefit from trade opportunities, were not simply a matter of choice; Judah was expected to bow to Assyria's will.[1] Also unlike earlier economic cycles in Palestine's history, in which urban communities with no obvious cooperative connection attempted to benefit from heightened trade activity, the late eighth and early seventh centuries witnessed the development of an advanced agrarian society that produced valuable goods that were exported throughout the Near East and the greater Mediterranean world.

Judah's entrance into the Assyrian Empire, and the growing world system to which it was connected, probably occurred in the 730s, coinciding with the reign of the Assyrian King Tiglath-Pileser III and King Ahaz of Judah.[2] This dating dovetails with the Assyrian campaign into the southern Levant in 734, during which Judah became a vassal and settlements along Assyria's trade routes enjoyed increased prosperity.[3] Blakely and Hardin write that as Assyria moved through Judah, as well as the Philistine and Transjordanian states, the empire "reorganized the polities of the

---

[1] Blakely and Hardin, "Southwestern Judah in the Late Eighth Century B.C.E.": 42-43.

[2] Finkelstein and Silberman, "Temple and Dynasty": 265.

[3] Elat, "The Economic Relations of the Neo-Assyrian Empire with Egypt": 26. Gitin and Dever, "Recent Excavations in Israel: Studies in Iron Age Archaeology": 43.

117

area to suit their established imperial ambitions."[4] The ambitions of the Assyrian Empire for southwestern Judah are reflected in extra-biblical literary evidence.

One sign of Judah's incorporation into the Assyrian economy was the establishment of trade emporiums in the region, which Finkelstein and Silberman believe to have been part of a larger strategy to incorporate Judah into the Assyrian-dominated Arabian trade network.[5] When the Assyrian king Sargon II conquered Gaza in 720, he established a trading emporium between Gaza and the border of Egypt. Describing the events of that year, Sargon proclaimed, "The sealed [ka]r-ri of Egypt I opened. Assyrians and Egyptians I mingled together and I made them trade."[6] Dovetailing with Finkelstein and Silberman's view on bringing Judah into the Assyrian-Arab trade network, Diana Edelman concludes that this trade emporium was placed between Gaza and Egypt to "obtain revenue from the Arabian trade that might have been diverted to this newly settled region instead of moving into Gaza [an independent city-state where the Assyrians could not benefit from taxes]," to create a trading diaspora there.[7] Blakely and Hardon claim that the creation of such emporiums and extending Assyria's trade sphere was one of the main economic motivations for the campaign of Tiglath-Pileser III in the 730s.[8] As in the Bronze Age, Palestine's location between empires made the area attractive to foreign economic interests, which appear to have had a profound effect on economic activity in Judah.

Unlike the developmental cycles of the Bronze Age, archaeological evidence suggests that the transformations that took place under Assyrian vassalage were more transformative, from a socio-anthropological perspective. Finkelstein and Silberman claim that

---

[4] Blakely and Hardin, "Southwestern Judah in the Late Eighth Century B.C.E.": 42.

[5] Finkelstein and Silberman, "Temple and Dynasty": 265.

[6] Elat, "The Economic Relations of the Neo-Assyrian Empire with Egypt": 27.

[7] Edelman. "Tyrian Trade in Yehud Under Artaxerxes I: Real or Fictional? Independent or Crown Endorsed?" 222.

[8] Blakely and Hardin, "Southwestern Judah in the Late Eighth Century B.C.E.": 43.

as a result of Assyrian domination of Palestine in the late eighth century BCE, Judah experienced a rise into full-blown statehood, as evidenced by

> ...the growth of Jerusalem into a major urban centre, the dramatic expansion of the Judahite population, and the establishment of a centralized bureaucracy which required extensive literacy and scribal activity. None of this is apparent before the late eighth century BCE.[9]

The threat of Assyrian power, the opportunities that it presented, and the desire to rebel against this foreign empire all had serious implications for Judean society and its economic strategies.

Societal Transformation in Judah

Due to the rapid development of political and economic structures, the inhabitants of Judah witnessed major societal advances that are not evidenced prior to the late eighth century. As Assyrian influence grew throughout Palestine, Judah appears to have been transformed from a land of scattered agrarian communities into a state, with flourishing urban-based economic activity. While evidence of an advanced economy specializing in secondary products, such as olive oil and wine, are absent from early eighth-century Judah, the late eighth century presents a very different picture.[10] The reasons behind this level of growth connect to both the effects of Assyrian expansion and also what is often one of the key instigators of societal change: population growth.

Demographic Upheaval

The late eighth century ushered in a period of heightened economic activity in Judah, with advances in production, the building of monumental works, and what appears to have been a centralization of administrative power.[11] A major change that took place dur-

---

[9] Finkelstein and Silberman, "Temple and Dynasty": 277.

[10] Finkelstein and Silberman, "Temple and Dynasty": 263.

[11] Beyond the archaeological evidence for a centralization of administrative power that is presented below, such centralization is almost always

ing this time, and would have helped to bring about these transformations, was a massive increase in population density. Jerusalem
was one area that experienced impressive increases in population
and urban development. Yigal Shiloh notes that from the tenth to
the eighth centuries BCE, the settled area of Jerusalem, not including the Temple Mount, was about 60 dunams, or 6 hectares.[12]
Shiloh writes that with the addition of the inclusion of the western
hill, "in the days of Hezekiah, the fortified area of the city increased
by about 460 dunams [46 hectares]."[13] Although population levels
of ancient sites are extremely difficult to determine, Liverani estimates that by the end of the eighth century, in the space of a single
generation, the population of Jerusalem grew fifteen-fold from one
thousand to fifteen thousand.[14] To facilitate such a population increase, new organizational strategies and administrative projects
would have been required, as illustrated below.

The dramatic level of population growth in Jerusalem was not
limited to urban centers during the late eighth century , but appear
to have occurred throughout the Judean countryside as well.
Finkelstein and Silberman note that "settlements in the hill country
to the south of Jerusalem swelled from perhaps 34 in Iron IIA to
122 in the late eighth century."[15] One theory as to the cause of
Judah's population boom focuses on the destruction of Samaria.
Several scholars believe it is probable that a wave of refugees from
southern Samaria entered into Judah as a result of the destruction
of the Northern Kingdom in the 720s, resulting in unprecedented

---

required in order to produce monumental works and production advances.

[12] Shiloh, *Excavations at the City of David* (vol. 19; Jerusalem: Institute
of Archaeology, Hebrew University of Jerusalem, 1984), 3.

[13] Shiloh, *Excavations at the City of David*, 3.

[14] Liverani, *Israel's History and the History of Israel* (London: Equinox,
2007), 152. There are other estimates on the scale of growth that took
place during this period. Finkelstein and Silberman suggest that Jerusalem's population grew from one thousand to ten thousand (Finkelstein
and Silberman, "Temple and Dynasty": 265).

[15] Finkelstein and Silberman, "Temple and Dynasty": 265.

population growth and density.[16] Regardless of the catalyst for this growth, such a rapid increase in population would have created a societal shock, resulting in a demand for the types of administrative strategies that were addressed in Chapter Two. These would include the creation of a distributive system to manage the increased strain on the land's carrying capacity. The response taken by the inhabitants of Judah appears to follow that most commonly found in cultural evolution: a strengthening of the political economy, which facilitates the sustenance of a society that has exceeded the narrow boundaries of a subsistence economy.[17] As detailed in Chapter Two, when subsistence-centered economies transform to become more dependent on a political economy the productive energies that had once focused on the benefit of the local family group becomes redirected toward the benefit of a centralized administrative class.[18]

---

[16] Broshi, "The Expansion of Jerusalem in the Reigns of Hezekiah and Manasseh," no. 24 (1974). Finkelstein and Silberman, "Temple and Dynasty": 264. Liverani, *Israel's History and the History of Israel*, 152. King, "The Eighth, the Greatest of Centuries?": 5. Younker, "The Iron Age in the Southern Levant," in *Near Eastern Archaeology: A Reader* (ed. Richard; Winona Lake, IN: Eisenbrauns, 2003), 379. It should be noted that a Judean hills survey that was conducted by Avi Ofer found that the region's population had doubled each century from the eleventh to the eighth centuries, experiencing a sharp decline in the seventh century (Ofer, "The Monarchic Period in the Judean Highland: A Spatial Overview," in *Studies in the Archaeology of the Iron Age in Israel and Jordan* [ed. Mazar; Sheffield: Sheffield Academic Press, 2001]). This could be taken to mean that although the population increase was significant, it may not have been entirely unique. However, the sudden rise in population from a neighbouring area, alongside evidence of economic and political developments at the same time, suggest that a tipping point was reached, causing caused societal change in Judah.

[17] Johnson and Earle, *The Evolution of Human Societies*, 24-26.

[18] Fried, *The Evolution of Political Society* (New York: Random House, 1967), 186. Sanderson, *The Evolution of Human Sociality: A Darwinian Conflict Perspective* (Lanham, Maryland: Rowman & Littlefield Publishers, 2001), 300-01.

Increased Agrarian Intensification and Trade

The late eighth century ushered in a period of increased economic activity that was probably the result of both population growth and Assyrian influence over Judah. Notable economic developments during this period include the first signs of mass-produced pottery in Judah, centralized olive oil production in the Shephelah, and the introduction of standardized weights, each of which point to the development of a political economy.[19] These economic advances suggest that much of Judah had surrendered subsistence agriculture as its central economic strategy in favor of export-oriented specialized farming, which would have been beneficial to Judah's Assyrian clients, who sought raw materials for both trade and domestic consumption.[20] The importation of luxury items into the region provides evidence of such trade activity in Judah.

Judah's involvement in long-distance trade, either through private or administrative channels, is indicated by the import of dietary goods into Jerusalem. Excavations have revealed that fish and shellfish were imported into the city from various distant regions. Faust and Weiss explain that a large number of fish bones, representing a wide variety of species, were found in "the City of David and in the Ophel at Jerusalem."[21] Considering the quantity and variety of fish that were consumed by Jerusalemites, Hanan and Omri Lernau conclude that Jerusalem enjoyed a well-organized fish trade.[22] Henk Mienis notes that the seashells discovered in Jerusalem also indicate that the city was engaged in significant trade activity, overall. According to Mienis, the shells discovered in Jerusalem originated from various distant locations, including the Medi-

---

[19] Finkelstein and Na'aman, "The Judahite Shephelah in the Late 8th and Early 7th Centuries BCE," *Tel Aviv* 31, no. 1 (2004): 73-75. Kletter, *Economic Keystones: The Weight System of the Kingdom of Judah* (vol. 276; Sheffield: Continuum International Publishing Group, 1998).

[20] Sherratt and Sherratt, "The Growth of the Mediterranean Economy in the Early First Millennium BC": 366-71.

[21] Faust and Weiss, "Judah, Philistia, and the Mediterranean World: Reconstructing the Economic System of the Seventh Century B.C.E.": 75.

[22] Lernau and Lernau. "Fish Remains," in *Excavations at the City of David 1978-1985* eds. de Groot and Ariel; Jerusalem: Institute of Archaeology, Hebrew University of Jerusalem, 1992), 136.

terranean Sea, the Red Sea, and the River Nile, indicating intensive trade between distant shores and the people of Jerusalem.[23] In addition to food goods, other luxury materials were imported into seventh-century Judah. Avraham Faust and Ehud Weiss note that luxury woods were imported into Jerusalem from great distances, originating from as far as South Arabia, North Syria, and perhaps even Greece.[24] In order to support a diet of seafood, an active long-distance trading community that is not evidenced in Iron IIA would have been required. Finds such as these indicate that Jerusalem's economic activities in the eighth century went beyond those of a simple agrarian society that is focused on local consumption. Increased trade activity was not limited to Jerusalem in the eighth and seventh centuries but is found in other areas of Judah as well.

Evidence of long-distance trade is also found in the remote and arid Beer-sheba region, where luxury wood that was imported from Lebanon has been discovered. Nili Liphschitz and Gidion Biger claim that the presence of cedar in such a remote area "indicates the wealth and widespread commercial activities of a regime which was able to use such an expensive import in the building of monumental constructions."[25] The ability to engage in the types of economic activities attributed to the eighth and seventh centuries, from the development of weights to the importation of luxury goods, suggests that massive developments occurred in Judah during this time. As Assyrian expansion spread throughout Palestine, Judah experienced significant societal change as production energy was refocused from more locally centered subsistence strategies to generating revenue through trade and the accumulation of luxury goods.[26] In order to facilitate such dramatic economic advances in

[23] Meinis. "Molluscs," in *Excavations at the City of David 1978-1985* eds. de Groot and Ariel; Jerusalem: Institute of Archaeology, Hebrew University of Jerusalem, 1992), 129.

[24] Faust and Weiss, "Judah, Philistia, and the Mediterranean World": 75.

[25] Liphschitz and Biger, "Cedar of Lebanon (Cedrus Libani) in Israel During Antiquity," *Israel Exploration Journal* 41, (1991): 172.

[26] The word "revenue" is used liberally here. Since there is no evidence of a monetary system in Judah at this time, goods would have been traded for other goods, rather than monetary compensation.

a relatively short period of time in Judah, significant administrative developments would have to have taken place.

Considering the developments that took place in Ekron and Ashkelon during the eighth and seventh centuries, the Judean countryside probably experienced significant changes in its economic activities. The appearance of Judean engagement in state-controlled olive-oil production in the eighth and seventh centuries[27] would have changed the way Judean farmers managed, if not controlled, their land. Increased levels of economic organization are evidence for such societal changes in rural Judah. Avraham Faust writes that "we see a great deal of organization in the processing of agricultural products within agricultural installations and industrial zones" in rural regions of eighth-century Judah.[28] This, Faust suggests, indicates levels of organization that exceed the bounds of family.[29] Economic goals shifting from beyond the family unit to centralized organization is a key development in the evolution of agrarian societies, and often brings with it elite-based policies like latifundialization.

Centralization of Judean Society and Structural Projects

The demographic and economic developments that Judah witnessed in the late eighth and early seventh centuries would not have been attainable without the strengthening or the creation of Judah's governing structure. As explained in Chapter Two, the organizational demands placed upon a subsistence-focused agrarian society by rapid increases in population density and trade activity require the development of a more complex administrative infrastructure. To meet these demands, as Johnson and Earle note,

---

[27] Na'aman, "Ekron Under the Assyrian and Egyptian Empires": 81. Finkelstein and Silberman, "Temple and Dynasty": 265. Gitin and Dever, "Recent Excavations in Israel: Studies in Iron Age Archaeology": 50-51. Finkelstein and Na'aman, "The Judahite Shephelah in the Late 8th and Early 7th Centuries BCE": 73-75.

[28] Faust, "The Rural Community in Ancient Israel During Iron Age II," *Bulletin of the American Schools of Oriental Research* 317 (2000): 23.

[29] Faust, "The Rural Community in Ancient Israel During Iron Age II": 23.

agrarian societies organize under a central authority, as an administrative class either gains strength or comes into being.[30] Such a cultural development appears to have occurred throughout Judah in the eighth century with lasting effect.

While traditional interpretations of Judah's history find that the eighth century BCE represented a time in which Judah's power gained strength, recent alternative interpretations find that it was during this period that a Judean state first came into being. Finkelstein and Silberman, for example, argue that Judah experienced a rise to full-blown statehood during the second half of the eighth century.[31] Supporting their assumption with a wide range of archaeological evidence, Finkelstein and Silberman write that the developments that Judah experienced during this period included

> ...the growth of Jerusalem into a major urban center, the dramatic expansion of the Judahite population, and the establishment of a centralized bureaucracy, which required extensive literacy and scribal activity. None of this is apparent before the late eighth century BCE.[32]

According to Na'aman, this state, with its centre in Jerusalem, continued to develop until

> ...the centrality of Jerusalem in the Kingdom of Judah was so remarkable that we can speak of the kingdom as being a kind of a city-state, in which the great capital city dominated a large territory that supplied all the needs of its population and elite.[33]

The transformation from a region of scattered agrarian communities to a land with such a highly centralized governing system would have led to dramatic changes for the inhabitants of Judah, from administrators to farmers.

---

[30] Johnson and Earle, *The Evolution of Human Societies: From Foraging Group to Agrarian State*, 248-51.

[31] Finkelstein and Silberman, "Temple and Dynasty": 277.

[32] Finkelstein and Silberman, "Temple and Dynasty": 277.

[33] Na'aman, "The Distribution of Messages in the Kingdom of Judah in Light of the Lachish Ostraca," 53, no. 2 (2003): 172.

While Samaria had adopted a highly organized administrative and bureaucratic system by the early eighth century, as indicated by the Samaria ostraca[34] and the Megiddo horse-breeding and training industry,[35] evidence of centralized administration in Judah prior to late eighth century is sparse. In contrast to Samaria, Judah lagged behind in state development, which is suggested by the Judahite Deuteronomistic Historian's acceptance of Samarian superiority over Judah in the story of King Amaziah of Judah and King Joash.[36] As explained above, Jerusalem was limited to six hectares prior to the late eighth century, urban sites were absent in the highlands, and only sparse urban activity took place in the Beer-sheba Valley.[37] Without evidence of state apparatuses, several scholars find it difficult to visualize a fully centralized state and integrated economy prior to the late eighth century .[38] Incorporation into the Assyrian world system, and a subsequent desire to rebel against it,

---

[34] Finkelstein and Silberman, "Temple and Dynasty": 262.

[35] Finkelstein and Silberman, "Temple and Dynasty": 262. Lester Grabbe explains that the Samaria ostraca is often explained as administrative documents detailing the importation of oil and wine (Grabbe, *Ancient Israel: What Do We Know and How Do We Know It?* [London: T&T Clark, 2007], 129), while Niemann argues that these ostraca were receipts for wine and oil that "document attempts by Jehoash and Jeroboam II to integrate the traditional tribal links into their personal power network" (Niemann. "Royal Samaria: Capital or Residence? or: The Foundation of the City of Samaria by Sargon II," in *Ahab Agonistes: The Rise and Fall of the Omri Dynasty* [ed. Grabbe; London: T&T Clark International, 2007]). Whether the Samaria ostraca documented trade or the strengthening of alliances, both activities suggest the presence of an advanced economic and political system.

[36] 2 Kgs. 14.9–10.

[37] Finkelstein and Silberman, "Temple and Dynasty": 262.

[38] Lemche, "From Patronage Society to Patronage Society," in *The Origins of the Ancient Israelite States* eds. Fritz and Davies; Sheffield: Sheffield Academic Press, 1996), 106-8. Hopkins, "Bare Bones: Putting Flesh on the Economics of Ancient Israel," in *The Origins of the Ancient Israelite States* eds. Clines, Davies and Jarick; vol. 228 of *JSOTSS*; Sheffield: Sheffield Academic Press, 1996), 121-32. Whitelam, "Constructing Jerusalem," in *Flowing with Milk and Honey: Visions of Israel from Biblical to Modern Times* (eds. Greenspoon and Simkins; Durham, North Carolina: Duke University Press, 2002).

would quickly accelerate Judah's relatively slow state development. Evidence of these changes is found in a rise of large urban projects, monumental architecture, and increased settlement in more arid regions.

During the late eighth century urban projects and the construction of fortresses took shape throughout Judah, with particularly high levels of activity in the south. As Jerusalem expanded in both population and size, a formidable seven-meter thick wall was constructed on the western slope to protect newly constructed quarters.[39] Two other protective walls were also built on Jerusalem's eastern slope during this time.[40] Another impressive urban project that is believed to have taken place in Jerusalem in the late eighth century was the creation of the Siloam tunnel. David Jamieson-Drake points out that this project was unique in that it was not merely created to store water but to channel it.[41] This endeavor to supply water to Jerusalem, which involved two teams of excavators tunneling toward each other, was, in the words of Liverani, a "remarkable work of hydraulic engineering."[42] Such developments in Jerusalem attest to the social organization and capital that was available in the late eighth-century BCE.

The Shephelah also experienced a surge in urban projects in the late-eighth century with the impressive fortification of Lachish's defenses. Liverani notes that at the end of the eighth cen-

---

[39] Avigad, *Discovering Jerusalem* (Oxford: Blackwell, 1984), 46-53. Liverani, *Israel's History and the History of Israel*, 152.

[40] Shiloh, *Excavations at the City of David*, 19.

[41] Jamieson-Drake, *Scribes and Schools in Monarchic Judah: A Socio-Archeological Approach* (109; eds. Clines and Davies; Sheffield: Almond Press, 1991), 97.

[42] Liverani, *Israel's History and the History of Israel*, 152. It should be noted that John Rogerson offers an alternative view of the construction of the Siloam tunnel, suggesting that it was built several centuries later during the Hasmonean period. Even if this were to be the case, it still places the construction of the tunnel in a period of time that required protection from a powerful empire (Roman) that had created a prosperous world system. For more information on Rogerson and Davies' theory see Rogerson and Davies, "Was the Siloam Tunnel Built by Hezekiah?" *The Biblical Archaeologist* 59, no. 3 (1996).

tury the city was "enclosed by an imposing wall, with a double city gate: an inner one with six rooms, and an outer one with an hairpin ramp. The gate led into a square from which one entered the palace complex through a second six-roomed gate."[43] Such elaborate defense architecture indicates Lachish's administrative importance, as well as the organizational ability and the available resources to undertake such a project. Such feats of engineering and construction would not have been possible, or necessary, without a centralized organization of labor and administrative duties. While urban centers enjoyed various improvements during this transformative period, rural areas also experienced development, which can be attributed, at least in part, to increased population density.

Although populations in Palestine appear to have experienced a slow, steady growth during at the beginning of Iron II, the late eighth century ushered in a period of accelerated growth in the countryside.[44] As Judah reached its carrying capacity, agrarian communities were forced to expand into less favorable farmlands. In order to cope with the hardship of farming land in semi-arid areas, greater societal organization was required. For example, the construction of dams, which had already been brought into use in Iron Age I, were used on a wider scale to help farmers to adapt to dry-land farming.[45] Rural projects, however, were not only geared toward sustaining Judean population, but also toward facilitating trade. Liverani notes that fortresses were constructed in the desert areas of the Negev to protect the frontier and to help control caravan routes.[46] It is very likely that these rural projects would have required a centralized administrative body to orchestrate their construction and use.

From the construction of city walls and advanced water systems to the expansion of settlements into less desirable areas for farming, such developments represent the conditions that tend to ignite the reoccurring patterns that occur when agrarian societies undergo rapid economic development, as well as the abuses that

---

[43] Liverani, *Israel's History and the History of Israel*, 154.
[44] Finkelstein and Silberman, "Temple and Dynasty": 262.
[45] Liverani, *Israel's History and the History of Israel*, 155.
[46] Liverani, *Israel's History and the History of Israel*, 155.

accompany them. Such connections further suggest that Judah had experienced a period of significant cultural evolution in the late eighth century BCE.

Eighth-Century Judean Transformation As Cultural Evolution

The presence of a profound period of societal transformation in eighth-century Judah is not only supported by material evidence of urban projects and state activity during this time, but by the lack of such evidence before the late eighth century. The uniqueness of these events in Judean society highlights the impact that such changes would have had on Judean communities. From dramatic increases in population levels to the development of urban sites and monumental projects, the events that took place in the late eighth and early seventh-century Judah dovetail with the recurring patterns that cultural-evolutionary theorists find as agrarian societies undergo increased agricultural centralization. This subsection considers potential connections between the evidence given above and what anthropologists Allen Johnson and Timothy Earle consider to be the key elements of a developing regional polity.

Water Systems and Proximity to Trade Centers

The first characteristic to be addressed has to do with water control and access to maritime trade and markets. Johnson and Earle write that a basis for the development of a regional polity is an environment that has developed

> ...(a) rich resources like irrigated land or bottom alluvium [soil or sediments deposited by running water that are often highly rich in nutrients], or (b) opportunities for trade resulting from water-based transport or proximity to markets and trade routes.[47]

Both of these economic benefits facilitate the development of specialized farming, which enable societies to produce greater volumes of goods for trade and support the growth of urban centers. The

---

[47] Johnson and Earle, *The Evolution of Human Societies*, 248-49.

development of water systems and Judah's proximity to inland and
maritime trade were both increased in the late eighth century BCE.

Although Judean farmers employed various means of water
preservation prior to the eighth century, such as terracing and the
construction of large water catchment basins,[48] the rapid development and sophistication of these projects in the eighth century attest to greater levels of administrative control. Water retention
strategies were developed in the eighth century as dams were used
to preserve water and soil in the flood-prone areas into which
Judean farmers were expanding.[49] Furthermore, it was not until the
eighth century that elaborate water systems were used to supply
cities, as evidenced in Jerusalem, Gibeon, Gezer, Hazor, and
Megiddo.[50] Rather than simply channeling water from a collected
source or retaining water in the fields, Judeans were channeling
water directly into their urban centers in the late eighth century.
While the region enjoyed an increase in the development of water
systems, entrance into Assyrian vassalage appears to have also
brought increased access to markets.

The development of communities alongside Assyrian trading
routes during Tiglath-Pileser III's campaign in the 730s, the construction of trade centers, the importation of seafood from as far
away as Egypt, and a heightened maritime economy at nearby Ashkelon all suggest that the inhabitants of Judah gained greater access
to interregional markets.[51] It is important to reiterate that the con-

---

[48] Amiran, *Early Arad* (Jerusalem: Israel Exploration Society, 1978),
13-14. Miller, "Water Use in Syria and Palestine from the Neolithic to the
Bronze Age," 11, no. 3 (1980): 336. Broshi and Gophna, "The Settlements
and Population of Palestine during the Early Bronze Age II-III," no. 253
(1984): 50. Faust, "The Rural Community in Ancient Israel During Iron
Age II": 23.

[49] Liverani, *Israel's History and the History of Israel*, 155.

[50] McNutt, *Reconstructing the Society of Ancient Israel* (Louisville: West-
minster John Knox Press, 1999), 153-54. Liverani, *Israel's History and the
History of Israel*, 152. Jamieson-Drake, *Scribes and Schools in Monarchic Judah:
A Socio-Archeological Approach*, 97.

[51] Elat, "The Economic Relations of the Neo-Assyrian Empire with
Egypt": 26. Lernau and Lernau. "Fish Remains," 136. Meinis. "Molluscs,"

cept of "market," as referred to by Johnson and Earl, was quite different from modern-day retail stores. Hayah Katz notes a lack of evidence for structures built for commerce and that 62.5% of Judean weights were found in domestic assemblages while only 4.8% were found in public places, it is likely that goods were traded in open air markets or at the door of merchants' homes.[52] Judah's subjugation to vassalage under their Assyrian masters, as well as the will to rebel against them, also suggest that Judah's incorporation into the Assyrian world system created new opportunities for trade and development.

It is probable that Judah was able to take advantage of a vibrant maritime economy. Master notes that although it is unlikely that Judah had direct trade relations with Ashkelon, products made from Judean agricultural goods probably travelled through the port city via intermediary sites in the Shephelah.[53] Ekron likely served as such an intermediary, where Judean olives would have been processed before being transported to Ashkelon.[54] Increased shipments of olive oil leaving from Ashkelon's port demanded greater volumes of olive oil from Ekron. As suggested by Fantalkin, the nearby fertile lands of Judah would have been a logical place for Ekron to turn to increase its olive supplies.[55] Evidence of a vibrant seafood trade in Jerusalem and Greek pottery throughout the highlands further suggest Judah's ability to have taken greater advantage

---

129. Stern, *Archaeology of the Land of the Bible* (vol. 2: The Assyrian, Babylonian, and Persian Periods; New York: Random House, 2001), 214, 216.

[52] Katz, "Commercial Activity in the Kingdoms of Judah and Israel," *Tel Aviv* 31, no. 2 (2004): 272-75.

[53] Master, "Trade and Politics": 60.

[54] Na'aman, "Ekron Under the Assyrian and Egyptian Empires": 81. Finkelstein and Silberman, "Temple and Dynasty": 265. Gitin and Dever, "Recent Excavations in Israel": 50-51. Finkelstein and Na'aman note that although Judah had its own olive oil processing facilities before Ekron's revitalization in the seventh century, but after the destruction of the Shephelah by Sennacherib in 701 and the rise of Ekron processing was likely transferred to the Philistine city. Finkelstein and Na'aman, "The Judahite Shephelah in the Late 8th and Early 7th Centuries BCE": 73-75.

[55] Fantalkin, "The Final Destruction of Beth Shemesh and the *Pax Assyriaca* in the Judahite Shephelah": 255.

of maritime trade.[56] Both increased inland and maritime trade indicate that Judah had experienced greater access to the trade networks that had developed into a powerful world system in the
eighth and seventh centuries BCE. Such improved access to foreign luxury items and revenue production had a profound effect on
a region that had not long before been composed of scattered
agrarian communities.

Increased Population Density

Another key characteristic that Johnson and Earle attribute to regional polities is increased population density, dovetailing with the
dramatic levels of population growth that were experienced
throughout Judah.[57] The sudden leap in population levels in both
urban and rural areas of Judah, the expansion of farming communities into previously uninhabited regions, and the growth of administrative centers, suggest that Judah needed to adapt to its changing
circumstances.[58] In order to manage the strain that such population
growth would have placed on the land, Judah would have required
a higher level of administrative power. Such movement toward
increased administrative control is indicated by the development of
city walls, fortresses and towers, urban water systems, and other
public works.[59] The undertaking of such developments in response
to increased population density would have had a profound effect
on the daily lives of the inhabitants of Judah.

---

[56] Lernau and Lernau. "Fish Remains," 136. Meinis. "Molluscs," 129.
Stern, *Archaeology of the Land of the Bible*, 214, 216.
[57] Johnson and Earle, *The Evolution of Human Societies: From Foraging
Group to Agrarian State*, 249.
[58] Shiloh, *Excavations at the City of David*, 19. Finkelstein and Silberman, "Temple and Dynasty": 265. Liverani, *Israel's History and the History of
Israel*, 152.
[59] Avigad, *Discovering Jerusalem*, 46-53. Liverani, *Israel's History and the
History of Israel*, 154-55. Finkelstein and Silberman, "Temple and Dynasty":
263. Jamieson-Drake, *Scribes and Schools in Monarchic Judah: A Socio-
Archeological Approach*, 97.

Pronounced Social Stratification

Directly related to increased trade activity and population growth is social stratification. As mentioned above, a greater level of administrative control leads to the development of a non-productive segment of society that manage the harvesting, redistribution, and trade of goods. Johnson and Earle write that

> ...with the emergence of complex chiefdoms and states comes the division [of citizens] into classes: a ruling segment that owns and manages much of the wealth and productive resources and a commoner segment that works in the fields and at other productive tasks.[60]

Although such class divisions almost certainly existed to some extent in Judah prior to Iron Age II, considering that cycles of urban growth and trade activity predate this time, late eighth-century Judah appears to have experienced unprecedented levels of urbanization and interregional trade.

Aside from development projects in administrative centers, which almost always accompany increased social stratification,[61] other indicators in the archaeological record evidence the rise of a ruling elite class in eighth-century Judah. One indication of the development, or at least intensification, of hierarchies is found in the advancement of literacy, which strengthens the gulf between administrative classes and the so-called *commoners* in agrarian societies.[62] Lenski writes that in ancient agrarian societies limited literacy was the rule, and as a result, "...the cultural unity of agrarian societies was seriously weakened, and a divided cultural tradition emerged."[63] In the end, such divisions work to benefit the elite,

---

[60] Johnson and Earle, *The Evolution of Human Societies: From Foraging Group to Agrarian State*, 250.

[61] Plattner. "Markets and Marketplaces," in *Economic Anthropology* (ed. Plattner; Stanford: Stanford University Press, 2002), 180-81. Berdan. "Trade and Markets in Precapitalist States," in *Economic Anthropology* (ed. Plattner; Stanford: Stanford University Press, 2002), 79-80. Lenski, *Power and Privilege: A Theory of Social Stratification*, 79-82. Johnson and Earle, *The Evolution of Human Societies: From Foraging Group to Agrarian State*, 247-48.

[62] Lenski, *Power and Privilege: A Theory of Social Stratification*, 208.

[63] Lenski, *Power and Privilege: A Theory of Social Stratification*, 208.

who can use cultural division to strengthen their hold on power and justify the control of resources over another group. Prior to the late eighth century BCE, any evidence of literacy in Judah is lacking, aside from a very small collection of seals and ostraca.[64] In contrast to the early eighth century, Finkelstein and Silberman note that the latter part of the century reveals "monumental inscriptions – in the Siloam tunnel and on the facades of the Siloam tombs – appear at that time and the number of seals, [both] seal impressions and ostraca grow dramatically."[65] This sudden increase in evidence of written material, in correlation with urban developments like the building of interior and exterior walls and common societal patterns, further suggests that the late eighth century witnessed a strengthening of hierarchical systems in Judah.

Sanctification of the Regional Polity

The final characteristic of a regional polity that correlates with the developments that took place in late eighth-century Judah is the establishment of a sacred connection between the state and religious institutions. Johnson and Earle write, "Sanctity in the regional polity is deployed most dramatically, in sacred ceremonies intended to create a sense of common origins, purpose, and destiny among strangers and to sanctify the class divisions of society."[66] While sanctity at the local group level mainly reinforces the ties that bind families into larger groups, Johnson and Earl write that at the level of the regional polity "sanctity is mainly about encouraging the compliance of commoners with elite policies and privilege."[67] Religion is closely linked with economic activity in agrarian societies, often manifested through sacred systems of land management and rituals or festivals that influence sowing and harvest schedules.[68]

---

[64] Finkelstein and Silberman, "Temple and Dynasty": 263.

[65] Finkelstein and Silberman, "Temple and Dynasty": 264.

[66] Johnson and Earle, *The Evolution of Human Societies*, 250.

[67] Johnson and Earle, *The Evolution of Human Societies*, 250.

[68] Rappaport, "The Sacred in Human Evolution," 2, (1971). Knapp. "Copper Production and Eastern Mediterranean Trade: The Rise of Complex Society in Cyprus," in *Sate and Society: The Emergence and Development of Social Hierarchy and Political Centralization* eds. Gledhill, Bender and

Rather than simply serve as a guide for agrarian practice, the use of the sacred in political and economic organization also plays a pivotal role in establishing the dominance of elite members of a society over their subjects.

Following this common connection between economic and religious practice, religion in the ancient Near East, and temples in particular, played a key role establishing the power of ruling elites over the rest of society. Anthropologist Kajsa Ekholm-Friedman notes that ever since the development of ancient Mesopotamian societies, the process of social evolution into hierarchical systems has included an otherworldly element. One of the initial steps in establishing a hierarchy in the ancient Near East was to create a higher sense of unity. Ekholm-Friedman writes, "First a *higher unity* in the form of a symbolic space is created, and then this 'empty' space can be filled with economic and political content. The process of change in southern Mesopotamia encompasses an early transformation of this type."[69] Through creating a mystical authority that exists outside of a society's tangible reality, that tangible reality can be recreated to justify the hierarchical, economic, and political activities of the society's elite. Ekholm-Friedman further explains that "when a point of centralization was established 'above' existing social groups, it was beyond their reach and could gain enough autonomy to develop on its own. It then transformed the former power structure, giving rise to a new type of society."[70] The manipulation of a sacred other to establish political and economic goals within a society is found in modern agrarian societies such as Libya and Tunisia, where leaders have manipulated religious norms and festivals in order to pursue their economic objec-

---

Larsen; London: Unwin Hyman, 1988), 157. These sorts of connections are not surprising, considering the important central role that farming plays in such cultures.

[69] Ekholm-Friedman. "On the Evolution of Global Systems, Part I: the Mesopotamian Heartland," in *World System History: The Social Science of Long-Term Change* eds. Denemark, Friedman, Gills and Modelski; London: Routledge, 2000), 161.

[70] Ekholm-Friedman. "On the Evolution of Global Systems, Part I": 161.

tives.[71] Considering the political and economic advantages of centralizing worship and sanctifying the regional polity, perhaps it is not a coincidence that the Hebrew Bible attributes King Hezekiah's centralization of the cult of YHWH in Jerusalem to this period of rapid societal development.

The historical accuracy of Hezekiah's temple reform is a subject of debate. Ze'ev Herzog's and Finkelstein and Silberman's interpretations of archaeological evidence allow for the possibility that the destruction of the sanctuaries in Arad and Beer-sheba took place in the late eighth century during Hezekiah's reign, suggesting that such a policy may have been enacted at that time.[72] As seen above, such a move on King Hezekiah's part would have made economic sense. Through eliminating these competing centers of cultic power, removing the בָּמוֹת,[73] and destroying various cult objects, as suggested in the third and fourth chapters of 2 Kings, Judah's ruling elite would have been able to focus the religious activity of Judah on Jerusalem and centralize religious control under a central authority. Finkelstein and Silberman claim that archaeological evidence of the destruction of countryside shrines dovetails with the biblical account and interpret these activities as an effort to centralize religious authority in Jerusalem. Such moves, Finkelstein and Silberman write,

> ...would have been aimed at strengthening the unifying elements of the state – the central authority of the king and the

---

[71] Anderson, *The State and Social Transformation in Tunisia and Libya: 1830-1980* (Princeton: Princeton University Press, 1986), 266. Tozy. "Islam and the State," in *Polity and Society in Contemporary North Africa* eds. Zartman and Habeeb; Boulder: Westview Press, 1993), 110.

[72] Arguments for the correlation between the destruction of these sanctuaries and Hezekiah's reforms include, in part, Herzog, "The Fortress Mount at Tel Arad: An Interim Report," *Tel Aviv* 29, (2002): 35, 40, 69-72. Finkelstein and Silberman, "Temple and Dynasty": 271-72. Arguments against a correlation come, in part, from Na'aman, 'The Abandonment of Cult Places in the Kingdoms of Israel and Judah as Acts of Cult Reform," 34, (2002): 585-92, 593-95.

[73] "High places," often referring to sites of worship and cultic activity. Hezekiah's removal of the בָּמוֹת are referred to in 2 Kgs. 18.22; 21.3; 2 Chr. 31.12; 33.3; Isa. 36.7.

elite in the capital – and at weakening the old, somewhat autonomous, clan-based leadership in the Judahite country-side.[74]

Finkelstein and Silberman's thesis dovetails with the motivations behind centralizing the sacred as proposed by Ekholm-Friedman, in pertaining to the evolution of global systems: creating a space through which the ruling elite can both solidify and justify their power while reinforcing hierarchical structures that are centered on themselves.

Many of the variables of a regional polity, such as the development of water systems, access to maritime trade, high population density, pronounced stratification, and the sanctification of the regional polity were not only present in late eighth and early seventh-century Judah but appear to have experienced significant development during that time. Such developments of a regional polity go together with the recurring societal patterns that lead to the abandonment of subsistence strategies, the consolidation of land, and the hoarding of wealth by elites. Whereas many agrarian societies simply experience these changes as an outcome of increased population density, the added pressure of the Assyrian threat may have accelerated the pace with which Judah transformed itself, inspiring the fortification of urban centers and the development of impressive water systems to protect cities like Jerusalem during periods of foreign aggression.

The presence of these variables, in tandem with evidence of specialized cultivation, the production of secondary agricultural and luxury goods, and increased systems of hierarchy, indicate the potential for Judah to have experienced the presence of the recurring societal patterns that are attributed to cultural evolution in agrarian societies and their subsequent patterns of exploitation. As a result, it is worth considering that late eighth-century Judean farmers who had been accustomed to mixed-subsistence farming would have been required to change their agricultural strategies and lifestyles, to varying degrees, for the sake of economic development.

---

[74] Finkelstein and Silberman, "Temple and Dynasty": 274.

D. CONCLUSION

This chapter has demonstrated that evidence for cycles of societal change as a result of increased economic activity, like those referred to by Chaney and Premnath, can be found in Palestine dating back to the Early Bronze Age and continuing on into the late eighth century BCE. The effects of waxing and waning empires and the development of an Iron Age II world system strengthen the arguments of economists and anthropologists like Joachim Rennstich, George Modelski, and William Thompson, who argue that what is referred to as "globalization" today is not an entirely new phenomenon but the current evolutionary cycle of a long series of interregional world systems.[1] In the Bronze Age, the inhabitants of Palestine appear to have restructured their social order and goals to benefit from increased trade activity as new economic opportunities arose. As a result, the inhabitants experienced movements back and forth along an economic continuum with subsistence-centered farming in scattered highland communities on one end, and specialized cultivation for trade based economic activity, along with the establishment and strengthening of hierarchical systems, on the other. These cycles continued to ebb and flow, leading up to the major societal shifts witnessed in late eighth-century Judah as the Neo-Assyrian Empire dominated Palestine, creating new trade opportunities in an expanding world system.

Although systems of trade and urbanization have been carried out on a much larger and more efficient scale in the twentieth and twenty-first centuries CE, subsistence farmers in agrarian societies appear to experience similar challenges as political and economic elites gain power and exchange subsistence agriculture for more lucrative export strategies, as seen in the modern developing world. Whether under modern-day international capitalism or the primitive trade systems of the fourth millennium BCE, several anthropologists have found that some common outcomes appear to have recurred for agrarian producers as societies, and the cultures that

---

[1] Rennstich. "Three Steps in Globalization: Global Networks from 1000 BCE to 2050 CE," 204-8. Modelski. "World System Evolution," 35-37.

are attached to them, evolve. The theory of cultural evolution argues that agrarian societies tend to transform in similar ways as they face challenges such as population growth and increased trade opportunities, including the abandonment of subsistence practices, land exploitation, and the development of hierarchies that concentrate wealth among a select few. It is the issue of land exploitation that cannot be evidenced in eighth-century Judah, at least directly, due to a lack of data pertaining to landownership practices at that time. It is possible, however, that the modern example might offer some insights into this matter.

In order to pursue such a goal, and before a modern society can be applied as an interpretive tool for understanding the socio-economic contexts behind prophetic complaints against land ownership abuse, a degree of knowledge about issues that traditionally lay outside the scope of biblical studies is required, namely the modern economic policies and structures that serve as the foundation of the currently dominant world system: corporate globalization. The following chapter will give an overview of the history, development, and the effects that corporate globalization has had on the developing world. Although corporate globalization has its roots in European colonialism, this thesis will concentrate on its development since the Bretton Woods Conference of 1944, as it was then that this world system took its present form through the creation of its currently used rules and regulatory bodies.[2]

---

[2] For information on the pre-war development of corporate globalization, see Flynn and Giráldez. "Globalization Began in 1571," in *Globalization and Global History* eds. Gills and Thompson; *Rethinking Globalization*, ed. Gills; London: Routledge, 2006). O'Brian. "Colonies in a Globalizing Economy, 1815-1948," in *Globalization and Global History* eds. Gills and Thompson; *Rethinking*, ed. Gills; London: Routledge, 2006). Hopkins. "The History of Globalization - and the Globalization of History?," in *Globalization in World History* (ed. Hopkins; London: Pimlico, 2002).

4 TWENTIETH-CENTURY CORPORATE GLOBALIZATION

Trade and all of the components that make it possible, from the organized production to their distribution, have had profound societal effects for millennia. The current manifestation of this process is found in corporate globalization. It is difficult to dispute that corporate globalization of the twentieth and twenty-first centuries is a unique economic phenomenon. The level of trade that is currently conducted around the globe involves previously unknown levels of technological and legal sophistication. Although advances in communication, transportation, and international cooperation have brought the art of interregional trade to a whole new level, the impressive power and influence of corporate globalization often distracts from its ancient roots. Economic analysts, such as Francis Fukuyama, Kenichi Ohmae, and Susan Strange, have referred to globalization as an entirely new phenomenon: a creation of the twentieth century.[1] Although some of the most impressive aspects of corporate globalization may be new, its roots go far deeper than the past one hundred years.

Societies across the world have experienced radical levels of economic change since the end of the Second World War. A global trade nexus has emerged alongside the development of agrarian, communication, and transportation technologies that rivals previous world systems in both its efficiency and range of influence. This sort of rapid economic growth, which involves a marked rise

---

[1] Fukuyama, *The End of History and the Last Man* (London: Penguin, 1992), 202. Ohmae, *The End of the Nation State: The Rise of Regional Economies* (London: HarperCollins, 1996). Strange, *The Retreat of the State: The Diffusion of Power in the World Economy* (Cambridge, 1996).

in trade activity, is not unique; it is the latest evolutionary cycle in a long line of world systems, in which a core society, or group of societies, orchestrates the economic activities of secondary communities, dating as far back as the fourth millennium BCE.[2]

Agrarian societies rarely develop a strong political economy independently, but rather through their interactions with neighbouring societies. As these societies interact through either mutual interest or some form of domination, economic opportunities arise that lead to development and growth, as has been displayed in the above examples of ancient Near Eastern cyclical development. From the intensification of regional divisions and labor that came with beginnings of what Christopher Chase-Dunn et al. refer to as the "merchant capitalism" of the Old Babylonian period[3] to the trans-global trade networks established through European colonialism,[4] world systems have continued to evolve and have had a profound influence on subsistence-based agrarian communities. With each subsequent cycle the evolution of these phases has led to trade expansion over greater areas of land and water, more complex systems of specialization and hierarchy, and increased social integration between societies, as seen in the spread of Islam during the Ottoman Empire or the current diffusion of English as the word's *lingua franca*.[5] As these cycles wax and wane, and during each

---

[2] Chew. "Neglecting Nature: World Accumulation and Core-Periphery Relations, 2500 BC to AD 1990," in *World System History: The Social Science of Long-Term Change* eds. Denemark, Friedman, Gills and Modelski; London: Routledge, 2000). Modelski. "World System Evolution," in *World System History: The Social Science of Long-Term Change* eds. Denemark, Friedman, Gills and Moldeski; London: Routledge, 2000), 25-26.

[3] Chase-Dunn, et al. "Growth/Decline Phases and Semi-Peripheral Development in the Ancient Mesopotamian and Egyptian World-Systems," in *Globalization and Global History* eds. Gills and Thompson; *Rethinking Globalization*; London: Routledge, 2006), 224-26.

[4] Flynn and Giráldez. "Globalization Began in 1571," in *Globalization and Global History* eds. Gills and Thompson; *Rethinking Globalization,* ed. Gills; London: Routledge, 2006).

[5] Bosworth. "The Evolution of the World-City System," in *World System History: The Social Science of Long-Term Change* eds. Denemark, Friedman,

new period of intensification, lessons from previous world systems are integrated and improved upon.[6]

As the rise and fall of these economic world systems repeat themselves, causing participating agrarian societies' dependence on their political economies to evolve and devolve, the economic issues highlighted by structuralist and ecological theorists emerge on a trans-societal level. Whereas these philosophies as pertaining to decision-making on the domestic level were discussed in Chapter Two, in a world system such decisions are often made by a core society and dictated to its peripheral communities. As in previous world systems, corporate globalization repeats this pattern, allowing the world's core (the wealthiest nations/financial institutions) to develop, organize, and dictate the economic activities of the world's periphery societies (the world's poorest nations/citizens), and to great effect. But unlike previous world systems, which did not take the wellbeing of peripheral societies into account, the foundations of twentieth-century corporate globalization were built upon notions of sustainable and equitable development. While this has created prosperity for some of those who live in the system's peripheral societies, such as those in India who have made their fortunes from the information technologies boom in the past decade, many more have suffered displacement and alienation.[7] This chapter will address the development, policies, effects, and the egalitarian ethos upon which the current world system was built so that comparisons and contrasts with the Mediterranean world system that developed in Iron Age II can be better understood.

Gills and Modelski; London: Routledge, 2000), 276-79. See also Modelski. "World System Evolution."

[6] Joachim Rennstich places the roots of this cycle in the Phoenician maritime commercial system, which he claims "provided an important nucleus for the evolution of a global maritime-based external network system, which is currently transforming into an external network system based on digital communication networks" (Rennstich. "Three Steps in Globalization: Global Networks from 1000 BCE to 2050 CE," in *Globalization and Global History* eds. Gills and Thompson; vol. 2 of *Rethinking Globalizations*, ed. Gills; London: Routledge [2006], 203).

[7] Chossudovsky, *The Globalization of Poverty* (Pincourt, Québec Global Research, 2003).

A. THE DEVELOPMENT OF TWENTIETH-CENTURY CORPORATE GLOBALIZATION

The roots of modern-day corporate globalization are found in European colonialism.[1] The great European empires of the sixteenth to the mid-twentieth centuries connected distant parts of the globe through opening vast trading networks throughout Africa, Asia, the Americas, and Oceania. As a result, the European powers profited handsomely from greater access to raw materials and an increased labor supply, both free and slave.[2] It was the global trade networks and hierarchies that were developed out of European colonialism that laid the foundation for twentieth-century corporate globalization.

Unlike European colonialism and the world systems that developed before it, the nucleus around which corporate globalization revolves is not a single state, at least at the outset,[3] but a collaborative core that is made up of powerful nations and international financial institutions (IFIs). The Group of Eight (G8), for example, made up of Canada, France, Germany, Italy, Japan, Rus-

---

[1] A useful survey of the connections between colonialism and modern globalization is found in Hopkins. "Globalization With and Without Empires: From Bali to Labrador," in *Globalization in World History* (ed. Hopkins; London: Pimlico, 2002).

[2] Ballantyne. "Empire, Knowledge and Culture: From Proto-Globalization to Modern Globalization," in *Globalization in World History* (ed. Hopkins; London: Plimco, 2002). Drayton. "The Collaboration of Labour: Slaves, Empires, and Globalizations in the Atlantic World, c. 1600-1850," in *Globalization in World History* (ed. Hopkins; London: Plimco, 2002).

[3] There are many who view the United States, especially after the collapse of the Soviet Union, as the world's dominant empire, using military and economic power to exert its will over the rest of the world. This idea is certainly relevant to the overall thesis of this book, but will not be explored in any great detail. For more on this topic see Chomsky, *Failed States: The Abuse of Power and the Assault on Democracy* (London: Penguin Books, 2007). Hardt and Negri, *Empire* (Cambridge, MA: Harvard University Press, 2000), and Harvey, *The New Imperialism* (Oxford: Oxford University Press, 2003).

sia, the United Kingdom, and the United States of America, is currently among the most powerful and influential collaborative economic powers in the world.[4] However, instead of making unilateral economic decisions, as world system cores have traditionally done, the G8 encourages its members to coordinate their fiscal activities in order to achieve common financial, and ultimately political, goals. Helping to ensure cooperation between organizations like the G8 and the developing world, international agreements are used to dictate trade practices and wealth distribution. In doing so, hierarchical structures are maintained, and agrarian-based societies are often made subject to foreign financial interests.[5] However, as mentioned above, the subjugation of weaker economies to dominant powers was not the original mandate, or at least the stated intent, of the IFIs that facilitate the international agreements that drive the current world system.

An understanding of the progression from the stated intent to create equitable growth to the development of a system that suppresses the workers of developing nations for the benefit of the world's wealthiest people will help to aid the process of analogy by shedding light on the changes that developing nations face as they become active participants in corporate globalization. Additionally, the disparity between the written intent and the reality of today's dominant world system serves to highlight the obstinacy of the recurring societal patterns that appear as agrarian societies experience increased trade activity, which will highlight the probability of the occurrence of such patterns in eighth-century Judah. Before these issues can be addressed, it is necessary to consider the development of two of the world's most influential IFIs: the International Monetary Fund (IMF, or "the Fund") and the World Bank. Beyond regulating trade, economic development, and the management of national debt, these two institutions have created policies that are designed to restructure the economies of developing countries.

---

[4] China and India are two of the world's largest economic powers. They are both conspicuously not included in the Group of Eight, thus far.
[5] Chossudovsky, *The Globalization of Poverty*, 4-12.

Development of the IMF and the World Bank

The International Monetary Fund and the World Bank were the fruition of the United States and the United Kingdom's desire to put an international monetary organization into place that would assist in reconstruction and development after the Second World War.[6] As it became apparent that the military prowess of Nazi Germany and Imperial Japan were on the decline, economists and international governing bodies began to prepare for the economic needs of the post-war era.[7] In July 1944, forty-four Allied nations sent delegates to the United States to partake in the United Nations Monetary and Financial Conference at the Bretton Woods Resort in New Hampshire.[8] The central objective of the conference was to devise a fiscal strategy that would enable the world to cope with the needs of a post-war global economy. Considering the devastation that had been caused during the war and both the human and material resources that were expended in fighting it, realizing the conference's objectives would be a daunting task.

Objectives of the Bretton Woods Conference

The Bretton Woods delegates agreed that an increase in international trade and investment would be needed in order to ensure lasting economic stability in Europe and Asia, as well as sustained growth throughout the developing world.[9] D.A. MacGibbon noted that the delegates to Bretton Woods commonly believed that facilitating trade and international investment would provide opportunities for generating employment for returning troops, increase reve-

---

[6] Bernstein, "The International Monetary Fund," *The American Economic Review* 22, no. 1 (1968): 97.

[7] Among these governing bodies were the Economic, Financial, and Transit Department of the League of Nations, the International Labor Office, the United Nations Interim Commission on Food and Agriculture, and the United Nations Relief and Rehabilitation Administration. See Beckhart, "The Bretton Woods Proposal for an International Monetary Fund," *Political Science Quarterly* 59, no. 4 (1944).

[8] Stern, "The Agreements of Bretton Woods," *Economica* 11, no. 44 (1944): 165.

[9] Smithies, "The International Bank For Reconstruction and Development," *The American Economic Review* 43, no. 4 (1944): 785-86.

nue for the reconstruction of war-torn areas, and encourage growth and political stability in the developing world.[10] Level economic growth, through the eradication of destabilizing factors such as poverty and hunger, was viewed as the path to a much-desired lasting peace.[11] Legal specialist Arthur Kuhn reflected this sentiment as he clarified the goals of the delegates shortly after the Bretton Woods Conference commenced, highlighting that the conference would seek to advance a spirit of international monetary cooperation that would promote stability through a balanced growth of international trade and, ultimately, the correction of nation-members' balance of payments.[12] Focusing both on the needs of those whose infrastructure was destroyed during the war, as well as areas suffering from *stunted* economic growth in developing parts of the world, the ideals of the conference took an egalitarian approach to international development.[13] To cope with such an ambitious set of objectives, the delegates initiated the creation of two financial organizations: the International Monetary Fund and the International Bank for Reconstruction and Development (IBRD), the latter of which came to be known as the World Bank.

The purpose of the IMF was to promote uniform economic growth by helping member states to settle their balances due and to promote exchange-rate stability. Edward Brown explained that this was to be accomplished by facilitating "the extension of a balanced growth of international trade."[14] Since the war had destroyed much of Europe and Asia's industrial and economic infrastructures, se-

---

[10] MacGibbon, "International Monetary Control," *The Canadian Journal of Economics and Political Science* 11, no. 1 (1945).

[11] Fellner, "The Commercial Policy Implications of the Fund and Bank," *The American Economic Review* 35, no. 2 (1945).

[12] Kuhn, "United Nations Monetary Conference and the Immunity of International Agencies," *The American Journal of International Law* 38, no. 4 (1944): 663.

[13] In line with the ecological view of economic motivation, the conference appeared to understand the connection between the fulfillment of basic biological needs, such as food and shelter, and stabilizing social institutions, like national governments.

[14] Brown, "The International Monetary Fund: A Consideration of Certain Objection," 17, no. 4 (1944): 199.

curing stable exchange rates would be a difficult task. The IMF sought to overcome this obstacle by demanding that its members base their exchange rates on a gold standard, from which they could not permit their rates to fluctuate above or below one percent.[15] Such financial policing helped trade to be conducted efficiently, allowing Europe and Asia to recover from the devastation of the war and to restore the economic footing of the world's most developed nations. The IMF has continued to function as a regulatory body for trade and currently plays a major role in shaping trade negotiations and development programs that are designed to assist member states in periods of financial turmoil. As their mission statement proclaims, "The IMF is an organization of 185 countries, working to foster global monetary cooperation, secure financial stability, facilitate international trade, promote high employment and sustainable economic growth, and reduce poverty."[16] As evidenced below, many farmers, scholars, and politicians in both the developing world and in highly developed countries contest whether the IMF has lived up to this mission.

The purpose of the IBRD, which was made up of the same member countries as the IMF, was to complement the IMF as the other half of a cooperative effort to ensure equitable economic growth and sustained stability throughout the world. Arthur Smithies notes that whereas the IMF was designed to promote and regulate trade between member states, the IBRD was designed to provide aid to member states that had either been destroyed or economically stunted by the Second World War.[17] In addition to assisting war-torn nations, the IBRD would promote economic growth in the developing world by encouraging wealthier states to export capital to countries in need of financial assistance.[18] To achieve

---

[15] Bernstein, "A Practical International Monetary Policy," *The American Economic Review* 34, no. 4 (1944): 781.

[16] IMF, *International Monetary Fund Homepage* ([March 5, 2010]); available from http://www.imf.org/external/about.htm.

[17] Smithies, "The International Bank For Reconstruction and Development": 787.

[18] Kuhn, "United Nations Monetary Conference and the Immunity of International Agencies," *The American Journal of International Law* 38, no. 4

these goals, the IBRD acted as an intermediary between lending agencies and borrowing nations. During its inception in 1944, E.M. Bernstein explained that the IBRD would "encourage private investors to undertake international investment by guaranteeing loans through the usual investment channels and by participating with private investors in such loans."[19] Rather than competing with private investors, the IBRD worked with lending institutions as a sort of co-signer to secure affordable loans for nations that might otherwise be forced to accept abusive interest rates.[20]

Like the IMF, the IBRD worked to realize uniform and sustainable economic growth throughout the world in the hopes of promoting peace and prosperity. Since the post-war reconstruction, the World Bank's primary mission has been to design development programs that are intended to relieve poverty and create sustainable growth. The Bank has been involved in projects throughout the developing world, ranging from the creation of power stations in India to shaping educational policies in Latin America.[21]

Bretton Woods in Contrast to Eighth-Century Judah

The economic framework that was developed at the Bretton Woods Conference is vastly different from the suzerain/vassal relationships of the ancient Near East. Whereas the IMF and World Bank looked for nations to voluntarily participate and found strategic value in equitable international development, the Neo-Assyrian Empire into which Judah was incorporated used its military might to either destroy the civilizations of the Levant or threaten them

---

(1944): 663. Grey, "The Monetary Conference and China," *Far Eastern Survey* 13, no. 18 (1944): 165.

[19] Bernstein, "A Practical International Monetary Policy," *American Economic Review* 34, no. 4 (1944): 782.

[20] Smithies, "The International Bank For Reconstruction and Development": 790-91.

[21] Mosley, et al., *Aid and Power: The World Bank & Policy-Based Lending* (2vols.; vol. 1 & 2; London: Routledge, 1991), 27. Bujazan, et al., "International Agency Assistance to Education in Latin America and the Caribbean, 1970-1984: Technical and Political Decision-Making," *Comparative Education* 23, no. 2 (1987): 164.

into submission.[22] As addressed in the previous chapter, the Assyrians would have taken no interest in sharing the economic benefits of their expansion with those who farmed the soil of their conquered territories, nor, save exceptions like Ekron and Ashkelon, would they have nurtured the economic development of their vassal lands.[23] However, despite the IMF and IBRD's stated intent to create equal prosperity throughout the world, farmers in the developing world have suffered from the same set of recurring abuses that cultural-evolutionary theorists would expect to have occurred during the massive growth that took place around the late eighth-century BCE in Judah.

Bretton Woods' Vision Versus Actualization

The objectives of the IMF and the World Bank have not lived up to the ideals of equitable growth and poverty alleviation that were set at the Bretton Woods Conference. Rather than assisting nations that have fallen into financial crisis, many argue that the policies of these two IFIs have served the world's wealthiest nations by keeping poorer states in a position of dependence and through maintaining international hierarchies, whether or not this was their intent. One of the aspects of the IMF and the World Bank that might facilitate these problems is revealed in the complaints of member

----

[22] Holladay, "Assyrian Statecraft and the Prophets of Israel," *The Harvard Theological Review* 63, no. 1 (2002): 37. Oppenheim. "Babylonian and Assyrian Historical Texts," in *Ancient Near Eastern Texts Relating to the Old Testament* (ed. Pritchard; Princeton: Princeton University Press, 1969), 287. Schloen, *The House of the Father as Fact and Symbol: Patrimonialism in Ugarit and the Ancient Near East* (2; ed. Schloen; Winona Lake, IN: Eisenbrauns, 2001), 147, n.18.

[23] Schloen, *The House of the Father as Fact and Symbol: Patrimonialism in Ugarit and the Ancient Near East*, 146. Master, "Trade and Politics: Ashkelon's Balancing Act in the Seventh Century BCE," *Bulletin of the American Schools of Oriental Research* no. 330 (2003): 50. Gitin. "Tel-Miqne - Ekron in the 7th Century B.C.E.: The Impact of Economic Innovation and Foreign Cultural Influences on a Neo-Assyrian Vassal City-State," in *Recent Excavations in Israel: A View to the West* (ed. Gitin; Dubuque: Kendall/Hunt, 1995), 50. Elat, "The Economic Relations of the Neo-Assyrian Empire with Egypt," *Journal of the American Oriental Society* 98, no. 1 (1978): 33.

states from Turkey to Latin America: that the institutions' lack transparency, maintain an imbalanced leadership structure, and have failed to respect the sovereignty of borrowing nations.[24] A significant sign of managerial trouble is that an overwhelming share of the governance and influence in policy-making decisions in the IMF and World Bank is held by the world's wealthiest nations, leaving the developing world with little control over the major economic decisions that affect their ways of life.

Imbalanced Representation

During its formation, several proposals were put forth as to how the IMF should be governed.[25] The proposal that was eventually adopted into the Fund's Articles of Agreement, and is still followed to this day, declared that each member-state would have 250 votes, plus an extra vote for each part of its quota equivalent of US$100,000.[26] MacGibbon explains that it was argued that a system of 250 basic votes alongside a quota count would create a space for poorer nations to share in decision-making power.[27] Such a provision, as will be displayed below, failed to create such equitable gov-

---

[24] Buira. "An Analysis of IMF Conditionality," in *Challenges to the World Bank and IMF: Developing Country Perspectives* (ed. Buira; London: Anthem Press, 2004), 59. Mosley, et al., *Aid and Power*, 68-72.

[25] For more on the various forms of governance that were tabled at the conference see McIntyre, "Weighted Voting in International Organizations," 8, no. 4 (1954): 487. George, "The International Monetary Fund," *The Review of Economics and Statistics* 26, no. 4 (1944): 170. Buira. "The Governance of the IMF in a Global Economy," in *Challenges to the World Bank and IMF: Developing Country Perspectives* (ed. Buira; London: Anthem Press, 2004), 14.

[26] Beckhart, "The Bretton Woods Proposal for an International Monetary Fund": 503. IMF, *Articles of Agreement of the International Monetary Fund: Article XII, Section 5(a)* (1990 [March 1, 2010]); available from http://www.imf.org/external/pubs/ft/aa/aa12.htm#5. For information on plans that were rejected, or used to create this final version, see McIntyre, "Weighted Voting in International Organizations": 487. George, "The International Monetary Fund": 170. Buira. "The Governance of the IMF in a Global Economy," 14.

[27] Gold, "Voting and Decisions in the International Monetary Fund," (Washington D.C.: IMF, 1972).

ernance, giving an insignificant share of voting power to the poorer nation-members of the Fund.

Some economists were skeptical of the motives and future outcomes of the quota policy from its inception. In 1945 MacGibbon stated his suspicion that the end result of Bretton Woods would be to "strengthen the position of the creditor countries in determining the policy of the Fund"[28] and that the final decision "stipulated that the distribution of voting power should be closely related to the quotas."[29] The editors of *The Economist* also saw the potential for abuse in the IMF's voting policy, calling it "ludicrous," writing that "the determination of the quotas resembled the process of political chaffering more than an objective attempt to achieve equity."[30] An example of such political wrangling is found in the US$1.2 billion quota that was given to the economically ruined Soviet Union against the US$1.3 billion quota that was given to the British. The editors of *The Economist* complained that such a move had abandoned economic reason in supposing that the USSR's "part in the financial transactions of the world either is, or for a very long time will be, at all comparable with that of the United Kingdom."[31] Such actions indicate that not only was the voice of developing nations being marginalized by the voting system that the Bretton Woods Conference had agreed upon, but fiscal interests were also being undercut by political positioning, as politics played a central role in determining how key decisions in the Fund would be made. Despite the 250 basic votes that had been allocated to all of the members of the IMF, the ability of wealthier nations to buy up large numbers of quota votes ensured that the lending nations maintained greater control in the Fund's decision-making process.

The concerns that were voiced by MacGibbon and *The Economist* appear to have been justified, as the quota system has produced an uneven playing field in creating IMF policy, giving the world's most powerful states power over the developing world.

---

[28] MacGibbon, "International Monetary Control": 7.
[29] MacGibbon, "International Monetary Control": 8.
[30] Economist, "Bretton Woods," CXLVII, no. 5266 (1944): 138.
[31] Economist, "Bretton Woods": 138.

Arial Buira, former executive director of the IMF and former director of the G24 (Group of 24 [developing] Nations), claims that a
concentration of power in the Fund is evident in the distribution of
basic votes. Buira writes that, even with "…the nearly 37-fold increase in quotas [since the Bretton Woods Conference], the share
of basic votes in the total has declined from 11.3 to 2.1 percent [of
total votes cast], despite the quadrupling of the IMF's member-
ship."[32] Such figures indicate that those who are able to purchase
the most quota votes have effective control over the decision-
making powers of the IMF, often shutting out the interests of the
developing world. International law scholar Ebere Osieke highlights the danger that this imbalance poses to developing countries
by pointing out that

> …if the votes of say 20 members with the largest quotas con-
> stitute the majority of the votes in the Fund, a decision of the
> Board of Governors could be properly adopted by the votes of
> such 20 members, irrespective of the actual number of Mem-
> ber States taking part in the vote.[33]

Such a concentration of power among the wealthiest members is
contrary to the Bretton Woods goals of equitable development.

As a result of the imbalanced distribution of voting powers in
the IMF, creditor countries are able to dictate the terms of the
IMF's lending policies, offering little or no protection to poorer
countries as they approach the Fund for emergency loans, which
has resulted in stunted growth in the developing world.[34] Under an
economic philosophy that focuses on growth through the strengthening of international trade and the liberalization of markets, the

---

[32] Buira. "The Governance of the IMF in a Global Economy," 15.

[33] Osieke, "Majority Voting Systems in the International Labour Organization and the International Monetary Fund," *The International and
Comparative Law Quarterly* 33, no. 2 (1984): 397.

[34] Parkinson, "The International Monetary Fund in Economic Development: Equality and Discrimination," *Journal of African Law* 26, no. 1
(1982): 22. A detailed account of the governance of the IMF can be found
in Mohammed. "Who Pays for the IMF?," in *Challenges to the World Bank
and IMF: Developing Country Perspectives* (ed. Buira; London: Anthem Press,
2003).

policies of the IMF and World Bank have allowed the macro-management of developing economies.[35] Despite the egalitarian spirit that was nurtured at the Bretton Woods Conference and led to the development of two major financial institutions to facilitate equitable trade and growth, the IMF and the World Bank have been accused of facilitating the same recurring sociological patterns that have unfolded in previous world systems.[36] The important difference is that previous world systems did not even attempt to apply such principles: the abandonment of subsistence farming, the consolidation of land into latifundia, and the hoarding of benefits among elites as hierarchical systems are developed and emboldened.[37] These patterns often unfold as a result of the conditions that the IMF and World Bank place on their loan agreements with the nations that approach them for economic aid.

---

[35] Mamdani. "Uganda: Contradictions in the IMF Programme and Perspective," in *The IMF and the South: The Social Impact of Crisis and Adjustment* (ed. Ghai; London: Zed Books Ltd., 1991), 201-03.[35] Redclift and Sage. "Resources, Environmental Degradation, and Inequality," in *Inequality, Globalization, and World Politics* eds. Hurrell and Woods; Oxford: Oxford University Press, 1999), 127-28. Collier and Quaratiello, *Basta!: Land and the Zapatista Rebellion in Chiapas* (Oakland: Food First Books, 2005), 45-52.

[36] Buira. "An Analysis of IMF Conditionality," 59. Mosley, et al., *Aid and Power*, 68-72. Kahler. "External Influence, Conditionality, and the Politics of Adjustment," in *The Politics of Economics Adjustment* eds. Haggard and Kaufman; Princeton: Princeton University Press, 1992), 131. Bardhan. "Efficiency, Equity and Poverty Alleviation: Policy Issues in Less Developed Countries," in *Poverty, Agrarian Structure, & Political Economy in India: Selected Essays* (ed. Bardhan; New Delhi: Oxford University Press, 2003), 9-11. Woods. "The Challenge to International Institutions," in *The Political Economy of Globalization* (ed. Woods; New York: St. Martin's Press, 2000), 205. Redclift and Sage. "Resources, Environmental Degradation, and Inequality," 127-28. Collier and Quaratiello, *Basta!*, 45-52.

[37] Chaney, "Micah - Models Matter: Political Economy and Micah 6:9-15," in *Ancient Israel: The Old Testament in its Social Context* (ed. Esler; London: SCM Press, 2005). Premnath, "Latifundialization in Isaiah 5.8-10," in *Social-Scientific Old Testament Criticism* (ed. Chalcraft; Sheffield: Sheffield Academic Press, 1997).

Conditionality and Social Change in the Developing World

Some of the great discrepancies between ancient and modern economic systems can reveal valuable analogies. Although the world's
most powerful countries no longer subject weaker nations to vassal
treaties, like the great empires of the ancient Near East, the conditionality clauses that are attached to IMF and World Bank loans
have resulted in exploitative relationships that exhibit similar motivations and levels of dominance.

A vassal treaty allowed a suzerain power to exercise a high
level of economic and political control over its vassal in return for
protection from the suzerain itself, or from a common enemy, as
appears to have been Judah's case when it entered into vassalage
under Assyria in return for protection from the northern kingdom
of Israel.[38] Although some people within vassal societies may have
benefited economically from increased interaction with the suzerain power, the suzerain did not actively seek to provide any extra
benefits for its vassals. A modern-day conditionality clause, conversely, is created with the intent of helping a borrowing nation to
achieve sustained growth and eventual self-reliance by allowing
lending institutions like the IMF and the World Bank to attach
economic and political stipulations onto loan agreements. In the
end, however, these conditions often render the borrower as the
economic subservient of the institutions or wealthy nations that
fund the loan.

The Two Sides of Conditionality Clauses

In essence, a conditionality clause is a form of financial security
that was developed to protect the IMF and World Bank's lending
partners from risk in light of the difficulties that are involved in
securing collateral and guaranteeing timely payments from faltering
national economies. Economists Paul Mosley, Jane Harrigan, and
John Toye explain that traditional means of securing the repayment
of loans, such as threatening to refuse follow-on finance or de-

---

[38] Blakely and Hardin, "Southwestern Judah in the Late Eighth Century B.C.E.," *Bulletin of the American Schools of Oriental Research* no. 326
(2002): 41-56.

manding government guarantees, are not always effective when dealing with impoverished nations.[39] Since the IMF and the World Bank are limited in their ability to secure repayments, they will impose pro-market policy conditions that are designed to ensure that the indebted nation can make timely payments on a loan's primary and interest.[40] In order to assist with this process, the stipulations within conditionality clauses are designed to help foster positive economic growth in the borrowing nation.

Injecting money into a broken economy, without addressing the root causes of the crisis, is like treating a symptom without curing the disease; the symptom may be remedied for a short time, but it will keep recurring. Economist Cheryl Payer writes that conditions can be highly useful in their ability to "change host government policies [that are] adverse to foreign investment, including unwillingness to release promising acreage to exploration."[41] The financial expertise and technological assistance that the IMF and the World Bank offer can be very beneficial for a Highly Indebted Poor Country (HIPC), helping it to dislodge deep-seated impediments to growth, like corruption or dysfunctional systems of patronage.[42] Buira agrees that conditionality clauses can be highly beneficial when conditions are welcomed, allowing the IMF and World Bank to work as positive mentors.[43] However, many of the

---

[39] Mosley, et al., *Aid and Power*, 66.

[40] Mosley, et al., *Aid and Power*, 66.

[41] Payer, *The World Bank: A Critical Analysis* (New York: Monthly Review Press, 1982), 204.

[42] Even for nations that do not fall into the HIPC category, conditionality clauses can be a positive force. During the Asian economic crisis of the 1990s, the IMF placed conditions on loans given to struggling Asian countries. In a report on its management of the Asian Crisis the IMF claimed that it was able to use policy-based conditions to "remove features of [borrowing nations' economies] that had become impediments to growth (such as monopolies, trade barriers, and non-transparent corporate practices)." Mosley, et al., *Aid and Power*, 70.

[43] Buira. "An Analysis of IMF Conditionality," 60. The conditions placed upon these loans allowed Asian countries to make their economies more efficient and accelerate the growth of their markets. Again, these aspects of conditionality clauses appear to be the antithesis of the international economic relationships of the eighth century BCE.

arguments in favor of conditionality clauses are double-edged swords.

Despite the positive changes that conditionality clauses can bring to a struggling economy, they are often criticized for penetrating too deeply into the political and economic workings of the borrowing country. As a result, the borrower societies' cultures and their agrarian workers' ways of life become threatened. Ralph Carter notes that certain socio-economic features that may be perceived as impediments to the health of a borrowing nation's international markets, such as protectionist measures or land-management strategies, can serve as lifelines for small-scale farmers and who are unable to compete with the technologically advanced agrarian sectors of wealthier nations.[44] Even the land that subsistence farmers depend upon can be put at risk. As Payer stated above, lands protected by domestic conservation laws can be opened up to oil or mineral exploration if it is thought to be beneficial to domestic and global markets.[45] Conditionality clauses often tear down protections and risk-reducing strategies, as farmers in the developing world are left vulnerable to foreign markets and financial interests. As a result, conditionality clauses that are intended to encourage development in impoverished areas often instigate the common evolutionary patterns referred to in Chapter Two: as subsistence-based communities develop to accommodate

---

[44] Carter, "Leadership at Risk: The Perils of Unilateralism," 36, no. 1 (2003): 18. This is especially true, considering that wealthier nations tend to shelter their farmers under protectionist policies.

[45] Payer, *The World Bank: A Critical Analysis*, 204. An example of this is found in the struggle of the U'wa people of Columbia. Although not directly tied to the IMF or World Bank, as a result of corporate globalization, Occidental Petroleum was able to overturn centuries old treaties that gave the U'wa rights to their land. When Occidental ignored the U'wa's concern that to drill for oil on their land would be tantamount to bleeding their sacred mother, the U'wa threatened to commit collective suicide. For more on the U'wa and their struggle, see Rodríguez-Garavito and Arenas. "Indigenous Rights, Transnational Activism, and Legal Mobilization: The Struggle of the U'wa People in Columbia," in *Law and Globalization from Below* eds. de Sousa Santos and Rodriguez-Garavito; Cambridge: Cambridge University Press, 2005), 267-68.

market strategies, economies previously focused on the wellbeing of the producer become refocused on the wellbeing of the markets, leading to increased levels of poverty in both rural and urban areas.[46]

Beyond the negative effects that conditionality clauses can have on the rural communities of borrowing nations, others complain that these loan clauses can infringe on the sovereignty of a country as a whole. Despite the potential advantages that Buira finds in the use of conditionality clauses, as mentioned above, he is well aware of their potential for abuse. Buira writes,

> Conditionality may be defined as a means by which a party offers support and attempts to influence the policies of another in order to secure compliance with a program of measures; a tool by which a country is made to adopt specific policies or to undertake certain reforms that it would not have [otherwise] undertaken, in exchange for support.[47]

Buira's definition reveals the coercive nature of conditions, and how they can infringe upon national sovereignty through compelling borrowing nations to agree to terms that are set by wealthier countries, often for their own long-term advantage. Evidence of such intrusiveness and opportunism stemming from IMF loan conditions is illustrated by the consequences that Argentineans suffered as a result of the loans that their country received after President Isabel Perón was ousted in a military coup in 1974. The conditionality clauses that were attached to those IMF loans demanded that the Argentinean government lower its workers' wages, devalue the peso, raise taxes, and cut funds to social services, all of which created more favorable trading conditions for foreign nations.[48] Although it was believed that these conditions would attract in-

---

[46] Fried, *The Evolution of Political Society* (New York: Random House, 1967), 186. Sanderson, *The Evolution of Human Sociality: A Darwinian Conflict Perspective* (Lanham, Maryland: Rowman & Littlefield Publishers, 2001), 300-01.

[47] Buira. "An Analysis of IMF Conditionality," 58.

[48] Conklin and Davidson, "The I.M.F. and Economic and Social Human Rights: A case study of Argentina, 1958-1985," 8, no. 2 (1986): 237.

vestment from overseas, they resulted in a dramatic decrease in poor people's standards of living as the Argentina's developmental efforts became focused on creating a trade environment that favored foreign financial interests.

Abusive policy practices associated with conditionality clauses are not limited to Argentina's experience but have resulted in suffering throughout the world. Riots erupted around the globe in the 1970s and the 1980s because of the unfavorable implementation of conditions and the negative consequences that conditionality clauses had on the poorer sectors of developing nations.[49] Venezuela alone suffered nearly four hundred deaths due to the violence that broke out during the IMF riots of 1989.[50] In response to the anger and loss of life around the globe, former Venezuelan president Carlos Andrés Pérez wrote a formal letter of complaint to Michel Camdussus, who was the managing director of the IMF at that time. Pérez condemned both the suffering that loan conditions had caused among the poor and also the counterproductive uniform framework that the IMF used in their implementation. Pérez wrote that the IMF's clauses

> ...take no account at all of the international economic environment within which they have to be applied, or of economic realities in the countries where they are implemented... There is thus a serious impact on the poorest sectors of [developing] countries, which explode with despair, fostered by injustice, in the appalling violence we have seen on the streets of Caracas, and which we are sure to see and experience again in cities elsewhere in the developing world.[51]

The failure of the IMF to ensure that their loan conditions matched the needs of borrowing nations' economic problems had fatal con-

---

[49] Petras and Brill, "The IMF, Austerity and the State in Latin America," 8, no. 2 (1986): 428-30. Skogly, "Structural Adjustment and Development: Human Rights - An Agenda for Change," *Third World Quarterly* 15, no. 4 (1993): 756-57 n. 26.

[50] Officer, "The International Monetary Fund," *Proceedings of the Academy of Political Science: International Trade: The Changing Role of the United States* 37, no. 4 (1990): 34.

[51] Pérez, "Letter to Michel Camdessus," (1989).

sequences. The IMF riots, which resulted from the Fund's failure to fully understand the socio-economic nuances of developing nations' financial crises, display the difficulties and dangers that can arise when foreign bodies dictate regional policy, regardless of their stated intentions.

Conditionality Loans and the Ancient World

The differences between conditionality loans and vassal treaties are vast, and engaging in analogies between such two different systems of domination can understandably be viewed as precarious at best and irresponsible at worst. However, analogies can be found in the motivations behind their implementation and the effects that they have on vulnerable states. It should be clarified that any analogies drawn here are not intended to demonstrate that conditionality loans are the modern manifestation of vassal agreements, as they are not. The purpose of this comparative exercise is to consider that coercion and exploitation will develop when world systems bring core and peripheral economic powers together, even in instances when the policy-making members of the dominate party make specific attempts to avoid the exploitation of their subordinates.[52] The following analogies are not intended to demonstrate equivalence, but to reveal common characteristics and expose similarities between political and economic relationships in the modern and ancient contexts.

The differences that exist between the conditions placed on IMF and World Bank loans and suzerain treaties are numerous. First, a country in financial crisis often has survivable alternatives to entering into an IMF or World Bank conditionality loan since private lenders are available. In fact, as F. Parkinson notes, despite the fact that the IMF was created, in part, to protect indebted nations from the exploitative practices of private creditors, the intrusiveness of IMF conditions has led some HIPCs to go to transnational banks for financial assistance. Parkinson explains that these indebted countries are "prepared to put up with high interest

---

[52] *Subordinate* is not to imply that developing or indebted nations are subordinate by nature, but that through entering into debt, a person or state assumes a subordinate position, dominated by its creditor.

rates and with commercial criteria in general, so long as they could be left unmolested in the choice of their economic policies."[53] Second, as illustrated above, conditionality clauses can provide a valuable assistance to HIPCs by creating long-term prosperity for nations that need help restructuring their financial sectors. The financial experts at the IMF and the World Bank can play a positive role in helping countries rid themselves of corruption and other unwanted obstacles to prosperity. It is difficult to imagine an ancient suzerain state either offering its potential vassal the option of not entering into a treaty or taking an interest in the vassal state's well-being and long-term development.

Despite the good that conditionality clauses can and have produced for indebted countries, their strict adherence to free-market principles and their uniform approach to implementing structural adjustment does not produce positive results in all situations, but has led to disastrous outcomes for many borrowing nations and, in particular, for their poorest citizens. It is in this aspect of conditionality loans, in which the conditions end up aiding the lending nations more than those that they are intended to assist, that analogies can be drawn between the powers that a suzerain exercises over its vassal and an IFI can wield over those who come to them in times of financial crisis.

Analogous to the exploitative nature of a vassal treaty, conditional lending is made possible only because one party is in a state of distress and is therefore willing to, as Buira phrases it, "adopt specific policies or to undertake certain reforms that it would not have undertaken."[54] In a conditionality clause, the subordinate state is coerced into complying with the specific demands of the dominant state, or in the case of the IMF and World Bank, the dominant *states* that control the policy decisions of these two IFIs. A significant difference between these ancient and modern means of coercion is that a conditionality loan should not attempt to control the subordinate's political infrastructure, only its economic activities. This outcome, however, is not often the case.

---

[53] Parkinson, "The International Monetary Fund in Economic Development": 217.

[54] Buira. "An Analysis of IMF Conditionality," 58.

Evidence of Coercion and Overreaching in Conditionality Agreements

In 1998 a commission of economic experts, headed by economist Allen Meltzer, was formed at the behest of the United States Congress to make recommendations on US policy toward the world's most powerful IFIs. In its report, the Meltzer Commission expressed dire concerns over the coercive and intrusive activities that the IMF had engaged in through the use of its conditionality loans. The commission found that beyond implementing economic policy, the Fund sometimes takes control over matters that fall under the authority of borrowing nations' political institutions. They reported that the far-reaching power of IMF conditionality clauses stretches beyond the limits of economic nation building, wielding "too much power over developing countries' economic policies" and that "the use of IMF resources and conditionality to control the economies of developing nations often undermines the sovereignty and democratic processes of member governments receiving assistance."[55] The fact that the Meltzer Commission, which was composed of anything but a group of anti free-market ideologues, found conditionality loans to be a serious threat to the national sovereignty of borrowing nations suggests that a strategy that had originally been designed to provide assistance to HIPCs had devolved into a mechanism that reshapes political structures to the advantage of lending countries. The members of the Meltzer Commission are not alone in their criticism of conditionality loans. Ngaire Woods, Michel Chossudovsky, and Lester Thurow also find IMF and World Bank loan conditions to be excessively intrusive.[56]

---

[55] Meltzer Commission, "The Meltzer Report," (Washington D.C.: United States Congress, 1999).

[56] Woods. "The Challenge to International Institutions." Thurow, *The Future of Capitalism: How Today's Economic Forces Shape Tomorrow's World* (New York: William Morrow and Company, Inc., 1996). Study on the IMF and World Bank's influence on seemingly extraneous governmental functions to economic development that could endanger national sovereignty, such as national education and military policies, can be found in Kempner and Jurema, "The Global Politics of Education: Brazil and the World Bank," *Higher Education* 43, no. 3 (2002), and Biersteker. "Globalization as a Mode of Thinking," in *The Political Economy of Globalization* (ed.

Like the Meltzer Commission, Woods concludes that beyond justifying particular macroeconomic indicators or results, conditions are being used to force countries to shape domestic policies in order to comply with international standards that favor the financial interests of the world's wealthiest and most powerful nations, disrupting domestic political structures.[57] As a result of these activities, Chossudovsky notes, countries are coerced into dismantling their own protective trade barriers, abandoning their traditional methods of landownership, and deregulating their central banks to enable debt collection so that powerful lenders can profit from the poorer nations of the world.[58] Thurow explains that as a consequence, "Instead of a world where national policies guide economic forces, a global economy gives rise to a world in which extra-national geo-economic forces dictate national economic policies."[59] This is to say that the current world system creates a socio-economic environment in which the system itself, in this case corporate globalization, becomes the dominant political power structure. As a result, regional powers are weakened under the weight of foreign financial interests.

Although borrowing countries are allowed to keep their governments, their leaders are often forced to surrender key policy-making authorities and accommodate economic changes that are to the advantage of more powerful nations. There is no direct threat of war if a country in financial difficulty refuses to comply, as there may have been in a vassal-suzerain relationship, but the loss of sovereignty and forced economic restructuring for the sake of the dominant group provides useful analogies for the economic domi-

---

Woods; New York: St. Martin's Press, 2000), 155-56. Amuzegar, "The IMF Under Fire," *Foreign Policy* no. 64 (1986): 118. Woods. "The Challenge to International Institutions," 212. Hurrell. "Security and Inequality," in *Inequality, Globalization, and World Politics* eds. Hurrell and Woods; Oxford: Oxford University Press, 1999).

[57] Woods. "The Challenge to International Institutions," 212.

[58] Chossudovsky, *The Globalization of Poverty*, 54-57.

[59] Thurow, *The Future of Capitalism*, 127.

nance that tends to be practiced as world systems evolve, and is manifest through the policies of the IMF and the World Bank.[60]

Insights to be Gained

Although differences between terms of a conditionality loan and those of an ancient vassal treaty are significant, both the comparisons and contrasts between them reveal some useful insights. Despite having been formed with the mandate to foster uniform economic development and balanced trade for all of its members, the IMF and the World Bank have participated in economic and political exploitation by shaping the domestic policies of poorer countries for the benefit of the world's wealthiest nations. Agrarian societies that have struggled while attempting to evolve into viable participants in the rising global economy and have become dependent on loans, find themselves trapped into accepting conditions that force them to abandon subsistence strategies, consolidate land into latifundia, and channel the benefits of these changes among regional and foreign elites, as has recently occurred in rural communities from Vietnam to Mexico.[61] This discrepancy between

---

[60] However, Noam Chomsky would argue that small wars and insurgencies that are funded by the United States and the CIA are waged to keep less developed nations in line with American economic interests. Chomsky, "World Order and Its Rules: Variations on Some Themes," *Journal of Law and Society* 20, no. 2 (1993).

[61] Hernández Castillo and Nigh, "Global Processes and Local Identity Among Mayan Coffee Growers in Chiapas, Mexico," *American Anthropologist* 100, no. 1 (1998): 140. Chossudovsky, *The Globalization of Poverty*, 180-83, 221-22. It should be noted that these conditions are sometimes used by governments, or a minority voice within a government that want to force through economic-liberalizing agendas that are converse to the will of their people. An example of this is found in the case of the 1990s loan negotiations undertaken by Uruguay's reformist president, Luis Alberto Lecalle. Lecalle circumvented the will of his government, his party, and his people by using the conditions attached to a US$150 Million IMF loan in order to undermine labor leaders and forcefully implement much of his liberalizing agenda, despite great unpopularity among his people. Vreeland, "Why Do Governments and the IMF Enter Into Agreements?: Statistically Selected Cases," *International Political Science Review* 24, no. 3 (2003): 328-29.

the stated intent of the IMF and the World Bank and the consequences of their conditionality loans may attest to the power of the
cyclical patterns that emerge during periods of increased economic
growth and centralization. Even when attempts are made to curb
the negative side effects that world systems are known to produce,
they appear to be inescapable.

Conditionality loans are but one example of the way that the
current world system has allowed core nations to exercise power
over peripheral states despite the original stated-intent to avoid
such exploitative practices. Opportunism and the effects that the
actions of core nations have on the world's agrarian societies can
be found in the handling of the 1980s Debt Crisis. The causes,
management, and consequences of this international crisis demonstrate how the neoliberal policies of corporate globalization affect
agrarian societies as they evolve to survive new economic conditions and challenges.

Naturally, the 1980s Debt Crisis will not provide insights into
the actual economic conditions of eighth-century Judah itself. The
Assyrians would not have needed to exploit financial vulnerabilities
to force less powerful lands, like Judah, into subjugation; the
Assyrians maintained an effective professional military for that very
purpose. However, the nurturing of hierarchies and the opportunism that is demonstrated throughout the development and management of the Debt Crisis represents the recurring patterns that
exist in world systems and cultural evolution, even when a concerted effort was made to prevent their manifestation. They also
characterize many of the abuses that Chaney and Premnath attribute to the eight-century Judean context in their interpretations of
Isa. 5. 8–10 and Mic. 2.1–2.[62]

---

[62] Chaney, "Bitter Bounty: The Dynamics of Political Economy Critiqued by the Eighth-Century Prophets," in *Reformed Faith and Economics*
(ed. Stivers; Lanham: University Press of America, 1989), 24-27.
Premnath, *Eighth Century Prophets: A Social Analysis* (St. Louis: Chalice,
2003), 95-96.

B. THE 1980S DEBT CRISIS AND CULTURAL-EVOLUTIONARY THEORY

Although the great European colonial empires slowly dissolved in the decades preceding and following the Second World War, the world's centers of economic power, in Europe and North America, have remained relatively the same. Aside from the recent levels of economic dominance enjoyed by China and India, many of the nations who controlled international finance from the seventeenth to the mid-twentieth centuries are largely in control of the global economy today. The reasons behind this maintenance of power structures, and the tensions that it has produced, are connected to the theories of economic motivation and cultural evolution that were detailed in Chapter Two. The conflict between those who work to maintain their positions of advantage through ensuring the survival of hierarchical systems and those who struggle to guarantee sustenance and an acceptable living standard is played out through the policies of the IMF and World Bank. This power struggle is clearly evidenced in the creation and managing of the 1980s Debt Crisis, which had a devastating impact on the economies of the developing world.

The 1980s Debt Crisis in the developing world was the product of both internal and external factors. Internal factors included faulty political decisions, natural disasters, excessive borrowing, and overspending in the developing countries. The external factors were rooted in the wealthiest countries' economic policies, some of which fostered an environment of economic opportunism, like excessive lending. The largest single external factor that contributed to the 1980s Debt Crisis was the oil shocks of the 1970s, which created an uneven field of trade that was heavily weighted toward the advantage of highly industrialized nations.

The Roots of the Debt Crisis

The economic policies of the world's most advanced industrial nations resulted in a boom of non-oil primary commodities in the early 1970s that led to a strong period of inflation. As a result, the Organization of Petroleum Exporting Countries (OPEC) felt the strain of these events and responded by raising petroleum prices threefold, leading to the oil shocks of 1973 and 1979. While oil-producing countries enjoyed a dramatic increase in revenue, Mosley et al. note that the resulting high fuel costs slashed the real growth output of many countries.[63] Poorer nations, which tend to rely on the export of raw materials, fell into recession as the price of primary commodities failed to match sharp increases in production and shipping costs. Timothy Gorringe notes that the price of raw materials collapsed worldwide, leading to an overvaluation of currencies and a decrease in labor wages.[64] To make matters worse, Brian Crisp and Michael Kelly write, the oil shocks "quickly consumed available foreign exchange [leading governments to turn] to international loans to pay for petroleum and other imports as well as to support government spending," making it difficult for poorer nations to secure such funding.[65] Just when the developing world was in desperate need of assistance, available credit had become scarce and, therefore, expensive.

While highly developed western nations profited from decreased labor costs and a sharp drop in the price of goods, the developing world suffered under an economic collapse. According to Carol Thompson, "…the purchasing power of one tonne of copper, coffee, or cotton for barrels of oil [in southern Africa] fell 50 percent from 1975-80."[66] This sudden reduction in the purchasing power of raw materials caused the rate of growth in sub-Saharan Africa to slow down to a mere 0.5 to 1.8 percent.[67] As in southern African countries, the effects of the oil shocks had devastating effects across the rest of the developing world, effects that continued into the 1980s.

---

[63] Mosley, et al., *Aid and Power*, 5-6.

[64] Gorringe, *Fair Shares: Ethics and the Global Economy* (New York: Thames & Hudson, 1999), 65. Thompson, "Regional Economic Policy Under Crisis Conditions: The Case of Agriculture within SADCC," *Journal of Southern African Studies* 13, no. 1 (1986): 83.

[65] Crisp and Kelly, "The Socioeconomic Impacts of Structural Adjustment," *International Studies Quarterly* 43, no. 3 (1999): 534.

[66] Thompson, "Regional Economic Policy Under Crisis Conditions: The Case of Agriculture within SADCC": 83.

[67] Mkandawire. "Crisis and Adjustment in Sub-Saharan Africa," in *The IMF and the South: The Social Impact of Crisis and Adjustment* (ed. Ghai; London: Zed Books Ltd on Behalf of The United Nations Research Institute for Social Development, 1991), 82.

Between 1980 and 1986 the gross domestic product (GDP) of Sub-Saharan nations declined by roughly 20 percent as exports fell 30 percent and imports declined by almost 75 percent.[68] In Latin America the crisis resulted in similar consequences as Bolivia, Nicaragua, and Haiti also suffered from a 20 percent decline in GDP.[69] Despite a severe reduction in the inflow of funds, between 1982 and 1986, debtor countries had to make huge interest payments that, as Stanley Fischer explains, frequently amounted to six percent of their individual GDPs. Such crippling debt expenditures made it even more difficult to accrue capital.[70] As a result, standards of living decreased dramatically, causing social and political unrest as the developing world became even more financially dependent on the wealthier countries.

The problems of the developing world mounted even further as the world's wealthiest nations implemented protectionist measures and increased the production of weapons and food to offset a global decline in the profitability of capital goods, which had prohibited them from meeting their economic expectations.[71] These increases created a hostile environment for farmers in Latin America and Africa, who were unable to compete with the heavy government subsidies that advanced capitalist-states were giving to their own farmers. The European Economic Community (ECC), for example, directed two-thirds of its budget to the subsidization of export crops. This move by the ECC essentially erased any competitive edge that developing world farmers had previously

---

[68] World Bank, *World Development Report 1988* [March 2, 2010]); http://econ.worldbank.org/external/default/main?pagePK=64165259&t heSitePK=469372&piPK=64165421&menuPK=64166322&entityID=00 0178830_98101912131965.

[69] Ghai and Alcántara. "The Crisis of the 1980s in Africa, Latin America, and the Caribbean: An Overview," in *The IMF and the South: The Social Impact of Crisis and Adjustment* (ed. Ghai; London: Zed Books Ltd on Behalf of The United Nations Research Institute for Social Development, 1991), 19.

[70] Fischer, "Sharing the Burden of the International Debt Crisis," *The American Economic Review* 77, no. 2 (1987): 165.

[71] Thompson, "Regional Economic Policy Under Crisis Conditions": 83.

enjoyed in the international food markets.[72] The combination of higher oil prices, a devaluation of raw materials, and the inability of farmers in the developing world to compete in global food markets created a vicious cycle of debt for many of the world's poorest countries.

Despite the IMF's obligation to control interest, the debt cycle spiraled out of control as interest rates became inflated around the world, rendering poorer nations unable to honor their loan agreements. Countries that had entered into loan agreements in the 1970s, when real interest rates were exceedingly low or even negative, found themselves in serious trouble.[73] As variable interest rates grew, Mosley et al. note, "...the combination of a rising nominal interest rate with a falling rate of inflation (consequent on slower growth plus monetary restriction) created an alarming increase in the real cost of borrowing."[74] Combined with faltering exports caused by the oil shocks, developing nations were unable to honor their increasing loan obligations. As interest accumulated while currencies became devalued, much of the developing world fell into debilitating levels of debt. What was a nightmare scenario for poorer countries, however, created a position of advantage that was exploited by the world's wealthiest nations.

Crisis Management and Perpetuation

The debt that the developing world was quickly accumulating did not go unchecked. In accordance with their duties, the IMF and the World Bank worked together with donor nations to ensure that HIPCs would receive assistance in honoring their loan agreements. The actions that were ultimately taken are indicative of the motivations that drive world systems and lead to recurring cultural-evolutionary abuses. Rather than facilitating equitable growth, as is the mandate of the IMF and World Bank, the policies that they implemented were first and foremost profitable for the world's

[72] United Nations, The, "Organization, Food, and Agriculture," *World Food Report* (Rome: United Nations, 1984), 13.

[73] Dornbusch, et al., "Mexico: Stabilization, Debt and Growth," *Economic Policy* 3, no. 7 (1988): 244.

[74] Mosley, et al., *Aid and Power*, 8.

wealthiest nations, with potential trickle-down effects for poorer countries. Again, there is no reason to suspect that Judah or the Neo-Assyrian world system engaged in the same methods of exploitation. However, the actions of today's core states attest to the prevalence of the exploitative patterns that world systems have inflicted on agrarian societies for millennia; although the weapons that are used today may be different, the wounds that they inflict on agrarian communities appear to be common.

The IMF and World Bank's Crisis Strategy

There are several strategies that the international community has used to approach the problem of debt, and each of these reveals the motivations of the creditor. The three most commonly used methods for handling national debt are market solutions,[75] the implementation of structural adjustment in the indebted nation,[76] and the use of structural adjustment in donor countries.[77] In response

---

[75] Market solutions rely on the power of the markets to rectify the problem, trusting that the markets will punish the indebted nation for irresponsible spending, and the lender parties for irresponsible lending. See Martinez, "Debt and Foreign Capital: The Origin of the Crisis," *Latin American Perspectives* 20, no. 1 (1993). Bird. "Introduction," in *Third World Debt: The Search For A Solution* (ed. Bird; Worchester: Edward Elgar Publishing Limited, 1989), 8. Türk, *The Realization of Economic, Social, and Cultural Rights* (United Nations, 1992 [March 2, 2009]); available from http://www.unhchr.ch/huridocda/huridoca.nsf/(Symbol)/E.CN.4.SUB. 2.1992.16.En?Opendocument. Dávila. "The Developing Countries and the International Financial System: 25 Years of Hope, Frustration, and Some Modest Achievements," in *G-24: The Developing Countries in the International Financial System* (ed. Mayobre; Boulder: Lynne Rienner Publishers, 1999).

[76] Structural adjustment restructures economic and production institutions in the indebted nation to enable growth. This method will be described in greater detail below.

[77] This solution works to restructure the way trade is practiced in wealthier nations to make an even playing field for poorer countries. Although this solution appears to be in line with the outcomes of the Bretton Woods Conference, it is rarely used. See Bird. "Introduction." and Deacon. "Social Policy in a Global Context," in *Inequality, Globalization, and*

to the 1980s Debt Crisis, structural adjustment programs (SAPs) were used, and their implementation involved a free-market philosophy that heavily favored the donor countries that effectively govern the IMF and the World Bank. As a result, the most vulnerable citizens of debtor countries lost what little economic protection they had as special attention was given to the health of these impoverished countries' markets.

Congruent with the intention of conditionality loans, a structural adjustment program is designed to dislodge any political or cultural impediments to sustained economic growth, thus ensuring that loan obligations are met; it is for this reason that conditionality loans are often used as an engine for SAPs. As John Williamson explains, advocates of SAPs argue that through demanding strong fiscal discipline, shifting public spending priorities, implementing tax reform, liberalizing trade, and employing programs of privatization and deregulation, both short-term relief and a long-term financial stability can be achieved.[78] The hope for such positive results is based on the free-market practices that encourage a gradual balance of payment by encouraging exports through trade liberalization while discouraging imports through currency devaluation.[79] However, this financial regimen often serves to create a definite advantage for the trade interests of local authorities and lending countries while harming local producers. In the end, SAPs often create significant problems for the countries that they are designed to benefit. Graham Bird lists three of the negative effects that frequently result from SAPs: the heavy-handed nature of their demands on the borrowing nation, their negative effect on living standards, and the ultimate ineffectiveness in bringing long-term change.[80] Considering that these consequences dovetail with the

---

World Politics eds. Hurrell and Woods; New York: Oxford University Press, 1999).

[78] Williamson, "On Seeking to Improve IMF Conditionality," The American Economic Review 73, no. 2 (1983): 354-58.

[79] Crisp and Kelly, "The Socioeconomic Impacts of Structural Adjustment": 534.

[80] Bird. "Introduction," 8.

recurring sociological pattern attributed to increased trade, they will be considered here as potential points of interpretation.

Decreased Standards of Living

As a result of a forced reduction of imports, the populations of borrowing nations typically experience a sharp decline in living standards. According to Judith Marshall, because of the Mozambique government's failure to assess the appropriateness of the IMF conditions that directed resources to rural areas, both cities and towns experienced increased living costs.[81] Because of this failure, the urban poor suffered from lower salaries, faltering health care, reduced nutritional intake, and a slowdown in the construction industry.[82] Similar SAPs implemented in Ghana led to a massive increase in suffering and unemployment as the IMF demanded large cuts in public spending, including money for medicine in rural areas.[83] As a result, the poorest sectors of society suffered as they bore the greatest weight of the IMF's plans for structural adjustment.

A disproportionate human cost is a common outcome of SAPs as wage labors and farmers experience a decrease in standards of living while economic and political elites experience relatively little change. Harry Sanabria suggests that this is due to the workings of neoliberalism, which favors capital interests over those of the wage laborers or farmers upon whom a large share of the adjustment burden rests.[84] Chossudovsky finds an example of this in the devaluation of currency, of which the effects are "brutal and immediate [as] the domestic prices of food staples, essential drugs,

---

[81] Marshall, "Structural Adjustment and Social Policy in Mozambique," *Review of African Political Economy* 47 (1990): 28-43.

47, (1990): 30.

[82] Marshall, "Structural Adjustment and Social Policy in Mozambique."

[83] Boafo-Arthur, "Ghana: Structural Adjustment, Democratization, and the Politics of Continuity," *African Studies Review* 42, no. 2 (1999): 51.

[84] Sanabria, "Consolidating States, Restructuring Economies, and Confronting Workers and Peasants: The Antinomies of Bolivian Neoliberalism," *Comparative Studies in Society and History* 41, no. 3 (1999): 538.

fuel, and public services increase overnight."[85] Despite the seemingly good intentions behind SAPs, more vulnerable populations
within the target country have no power in the creation of the adjustment program. Manuel Pastor, Jr. and Gary Dymski explain
that when an SAP is negotiated, political leaders face the powerful
temptation to place the burden of adjustment on the lower classes
rather than on themselves.[86] As a result, the elites benefit from the
change and hoard the spoils while farmers and wage laborers pay
the social cost.

A sign that many SAPs are inherently unable to improve conditions for the impoverished, and that the system is often geared
toward the interests of the elite, is found in the fact that their indicators can point to positive economic growth while the population
becomes increasingly impoverished. Crisp and Kelly note that even
when a SAP successfully reduces debt, restores growth, lowers inflation, and provides long-term economic development for a country, it often simultaneously exacerbates poverty and inequality.[87]
The small-scale farmers and other laborers of the target country
experience what commonly occurs during heightened trade activity,
whether in an ancient agrarian economy or a modern capitalist system: their well-being is sacrificed for the well-being of the markets.[88]

Threats to Societal Instability

One of the consequences of reduced standards of living is the
threat of social unrest, and this was one of the outcomes of the
1980s Debt Crisis. Bird notes that as SAPs force reduced imports,

---

[85] Chossudovsky, *The Globalization of Poverty*, 48.
   [86] Pastor and Dymski, "Debt Crisis and Class Conflict in Latin America," *Review of Radical Political Economics* 22, no. 1 (1990): 161.
   [87] Crisp and Kelly, "The Socioeconomic Impacts of Structural Adjustment": 537.
   [88] Fried, *The Evolution of Political Society*, 186. Sanderson, *The Evolution of
Human Sociality: A Darwinian Conflict Perspective*, 300-01. Plattner. "Markets
and Marketplaces," in *Economic Anthropology* (ed. Plattner; Stanford: Stanford University Press, 2002), 180. Berdan. "Trade and Markets in Precapitalist States," in *Economic Anthropology* (ed. Plattner; Stanford: Stanford
University Press, 2002), 79-81.

"...living standards, or at best, the rate of growth of living standards in [borrowing nations] will fall," which can test the patience of a country's citizens.[89] When patience with these SAPs and their effects on a country's standard of living runs out, and in line with the recurring pattern that John Kautsky attributes to sudden trade activity in agrarian societies,[90] political unrest erupts and undermines the local governments for whom these policies were created to help. As Dharam Ghai and Hewitt de Alcántara note, suffering caused by IMF adjustments has provoked guerrilla movements and, at times, the takeover of entire regions by either criminal organizations or political factions, like the Shining Path movement in Peru.[91] While the donor nations profit from improved trade conditions, HIPCs are threatened by the decreased living standards and political instability that structural adjustment often produces. However, social instability resulting from SAPs is not merely limited to threats of rioting or revolution amongst the poor, but also amongst the segments of the economic elite as class structures become destabilized.

While the SAPs that were adopted in Latin America and Africa brought new trade opportunities that favored many local elites, the deflation of currencies and patronage systems that accompanied these developments caused some members of the upper economic strata to lose their social status. Those members of the elite who had their fortunes invested domestically suffered substantial losses as currencies were devalued; some upper-class families found themselves moving downward into the middle class. Conversely, as Ghai and de Alcántara note, the devaluation of local currencies increased the return of wealth held in foreign investment; those who had invested outside their own borders saw their capital in-

---

[89] Bird. "Introduction," 9.

[90] Kautsky, *The Politics of Aristocratic Empires* (New Brunswick: Transaction Publishers, 1997), 289.

[91] Ghai and Alcántara. "The Crisis of the 1980s in Africa, Latin America, and the Caribbean," 36. Morales, "Coca and Cocaine Economy and Social Change in the Andes of Peru," *Economic Development and Cultural Change* 35, no. 1 (1986).

crease spectacularly.[92] Despite the growing poverty that these countries experienced, new markets for luxury goods and services appeared incongruously to the developing crisis, creating "startling
manifestations of advancing polarization."[93] Although, on a life or
death scale, the movement from the upper echelons of society to
the middle class does not compare to the suffering experienced by
those living in poverty who lost their access to affordable food and
medical services. However, on a societal level, the psychological
strain of losing one's class standing while others see their wealth
increase can have a profound effect. Jorge Schvarzer notes that this
split in the upper classes resulted in unrest among members of the
elite and contributed to a serious threat to stability and democracy
in borrowing countries.[94]

The fact that members of various elite groups can lose their
status as agrarian societies develop is rarely addressed when considering the changes that took place in eighth-century Judah. Alongside the effects of sudden development on rural peasants or workers, instances in which elites have lost their influence or class standards as a result of corporate globalization raise new questions
about prophetic complaints attributed to the eighth century BCE.
Such potential insights will be addressed in greater detail in Chapter
Six.

Failure to Produce Positive Change for Developing Economies

Beyond the disproportionate economic growth and suffering that
SAPs can cause in the developing world, several economists call
the overall economic value of structural adjustment into question.
Buira argues that SAPs are often implemented with too many con-

---

[92] Ghai and Alcántara. "The Crisis of the 1980s in Africa, Latin
America, and the Caribbean," 26.

[93] Ghai and Alcántara. "The Crisis of the 1980s in Africa, Latin
America, and the Caribbean," 26.

[94] Schvarzer. "Economic Crisis and the Commonwealth Caribbean:
Impact and Response," in *The IMF and the South: The Social Impact of Crisis
and Adjustment* (ed. Ghai; London: Zed Books Ltd on Behalf of The
United Nations Research Institute for Social Development, 1991).

ditions attached to their loans.[95] Between the 1970s and 1980s the average number of conditions attached to an IMF loan rose from six to ten,[96] and reached its peak in the 1990s, when an average of sixteen conditions were imposed on countries seeking emergency assistance.[97] Noting that these increases were met in equal proportion with a decline in program success, Buira claims that the correlation is obvious, writing, "…the greater the number of performance criteria, structural benchmarks and other targets, the greater the chance that some will not be met."[98] Imposing a large number of new policy objectives on a country that is already struggling with a crisis can exacerbate problems rather than alleviate them. The Meltzer Commission supports Buira's concerns, concluding in its report to the US Congress that "detailed conditionality (often including dozens of conditions) has burdened IMF programs in recent years and made such programs unwieldy, highly conflictive, time-consuming to negotiate, and often ineffectual."[99] Rather than producing positive structural reform for the developing world, SAPs can demand too much, thus demoralizing weakened nations by creating unnecessary obstacles to development.[100]

Woods' concerns are raised by the inevitable inefficiencies that appear when foreign bodies, removed from the domestic realities of the crisis, impose policies that may be intellectually sound but practically unfeasible or harmful.[101] She notes that some internal problems cannot be solved through external pressure, writing that "the only agency which has the capacity to ensure that human rights, environmental standards, or banking supervision guidelines

---

[95] Buira. "An Analysis of IMF Conditionality," 61-63. Woods. "The Challenge to International Institutions," 213.

[96] Buira. "An Analysis of IMF Conditionality," 62. See Figure 2.

[97] Kapur and Lewis, "Governance-Related Conditionalities of the International Financial Institutions," *G-24 Discussion Paper Series* 6, (2000).

[98] Buira. "An Analysis of IMF Conditionality," 63.

[99] Meltzer Commission, "The Meltzer Report."

[100] In addition to the number of conditions placed on borrowing nations, Bird notes that rapid nature with which adjustment is implemented is "unlikely to induce the structural changes which may be required and it may therefore be anti-developmental." Bird. "Introduction," 9.

[101] Woods. "The Challenge to International Institutions," 213.

are systematically respected within any country is the state and the government of that country."[102] Try as they might, foreign IFIs cannot fully understand all of the socio-political and historical realities that are involved in a country's economic crisis, and inherently bring their own economic interests and cultural paradigms into the solution. Schvarzer finds evidence of the latter problem in the fact that SAPs almost exclusively focus on foreign investment and the privatization of state industries, or the sale of these industries to foreign states and corporations.[103] These foreign-based strategies have profound effects on domestic standards of living and political stability, forcing governments to cut back on the social services that their poorest citizens depend upon.[104]

Attempts to Address the Negative Outcomes of Structural Adjustment

It has been established that despite the IMF and World Bank's mandates to alleviate poverty and create equitable growth, in many cases the opposite has held true. Acknowledging the suffering and uneven growth that has been caused as a direct result of their programs, the IMF has worked to address these outcomes by inserting "social safety nets" into their SAPs. Through adding benefits for the vulnerable, such as food coupons and medical subsidies, the IMF has worked to ensure that even the most impoverished are able to benefit from the development process.[105] Despite the IMF's positive response to concerns over their policies' deficiencies, the effectiveness of the social safety nets has drawn skepticism. The United Nations Commission on Human Rights (UNCHR) has stated that, while social safety nets are welcomed attempts to mitigate the negative impact of structural adjustment on the rights of the poor, SAPs continue "...to have a daunting effect on human

---

[102] Woods. "The Challenge to International Institutions," 216.
[103] Schvarzer. "Economic Crisis and the Commonwealth Caribbean," 76.
[104] Schvarzer. "Economic Crisis and the Commonwealth Caribbean," 76.
[105] Pfeiffer, "How Tunisia, Morocco, Jordan and Even Egypt Became IMF 'Success Stories' in the 1990s," *Middle East Report* no. 210 (1999): 26.

rights and upon the capacities of legal regimes with obligations to fulfill and respect these rights."[106] The UNCHR found that the social safety nets' failure to negate the negative impact of IMF's programs on the poor was due to the inherent nature of structural adjustment, which undermines national sovereignty and diminishes the target nation's control over its own economic practices.[107] By failing to consider the individual needs of those who approach the IMF for assistance and through weakening the power of regional leaders to create positive change within their own countries, policies that worsen living conditions for the poor eclipse the IMF's attempts to ease the suffering that they create.

In the end, while wealthy nations enjoy increased profits from lowered tariffs and devalued currencies while the most vulnerable are left to pay the social cost. Rather than create equitable growth, Crisp and Kelly write, "the IMF merely [continues] perpetuating a system of international debt peonage."[108] The changes that are needed to improve economic conditions in developing nations often require long-term planning rather than the quick fixes that SAPs try to provide. In the past few decades, the shortsighted demands of structural adjustment have led to catastrophic program failures.[109] The only apparent benefactors of these policies are the donor nations and local elites who design them to work in their favor.

---

[106] Türk, "The Realization of Economic, Social, and Cultural Rights," in *Economic and Social Council, Commission on Human Rights* (New York: United Nations, 1992).

[107] Türk, "The Realization of Economic, Social, and Cultural Rights."

[108] Crisp and Kelly, "The Socioeconomic Impacts of Structural Adjustment": 534.

[109] Woods. "The Challenge to International Institutions," 217. Pérez, "Letter to Michel Camdessus." Kapur and Lewis, "Governance-Related Conditionalities of the International Financial Institutions."

C. CONCLUSION

This chapter has explained how the current cycle of increased trade activity, manifested through corporate globalization, functions and adversely affects agrarian communities and states. From the inception of the IMF and the World Bank at the Bretton Woods Conference in 1944 to their management of the 1980s Debt Crisis, the course that these two IFIs have taken attests to the perseverance of the recurring patterns that cultural-evolutionary theorists describe. Through the use of loans and the policies of those institutions that are charged with ensuring equitable growth and development, agrarian communities throughout the developing world have been coerced into abandoning mixed-subsistence farming for specialized agriculture and the demands of international markets, enduring the consequences of latifundialist policies, and have seen the fruits of development concentrated in the hands of a minority elite.[1] The same institutions under which the protection of the developing world was entrusted have instigated policies that favor the core states of the current world system. Rather than enabling sustainable growth for member states from the developing world through the creation of even-handed trade policies and controlled interest rates, the IMF and the World Bank brought HIPCs further into debt through allowing the world's wealthiest nations to essentially set the terms of the contracts. Even those policies that are directed toward helping the poor by combating the negative effects of SAPs, like the introduction of social safety nets, were unable to improve conditions. As the most basic biological needs of the majority of those in the developing world were ignored or left unfulfilled, the wealthiest nations' desire to maintain hierarchical economic structures was satisfied.

---

[1] Carter, "Leadership at Risk: The Perils of Unilateralism": 18. Hernández Castillo and Nigh, "Global Processes and Local Identity Among Mayan Coffee Growers in Chiapas, Mexico": 140. Chossudovsky, *The Globalization of Poverty*, 180-83, 221-22. Crisp and Kelly, "The Socioeconomic Impacts of Structural Adjustment": 534. Meltzer Commission, "The Meltzer Report," Schvarzer. "Economic Crisis and the Commonwealth Caribbean," 76.

The failure of the IMF and the World Bank to protect developing nations and their most vulnerable citizens from the negative effects that rapid development tends to inflict on local and inter-regional levels, including the recurring patterns of subsistence abandonment, latifundialization, and the hoarding of wealth, offers a couple of interesting insights into the nature of economic exploitation as agrarian societies enter into trade systems. Such a failure has particular value for the thesis that is proposed in this book. First, as mentioned above, an inability or lack of resolve to protect developing nations, despite a concerted effort, attests to the recurring strength of these patterns. Not only did institutions charged with alleviating the negative consequences of rapid economic growth fail to protect peripheral states and small-scale farmers, but attempts to correct these errors failed as well. These failures could simply represent an isolated problem such as a lack of will on behalf of the IMF and World Bank to see that all member states benefit from development. However, considering that the rise of world systems and increases in trade involves catering to the demands of foreign consumers, be they individuals or states, economies will adapt to produce the most lucrative products in volumes that match that demand. This would signal that the problems that the IMF and World Bank faced in trying to provide equitable growth and development were insurmountable – for they appear to be inherent to the system. As the UNCHR reported, SAPs fail to produce positive results for developing countries and the majority of their citizens because, while attempting to encourage positive growth, they focus on enacting policies of trade liberalization and currency devaluation, which undermine national sovereignty and increase the cost of living.[2] The UNCHR's observations support the theory that during periods of heightened trade the wellbeing of producers becomes refocused on the wellbeing of the markets.[3] Although entrance into a world system can produce benefits, the drawbacks appear to be difficult, if not impossible, to mitigate.

---

[2] Türk, "The Realization of Economic, Social, and Cultural Rights."
[3] Fried, *The Evolution of Political Society*, 186. Sanderson, *The Evolution of Human Sociality: A Darwinian Conflict Perspective*, 300-01.

Second, the IMF's and the World Bank's failures to reduce the negative effects of the rapid developments that accompany the current world system suggests that the primary producers of earlier world systems, which did not attempt to alleviate such suffering, would have experienced even greater levels of oppression. For an example that lies within living memory, consider European colonialism. Less than two hundred years ago agrarian societies did not only lose land rights and the ability to pursue a subsistence lifestyle in Africa and Latin America, but an entire industry was based on their enslavement, either by domestic or foreign agents. More recently, in 1919, British military commander General Reginald Dyer responded to an illegal assembly of unarmed men, women, and children in an Indian garden by ordering his troops to shoot, without warning, concentrating on the thickest areas of the crowd and the exits.[4] After ten minutes of open fire, this peacetime massacre left several hundred Indian civilians dead and well over a thousand wounded.[5] The fact that slavery and civilian massacres are no longer considered an acceptable part of the current world system, although they do take place under the watch of the core states, displays changing paradigms on human rights, which are reflected in the mandates of the IMF and the World Bank.

Considering that the economic policies of our current world system lead to starvation and decreased access to medical care, despite safeguards that have been put in place by regulating IFIs, abuses inflicted upon mixed-subsistence farmers during the period to which Isa. 5.8–10 and Mic. 2.1–2 are attributed, eighth-century Judah, would be not be unexpected. This is not to argue that these books were necessarily written during this time. Due to the recur-

---

[4] Tuteja, "Jallianwala Bagh: A Critical Juncture in the Indian National Movement," *Social Scientist* 25, no. 1/2 (1997): 25.

[5] Tuteja, "Jallianwala Bagh: A Critical Juncture in the Indian National Movement": 25. Althoguh War-time massacres of civilians have been carried out by the dominate powers of corporate globalization, such as Mi Lai massacre carried out by US troops in Vietnam, they did not inspire popular movements to present the instigator with a purse and tokens of honour, as in the case of General Dyer (Collett, *The Butcher of Amritsar: Brigadier-General Reginald Dyer* (London: Hambledon and London, 2005), 387).

ring nature of the abusive patterns that result from a switch to specialized farming, latifundialization, and the hoarding of any resulting profits, they could have related such abuses taking place in the
Persian or Hellenistic periods back to an eighth-century example,
as addressed in Chapter One.

The Assyrian Empire did not engage with peripheral lands in
the same way that either the core states or the IFIs of corporate
globalization engage with the developing world today. But, although SAPs were not a part of the eighth-century world, the nature of their failure to provide assistance to modern farmers raises
useful questions about the recurring patterns that arise as political
economies and foreign financial interests gain power and influence
in agrarian societies.

Despite culture or time, it appears that as societies are thrust
into development and economic centralization, primary producers
become caught in the wake of the financial interests of the powerful. This chapter has examined motivations and activities of twentieth-century corporate globalization to provide a socio-economic
background for the experiences of the country that will be used to
explore whether or not a modern case study can provide a constructive tool for interpreting prophetic complaints against landownership abuse and help further the work of those who use cultural-evolutionary theory in biblical interpretation.

Using a modern society with a strong tradition of mixed-
subsistence culture to interpret ancient texts like Isa. 5.8–10 and
Mic. 2.1–2 is an arduous task indeed: cultural, economic, and technological differences between the current world system and the
system in which the Neo-Assyrian Empire participated are vast.
The best way to uncover new interpretive questions and insights is
to choose a society that shares as many general commonalities[6]
with the ancient culture as possible. In order to narrow down potential case studies, the search first focused on modern agrarian

---

[6] "Commonality" has to be used in the most liberal sense of the word
since there are so many factors that we do not know about the ancient
world. Commonalities pertaining to weather patterns or topographical
features are somewhat safer to determine than those pertaining to societal
norms or values.

societies that shared similar agrarian environments, from topographical and weather features to crop selection. The secondary criterion, which is far less stable, has to do with cultural concerns. For purposes of biblical interpretation, a modern society that held a strong religious-based landownership tradition, values land inalienability, and inheritance laws, which is found in the Hebrew Bible, needs to be studied.[7] The country that seemed to best suit these criteria was the Mediterranean country of Tunisia, in North Africa, which experienced major changes after its independence from French colonialism and its subsequent entrance into corporate globalization as an autonomous state.

As a result of the Tunisian government's moves to take advantage of interregional markets in the mid-twentieth century, the country gave up aspects of its religious identity and restructured its agrarian sector to increase revenue through trade. Consequently, religious traditions that protected vulnerable citizens were overturned as subsistence farmers who had enjoyed access to arable land for generations were reduced to wage laborers or left unemployed. The following chapter will address how the current world system reshaped the lives of Tunisia's subsistence farmers as their country was thrust into rapid development through both internal and external political and economic forces.

---

[7] The land ownership laws found in Leviticus could have been written after Isa. 5.8–10 and Mic. 2.1–4 were produced and may not have been a part of the eighth-century paradigm. The study of a modern culture without such an inalienable concept of landownership may provide a useful contrast. For the purposes of this particular study, these criteria are used since either one of the original authors or a redactor of Mic. 2.2 referred to the loss of a man's inheritance.

5 RESHAPING LANDOWNERSHIP IN TUNISIA

Times have changed. Morality has changed. The rich don't feel anything for the needy. They even fear the poor. They don't want the poor living near them or having land near them because they will ask for things. They don't even want the poor to raise a chicken near them because it would sneak on their land. Hajj Naouar [a wealthy land owner], who lives next door, wants us all to move. His workers only work the land [and do not farm for themselves].[1] He said, 'Don't raise your animals and let them eat my grass.' Some of his workers had to sell their cows and look for other work. All he does is give the zakat.[2] It's probably the full one-tenth, but that's it.[3]

> – Majoub, late twentieth-century Tunisian peasant

A. A BRIEF INTRODUCTION TO LAND TENURE IN TUNISIA

Since gaining independence in 1956, Tunisia has gone through a series of changes in its approach to land management. Internally, Tunisia's government has played a significant role in altering the face of traditional landownership through a series of failed reforms, each of which led to a new strategy.[4] Externally, international fi-

---

[1] Brackets belong to King.

[2] Arabic for 'alms for the poor': part of a Muslim's charitable obligation.

[3] King, *Liberalization Against Democracy: The Local Politics of Economic Reform in Tunisia* (Bloomington: Indiana University Press, 2003), 86-87.

[4] King, *Liberalization Against Democracy*, 2-7.

nancial institutions, including the International Monetary fund and the World Bank, have worked with the Tunisian government to facilitate economic liberalization.[5] These foreign and domestic forces have implemented neoliberal programs that are aimed at bringing this relatively new nation into the fold of corporate globalization, with outcomes that have had profound transformative effects on Tunisia's agrarian communities.[6] The past six decades have seen major changes in how Tunisian farmlands are owned and operated, and for whom the benefits are obtained.

Why Tunisia Is A Useful Case Study

One aspect that makes Tunisia's transition from mixed-subsistence farming to a centralized agrarian effort a particularly interesting case study is that the transformation did not come all at once; it evolved through a series of economic and structural reforms.[7] In an almost trial-and-error fashion, the Tunisian government adopted various approaches for attaining economic liberalization as it attempted to secure a more lucrative and sustainable alternative to traditional semi-subsistence strategies.[8] Such an assortment of failed strategies offers a variety of insights into how cultural evolution can unfold while displaying that although strategies may vary, the consequences for subsistence farmers are often homogeneous. Additionally, the multiple strategies that were employed by the Tunisian government offer a variety of examples through which to consider potential interpretations of biblical texts and their socio-economic contexts.

　　Another useful feature of the Tunisian landownership reforms is their religious significance. At the time of Tunisian independ-

　　[5] Payne. "Economic Crisis and Policy Reform in the 1980s," in *Polity and Society in Contemporary North Africa* eds. Zartman and Habeeb; Boulder: Westview, 1993), 143-46. King, *Liberalization Against Democracy: The Local Politics of Economic Reform in Tunisia*, 115.

　　[6] Radwan, et al., *Tunisia: Rural Labour and Structural Transformation* (London: Routledge, 1991), 2.

　　[7] Radwan, et al., *Tunisia: Rural Labour and Structural Transformation*, 3-4.

　　[8] Anderson, *The State and Social Transformation in Tunisia and Libya: 1830-1980* (Princeton: Princeton University Press, 1986), 231-50.

ence, one-fifth of the country's arable lands were under the control of Muslim-based cooperatives, which the new government quickly overturned in order to make room for federally controlled latifundia.[9] Despite protests from members to Tunisia's religious establishment, Muslim sensibilities were ignored as lands that had been set aside for the wellbeing of subsistence communities were reallocated for the benefit of Tunisia's wealthiest citizens. Although the voices of Tunisia's religious leaders should not be borrowed to replicate those in Isa. 5.8 and Mic. 2.2, the ire that these twentieth-century CE land grabs inspired in Muslim leaders may provide useful material for considering the effects that eighth-century BCE land grabs may have had on YHWHist religious leaders. The complaints lodged by Tunisian imams highlight the religious casualties that often occur as traditional economic and agrarian strategies are upset.

Tunisia and ancient Judah have similar agrarian environments. Considering the multilinear notion that societies with similar environmental challenges tend to develop and evolve in similar ways, the arid and unpredictable weather patterns of Tunisia make for a useful comparison. Like Judean farmers, Tunisian agriculturalists have had to deal with a particularly harsh growing environment. Out of the over one-hundred-thousand square miles of land that lie within Tunisia's borders, only thirty percent is arable, and forty-five percent of that land was covered by trees as of the late 1990s.[10] Due to this lack of available farmland, any shift in agrarian strategy will have a significant impact on the region's agrarian communities.

Tunisia and ancient Judah also share similar meteorological challenges. As in Judah, unfavorable weather patterns have led Tunisian agriculturalists to develop farming techniques and risk-reducing strategies that are specifically adapted to the local envi-

---

[9] Anderson, *The State and Social Transformation in Tunisia and Libya*, 235. Powers, "Orientalism, Colonialism, and Legal History," *Comparative Studies in Society and History* 31, no. 3 (1989): 536.

[10] Zaibet and Dunn, "Land Tenure, Farm Size, and Rural Market Participation in Developing Countries: The Case of the Tunisian Olive Sector," *Economic Development and Cultural Change* 46, no. 4 (1998): 833.

ronment and can help to ensure successful harvests.[11] When such strategies are disrupted by the demands of specialized agriculture, farmers find themselves vulnerable to both the weather and the markets. Such a dilemma, suggested by Chaney and Premnath in the Judean context, is found in modern Tunisia.[12] It appears that both modern and ancient farmers along the Mediterranean have experienced hardship as a result of increased commercialization.

Traditional Land Tenure in Rural Tunisia

As is often the case in agrarian states, Tunisian land-tenure management was not limited to a single system.[13] While some landownership systems favored the interests of wealthy and powerful families, supporting and maintaining established systems of hierarchy, others were designed to provide for the needs of small-scale farmers who practiced mixed-subsistence agriculture. Both of these models were represented under the *habous* system of land management. It is these Muslim-based land endowments, embedded in

---

[11] D. Ashbel, "Israel: Land of Climate." *Encyclopedia Judaica* 9:181-94, 185. Anderson, *The State and Social Transformation in Tunisia and Libya*, 44. Johnson, et al., "Rangeland and Marginal Cereal Cropland in Central Tunisia," *Rangelands* 11, no. 5 (1989). Falkenmark, "Rapid Population Growth and Water Scarcity: The Predicament of Tomorrow's Africa," 16, Supplement: Resources, Environment, and Population: Present Knowledge, Future Options, (1990).

[12] Chaney, "Bitter Bounty: The Dynamics of Political Economy Critiqued by the Eighth-Century Prophets," in *Reformed Faith and Economics* (ed. Stivers; Lanham: University Press of America, 1989). Premnath, *Eighth Century Prophets: A Social Analysis* (St. Louis: Chalice, 2003). King, *Liberalization Against Democracy*, 117. Micaud, "Leadership and Development: The Case of Tunisia," 1, no. 4 (1969): 477. Hopkins, "Tunisia: An Open and Shut Case," *Social Problems* 28, no. 4, Development Processes and Problems (1981): 386.

[13] This follows David Hopkins' observations on the presence of multiple economies existing within single agrarian societies in the ancient Near East (Hopkins. "Bare Bones: Putting Flesh on the Economics of Ancient Israel," in *The Origins of the Ancient Israelite States* eds. Clines, Davies and Jarick; vol. 228 of *JSOTSS*; Sheffield: Sheffield Academic Press, 1996), 124-29).

Tunisia's religious establishment, which are of the greatest interest to this thesis.

The origins of the *habous* date back to the dawn of Islam in the first century AH (622-719 CE).[14] The *habous* land endowments were formed, in part, to give peasants the right to share land communally and enjoy the fruits of their labor while providing for both the material and spiritual needs of rural communities.[15] Made inalienable from their inception, David Powers explains that when a *habous* was formed,

> ...a (*waqif*) [founder] would assign the usufruct of a revenue-producing property to either a person or an institution in a way considered 'pleasing to God,' while sequestering the property itself in such a manner that it became inalienable in perpetuity and could not be sold, given away as a gift, or inherited.[16]

Although the differences between the *habous* and the methods of land tenure that are put forth in the Hebrew Bible may be great, they share a religious-based inalienable approach that is supposed to ensure that even poorer families have access to arable land.[17] Whether or not these are of any value for comparison will be explored below.

The integration of *habous* land management into Tunisian agrarian culture occurred during the Ottoman Empire, when the Ottomans set up *habous* endowments to ensure that everyone could benefit from the region's most fertile lands. To ensure that their intent was realized, Ghazi Duwaji writes, "...*waqif* (or *habous*) lands [were] dedicated in perpetuity to religious or charitable purposes."[18] To a large extent the Ottomans were successful in creating a lasting system of welfare for the poorer farmers in Tunisia, particularly in the case of the public *habous*. The public *habous* perpetuated a charitable spirit of providing for the spiritual and material wellbeing of

---

[14] Powers, "Orientalism, Colonialism, and Legal History": 536.

[15] Powers, "Orientalism, Colonialism, and Legal History": 536.

[16] Powers, "Orientalism, Colonialism, and Legal History": 536.

[17] Lev. 25.23, Num. 27.1-11; 36.1-12, and Josh. 17.3-6

[18] Duwaji, "Land Ownership in Tunisia: An Obstacle to Agricultural Development," 44, no. 1 (1968): 129.

the communities they served. These land endowments did not only supply semi-subsistence farmers with arable land; they funded schools, hospitals, and other charitable programs.[19]

Not all of the *habous* served the rural communities of Tunisia with the same charitable spirit of the public *habous*. Familial *habous* were used to secure the wealth of powerful families, often from the higher ranks of the religious elite. Although they were not owned directly by the families that ran them, familial *habous* were passed down through the family line until that line became extinct.[20] Although the prominence of the *habous* lands deteriorated with the emergence of European colonialism, it was still the predominant method of managing Tunisian lands up until shortly after Tunisian independence.[21] With the emergence of a free Tunisia in 1956, however, the management of land ownership took a series of dramatic turns.

It must be remembered that neither pre-independence Tunisia nor pre-colonial Tunisia, and almost certainly not in eighth-century Judah for that matter, were utopian agrarian societies in which its members shared and benefited equally from the land.[22] Definite power structures had been in place in Tunisia for centuries, and these structures, including the *habous*, had played to the advantage of Tunisia's religious and political establishments. Lisa Anderson notes that prior to the disbanding of the public and familial *habous* in 1956 and 1957, various patterns of sharecropping contributed to a hierarchical, stratified society and the unequal exchanges that ac-

---

[19] Powers, "Orientalism, Colonialism, and Legal History": 536. Duwaji, "Land Ownership in Tunisia": 129.

[20] Cannon, "Administrative and Economic Regionalism in Tunisian Oleiculture: The Idarat al Ghabah Experiment, 1870-1914," *The International Journal of African Historical Studies* 11, no. 4 (1978): 597.

[21] Nicolaï, "Approche structurelle et effet de domination Une application: la Tunisie," 7, no. 5 (1956): 748-49. Powers, "Orientalism, Colonialism, and Legal History."

[22] This arrangement must certainly not have been utopian for those who lost their lands for the creation of the *habous* after the Ottoman invasion. Such considerations and their value to biblical studies will be addressed later.

company clientelism.[23] Unlike in post-independence Tunisia, however, the absentee landlords for whom the sharecroppers worked did not attempt to obtain total control over the land, but allowed their employees to keep their own parcels of land, which were used by the peasants to grow food for their individual families.[24] Subsistence life is not ideal, but as often happens when agrarian societies retool themselves to maximize trade potential, the hardships that their members are accustomed to become amplified.

A series of different land reforms, religious ties to the ownership and management of land, and similar agrarian conditions in Tunisia and Palestine provide a range of avenues from which the Tunisian experience can be used to approach the eighth-century Judean context. Through exploring the various phases of Tunisia's agrarian transition from a semi-subsistence culture to a market-focused economy, this chapter will serve as a basis for understanding how the effects of modern-day corporate globalization can help to shed light on the ambiguous complaints against land-tenure abuse found in Isaiah and Micah. Before the interpretive value of independent Tunisia's experiences with land ownership reform can be assessed, the greater colonial context behind these events needs to be considered.

B. FRENCH PROLOGUE TO LAND ABUSES IN
INDEPENDENT TUNISIA

Latifundialization and other common outcomes of increased trade activity were not novel to independent Tunisia, but had already begun under French Colonialism, which brought significant cultural change to the North African country. Attempts made by the French to centralize agrarian production in the nineteenth and early-twentieth centuries foreshadowed the policies of the Tunisian government in the mid to late-twentieth century. Over seven decades before Tunisia gained its independence, French colonialism threatened the region's traditional landownership methods and subsistence strategies in the interest of increasing trade revenue. In

---

[23] Anderson, *The State and Social Transformation in Tunisia and Libya*, 43.
[24] Anderson, *The State and Social Transformation in Tunisia and Libya*, 43.

their bid to exploit the region's limited agricultural capabilities for the production of exportable cash crops, the French needed to overcome two main obstacles: attachment to traditional subsistence strategies and the *habous* land endowments.[25] Both of these obstacles were particularly difficult to navigate, for they were both rooted in the Muslim sensibilities of the Tunisian people.

A main concern of the French leadership in Tunisia was the avoidance of rebellion. In order to circumvent a revolt among Tunisia's native Muslim population, French legal experts and orientalists employed a method that had proved effective in Algeria: compromising the religious integrity of the *habous*.[26] French intellectuals in Algeria had argued that the *habous* perpetuated the wealth of an elite few, which was indeed true of the familial *habous*. In this way they were able to convince enough local Algerian leaders to pass legislation that opened up these arable lands for sale in the private sector.[27] The strategy proved to be a success in Tunisia as well and, in 1885, the French were able to pass an act that greatly reduced the size of the communally held public *habous*, giving foreigners the right to acquire these properties.[28] As a result, the *habous* were reduced from covering one-third of Tunisia's arable lands to covering one-fifth. Against the nature of the French colonialists' own argument, however, it was the land endowments that did *not* perpetuate wealth amongst the elite that were opened for privatization.

The 1885 land reform act altered the face of Tunisian agriculture as the management of land, the selection of crops, and the distribution of profits were shifted to favor international markets rather than local producers. Donald McKay's 1945 account of the French occupation of Tunisia explains the significance of these changes. In language that reflects the colonial sensibilities of his time, McKay praises the polices that overturned *habous* lands and led to a greater prevalence of specialized farming, writing that

---

[25] Anderson, *The State and Social Transformation in Tunisia and Libya*, 151.

[26] Powers, "Orientalism, Colonialism, and Legal History": 543.

[27] Powers, "Orientalism, Colonialism, and Legal History": 543.

[28] Harber, "Tunisian Land Tenure in the Early French Protectorate," 63, (1973): 311. McKay, "The French in Tunisia," 35, no. 3 (1945): 387.

"within fifty years the cultivated area in cereals more than tripled, the number of olive trees more than doubled," and the vineyards had increased by fifteen-fold.[29] These changes highlight the success of France's efforts to consolidate Tunisia's productive resources and make the Tunisian agriculture sector more lucrative. Land that had served to provide essential services for rural communities was now used to cultivate export crops. Between 1881 and 1938 the land allocated to the growth of olives increased over ten times, from fifty thousand to 550,000 hectares, while the previously uncommon cultivation of grapes became prominent in the region.[30] Nicola Ziadeh explains that the cultivation of grapes, which had been almost nonexistent before French colonization, covered forty thousand hectares of Tunisian farmland by the start of the Second World War.[31]

Effects of Colonialism on Tunisian Subsistence Farmers

While French colonists enjoyed a lucrative trade in agricultural goods, Tunisian subsistence farmers were evicted from the properties that their families had worked for generations with little legal recourse. Lisa Anderson explains that since there is little motivation to maintain proof of entitlement in regions where land is not a scarce resource, as had been the case in Tunisia, few Tunisian farmers actually held titles to the lands that they owned.[32] The French were able to use this lack of legal documentation to target those whose land claims were disputable.[33] As a result, many small-scale landholders were forced off of their lands and into urban areas to search for employment as migrant workers.[34] As described above, this kind of displacement that the Tunisian farmers faced at

[29] McKay, "The French in Tunisia": 387.

[30] King, *Liberalization Against Democracy: The Local Politics of Economic Reform in Tunisia*, 65.

[31] Ziadeh, *Origins of Nationalism in Tunisia* (Beirut: Librarie du Liban, 1969), 40.

[32] Anderson, *The State and Social Transformation in Tunisia and Libya*, 152.

[33] Anderson, *The State and Social Transformation in Tunisia and Libya*, 152.

[34] Ziadeh, *Origins of Nationalism in Tunisia*, 41.

the hands of the French is commonplace during such periods of economic development and imperial influence.

Despite the French land grabs, most farmlands were still controlled by Tunisian farmers. However, reforms ensured that the best lands went to French and Italian "colon" farmers. Reynold Dahl writes that

> ...the European sector which accounted for one-sixteenth per cent of the total population produced 95 per cent of the wine and 40 per cent of the cereals and accounted for one third of the total cash from income. So the Tunisian economy possessed the characteristics of a dual economy with a small modern sector and a large traditional sector.[35]

Rather than overrun Tunisian agricultural traditions entirely, the French restructured the landscape to ensure that the best lands went to the benefit of European farmers, leaving the lands of poorest quality to the native Tunisians. Such disparity of land wealth represents an inequality that Frances Berdan and John Kautsky associate with the commercialization of agriculture, as evidenced in thirteenth-century England and sixteenth-century Japan.[36] As the elites prosper from abandoning traditional subsistence strategies in favor of market-based plans, small-scale farmers are often left to struggle in the shadow of the newly developed economic paradigm.

Not all Tunisian families suffered under these new economic developments. Some of Tunisia's wealthier farmers were able to assimilate into the modern sector and profit from a market-driven economy.[37] But as an affluent class of farmers enjoyed the increased wealth and prestige that came with the ability to compete in

---

[35] Dahl, "Agricultural Development Strategies in a Small Economy: The Case of Tunisia," (Staff Paper, USAID, 1971), 32.

[36] Berdan. "Trade and Markets in Precapitalist States," in *Economic Anthropology* (ed. Plattner; Stanford: Stanford University Press, 1989), 79. Kautsky, *The Politics of Aristocratic Empires* (New Brunswick: Transaction Publishers, 1997), 288-92. Johnson and Earle, *The Evolution of Human Societies* (Stanford: Stanford University Press, 1987), 254-55. Hilton, "Peasant Movement In England Before 1381," 2, second series, no. 2 (1931): 122.

[37] King, *Liberalization Against Democracy*, 64.

the international markets, the majority of Tunisians suffered. Dahl notes that by the time of Tunisian independence in 1956, five thousand Tunisian families owned farms averaging seventy hectares each while 450,000 families owned plots averaging seven hectares.[38] As a result of these latifundialist policies, which often accompany rapid increases in trade, many Tunisians were forced to either farm plots of land that were too small and poor to sustain a family or move to cities in search of work.[39] The hardships caused by French efforts to commercialize Tunisia's agrarian sector reflect the recurring societal patterns discussed in Chapter Two, and were perpetuated by the Tunisian government when it took power in 1956.

C. TUNISIAN INDEPENDENCE AND LAND REFORMS

The ruling elites who emerged as Tunisia achieved independence shared a drive to compete and profit from an ever-shrinking global economy. However, the country's limited access to arable farmland was a key obstacle to achieving the coordinated production efforts that are required to compete in corporate globalization. In order to alleviate this problem, the Tunisian government sought to implement an ambitious reform plan that would streamline the nation's agrarian infrastructure by reshaping the way in which Tunisian farmland was managed.[40] Tunisia's political leaders believed that through increasing government control over the country's arable lands, they would be able to ensure that crops were produced with greater efficiency.[41] Controversially, this plan would require major changes in traditional agrarian practices and upset what had been a predominant domestic power structure: Tunisia's religious establishment.

---

[38] Dahl, "Agricultural Development Strategies in a Small Economy," 33.

[39] King, *Liberalization Against Democracy*, 64.

[40] Ashford, "Succession and Social Change in Tunisia," *International Journal of Middle East Studies* 4, no. 1 (1973): 26-27. Zaibet and Dunn, "Land Tenure, Farm Size, and Rural Market Participation in Developing Countries": 833-34.

[41] Zaibet and Dunn, "Land Tenure, Farm Size, and Rural Market Participation": 833-34.

A series of varied, and at times converse, reform strategies that were employed to increase agrarian productivity between 1956 and the 1990s have resulted in profound changes for Tunisian subsistence farmers. These small-scale farmers have been forced to endure several dramatic departures from their traditional methods of landownership and production, which are useful in exemplifying both the negative consequences of corporate globalization on subsistence farmers and the way in which these consequences relate to cultural-evolutionary theory. The evolution of Tunisia's state agrarian policy, according to Lokman Zaibet and Elizabeth Dunn, can be divided into three major phases: the initial reforms of 1956 and 1957, the Destourian socialist experiment of 1961-1969, and the subsequent move toward privatization in the 1970s.[42] Each of these phases had lasting impacts on the face of Tunisian agriculture, which are evidenced in the social consequences for the country's poorest citizens.

The Privatization of Traditional Collectives

After the French protectorate was disbanded in 1956, the newly formed Tunisian government faced significant international economic pressures. A main catalyst for Tunisian structural change was a sense of urgency to bring Tunisia into the "modern world." A mainstream economic view in the 1950s, shared by mid-twentieth century economists such as Daniel Lerner, Edward Shils, and Ghazi Duwaji, was that economic development in post-colonial nations had fallen behind the West as a result of an unhealthy attachment to traditional methods of agriculture and production.[43] Economists who held this view believed that developing countries were unable to benefit from the global economy due to a dysfunctional reverence for outdated principles and modes of production, which often focused on the needs of local producers

---

[42] Zaibet and Dunn, "Land Tenure, Farm Size, and Rural Market Participation": 834.

[43] Lerner, *The Passing of Traditional Society* (Glencoe: The Free Press, 1958), 87-89. Shils, "Political Development in the New States," *Comparative Studies in Society and History* 2, no. 3 (1960). Duwaji, "Land Ownership in Tunisia: An Obstacle to Agricultural Development."

rather than international-market strategies.[44] French economist André Nicolaï exemplified this attitude while expressing his disdain for the Tunisian agricultural system and its adherence to traditional methods, claiming that they were *"typiques d'un mode d'exploitation féodal. Par rapport à l'Europe occidentale la Tunisie est un pays arriéré."*[45] Intent on alleviating this "problem," international organizations such as the IMF and the IBRD pressured developing countries to modernize their economies so that these emerging nations would be able to participate in the expanding post-war global economy.[46] It was in this spirit of change and development that the government of Tunisia sought to restructure the nation's agrarian strategies, and through which the recurring patterns associated with cultural-evolutionary theory began to emerge.

The Elimination of the Habous

Tunisia's first president, Habib Bourguiba, was a staunch believer in modernization, and along with his government, agreed with the mid-twentieth century economic view that attachment to tradition was an obstacle to economic growth.[47] In order to bring Tunisia into a new era and achieve the level of agrarian efficiency that was required to compete in the global markets, President Bourguiba believed that the government would have to take three major steps: seize control of the nation's farmlands, undermine the cultural influence of the country's Muslim establishment, and weaken the authority of the old upper class. Bourguiba and his government realized that the most effective way to achieve each of these goals was to seize control over the *habous*. The seizure of these religious-

---

[44] Shils, "Political Development in the New States": 256-57. Duwaji, "Land Ownership in Tunisia": 129.

[45] "...typical of a feudal mode of exploitation. Compared to Western Europe, Tunisia is a backward country." Nicolaï, "Approche structurelle et effet de domination Une application: la Tunisie": 741.

[46] International Organization, "International Bank for Reconstruction and Development," 12, no. 3 (1958). Shils, "Political Development in the New States": 267.

[47] Parsons, "The Tunisian Program for Cooperative Farming," *Land Economics* 41, no. 4 (1965): 304.

based land endowments had drastic effects for the Tunisia's long-established hierarchies. Anderson notes that

> ...the weakening of the legal status of *habous* properties not only deprived the religious establishment of its independent financial base but undermined the old upper class, for the private *habous* had often been endowed to the benefit of the bourgeoisie of [Tunisia's capital city] Tunis.[48]

This shift in Tunisian land management was able to both advance Tunisia's global economic strategy while upsetting traditional power structures that had favored the religious establishment for centuries. Only six weeks after Tunisia gained independence, the government began to implement a land tenure system based on the private ownership of land, and within a year the *habous* had completely vanished.[49] As would soon prove to be the case, the privatization of these arable lands would benefit only an elite minority.

On May 31, 1956 the Tunisian government implemented the first of their land reforms and enforced a policy of latifundialization as all of the public *habous* were abolished and their lands were transferred to the *Office Des Domaniales*.[50] These charitable land endowments that had been established for Tunisia's small-scale farmers and the poor were declared an impediment to Tunisia's aspirations in the new world system and were dismantled in the name of progress.[51] Through transferring these properties to the *Office Des Domaniales*, the land could be allocated to wealthy landowners who would, in turn, assist in the process of centralizing the nation's agrarian sector.[52]

In the following year the government dissolved all of the familial *habous*. However, rather than transferring these elite-controlled *habous* to the *Office Des Domaniales*, the familial *habous*

---

[48] Anderson, *The State and Social Transformation in Tunisia and Libya*, 234.

[49] Zaibet and Dunn, "Land Tenure, Farm Size, and Rural Market Participation": 834.

[50] Parsons, "The Tunisian Program for Cooperative Farming": 304.

[51] Parsons, "The Tunisian Program for Cooperative Farming": 304.

[52] Zaibet and Dunn, "Land Tenure, Farm Size, and Rural Market Participation": 834.

were simply given to the affluent individuals who were next in line to inherit them. In essence, this reform gave Tunisia's wealthiest families the right to sell the lands that had been placed in their care for generations past.[53] The fact that the *habous* that had benefited Tunisia's wealthy elite were given to the next heir, while those that had ensured the wellbeing of the underprivileged were seized and redistributed to the rich, highlights the inequitable nature of the government's reforms. From the first year of independence it was apparent that the new government would act in the interests of the economic and political elite with little concern for the nation's poorer majority.

A Backlash Against the Government

The elimination of these religious endowments did not go unanswered by those who had lost access to their land and livelihood or the religious elite. While the peasants who worked on the *habous* depended upon them for employment and the charitable hospitals and schools that they provided,[54] the religious establishment depended on the revenue that these religious endowments generated as their financial base.[55]

Aside from the economic implications, the *habous* closures were perceived by many as a secular affront to traditional religious sensibilities, sparking outcries from around the Muslim world.[56] While many Muslim leaders charged President Bourguiba with a blatant disregard for the charitable principles of Islam and the traditions of Tunisia, Bourguiba vehemently denied their accusations. Savvy enough to appreciate the power of Tunisian religious sensibilities, Bourguiba attempted to attach a sense of Muslim piety to

---

[53] Duwaji, "Land Ownership in Tunisia': 130. Parsons, "The Tunisian Program for Cooperative Farming": 304.

[54] Powers, "Orientalism, Colonialism, and Legal History": 536. Duwaji, "Land Ownership in Tunisia": 129.

[55] Anderson, *The State and Social Transformation in Tunisia and Libya*, 234-35. Boulby, "The Islamic Challenge: Tunisia Since Independence," *Third World Quarterly* 10, no. 2, Islam & Politics (1988): 592.

[56] Roussier, "L'application du chra' au Maghrib en 1959," *Die Welt des Islams*, New Ser 6, no. 1/2 (1959): 50-54.

his reforms and project himself as a modernist reformer of Islam. Mohammad Tozy notes that rather than outrightly disrespecting the national religion, Bourguiba claimed that he was simply continuing Islam's long-standing tradition of reinterpretation.[57] While addressing an audience in Kairouan, President Bourguiba proclaimed,

> The progress of Islam and its evolution necessarily suppose an effort of constant research and free thinking in order to overhaul everything that can seem rigid and outmoded in legislation, everything that is no longer consistent with the requirements of a life under continuous renewal and that is no longer in tune with objective facts in constant evolution.[58]

Rather than portraying themselves as secularists, Bourguiba wanted to be seen as an active agent of Islam's ever-evolving interpretive tradition. Tozy writes that, as far as the government was concerned, "At no time was Islam to be explicitly called into question; even the operations considered by the observers to be frontal attacks on Islam can be seen as a reinterpretation [of Muslim doctrine]."[59] By casting his government's actions in this light, Bourguiba attempted to give himself license to carry out his secular plans, regardless of what they may be, under the guise of religious piety.

In his attempts to reform Islam, Bourguiba attempted to wed his government's policies to the Muslim ideal of caring for the impoverished. While the country's wealthiest citizens were enjoying increased land wealth at the expense of the poor, Bourguiba tried to marginalize accusations of religious insensitivity by telling an audience,

> At a time [when] we are struggling against poverty, setting up programs and drawing plans to escape from underdevelopment, demanding an accounting from those who do not produce enough and who limit freedom of enterprise, at the time

---

[57] Tozy. "Islam and the State," in *Polity and Society in Contemporary North Africa*, Boulder: Westview Press, 1993), 109-10.

[58] Tozy. "Islam and the State," 110.

[59] Tozy. "Islam and the State," 110.

when our life and death are at stake, at a time when the recovery of this Muslim nation depends on our tenacious work, I enjoin you to take advantage of a dispensation clearly defined by a healthy conception of the religious laws.[60]

In an Orwellian use of language, Bourguiba tried to rally his people around the development of a Muslim-based capitalist vision[61] and reassure them of the government's religious integrity as his government simultaneously dismantled key Muslim structures. Rather than detracting from Islam, Bourguiba's demands were to be viewed as helping Islam to realize Allah's will in the twentieth century, which apparently coincided with his school of free-market capitalism.

In order to lend an appearance of spiritual legitimacy, Tunisia's ruling elite demanded that the religious establishment endorse the party line and their new interpretations of Muslim doctrine. When many of the country's more pious religious leaders refused to comply, the government forced them to resign from their posts and weakened their educational institutions.[62] Marion Boulby writes,

> The government's moves both weakened the political influence of the *ulema* [the country's Muslim legal scholars] by depriving them of their traditional role as Tunisia's educators as well as laid the foundation to create an educational system that would support the country's changing economic goals.[63]

Commenting on Bourguiba's actions against the religious elite, Tunisian scholar Elbaki Hermassi states that "out of all the Arab countries, Tunisia is the only one where the modernist elite deliberately attacked the intuitions of Islam and dismantled its infrastructure in the name of systematic reform of the social and cultural

---

[60] Debbasch, *La République Tunisienne* (Paris: CNRS, 1962), 148.

[61] It could be equally argued that his was a capitalist-based Muslim vision.

[62] The Zeitouna mosque university system was hit particularly hard by these reforms. Tozy. "Islam and the State," 105, 110.

[63] Boulby, "The Islamic Challenge": 592.

order."[64] It had become very clear to most that in independent Tunisia, the influence of the markets would outweigh the authority of religious tradition. Despite the president's attempts to present himself as a religious reformer, the radical moves taken against the *habous* and the religious establishment drew a negative response from the citizenry and led to fears of social unrest.

The impact of the privatization of the *habous* on Tunisia's mixed-subsistence communities was profound. As these lands were transferred into the hands of the wealthy elite, the hospitals and schools that had been run by the public *habous* collectives were closed, depriving Tunisia's poor of the important social welfare functions on which they had come to rely.[65] Despite the impact of these closures on Tunisia's poorest citizens, the government justified its policies of economic centralization and latifundialization on the premise that the short-term consequences would be vindicated by long-term benefits.[66] The Tunisian government claimed that latifundialization would allow the country to be competitive in the global markets and thus improve living standards for all Tunisians.[67] Any long-term benefits became increasingly difficult to see as the wealthy enjoyed greater advantages while the majority supported their gains.

By the end of the 1950s the government had realized that it was quickly running out of time to convince their people that all Tunisians would benefit from the cultural changes that they were implementing. Social unrest grew, and Tunisia's ruling class began to fear a revolt as the government's reforms became widely perceived as being for the good of the elite and at the cost of the poor.[68] According to Raymond Crist, these fears led the Tunisian

---

[64] Boulby, "The Islamic Challenge": 591. It is certainly arguable that Colonel Mu'ammar al-Qadhdhafi's actions in Libya during the 1970s constituted an attack on traditional Islamic institutions. His actions are addressed below.

[65] Zaibet and Dunn, "Land Tenure, Farm Size, and Rural Market Participation": 834.

[66] Roussier, "L'application du chra' au Maghrib en 1959": 55.

[67] Roussier, "L'application du chra' au Maghrib en 1959": 55.

[68] The threat of revolt was not only a danger for the rulers of Tunisia but for leaders all over the developing world. C.A. Chick observed that,

government to reconsider its strategy and explore alternative land tenure policies which could simultaneously benefit Tunisia's standing in the international economic community while restoring social stability.[69] The search for such a balance would bring a whole new approach to land management in the 1960s.

It is interesting to note that Crist concluded his study in the *American Journal of Economics and Sociology* on the effects of land privatization on Tunisian peasants in the late 1950s by quoting Isa. 5.8: "Woe unto them that join house to house, that lay field to field, till there be no place, that they may be placed alone in the midst of the earth."[70] Apparently Crist, a mid-twentieth-century CE economist who had approached Isaiah from a socio-economic perspective, saw commonalities between the effects of ancient and modern land privatization. Considering the economic events that took place in 1950s Tunisia through the lens of cultural evolutionary theory, Crist's observations appear to be rooted in a common societal phenomenon that has reoccurred throughout history. Although the interpretive value of the Tunisian experience will be addressed more fully in Chapter Six, it is useful to call attention to those aspects of the recurring sociological patterns associated with accelerated trade activity that have emerged out of Tunisia's land reforms.

1950s Land Reforms and Cultural-Evolutionary Theory

The divisions of wealth that were created by French colonists as they weakened the *habous* in order to provide profitable latifundia were expanded and accelerated in the first years of Tunisian inde-

---

since the Tunisian reforms were parallel to those being propagated by IFIs throughout the developing world, peasants in several countries were experiencing similar hardships, spreading unrest throughout the Middle East and North Africa in the late 1950s (Chick, "The West's Changing Attitude Toward Africa," 29, no. 2 (1960): 191-92). Moore, "The Neo-Destour Party of Tunisia: A Structure for Democracy?," *World Politics* 14, no. 3 (1962): 466.

[69] Crist, "Land for the Fellahin, XI: Land Tenure and Land Use in the Near East," *American Journal of Economics and Sociology* 19, no. 3 (1960): 322.

[70] Crist, "Land for the Fellahin, XI": 322.

pendence. Whereas the French eroded the power of the *habous*, transferring some of their best lands to the private sector, the Tunisian government eliminated these traditional landholdings altogether.[71] This radical shift on the part of Bourguiba's government continued to produce many of the societal problems that are highlighted by cultural-evolutionary theorists.[72] The government seized control of the nation's main productive resource, abandoned subsistence farming in favor of specialized cultivation, and concentrated the wealth gained by these changes among the newly established political and economic elite.

Seizing Control of Productive Capabilities

Unlike the French colonialists before them, Tunisia's newly established sovereign government enjoyed both the power of the law and the advantages that come with being a member of the indigenous population. Unlike the French, President Bourguiba's government was not a foreign entity that had taken control of the country by force, but was comprised of native Tunisians governing within their own homeland. The traditions and culture of the Tunisian people were, in part, their traditions as well.[73] The advantage of legitimacy that comes with being an indigenous member of a community would have given Bourguiba and his government a level of hubris that enabled them to implement culture-transforming reforms that the French were wary to enact, using their political power to overturn regional tradition in favor of economic progress. The land reforms that occurred in the first two

---

[71] Harber, "Tunisian Land Tenure in the Early French Protectorate": 387. Zaibet and Dunn, "Land Tenure, Farm Size, and Rural Market Participation": 834.

[72] Berdan. "Trade and Markets in Precapitalist States," 79. Johnson and Earle, *The Evolution of Human Societies*, 255. Nolan and Lenski, *Human Societies: An Introduction to Macrosociology* (Boulder: Paradigm Publishers, 2004), 159-60.

[73] I use "in part" because many cultures and traditions exist within a society. Those who rise to power are often born into positions of advantage and experience different cultural norms than the majority of their society's population. The traditions that Bourguiba's government overturned were cultural aspects that a majority of Tunisians had enjoyed.

years of Tunisian independence exemplify the cultural transformation that tends to occur as agrarian societies experience sudden economic growth. The recurring pattern of seizing a region's productive resources, manifested through the disbanding of the public *habous*, took place in the first weeks of Tunisia's independence.[74] Subsistence farmers experienced drastic changes as this phase of Tunisia's development allowed the government to restructure agrarian strategy to allow for the production of exportable goods.

Abandonment of Subsistence Strategies the Concentration of Wealth

Tunisia's rising political elite knew that changes to agrarian production strategies would be necessary if the country was to compete in international markets. Through opening up the familial *habous* for sale into the private sector and absorbing the public *habous* into the state, the Tunisian government ensured its control over the country's arable lands and their productive capability.[75] This control paved the way for an agrarian strategy that served the interests of the markets rather than the wellbeing of the producers as subsistence strategies were abandoned for specialized cultivation.[76] Following the recurring societal patterns found as agrarian societies are restructured for trade, the wealthy hoarded the benefits of the country's new economic goals. Similar to the events that unfolded in twelfth-century France, thirteenth-century England, and sixteenth-century Japan, only an elite minority benefited from the cultural changes that accompanied agricultural centralization.[77] As rulers altered religious and secular tradition in order to become the

---

[74] Anderson, *The State and Social Transformation in Tunisia and Libya*, 234.

[75] Parsons, "The Tunisian Program for Cooperative Farming": 304.

[76] Radwan, et al., *Tunisia: Rural Labour and Structural Transformation*, 30. Lenski, *Power and Privilege: A Theory of Social Stratification* (New York: McGraw-Hill Book Company, 1966), 220. Berdan. "Trade and Markets in Precapitalist States," 79. Kautsky, *The Politics of Aristocratic Empires*, 288-92.

[77] Berdan. "Trade and Markets in Precapitalist States," 80. Other works on this phenomenon include Johnson and Earle, *The Evolution of Human Societies*, 254-55 and Hilton, 'Peasant Movement In England Before 1381': 122.

sole benefactors of their own reforms, families that had depended upon mixed-subsistence agriculture for generations were left to shoulder the burden of change.

Abandonment of Religious Traditions

The Tunisian government's concerted efforts to weaken long-held religious traditions that were viewed as impediments to economic progress is also a common occurrence as agrarian societies evolve to develop stronger political economies. Due to the dire importance of a successful harvest in agrarian communities, agricultural practices are often incorporated into religious rituals that dictate sowing, harvesting, and land management.[78] Bernard Knapp explains that because connections develop between religious belief and farming strategy, "…ritual activities serve as the interface between religion and techno-economic or socio-political activities" in agrarian societies.[79] Anthropologist Roy Rappaport claims that ritual, social, and economic needs often become intertwined, causing economic concepts to be perceived to be as infallible as other religious beliefs.[80] As a result, the ritualization of an economic ideal or system imprints itself on the very essence of the deity to which the ritual is connected, as demonstrated in the sacred agricultural festivals that are prevalent in both ancient and modern agrarian societies.[81] When ritual and economic practice interconnect, it is very difficult to separate them from the socio-economic structures that they come to represent.

Due to the bridges that develop between religious and economic practice, as economic strategies evolve, various sets of religious norms and teachings are called into question. If the nature of a

---

[78] Rappaport, "The Sacred in Human Evolution," 2, (1971), 37-39.

[79] Knapp. "Copper Production and Eastern Mediterranean Trade: The Rise of Complex Society in Cyprus," in *Sate and Society: The Emergence and Development of Social Hierarchy and Political Centralization* eds. Gledhill, Bender and Larsen; London: Unwin Hyman, 1988), 157.

[80] Rappaport, "The Sacred in Human Evolution" 2 (1971), 32-37.

[81] Hughes, "Sustainable Agriculture in Ancient Egypt," *History of Agriculture and the Environment* 66, no. 2 (1992): 16. Rappaport, "The Sacred in Human Evolution," 37-39. Exod. 23.14-18.

society's development renders subsistence strategies deficient or undesirable, as if often the case, tensions begin to develop as those who stand to gain from economic change work to alter or eliminate religious customs that have become obstacles to either wealth accumulation or survival. These tensions were experienced across the world in the fifteenth century CE as agrarian societies across Europe and Asia abandoned religious dietary habits that obstructed wealth accumulation through increased trade opportunities.[82] Foods and spices that had been considered sacred and only for ritual use were opened to general consumption when lucrative markets began to demand them.[83] When religious and economic interests come into conflict, it is often the economy that prevails.

The dominance of economic interests over religious tradition is found in Tunisia's neighbor, Libya. Like President Bourguiba's move to close the *habous* in the 1950s, Colonel Mu'ammar al-Qadhdhafi nationalized the *waqif* lands,[84] which had been controlled by the religious establishment up until the late 1970s. When Libya's religious elite opposed the move, Anderson explains, Qadhdhafi took a similar approach to that of Bourguiba by accusing the religious authorities of "inaccurately interpreting the true meaning of Islam."[85] In a further show of power over Libya's religious establishment, Qadhdhafi changed the Muslim calendar to his liking, leaving it ten years out of sync with the rest of the Muslim world.[86] Through practices such as reinterpreting religious doctrine, altering educational institutions, and reforming traditional calen-

---

[82] Bayly. "'Archaic' and 'Modern' Globalization in the Eurasian and African Arena: c. 1750-1850," in *Globalization in World History* (ed. Hopkins; London: Pimlico, 2002), 52-53. Pomeranz, *The Great Divergence: Europe, China, and the Making of the Modern World Economy* (Princeton: Princeton University Press, 2000), 119-20. Sombat, *A History of the Economic Institutions of Modern Europe* (New York: F.S. Crofts and Co., 1933).

[83] Bayly. "'Archaic' and 'Modern' Globalization in the Eurasian and African Arena": c. 1750-1850), 53.

[84] *Waqif* lands are *habous*.

[85] Anderson, *The State and Social Transformation in Tunisia and Libya*, 266.

[86] Anderson, *The State and Social Transformation in Tunisia and Libya*, 266.

dars, Bourguiba and Qadhdhafi reshaped their nations' religious practices to coincide with a new economic climate. Such changes, however, are not always welcomed.

Threat of Civil Unrest

The threat of civil unrest among struggling farmers as a response to the Tunisian government's reforms is another common aspect of cultural evolution in agrarian societies. According to Kautsky, members of the poorest classes who have become accustomed to the oppressive conditions into which they were born will rarely revolt, except during periods of increased commercialization.[87] It is when the disenfranchised members of a society experience the sudden increases in exploitation that accompany heightened market activity that revolts tend to occur.[88] Rodney Hilton explains that revolts of this nature took place in thirteenth-century England when poor and middling peasants, who lived only above the subsistence level, were forced to endure increased labor and tax demands that lowered their already meager standard of living.[89] In the late 1950s Tunisian subsistence farmers found the increased hardships that they were experiencing, while the political and economic elite enjoyed newfound wealth, too great to bear.[90] As a consequence, the Tunisian government faced the prospect of losing power and was forced to reshape its modernization schemes.

The actions taken by Tunisia's rulers in the first few years of independence are not surprising in light of the recurring cultural-evolutionary patterns that tend to accompany rapid economic development. In their drive to modernize the Tunisian economy and become competitive in the international markets, the ruling elite had used their newfound power to alter Tunisia's agrarian landscape so as to increase their personal riches. Through an initial consolidation of land, abandonment of subsistence strategies, and

---

[87] Kautsky, *The Politics of Aristocratic Empires*, 288-92.

[88] Hilton, Peasant Movement In England Before 1381": 122. Kautsky, *The Politics of Aristocratic Empires*, 288-92.

[89] Hilton, "Peasant Movement In England Before 1381": 122.

[90] Chick, "The West's Changing Attitude Toward Africa": 191-92. Moore, "The Neo-Destour Party of Tunisia," 466.

consolidation of wealth, these elites created disproportionate growth, offended the religious establishment and its supporters, and nearly sparked a revolt among the citizenry. Although major changes to rectify these issues were to come in the 1960s, many of these same characteristics of cultural evolution would recur.

D. THE 1960S NÉO-DESTOURIAN SOCIALIST EXPERIMENT

Tunisia's second phase of land reform signaled a radically different approach, which largely reversed the privatization schemes of the late 1950s. Rather than rejecting the communal land-management strategies that were developed under the *habous*, the government embraced some of their aspects through an ambitious socialist experiment that attempted to wed communal-based management with internationally-focused market strategies.[91] The idea that the nation's wealthiest citizens didn't have to own everything for Tunisia to benefit from the global economy was put into practice.

Tunisia's socialist experiment sought to free the country from foreign influences while maintaining viabilities in the international markets. Lars Rudebeck explains that the advice and demands of IFIs were to be ignored while promoting a spirit of national cooperation, openness, freedom, and "the promotion of man."[92] The idea peaked interest among development experts, and much of the international community held high hopes for Tunisia's political reinvention, praising the government's grassroots strategy and spirit of national unity as a model for political development.[93] The government's mismanaged application of the program, however, would dash such expectations over the next several years. According to Steven King, the failure of Néo-Destourian socialism was caused by a series of unnecessary economic decisions that were ultimately directed at fulfilling the interests of the governing and economic elite.[94] The end result of this attempt to create equitable develop-

---

[91] King, *Liberalization Against Democracy*, 27-28.

[92] Rudebeck, "Developmental Pressure and Political Limits: A Tunisian Example," *The Journal of Modern African Studies* 8, no. 2 (1970): 181.

[93] Payne. "Economic Crisis and Policy Reform in the 1980s," 143-44.

[94] King, *Liberalization Against Democracy*, 25.

ment for the people of Tunisia resulted in even greater abuses than those experienced in the late 1950s.

The Rise of Néo-Destour Socialism

The second phase of Tunisian reforms brought a period of great hope to Tunisia in the early 1960s, as President Bourguiba's Néo-Destour Party came to be known to many within the international community as a champion of social justice.[95] In response to the frustration and distrust that had fermented amongst peasants during the first phase of reforms in the 1950s, the party created a Ten-Year Development Plan, with a wide-reaching land-management component that consolidated Tunisian farmlands into a cooperative socialist system.[96]

The idea behind this new cooperative system was to group small-scale farmers together as both owners and laborers of sections of land that were deemed to be, as Kenneth Parson explains, "of adequate scale, with appropriate technology and sufficiently effective management and marketing services to make modernized farming possible."[97] It was believed that this collective system could streamline production by simultaneously creating favorable conditions for Tunisia's rural communities. It initially appeared that the government had found a way to pursue its economic goals while satisfying the needs of its people.

Land Allocation

The Néo-Destour socialist system was designed to maximize agrarian efficiency and modern technology. Each of the proposed government cooperatives were roughly 1,250 acres in size, which was considered the optimal land area to benefit from the farming techniques and machinery that were being used in the world's most

---

[95] "Moore, "The Neo-Destour Party of Tunisia: A Structure for Democracy?"

[96] Moore, "The Neo-Destour Party of Tunisia": 461.

[97] Parsons, "The Tunisian Program for Cooperative Farming": 305.

highly developed countries.[98] In addition to providing Tunisia's farming communities with these collectives, the government demanded that wealthy Tunisian farmers make at least ten percent of the arable land on their large estates available to poorer families for subsistence cultivation.[99] It was hoped that providing these subsistence plots, from which any harvested food was to go directly to the peasants who worked on them,[100] would help to subdue the unrest that had developed under the privatization policies of the late 1950s and display the government's newfound commitment to equity and poverty reduction. A significant problem that was inherent to this socialist project was that to provide justice to one group, injustice would have to be dispensed to another segment of society.

In order to create the 1,250-acre cooperatives, which were designed to provide less affluent Tunisians with employment and a sense of ownership, that land would have to be seized from others, and with immediate repercussions. The Tunisian government passed a law in 1964 that made it illegal for anyone other than native Tunisians to own Tunisian land, nationalizing all of the land that had been held by the families of colonial settlers. This newly acquired land was then transformed into collectively owned latifundia for Tunisian natives.[101] French and Italian families, many of whom had legally inherited their homes and farmland from generations past, were outraged at this act of nationalization. In response to their protests, Bourguiba justified the move by claiming that the losses that these foreign landowners would sustain were miniscule in comparison to the benefits that would be gained by the Tunisian people.[102] The *New York Times* cited a speech by the Tunisian President, in which he claimed that the loss of Tunisian farmland

---

[98] Duwaji, "Land Ownership in Tunisia": 131. This brought back a tradition of land allocation to the poor that had been practiced before independence.

[99] New York Times, "Tunisian Harvests Cut by Seizures," *The New York Times*, July 26 1964, 13.

[100] New York Times, "Tunisian Harvests Cut by Seizures," 13.

[101] Zaibet and Dunn, "Land Tenure, Farm Size, and Rural Market Participation": 834. Duwaji, "Land Ownership in Tunisia": 131.

[102] New York Times, "France Suspends Aid to Tunis, Retaliating on Seizure of Land," *The New York Times*, 13 May 1964, 17.

was a minor inconvenience for France and Italy, "...but for Tunisia it was 'a question of life and death.'"[103] Bourguiba claimed that considering the economic advantages that Tunisia's former occupiers had enjoyed before Tunisian independence, "it ought not be an 'impossible effort' for France to compensate her nationals for the loss of their farms."[104] Bourguiba's refusal to offer any compensation for the seizure of over 700,000 acres of foreign-owned land came at a high cost.[105] In retaliation, the French worked to isolate Tunisia by suspending all financial aid to the country.[106] The consequences for upsetting Tunisia's former colonizers would prove very difficult for the young nation.

While relations with the French deteriorated rapidly, the nationalization of foreign-owned lands allowed the cooperative scheme to advance quickly. From 1964 to 1966 cooperative participation had almost doubled with a total of 779 operational cooperatives, which were operated by a total of 206,633 members.[107] The goal of combining a modernization of the agrarian sector with quasi-traditional landholding sensibilities, allowing Tunisia to function relatively independently from foreign influence while remaining competitive within the global markets, appeared to be within reach.

The Failings and Collapse of Néo-Destourian Socialism

The initial optimism and renewed Tunisian nationalism that accompanied the start of the cooperative system began to waver as signs of ill-planned policy and a lack of governmental foresight began to emerge less than two years into the project. President Bourguiba's decision to seize the lands of former French and Italian landowners had serious economic ramifications by souring rela-

---

[103] New York Times, "France Suspends Aid to Tunis, Retaliating on Seizure of Land," 17.

[104] New York Times, "France Suspends Aid to Tunis, Retaliating on Seizure of Land," 17.

[105] Ashford, "Succession and Social Change in Tunisia": 28.

[106] New York Times, "France Suspends Aid to Tunis, Retaliating on Seizure of Land," 17.

[107] Ashford, "Succession and Social Change in Tunisia": 29.

tions with Tunisia's two largest trading partners. Prior to these sweeping land grabs, France had bought much of Tunisia's wheat, fruit, and wine at preferential prices. As a consequence of Bourguiba's nationalization scheme, France discontinued its preferential arrangement and left Tunisia unable to find an alternative buyer.[108] To make matters worse, France recalled more than one hundred of the agricultural advisors that it had sent to help train Tunisians in techniques that would help the country to better cope with its adverse farming conditions.[109] Consequently, productivity was stunted in what had already been considered an unfavorable growing season, harvests failed to produce expected yields, and the Tunisian people suffered.[110] These problems were further compounded by governmental mismanagement.

Signs of Inequitable Growth

In addition to the losses that were sustained by the government's treatment of foreign nationals, internal problems arose. Despite the fact that the *Socialist Destour* cooperatives were created to allow all Tunisians to benefit from the new economy, it became apparent that the benefits were not distributed equally. Barbara Larson explains that one problem in distributing the fruits of trade equally throughout Tunisia was the remote locations of many of Tunisia's hamlets and villages.[111] While areas of Tunisia that were more accessible experienced the fruition of the socialist reforms, isolated villages did not receive any of the intended benefits. Larson notes that the village of Shibeka in the South, located far from governmental centers, was not only left relatively untouched by the government, but few of its three hundred inhabitants were even aware of developments taking place outside of their immediate locale.[112] In the areas of Béja and Jendouba, some of country's most impoverished people were removed from their land to build the coopera-

---

108 New York Times, "Tunisian Harvests Cut by Seizures," 13.

109 New York Times, "Tunisian Harvests Cut by Seizures," 13.

110 New York Times, "Tunisian Harvests Cut by Seizures," 13.

111 Larson, "Local-National Integration in Tunisia," *Middle Eastern Studies* 20, no. 1 (1984): 19-21.

112 Larson, "Local-National Integration in Tunisia": 20.

tives in that region, and then left out of the system altogether. Nicholas Hopkins writes that the disenfranchised Tunisians from these two communities

> ...suffered the shock of moving from a semi-subsistence pattern of agriculture to one based entirely on wage labor and cash purchases of food. The cooperative structure, to put it briefly, was a model developed by an urban elite for organizing rural people, and it was fairly insensitive to the delicate balances of rural life.[113]

The government's ability to fulfill its promise of equitable growth was hampered by the exclusion of many impoverished Tunisians and the fact that the system was designed by urban elites who could not fully understand the needs of Tunisia's rural poor. Due to the socio-economic disconnect between policy maker and producer, strategies that had been created with good intentions ended with harmful results for the rural poor.[114]

Although the government was able to stimulate the private sector and create jobs for the growing urban labor force, such advances were thwarted by the failure of shortsighted programs and economic decisions, which crippled the Tunisian economy.[115] As King notes, "...a large resource gap was created when the country tried to invest more resources than were saved domestically."[116] To add to the country's economic woes, the Tunisian government had relied on foreign loans to compensate for a misbalanced budget while taking on an arduous welfare system.[117] Unsound fiscal decisions such as these drove the nation more deeply into debt and ensured the ruin of Tunisia's socialist plan.

----

[113] Hopkins, "Tunisia: An Open and Shut Case": 386.

[114] Larson, "Local-National Integration in Tunisia": 20-21.

[115] Harik. "Privatization: The Issue, the Prospects, and the Fears," in *Privatization and Liberalization in the Middle East* eds. Harik and Sullivan; Bloomington: Indiana University Press, 1992), 211. King, *Liberalization Against Democracy*, 27.

[116] King, *Liberalization Against Democracy*, 27.

[117] Harik. "Privatization: The Issue, the Prospects, and the Fears," 212.

A Revolt Across Class Lines

In the end, the goals of Tunisia's socialist experiment failed due to the inability of the government to handle the strenuous nature of the task. As a result, discontent grew throughout Tunisia as many of the poor did not receive the benefits that had been promised to them, and economic elites who did not appreciate their personal financial growth stunted by failed socialist policies became resentful.[118] While pressure grew internally from both affluent and poor segments of Tunisia's agricultural sector, IFIs like the World Bank began to apply external pressure, calling for the government to dismantle its *Néo-Destourian* socialist experiment.[119] To the detriment of the architects of *Néo-Destourian* socialism, the movement collapsed in spectacular failure.

What had been hailed as a great national experiment in the early 1960s failed to live up to expectations. According to Charles Micaud, the two greatest mistakes of the *Socialist Destour* experiment were the government's attempts to appease more internal interest groups than was manageable and hurried planning, which led to unsound decision-making.[120] The resulting termination of Tunisia's socialist policy was expedited as large-scale landowners and the bourgeois began to place pressure upon the government with anti-cooperative demonstrations.[121] After a demonstration carried out by affluent landowners in 1969, the government felt compelled to fire the Minister of Planning and main promoter of Destour socialism, Ahmed Ben Salah.[122] Fearing the consequences of social unrest among wealthy Tunisian landowners and urban elites, the government implemented a policy shift that favored the liberalization

---

[118] Radwan, et al., *Tunisia: Rural Labour and Structural Transformation*, 30.

[119] Hopkins, "Tunisia: An Open and Shut Case": 386. Radwan, et al., *Tunisia: Rural Labour and Structural Transformation*, 30.

[120] Micaud, "Leadership and Development: The Case of Tunisia": 478. Zaibet and Dunn, "Land Tenure, Farm Size, and Rural Market Participation": 834.

[121] Hopkins, "Tunisia: An Open and Shut Case": 386.

[122] Entelis, "Reformist Ideology in the Arab World: The Cases of Tunisia and Lebanon," 37, no. 4 (1975): 545.

of the economy and the re-privatization of Tunisian farmlands.[123] In need of a scapegoat for the catastrophic meltdown of the cooperative reforms, the government stripped Ben Salah of all political influence before he was arrested and sentenced to ten years of hard labor.[124]

Despite the drastic differences between the strategies employed in the 1950s and the 1960s and attempts to create equitable growth, the Tunisian government furthered elite interests and perpetuated the recurring abuses that are associated with a rapid increase in trade activity. Over the following few years, the Tunisian government reversed the reforms that it had created during the previous decade, and by the end of the 1960s, Tunisian farmers experienced another 180-degree shift in land ownership policy.[125]

Socialist Destour and Cultural-Evolutionary Theory

Similar to the failings of the World Bank and the IMF to protect the vulnerable from the abuses that accompany periods of increased trade, the Tunisian government's attempt to integrate traditional communal strategies with a market-driven system failed to create equitable development for the country's small-scale farmers and, eventually, led back to the latifundialist strategies that are expected during periods of cultural evolution. A.E. Alpart explains that although the socialist experiment was intended to "raise the standards of production through the introduction of modern methods, new crops, fertilizers, machinery, and credit to traditional subsistence farmers," the final goal of production for export ran converse to centuries of family-based semi-subsistence culture.[126] In the end, rather than helping the country's poorer farmers, the techniques used in the *Socialist Destour* reforms brought increased risk and alienation for many of the country's poorer citizens.[127] This, as discussed in the previous chapter, attests to the power of

---

[123] Radwan, et al., *Tunisia: Rural Labour and Structural Transformation*, 30.

[124] Rudebeck, 'Developmental Pressure and Political Limits': 173.

[125] King, *Liberalization Against Democracy*, 28.

[126] Alport, "Socialism in Three Countries: The Record in the Maghrib," *International Affairs* 43, no. 4 (1967): 690.

[127] Hopkins, "Tunisia: An Open and Shut Case": 386.

these recurring patterns of abuse; even when a system attempts to act benevolently, the cultural evolution unfolds for the benefit of the elites and not the producers.

E. PRIVATIZATION, LIBERALIZATION, AND OPPRESSION IN THE 1970S

In order to compensate for the failed *Socialist Destour* policies of the 1960s, the Tunisian government initiated a series of reforms that favored the country's most affluent citizens. The desire to produce quick successes could be seen in the government's shift from long-term goals to an emphasis on short-term growth.[128] Micaud writes that the socialism and humanism of the 1960s was replaced with *bourguibism*, ushering in a series of stages that were "…geared to the realization of what is attainable now, and yet concurrently contributes to the reach of long-range objectives."[129] To assist with a quick change of economic policy, President Bourguiba appointed the head of the Central Bank, Hédi Nouira, as Prime Minister in 1971.[130] Nouira quickly became Bourguiba's champion of liberal economic policy through establishing increased trade links with European countries in hopes that, as Hopkins notes, the resulting prosperity "would trickle down to the population at large."[131] The outcomes of Bourguiba and Nouira's quick-fix plans, which included the privatization of farmland and the acceptance of World Bank conditions, worked to favor Tunisia's wealthiest citizens while creating hardship for the poor.

Land Privatization

In efforts to quickly undo what had become perceived as a burdensome cooperative system, the government began to introduce land-privatization schemes in 1969, with tragic consequences for Tuni-

---

[128] Radwan, et al., *Tunisia: Rural Labour and Structural Transformation*, 30.

[129] Micaud, "Leadership and Development": 471.

[130] Anderson, *The State and Social Transformation in Tunisia and Libya*, 241.

[131] Hopkins, "Tunisia: An Open and Shut Case": 387.

sia's small-scale farmers.[132] Radwan, Jamal, and Ghose note that from 1961-1962 to 1979-1980 a decline in the average size of land-holding was apparent as the lands held by the majority of Tunisians lessened while an affluent minority enjoyed an increase in average landholding size.[133] Such periods of latifundialization are common when unfettered control is given to wealthy landowners, often lead-ing to revolts. Highlighting this phenomenon, Ashford writes,

> As so often happens with abrupt shifts of policy over unpopu-
> lar decisions, a good many of the aggrieved took matters into
> their own hands. A number of recently organized agricultural
> production co-ops were forcefully dissolved by the members
> and the managers simply driven off the land. Fall planting in
> some areas was seriously disrupted, while in the cities several
> long established co-ops for marketing and commerce were re-
> turned to private hands.[134]

The hasty closure of cooperatives led to inefficiencies that ham-pered the production of food. While prosperous Tunisians would be more likely to weather such difficulties, those without sufficient financial resources, Ashford notes, had to struggle to sustain their families as they missed the beginning of the growing season due to a lack of labor, available land, and disorganization.[135] While the suffering of the country's poorer citizens increased, wealthier Tuni-sians enjoyed short-term benefits from privatization.

Beyond the takeover of cooperatives by individual members, the government moved to privatize a majority of Tunisia's arable lands in a bid to regain confidence among IFIs and the country's economic elite, which had become wary of bureaucratic land schemes in the 1960s.[136] Large farms that had operated under pri-

---

[132] Zaibet and Dunn, "Land Tenure, Farm Size, and Rural Market Participation": 834.

[133] Radwan, et al., *Tunisia: Rural Labour and Structural Transformation*, 37. Unfortunately, there are no records on landownership. Landholding and landowning are different, and it is landholding that is represented in this study.

[134] Ashford, 'Succession and Social Change in Tunisia': 36.

[135] Ashford, 'Succession and Social Change in Tunisia': 36.

[136] Micaud, "Leadership and Development": 481.

vate ownership were left to be managed by powerful landowners as latifundia. The government considered these changes to be a necessary response to the failure of the 1960s reforms, which had come to be perceived as too hasty, authoritarian, and bureaucratic.[137] In a move to accelerate the consolidation of Tunisia's productive capabilities under private ownership, the government allowed the nation's wealthiest minority to take control of the failed government cooperatives.

Despite the negative connotations that had become associated with the socialist cooperatives of the previous decade, they were not completely disbanded. Rather than abolishing all of these government-controlled latifundia, the government decided to keep those that had proved to be efficient and profitable. However, rather than allowing the workers to maintain their shares in the collective, control was given to a single individual.[138] Rudebeck explains that the 1970s cooperatives were owned and controlled by a single private owner who held all of the shares, which created "great economic and social differences between [the landowner] and the rest of the members," thus effectively negating the spirit of a cooperative.[139] These new cooperatives were not completely independent, but managed under the close administrative supervision of the Tunisian government to ensure that productive efforts were synchronized.[140] What came to be called a cooperative system of land management was nothing more than a governmental-dominated patronage scheme based upon a latifundialist policy. Such policies were not only encouraged by President Bourguiba and Prime Minister Nouira, they were celebrated by the World Bank and a number of the world's most powerful nations.

---

[137] Rudebeck, "Developmental Pressure and Political Limits": 173.

[138] Zaibet and Dunn, "Land Tenure, Farm Size, and Rural Market Participation": 834. Ashford, "Succession and Social Change in Tunisia": 36.

[139] Rudebeck, "Developmental Pressure and Political Limits:" 193.

[140] Ashford, "Succession and Social Change in Tunisia": 36.

Acceptance of World Bank Conditions

Western nations took a strong interest in helping the Tunisian economy to recover from the policy failures of the 1960s, as West Germany, the United States, and the United Kingdom reached out to offer both financial assistance and policy advice.[141] Using the World Bank as a conduit, as well as some private channels, these powerful countries pressured Tunisia to distance itself from the principles of *Socialist Destour* economics and embrace a neoliberal approach. While keeping the Tunisian government afloat through various loan arrangements, western nations paved the way for their own corporate interests, creating a favorable trade environment and leading the country to become increasingly dependent on foreign aid.[142] Hermassi notes that by 1972 Tunisia had yielded to international economic pressures at least twice. Tunisia first succumbed to international pressure when it accepted a stabilization program that devalued the country's national currency.[143] As Stallings and other economists point out, the devaluation of currency, which encourages an increase in exports, is a common initial step in liberalizing a developing nation's economy.[144] Tunisia submitted to international pressures once again as it accepted the conditions of a World Bank loan that dictated how the country's land reform should be managed.[145] As the Tunisian government made moves to embrace a neoliberal stance and benefit from interna-

---

[141] Kleve, "The Control of Annual Plans: The Experience of Tunisia," *The Journal of Modern African Studies* 9, no. 2 (1971): 306-7. Entelis, "Reformist Ideology in the Arab World": 538.

[142] Entelis, "Reformist Ideology in the Arab World": 538.

[143] Hermassi, *Leadership and Development* (Berkeley: University of California Press, 1972), 191.

[144] Stallings. "International Influence on Economic Policy: Debt, Stabilization, and Structural Reform," in *The Plitics of Economic Adjustment* eds. Haggard and Kaufman; Princeton: Princeton University Press, 1992). Crisp and Kelly, "The Socioeconomic Impacts of Structural Adjustment," *International Studies Quarterly* 43, no. 3 (1999): 534, 542. Corbo and de Melo, "Lessons from the Southern Cone Policy Reforms," *World Bank Research Observer* 2, (1985): 118.

[145] Hermassi, *Leadership and Development*, 191.

tional trade, the country's economic and political sovereignty began to be eclipsed by foreign financial interests.

Despite the control that the Tunisian government was handing over to IFIs and foreign countries, Tunisia's aim of achieving short-term economic successes was being realized. Anderson writes that the promotion of the private sector, as championed by Nouira, produced "a positive aggregate economic picture."[146] Between 1972 and 1976 the nation's GDP grew at an impressive rate of nine percent per annum, well over double the rate of growth in the 1960s.[147] This growth would take a drastic turn for the worse as the trickle-down effect that Nouira had forecasted never materialized.

Typical of the criticisms leveled against structural adjustment programs, Tunisia's World Bank loans focused on market interests while neglecting projects that have a direct impact on humanitarian need. For example, World Bank loans were used to improve the Tunisian luxury industry in hopes of stimulating tourism. In 1974 the World Bank granted Tunisia a US$5.6 million loan to finance a project that focused on training hotel personnel.[148] Although the tourism package helped Tunisia to acquire a positive net foreign exchange and some new employment opportunities, the loan's trickle-down approach failed to alleviate the urgent humanitarian needs the country was facing at that time, such as severely limited access to health care and increasing food prices.[149] The acceptance of this type of loan package reveals the economic priorities that were held by the Tunisian government at the time. Despite a seemingly strong GDP in the early 1970s, a combination of the government's privatization policies, a turbulent global economy, and a failure to aid Tunisia's poorest citizens led to economic failure and social unrest.

---

[146] Anderson, *The State and Social Transformation in Tunisia and Libya*, 241.

[147] Anderson, *The State and Social Transformation in Tunisia and Libya*, 241.

[148] New York Times, "World Bank Loans of $81.1-Million to 3 Nations," *The New York Times*, June 14 1974, 46.

[149] Jursa and Winkates, "Tourism as a Mode of Development," *Issue: A Journal of Opinion* 4, no. 1 (1974): 49.

Policy Failures, Resistance, and Violent Oppression

In line with the fate of the idealistic ambitions of the socialist experiment of the 1960s, the short-term goals of the economic reforms in the 1970s proved to be out of reach. By the end of the decade, like much of the rest of the developing world, the Tunisian economy had taken a serious hit from the oil shocks and was in a serious decline. Despite the impressive gains that the country had made between 1970 and 1976, in 1977 the GDP was cut by half, and unemployment grew by one hundred percent.[150] Such a dramatic economic meltdown had severe social consequences, including a rising populist movement with a strong Islamic ideology that was fuelled by an increasingly political and active working class and student population.[151] The government's response to the emerging voices of resistance was both harsh and swift.

In January 1978, the 500,000-member strong *Union Générale des Travailleurs Tunisiens* (UGTT) called a general strike that was met with violent resistance. According to Nigel Disney, government and non-governmental estimates suggest that between one hundred and five hundred demonstrators were killed in the confrontation. As a further show of strength, the government arrested 1,600 union members, three hundred of whom received prison sentences of up to seven years.[152] By the end of the 1970s torture and imprisonment were a regular part of the government's strategy to deal with those who opposed the nation's economic and social policies.[153] Despite, or perhaps as a result of, these harsh crackdowns, the resistance continued to grow.

The government's attempts to crush political opposition could not deter the persistent populist movement, which grew in strength and influence. King notes that Tunisia's empowered workers placed increasing pressure on the country's single-party system and

---

[150] Anderson, *The State and Social Transformation in Tunisia and Libya*, 242.

[151] Boulby, "The Islamic Challenge": 603-05.

[152] Disney, "The Working Class Revolt in Tunisia," no. 67 (1978): 12.

[153] Ahmad and Schaar, "Human Rights in Morocco and Tunisia: A Critique of State Department Findings," *Middle East Research and Information Project* no. 67 (1978). Disney, "The Working Class Revolt in Tunisia."

demanded greater democratic reform. As members of the political elite started to break ranks and join the campaign for democratic reform, a breakthrough came in the form of the country's first multi-party elections, held in 1981.[154] Despite this pivotal step forward, the ruling party rigged the elections to solidify Bourguiba's power.[155] Democratic reforms failed to take hold, and the voices of populism were marginalized as patronage-based authoritarian control was perpetuated throughout the countryside.[156] As a result, the Tunisian government continued its policies of economic liberalization, and cultural change in Tunisia continued to favor the interests of a wealthy and powerful minority.

Policies of the 1970s and Cultural Evolutionary Theory

The Tunisian government's actions in the 1970s, like those of the 1950s and the 1960s, reflect the recurring patterns of economic exploitation that are addressed by cultural-evolutionary theorists. In the wake of the catastrophic failure of the *Socialist Destour* experiment came a series of reforms that advanced the government's desire to consolidate Tunisia's farmlands into latifundia. As a result, many Tunisian farmers struggled as they were driven off of their lands and prohibited from continuing the semi-subsistence traditions that their families had practiced for generations.[157] Yet again, the Tunisian government enacted policies that concentrated land and the benefits of trade in the hand of an elite few.

Debt as a Tool for Latifundialization

The closure of urban cooperative markets made it difficult for small-scale farmers to sell their goods domestically, subsequently forcing these farmers to take out survival loans to meet the increased costs of growing produce that could be traded in the international markets. When these survival loans could no longer be

---

[154] King, *Liberalization Against Democracy*, 4.

[155] Waltz, "Antidotes for Social Malaise: Alienation, Efficacy, and Participation in Tunisia," *Comparative Politics* 14, no. 2 (1982).

[156] Anderson, *The State and Social Transformation in Tunisia and Libya*, 249.

[157] Ashford, "Succession and Social Change in Tunisia": 36.

honored, farmers were forced into foreclosure, and their lands were surrendered to the government or wealthier landowners.[158] These events lie in stark contrast to the situation in Mali in the 1970s, where, in many areas, land was still held communally under the control of the village. In the village of Kita, Mali, for example, a creditor could only claim revenue from a debtor, not seize the family's property.[159] Rather than attempting to trap farmers in a cycle of liability, it was thought to be in a Malian creditor's best interest to ensure that their debtors' production capabilities were sustainable so that a return could be made.[160] In contrast, the dire economic conditions that proved to be devastating for Tunisia's rural poor had served the Tunisian government's desire to create latifundia and become a more efficient competitor in the world of corporate globalization.

As explained in Chapter Two, debt is commonly used as a tool by which ruling or economic elites can seize the properties of small-scale farmers. Michael Hudson explains that debt foreclosure was the primary method through which communal subsistence lands were privatized in the ancient Near East, "passing [them] into the hands of public collectors and merchants when cultivators ran into problems."[161] As in the ancient world, by making it more difficult to avoid participation in the global markets the Tunisian government was able to exploit the expensive nature of specialized agriculture to force farmers into survival loans that they would not likely be able to repay.[162] As the lands were seized and either sold or gifted to the government's supporters, they were used to cultivate exportable goods such as dates, olives, citrus fruits, and grapes,

---

[158] Ashford, "Succession and Social Change in Tunisia": 36.

[159] Hopkins, "The Small Urban Center in Rural Development: Kita (Mali) and Testour (Tunisia)," 49, no. 3 (1979): 320.

[160] Hopkins, "The Small Urban Center in Rural Development": 320.

[161] Hudson. "Private Landownership, Debt, and Fiscal Crisis in the Ancient Near East," in *Property in Economic Context* eds. Hunt and Gilman; *Monographs in Economic Anthropology*; Oxford: University Press of America, 1998), 149.

[162] Ashford, "Succession and Social Change in Tunisia": 36.

rather than sustain the needs of villagers.[163] This is a pattern that has reoccurred throughout the ancient and modern world, as detailed above[164]

Negative Impact on Subsistence Farmers

A loss of land for small-scale farmers was accompanied by a loss of self-sufficiency, which is a highly valued principle in subsistence cultures. As the Tunisian government prioritized the growth of cash crops, those who could afford to compete in the global markets were given the best parcels of land while subsistence farmers were left with plots that could not adequately meet their needs.[165] Unable to provide for their families, the subsistence farmers from more economically depressed areas were driven to the labor sector, often to work in the then booming tourist industry.[166] Johnson and Earle note that such conditions take away "whatever remained of the self-sufficiency of the farm household."[167] As Tunisian farmers migrated to urban centers to find a means of survival, their options become more limited, as is evidenced in the one-hundred percent rise in unemployment that occurred between 1976 and 1977.[168] As

---

[163] King, *Liberalization Against Democracy.* Radwan, et al., *Tunisia: Rural Labour and Structural Transformation*, 75.

[164] Lenski, *Power and Privilege*, 220. Hudson. "Private Landownership, Debt, and Fiscal Crisis in the Ancient Near East," 149-50. Weber, *Ancient Judaism* (trans. Gerth and Martindale; London: The Free Press, 1952), 56-57. Chirichigno, *Debt-Slavery in Israel and the Ancient Near East* (141; eds. Clines and Davies; vol. 141; Sheffield: Sheffield Academic Press, 1993), 35.

[165] Johnson and Earle explain that the same thing happened in Brazil and Java when the two countries experienced a sharp rise in the export of sugar cane production; specialized production took over and farmers lost the ability to provide for their families (Johnson and Earle, *The Evolution of Human Societies*, 273).

[166] Radwan, et al., *Tunisia: Rural Labour and Structural Transformation*, 11.

[167] Johnson and Earle, *The Evolution of Human Societies: From Foraging Group to Agrarian State* (Stanford: Stanford University Press, 1987), 273.

[168] Anderson, *The State and Social Transformation in Tunisia and Libya:* 242.

mass production increased, the traditions of Tunisia's agrarian communities were lost, and people became displaced.

Like the policies of the late 1950s and the consequences of the reforms in the 1960s, the measures taken in the 1970s by the Tunisian government, a few of corporate globalization's core nations, and the World Bank exemplify the recurring outcomes of cultural evolution in agrarian societies. In order to take advantage of an expanding global economy and increase their personal wealth, Tunisia's political and economic leaders consolidated the country's arable lands by forcing farmers off of their property through schemes of debt and forced takeover. Instigating methods of both physical and political oppression, they exploited producers in ways that have been employed by ruling elites for thousands of years: overturning the rights and traditions of farmers in order to gain a monopoly on productive control and the benefits thereof.[169] As subsistence farming was rendered irrelevant in the new Tunisian economic model, unemployment grew and led to a greater disparity of wealth distribution.[170] The policies of the following decade would solidify the latifundialist reforms of the 1970s and lead to greater suffering in the country's agrarian communities.

---

[169] Chirichigno, *Debt-Slavery in Israel and the Ancient Near East*, 140. Rudebeck, 'Developmental Pressure and Political Limits:': 193.

[170] Anderson, *The State and Social Transformation in Tunisia and Libya*, 242.

F. SOLIDIFICATION OF SOCIETAL CHANGE IN THE 1980s AND ITS CONSEQUENCES ON STANDARDS OF LIVING

The economic reforms of the 1980s accelerated the liberalization of Tunisia's economy and the consolidation of the country's farmlands as patronage systems that had developed in the 1970s were solidified. Following a common pattern, Payne writes, "...the principal supporters of the Bourguiba regime [were] rewarded with control over the parastatal corporations that dominated the Tunisian economy or with the disbursement of public spending in its various forms."[1] Such gifts further consolidated the country's wealth under the control of those who will serve the interests of the government. While the solidification of these patronage systems benefited those who had enjoyed the government's favor, it had dire consequences for Tunisia's poorest farmers, who became increasingly vulnerable to elite interests as access to arable lands became more limited.[2] When those in power demanded a production increase in export crops from impoverished farmers, even against those farmers' own best interests, they had little choice but to comply.

The hardships suffered by Tunisia's small-scale farmers were not only the result of domestic planning. Rather than championing the interests of Tunisia's poorest citizens directly, in 1986 the IMF and the World Bank implemented a series of structural adjustment programs that accelerated the liberalization of the Tunisian economy, claiming that this would benefit Tunisia's poorest citizens.[3] The Bank expressed its eagerness to support the government's liberalizing policies, claiming that they would benefit the poor of both urban and rural areas.[4] In 1986 the World Bank issued a statement that claimed,

---

[1] Payne. "Economic Crisis and Policy Reform in the 1980s," 144.

[2] King, *Liberalization Against Democracy*, 38.

[3] King, *Liberalization Against Democracy*, 4.

[4] World Bank, *Republic of Tunisia, Agricultural Sector Adjustment Loan: Medium-Term Agricultural Sector Adjustment Program* (Washington, D.C.: World Bank, 1986).

(a) The rural poor, particularly in rain fed areas, will profit
from increased agricultural producer prices as well as from increases in agricultural production for import substitution and
exports; (b) the urban poor will profit from the increase in the
minimum wage introduced in mid-1986; and (c) both groups
will profit from the stimulating effects of the adjustment
measures on employment creation, as export industries, agriculture, and tourism are all relatively labor-intensive sectors.[5]

In theory, the liberalization of the Tunisian economy would allow
the country to participate more freely in the global economy, thus
producing significant benefits for its most impoverished citizens.
In the end, however, the World Bank's program would have the
opposite effect.

Effects of Accelerated Liberalization on Public Heath

The program of accelerated liberalization that was implemented by
the Tunisian government with the support of the World Bank's
SAP had dire consequences for the country's most vulnerable citizens. To facilitate the Bank's demand for a twenty-six percent increase in spending on debt interest, the government adhered to an
eighteen-percent cut in public investment, taking money out of
social programs and reducing the number of services available to
those in rural communities.[6] As a direct result of these spending
cuts, and only three years after the SAP was implemented, the
World Bank was declared responsible for a lethal decline in social
conditions. In 1989 the United Nations Children's Fund (UNI-
CEF) filed a complaint against the World Bank's Tunisian SAP,
which it blamed for a sudden rise in the country's infant mortality
rate.[7] UNICEF cited the World Bank's demands to liberalize Tuni-

---

[5] World Bank, *Report and Recommendation of the President of the International Bank for Reconstruction and Development to the Executive Directors on a Proposed Loan in an Amount Equivalent to U.S. $150.0 Million to the Republic of
Tunisia for an Agricultural Sector Adjustment Loan* (Washington D.C.: World
Bank, 1986), 16.

[6] Payne. "Economic Crisis and Policy Reform in the 1980s," 145.

[7] United Nations Children's Fund, *The State of the World's Children*
(New York: Oxford University Press, 1989).

sia's agrarian sector and reduce finances for social aid as the catalyst for increased food costs, decreased family wages, and a serious lack of access to medical services.[8] It became evident shortly after the 1986 plan to accelerate the economic liberalization of Tunisia that a positive outcome for Tunisia's poor would not materialize. Instead, the reforms ushered in an age that benefited the nation's affluent, especially those with political connections.[9] The outcomes of these structural adjustments were radically different from the benefits that the Bank had forecasted in 1986.

Not everyone was taken aback by the consequences of the World Bank's SAP for Tunisia. Public Health experts Kenneth Hill and Anne Pebley, who find a direct correlation between the World Bank's program and a decrease in Tunisian living standards, note that the final effects of the World Bank's moves to liberalize the Tunisian economy were predictable.[10] Hill and Pebley echo UNICEF's concerns that SAPs tend to make the impoverished even more vulnerable by implementing policies that focus on improving business sectors, like training hotel staff, while funding for social services, food subsidies, and medicine are allowed to falter.[11] The conditions that the World Bank helped the Tunisian government to create, which made nutritious food and medical services unaffordable, commonly raise child mortality rates in developing nations.[12] The priority that the World Bank placed on Tunisia's financial sectors is yet another example of how the engines behind corporate globalization can inadvertently facilitate the abusive patterns of cultural evolution that are common to agrarian societies.

Effects of Accelerated Liberalization on Wealth Discrepancy

In addition to the cuts in social spending, the land reforms that were instituted by the government resulted in a massive disparity in

---

[8] United Nations Children's Fund, *The State of the World's Children*.

[9] Payne. "Economic Crisis and Policy Reform in the 1980s," 144.

[10] Hill and Pebley, "Child Mortality in the Developing World," *Population and Development Review* 15, no. 4 (1989): 675.

[11] Hill and Pebley, "Child Mortality in the Developing World": 675.

[12] Hill and Pebley, "Child Mortality in the Developing World": 675-76.

land wealth. By 1989 the poorest forty-six percent held only eight percent of the country's arable lands while the wealthiest three percent enjoyed control of over thirty-five percent.[13] The increased inability of farmers to access land for personal use removed the insurance that subsistence farming can provide in hard times. King writes that Tunisia's land policy during the 1980s "…amounted to distributing the lion's share of privatized land to large landowners, while preserving a small percentage of farmland for small peasants to support their families."[14] Even when land did make it into the hands of poorer farmers, it did not usually take long before wealthier landholders found ways to reclaim the land. As poorer Tunisians soon discovered, farming in a market-based economy is far more expensive than subsistence agriculture. On top of the difficult task of gaining access to local markets, due to the closure of market cooperatives in the 1970s,[15] King notes that small-scale farmers found that export crops required "irrigation, refrigeration, and other resources that small farmers typically lack."[16] Due to such complications, land ownership became a luxury of the elite as traditional farming methods faded away.

Accelerated Liberalization and Cultural-Evolutionary Theory

The 1980s represented the solidification of the cultural changes that had been occurring over the previous three decades.[17] The reforms of privatization and liberalization that the Tunisian government had implemented with the help of IMF and World Bank SAPs helped the nation's ruling elite to achieve the cultural changes that they had wanted to create since independence in 1956. Through exploiting the political system and international financial

---

[13] Zaibet and Dunn, "Land Tenure, Farm Size, and Rural Market Participation": 835-36.

[14] King, *Liberalization Against Democracy*, 35.

[15] Ashford, "Succession and Social Change in Tunisia": 36.

[16] King, *Liberalization Against Democracy*, 117. The situation for small-scale farmers was made even more difficult as the patronage systems of the 1970s developed even further in the 1980s.

[17] And, for that matter, since the French became a colonial power in the region

interests, Bourguiba and his colleagues gained control over the productive capabilities of their country's agrarian sector by creating latifundia and consolidating wealth among the political elite and their supporters. Strengthened systems of patronage ensured that those who enjoyed large landholdings would use the land's productive power to further the Tunisian government's economic strategy to gain from increased international trade.

The events that led to increased privatization and economic liberalization in the 1980s reflect the evolutionary changes proposed by Lenski, Nolan, Johnson, Earle, and Plattner and offer evidence for their theories pertaining to the consolidation of land, the abandonment of subsistence farming, the concentration of wealth among an elite minority, and the strengthening of hierarchical systems.[18] These events in Tunisia offer further data to support the theory of recurring cultural-evolutionary patterns in developing agrarian societies. In line with the findings of cultural-evolutionary theorists, while an elite minority benefited from the country's increased interconnectedness with foreign markets, the majority of Tunisians carried the burden of these developments through increased financial vulnerability and decreased standards of living.

G. CONCLUSION

Although Tunisia's mixed-subsistence farmers experienced significant cultural changes as a result of French colonialism, the independent government of Tunisia brought more far-reaching trans-

---

[18] Johnson and Earle, *The Evolution of Human Societies: From Foraging Group to Agrarian State* (Stanford: Stanford University Press, 2001), 22-32. Nolan and Lenski, *Human Societies: An Introduction to Macrosociology*, 157-62. Plattner. "Markets and Marketplaces," in *Economic Anthropology* (ed. Plattner; Stanford: Stanford University Press, 2002), 180-81. As addressed through Anderson's work above, Tunisia had a powerful system of hierarchies before independence, revolving largely around the religious elite. In 1956 the old hierarchies were undermined and replaced by new ones that displayed less concern toward the needs of the nation's poor. It is also useful to note that these evolutionary events were not the result of a sudden increase in population growth, but technological advances and foreign financial interests, which often ignite the increased trade activity that leads to the same results.

formation, and at an accelerated pace. In the government's bid to
benefit from a new and expanding world system, and to the detriment of Tunisia's farming communities, the country's ruling elites
surrendered long-held religious beliefs and institutions in order to
restructure the agricultural sector for trade-based production. As
explained above, these changes were not entirely domestic. They
had been supported by several of corporate globalization's core
nations alongside the IMF and the World Bank, which had made
commitments to ensure that the abuses commonly associated with
increased international trade would be avoided. As the Tunisian
culture experienced rapid changes in its first three decades of independence, many of Tunisia's subsistence farmers who had enjoyed
access to land for generations were forced into wage labor or various degrees of unemployment.

Each phase of Tunisia's development reveals the government's motives behind modernizing Tunisia for involvement in
corporate globalization, and the obstinacy with which the recurring
patterns associated with such cultural-evolutionary patterns in
agrarian societies emerge. The socialist experiment of the 1960s
and the World Bank's efforts to improve conditions for Tunisia's
farmers in the 1980s not only failed to produce positive development for rural communities; these efforts actually worsened the
suffering of the people in these communities.

It must be made clear that the Tunisian farmers' experiences
are not those of the ancient Judean farmer. Eighth-century Judah
did not have an IMF or a World Bank, let alone an established
monetary system. Furthermore, Judah did not enjoy international
standards for human and worker's rights, nor could they have expected development aid from the Assyrians. The Tunisian situation
cannot reveal what happened in eighth-century Judah with certainty
or exactly what the prophetic authors who complained against land
ownership abuse were addressing. But because of the recurring
nature of cultural-evolutionary patterns and material evidence of
the presence of such a societal process in both Tunisia and eighth-
century Judah, the Tunisian experience can offer a point of reference from which to approach these prophetic writings and consider new interpretive possibilities. The following chapter will consider the voices of the oppressed and the oppressors in rural Tunisia to distinguish whether or not their perspectives can offer any

valuable insights for the interpretation of the land ownership abuses found in Isa. 5.8–10 and Mic. 2.1–2.

6 INSIGHTS TO BE GAINED THROUGH THE MODERN CONTEXT

A. INTRODUCTION

Biblical scholars who have employed cultural-evolutionary theory in their attempts to better discern the socio-economic contexts behind prophetic complaints against injustice that are attributed to eighth-century Judah, such as Chaney, Premnath, Gottwald, and Dearman, have been able to shed new light on these texts. Through considering the recurring patterns that take place as agrarian societies expand from subsistence-based farming to advanced political economies, which depend upon increased interregional trade and administrative centralization, new theories have developed as to what may have upset these prophetic authors. However, the social patterns and economic cycles proposed by cultural-evolutionary theorists are not phenomena of the past or those limited to the intellectual sphere, but are currently playing themselves out through the effects of corporate globalization. Agrarian societies throughout the world are being transformed by the modernization and economic liberalization of their agrarian and economic practices as they are brought into the vibrant international trade nexus of corporate globalization. Despite the existence of a modern-day example of this cultural-evolutionary phenomenon,[1] the potential value of considering this modern manifestation of cultural evolution, which has led to prosperity for some and grave levels of economic exploitation for others, has yet to be explored.

---

[1] Modelski. "World System Evolution," in *World System History: The Social Science of Long-Term Change* (eds. Denemark, Friedman, Gills and Moldeski; London: Routledge, 2000).

If biblical scholars are going to use cultural-evolutionary theory to interpret the intangible contexts of prophetic complaints attributed to the time of Judah's absorption into the Assyrian world system, it would seem logical to consider the evolutionary effects of a current world system on a modern, and thus tangible, agrarian society. Along with such an exercise, however, comes all of the very real problems and controversies that accompany studies based upon analogy, as described in Chapter Three; but through employing cultural-evolutionary theory, Chaney, Premnath, Dearman, and others have already crossed that line. As with the work of those who have used cultural-evolutionary theory to better understand prophetic complaints against injustice, it is important to remember that the use of a modern example cannot reveal the socio-economic contexts of eighth-century Judah. What a modern example can do is provide new insights and questions through which to interpret biblical material, archaeological data, and the interpretations of others.[2]

What Globalization and Tunisia Might Contribute

Apparent similarities between eighth-century Judah and modern Tunisia, such as religious-based land ownership systems, erratic weather conditions, and types of crops, have been explored above. One of the important differences between these two agrarian societies is that modern Tunisia offers the actual voices of farmers who have been affected by the negative recurring patterns that are commonly associated with periods of increased population growth and heightened trade activity. The protests of Tunisian farmers who have lost their land and the livelihood that they had once enjoyed as mixed-subsistence farmers may help to shed some light on the prophetic complaints found in Isa. 5.8–10 and Mic. 2.1–2, as

---

[2] David Clines coined the term "metacommentary" for the interpretation of other biblical commentator's material, which is a very important exercize. For more on metacommentary and its importance, see Clines, D.J.A. "Metacommentating Amos," in Interested Parties: The Ideology and Readers of the Hebrew Bible (ed. Cheryl Exum, JSOTSS; Sheffield: Sheffield Academic Press) 1995.

they appear to address similar economic events. A close examination of these issues may be able to produce a better understanding of the plight of the Judean farmer and the prophetic context as new avenues through which to approach these texts are opened.

Naturally, twentieth-century CE Tunisia and eighth-century BCE Judah are two very different societies. Modern Tunisia was born out of French colonialism into a world that was trying to repair international relations at the end of a devastating war and a holocaust that had brought human rights issues to the forefront of human consciousness, something that would have not been taken into consideration in the eighth century BCE. Additionally, technological advances such as refrigeration and efficient trans-continental transportation make the modern trading environment vastly different than that of the eighth-century context. Despite these very important differences, which must be acknowledged and used with caution, the shared similarities provide a basis for comparison.

As is the case in any agrarian society, the central productive unit of the Tunisian economy in the 1950s was arable land. As a result, the acquisition of land that farmers had worked on for generations became a key step in gaining control of the Tunisian economy. The priority given to this task is evidenced in the speed with which Tunisia's newly appointed rulers worked to further French efforts at the consolidation and the modernization of Tunisia's agrarian sector, as detailed in the previous chapter. The consequences of these efforts follow the recurring societal patterns that are found in agrarian societies as they begin to rely less on subsistence agriculture in favor of trade-friendly strategies, shifting the economy's priorities from the wellbeing of farmers toward the wellbeing of markets.[3]

Whereas political and economic elites will often choose from a variety of methods to seize and consolidate land, including land reform schemes, debt and foreclosure, or the more direct approach

---

[3] Fried, *The Evolution of Political Society* (New York: Random House, 1967), 186. Sanderson, *The Evolution of Human Sociality: A Darwinian Conflict Perspective* (Lanham, Maryland: Rowman & Littlefield Publishers, 2001), 300-01.

of physical coercion,[4] the Tunisian elite practiced a variety of these methods. As Tunisia's arable lands became more tightly concentrated under the control of a powerful minority, many Tunisian farmers suffered from unemployment,[5] displacement,[6] and fatal levels of poverty.[7] As has been experienced by other agrarian societies,[8] the cultural changes that resulted from latifundialization were solidified as the Tunisian elite ensured that the lands that they had seized remained under their control, particularly in the 1970s.[9] This bleak outcome for the majority of Tunisian farmers connects with the recurring patterns found in cultural-evolutionary theory and, in turn, with Chaney's and Premnath's cultural-evolutionary-based reconstruction of the socio-economic realities underlying Isa. 5.8–10 and Mic. 2.1–2. Other points of connection between Tunisia and ancient Judah include the relatively arid climates that these two agrarian societies share and a perceived offence against religious principles through the seizure of land: in the Tunisian context the religious *habous* land endowments; and in the Judean context, the divine rage against the land seizures as expressed by the authors of Isa. 5.9–10 and Mic. 2.3–4.

---

[4] Lenski, *Power and Privilege: A Theory of Social Stratification* (New York: McGraw-Hill Book Company, 1966), 220.

[5] Anderson, *The State and Social Transformation in Tunisia and Libya: 1830-1980* (Princeton: Princeton University Press, 1986), 242.

[6] Hopkins, "Tunisia: An Open and Shut Case," *Social Problems* 28, no. 4, Development Processes and Problems (1981): 386.

[7] United Nations Children's Fund, *The State of the World's Children* (New York: Oxford University Press, 1989).

[8] Lenski, *Power and Privilege*, 220. Zaccagnini, "The Price of Fields at Nuzi," *Journal of the Economic and Social History of the Orient* 22, no. 1 (1979): 19-20. Mamdani. "Uganda: Contradictions in the IMF Programme and Perspective," in *The IMF and the South: The Social Impact of Crisis and Adjustment* (ed. Ghai; London: Zed Books Ltd., 1991), 201-03. Pastor and Wise, "State Policy, Distribution and Neoliberal Reform in Mexico," *Journal of Latin American Studies* 29, no. 2 (1997): 441-42.

[9] Zaibet and Dunn, "Land Tenure, Farm Size, and Rural Market Participation in Developing Countries: The Case of the Tunisian Olive Sector," *Economic Development and Cultural Change* 46, no. 4 (1998): 834.

A Useful Discrepancy

Aside from offering the voice of suffering ferments, another important difference between the Tunisian example and interpretations of the events that took place in eighth-century Judah, as addressed in the preceding chapters, is that the world system, into which Tunisia entered was founded on principles of equitable growth and the alleviation of suffering among the vulnerable. Due to a realization among the architects of the current world system, that uneven growth and poverty often lead to war and civil unrest, the International Monetary Fund and the World Bank were designed, in part, to regulate trade and ensure that less developed areas of the world could benefit from a powerful new world system.[10] In stark contrast to this egalitarian vision for corporate globalization, the Assyrians would have perceived the world system into which Judah was absorbed as a means to increase Assyrian power and wealth through military and economic domination, nothing more.[11] The wellbeing of the Assyrian-conquered territories, vassal states, and even their foreign trading partners would not have been of concern to the expanding empire.[12]

---

[10] Kuhn, "United Nations Monetary Conference and the Immunity of International Agencies," *The American Journal of International Law* 38, no. 4 (1944): 663. Smithies, "The International Bank For Reconstruction and Development," *The American Economic Review* 43, no. 4 (1944): 790-91.

[11] This contrast in no way denies the realities of corporate globalization and the attitudes of its core states, only that institutions were created and have attempted to carry out protections for the world's most vulnerable people. Authors such as Noam Chomsky have written extensively on the use of American and western military power, from cracking down on socialist movements in Latin America to securing oil interests in the Middle East, to ensure that trade is conducted in a way that increases the strength of western powers. See Chomsky, *Hegemony or Survival: America's Quest for Global Dominance* (London: Hamish Hamilton, 2003).

[12] Schloen, *The House of the Father as Fact and Symbol: Patrimonialism in Ugarit and the Ancient Near East* (2; ed. Schloen; Winona Lake, IN: Eisenbrauns, 2001), 146. Grayson, *Assyrian Rulers of the Early First Millennium BC. II, (858-745 BC)* (vol. 3; Toronto: University of Toronto Press, 1996), 60, 163, 187. Oppenheim. "Babylonian and Assyrian Historical Texts," in *Ancient Near Eastern Texts Relating to the Old Testament* (ed. Pritchard; Princeton: Princeton University Press, 1969), 287.

Such discrepancies between these modern and ancient contexts could be seen as an indication that little is to be gained from using the consequences of corporate globalization in biblical studies. If the purpose of this thesis was to create a definitive historical picture of the eighth-century Judean socio-historical context, such a criticism would be merited. However, the intent here is to use the effects of corporate globalization as an interpretive tool, to illuminate valuable similarities and contrasts that can give insight into the ancient context. For example, if a world system organized around principles of human rights and equitable growth cannot protect modern farmers from land exploitation and famines caused by humans, it is unlikely that Judean farmers who labored within a world system that was openly centered upon exploitation would have been spared from the recurring patterns of injustice that tend to accompany heightened trade activity.

Although various characteristics of Tunisia's transformation in the twentieth century are not relevant to the exploration of the Judean experience,[13] two primary contextual themes will be addressed in detail below: the displacement of agriculturalists who relied on traditional methods of subsistence farming and the dismantling of a religious-based system of land management.[14]

---

[13] Several of these irrelevant characteristics will be addressed in detail in the following chapter.

[14] The issue of overturning religious land-tenure systems is one that deserves a thesis in and of itself, but for the sake of brevity will be addressed as but a single section within this chapter.

B. THE VOICES OF THE OPPRESSED

It is important to reiterate that the purpose of this chapter, and this book as a whole, is not to suggest that Tunisian and Judean farmers share identical experiences as a result of their respective societies' entrances into different world systems; the cultural and economic realities of these two agrarian societies are vastly different, and such discrepancies must be respected. At the same time, however, the potential similarities between these two societies should not be discarded. Since corporate globalization is not a unique phenomenon but the most recent stage of world systems evolution,[1] and the entrance into world systems has inflicted a recurring set of exploitative patterns upon subsistence farmers that traverse both time and culture,[2] the effects of these patterns stemming from corporate globalization can be used as an interpretive tool for understanding injustice attributed to such transitional periods in the ancient world.[3] Although the tools and methods used in modern trade may be vastly different from those of the first millennium BCE, the motivations of elites and the wounds that they inflict upon subsistence farmers appear to dovetail.

---

[1] Modelski. "World System Evolution."

[2] Goodfellow. "The Applicability of Economic Theory to So-Called Primitive Communities," in *Economic Anthropology: Readings in Theory and Analysis* eds. LeClair and Schneider; New York: Holt, Rinehard, and Winston, 1968), 57. Nolan and Lenski, *Human Societies: An Introduction to Macrosociology* (Boulder: Paradigm Publishers, 2004), 149-50. Berdan. "Trade and Markets in Precapitalist States," in *Economic Anthropology* (ed. Plattner; Stanford: Stanford University Press, 1989), 80. Woods. "The Challenge to International Institutions," in *The Political Economy of Globalization* (ed. Woods; New York: St. Martin's Press, 2000). Bell. "The Social Relations of Property and Efficiency," in *Property in Economic Context* eds. Hunt and Gilman; Oxford: University Press of America, Inc., 1998), 38-41.

[3] These could include the Assyrian, Babylonian, Persian, Hellenistic, or Roman eras.

Displacement of Subsistence Farmers and Altered Social Relations

The lack of an extra-biblical benchmark for land-tenure abuse in eighth-century Judah may be the reason that little variation can be found in commentators' interpretations of the socio-economic contexts behind Isa. 5.8–10 and Mic. 2.1–2. Examining the experience of displacement among Tunisian farmers might provide a useful point of reference outside of the biblical narrative with which to consider the identities of the victims and perpetrators in these prophetic texts and the consequences of their actions.

The initial Tunisian land reforms of the 1950s that had an immediate effect on longstanding and religious-based systems of land tenure and land management displaced a large segment of the Tunisian population. The land reforms that followed over the following four decades may not have dismantled religious land institutions,[4] but they provoked considerable anger and appear to reflect elements of the accusations found in Isa. 5.8–10 and Mic. 2.1–2. Two issues that will be addressed in this section are increased social stratification and the eviction of farmers from their land. Both of these events represent a change in the way that people interact with one another, an important societal issue that is not widely discussed in biblical commentary on land ownership abuse in ancient Judah.

The nature of Judean social relations, as pertaining to the issue of land ownership abuse, is indirectly referred to in Chaney's and Premnath's depictions of the Judean elites'[5] callous disregard for the needs of Judean subsistence farmers. This interpretation presents two classes in conflict as one hoards the spoils of trade while the other is left to suffer either as a disenfranchised member of society or as a wage-laborer for the affluent.[6] Through considering

---

[4] After the 1950s there were not any religious land endowments left to dismantle.

[5] Or, callous *merchants* as tends to be found in more traditional biblical commentary.

[6] Chaney, "Whose Sour Grapes? The Addressees of Isaiah 5:1-7 in the Light of Political Economy," in *The Social World of the Hebrew Bible: Twenty-Five Years of the Social Sciences in the Academy* eds. Simkins and Cook; *Semeia*, ed. Brenner; Atlanta: Society of Biblical Literature, 1999), 109.

the unfolding of such events in the modern example of Tunisia, a more complex situation is revealed.

It is important to reiterate that neither Tunisia nor Judah enjoyed a utopian existence before entering into their respective world systems. It is highly unlikely that there was ever a golden age of subsistence farming in which agrarian workers had all that they needed to live in an unfettered paradise, free of hunger and exploitation until forces of greed and self-interest entered into the equation and ruined everything. Although it is true that subsistence-based cultures, by their nature, tend to enjoy a more cooperative ethos than societies that are centered on a strong political economy, which is hierarchical and elitist in its nature,[7] to suggest that subsistence societies are free of societal ills, such as exploitation, conflict, famine, and disease, would be naïve. The development of a political economy in an agrarian society does not introduce such societal problems; it institutionalizes them, causing members to become more individualistic as they compete to benefit from new economic opportunities; as a result, hierarchies become reinforced.[8] Such developments tend to change the way that members of a society interact with one another. The disregard that the protagonists of Isa. 5.8 and Mic. 2.1–2 display toward the needs of their victims, when considered through the lens of cultural-evolutionary theory, may indicate such a common by-product of a developing political economy: a shift in traditional norms pertaining to social interaction.[9]

Kissane, *The Book of Isaiah: Translated from a Critically Revised Hebrew Text with Commentary* (2vols.; vol. 1; Dublin: Browne and Nolan Limited, 1941), 57.

[7] Nolan and Lenski, *Human Societies*, 227.

[8] Nolan and Lenski, *Human Societies*, 149. This is particularly the case in instances of increased population, as found in eighth-century Judah (Johnson and Earle, *The Evolution of Human Societies: From Foraging Group to Agrarian State* [Stanford: Stanford University Press, 2001], 13-14).

[9] Knapp. "Copper Production and Eastern Mediterranean Trade: The Rise of Complex Society in Cyprus," in *Sate and Society: The Emergence and Development of Social Hierarchy and Political Centralization* eds. Gledhill, Bender and Larsen; London: Unwin Hyman, 1988), 157. Rappaport, "The Sacred

Abuses and changed relations are common as agrarian communities begin to abandon traditional subsistence practices for more centralized economic strategies, but a lack of archaeological and literary evidence makes it difficult to determine to what degree, if any, the socio-economic changes of the late eighth century and early seventh century BCE affected the social relations of the inhabitants of Judah. In the case of twentieth-century CE Tunisia, however, there is a clear connection between shifting land management and ownership strategies and the way that Tunisians interacted with one another. Although the Tunisian example cannot reconstruct the realities of eighth-century Judah, it may allow what evidence pertaining to eighth-century Judah that does exist to be read in a different light.

Changing Attitudes Toward the Tunisian Poor

The effects of social exclusion, as a result of corporate globalization, are often addressed on an international level: how one nation becomes excluded as another enjoys the benefits of trade. The development of systems of social exclusion within a particular state, however, is equally damaging. Manuel Castells notes that the "black holes" of social exclusion that have been generated around the world by the development projects of the IMF and World Bank have not only prevented entire *countries* from benefiting from new technologies and trade, but also *communities* within nations as wealthy as the United States or Great Britain.[10] Such black holes formed within Tunisia as the country became more involved in corporate globalization and as Tunisia adopted the neoliberal policies that were promoted by the IMF and the World Bank.

Tunisia's ambition to become an active member of the global economic community led to rapid cultural changes, as is common when agrarian societies become more dependent upon political economies. Nolan and Lenski explain this phenomenon, noting that as greater revenue is generated to afford the import of luxury

---

in Human Evolution," *Annual Review of Ecology and Systematics* 2, (1971), 37-39.

   [10] Castells, *End of Millennium* (3vols.; vol. 3; Oxford: Blackwell Publishers, 2000), 164-8.

goods, societies tend to lose their sense of common purpose, which had previously been facilitated by subsistence strategies and their extended kin systems.[11] As economic strategies become more market-oriented in Tunisia, the communal sentiments experienced under the previous economic model become eclipsed by opportunism as individualism, rationalism, and competition become more prevalent.[12] Consequently, Tunisia experienced heightened social stratification as new systems of patronage developed that were centered on market opportunism rather than the country's traditional religious hierarchies.[13] The resulting decline in institutional piety meant that the Tunisia's poor lost many of the charitable resources upon which they had relied for centuries. One example of this post-independence shift and the opportunism that followed is found in the government's abolition of the Muslim-based *habous* land endowments in 1956. However, this takeover of over one-fifth of Tunisia's arable lands[14] did not only affect the changing state of relations between the country's political and religious power structures, as addressed in Chapter Five, it also had significant long-term effects on how people from varying social classes interacted with one another.

Considering the evolutionary connections between Judah and Tunisia, the recorded experiences of Tunisian farmers provide a useful starting point for exploring Tunisia's, and the greater phenomenon of corporate globalization's, potential as an interpretive model. Although the voices of those affected by modern globalization cannot resurrect the voices of disaffected farmers in eighth-century Judah, they may provide a useful means for assessing current assumptions about the experience of Judean farmers, inspire new theories that have not yet been considered, and provide fresh new ways of looking at the prophetic account. The following sec-

---

[11] Nolan and Lenski, *Human Societies*, 149.

[12] Again, these developments dovetail with periods of cultural evolution (Nolan and Lenski, *Human Societies*, 149).

[13] Boulby, "The Islamic Challenge: Tunisia Since Independence," *Third World Quarterly* 10, no. 2, Islam & Politics (1988): 592-96.

[14] Anderson, *The State and Social Transformation in Tunisia and Libya*, 235.

tion will consider the perspectives of deeply impoverished Tunisian peasants, an educated middle peasant, and members of the wealthy elite.

The Poorest of the Poor

One voice that directly addresses the economic consequences of losing traditional agrarian methods to market-driven reforms, and the subsequent changes in intra-community relationships, belongs to an elderly small-scale farmer named Majoub. Majoub witnessed a definite shift in intra-community relations in the northern town of Tebourba, which lies about twenty miles west from the capital city of Tunis, as his country experienced the various land reforms that took place between 1956 and the 1990s.[15] Whereas the wealthy citizens of Tebourba had once been interested participants in a "moral economy," they became more interested in engaging in competitive practices as new economic opportunities presented themselves.[16] In an interview with Stephen King, Majoub claimed that

> ...in the past the rich were kind. If they knew someone did not have clothes and food, then they would go find them to help them out. At harvest time, everyone helped out. Sometimes the rich would give you a piece of land and allow you to use their tractors.[17]

Although not all wealthy individuals in Tebourba would necessarily act so benevolently, this type of communal approach to land and labor reflects the common sense of purpose that is often found in subsistence-based economies.[18]

As Tunisia's economic strategies became more focused on the demands of global markets and generating capital, however, attitudes toward land management and the wellbeing of the poor began to change among the wealthier citizens of Tebourba. Pining for

---

[15] King, *Liberalization Against Democracy: The Local Politics of Economic Reform in Tunisia* (Bloomington: Indiana University Press, 2003), 86-87.

[16] King, *Liberalization Against Democracy*, 86.

[17] King, *Liberalization Against Democracy*, 86-87.

[18] Nolan and Lenski, *Human Societies*, 149.

the communal spirit that Majoub had enjoyed earlier in his life,
Majoub lamented,

> Times have changed. Morality has changed. The rich don't feel
> anything for the needy. They even fear the poor. They don't
> want the poor living near them or having land near them be-
> cause they will ask for things. They don't even want the poor
> to raise a chicken near them because it would sneak on their
> land. Hajj Naouar [a wealthy land owner], who lives next door,
> wants us all to move. His workers only work the land [and do
> not farm for themselves].[19] He said, 'Don't raise your animals
> and let them eat my grass.' Some of his workers had to sell
> their cows and look for other work. All he does is give the za-
> kat.[20] It's probably the full one-tenth, but that's it.

> I can't understand why the government didn't help the
> poor with the land. A man and his family can live on five hec-
> tares. Small farmers wanted a little land to live on. It's mainly
> who you know. Connections are very important around here.
> Even in agriculture, you can hardly get a job without knowing
> somebody.[21]

Bearing in mind that Majoub provides but a single perspective, several of the issues that he addresses could be useful to scholars that
are trying to piece together the socio-economic contexts that lay
behind prophetic complaints against land ownership abuse in prophetic literature. Four issues to which this information may contribute are those of 1) a moral change among the wealthy, 2) a desire among elites to live away from poorer farmers, 3) the displacement of farmers from their lands and livelihoods, and 4) altered approaches to religious practice.

---

[19] Brackets belong to King.

[20] Arabic for "alms for the poor": part of a Muslim's charitable obligation.

[21] King, *Liberalization Against Democracy*, 86-87.

Intra-Community Abuse

Majoub's observation of a shift in moral behavior among wealthier
Tunisians as a result of changing economic priorities could provide
new avenues through which biblical scholars might approach prophetic complaints against injustice. Mays, Smith, and Alfaro's
commentaries on Mic. 2.1–2 and Kissane, Herbert, and Kaiser's
commentaries on Isa. 5.8–10 present characters that lack the com-
plexities that are prevalent in instances economic exploitation.
These more traditional commentaries portray an innocent group of
farmers who are oppressed by the actions of a wealthy class, be
they merchants or political figures, who are consumed by their
greed; neither the victims nor the villains are very multi-
dimensional. Kissane's reference to the "rapacity of the rich"[22] and
Alfaro's vision of a family of "professional land-grabbers" that
seized land from the poor[23] suggest that Judean farmers had to
contend with people who were inherently nasty. These commentaries present a class of amoral individuals who had been removed
from the daily activities of the "poor" until the point at which they
began to seize land from other people. In the case of Mic. 2.1–2,
Francis Andersen and David Noel Freedman suggest that "the
prophet [was] exposing typical behavior on the part of these people"[24] Andersen and Freedman's view of "typical behavior" among
"these people" sums up a common view that these latifundialists
were bad by their very nature. If the perpetrators of these injustices
were of such a naturally unscrupulous disposition, their actions
against the rights of vulnerable Judeans would have been expected.
Looking at the perpetrators of passages like Mic. 2.1–2 through the
lens of Majoub's experience offers an interesting contextual consideration. If increased economic opportunities can have an effect
on people's moral behavior, causing them to abuse those whom
they previously assisted,[25] it is worth contemplating the possibility

---

[22] Kissane, *The Book of Isaiah*, 57.

[23] Alfaro, *Justice and Loyalty: A Commentary on the Book of Micah.* (Grand
Rapids: Eerdmans, 1989), 22.

[24] Andersen and Freedman, *Micah* (24E; eds. Albright and Freedman;
New York: Doubleday, 2000), 274.

[25] As Nolan and Lenski suggest and to which Majoub attests

that there is an element of personal betrayal in the accusations being made by the authors of Isa. 5.8 and Mic. 2.1–2 that has not been widely considered.

Personal Betrayal

The businessmen and merchants referred to in Smith and Kaiser's commentaries,[26] as well as the urban elites that Chaney offers,[27] all appear to exist outside of the victims' immediate subsistence community. While Majoub's statements about his life in Tebourba cannot address the Judean experience directly, when considered in the context of behavioral changes that commonly coincide with agricultural intensification, it raises questions as to whether the targets of accusations in Isa. 5.8 and Mic. 2.1–2 may have been active, and even positive, members of their victims' communities at one time. Perhaps those upon whom Judean subsistence farmers had relied and trusted in difficult times were the same people who took their land for personal gain. This is not to suggest that the economic drive that led to these abuses did not originate in urban centers like Jerusalem and Lachish, but that a developing political economy may have led to oppression from within the communities of more rural regions rather than being inflicted upon them by outsiders. The possibility of such a dynamic involving shifting moral climates in Isa. 5.8–10 and Mic. 2.1–2 offers a new dimension to current understandings of the socio-economic context behind these passages.[28]

---

[26] Smith, *Micah - Malachi* (eds. Hubbard, Barker, Watts and Martin; 58 vols.; vol. 32; Waco: Word Books, 1984), 24. Kaiser, *Isaiah 1-12: A Commentary* (London: SCM Press LTD, 1972), 65.

[27] Chaney, "Whose Sour Grapes?," 107. Chaney, "Bitter Bounty: The Dynamics of Political Economy Critiqued by the Eighth-Century Prophets," in *Reformed Faith and Economics* (ed. Stivers; Lanham: University Press of America, 1989), 24.

[28] Premnath's presentation of "wealthy landowners" or "landed elite" as the target of prophetic anger would fit better into such an intra-community conflict, if this was indeed the case. See Premnath, *Eighth Century Prophets: A Social Analysis* (St. Louis: Chalice, 2003), 101-02, 105-06. That being acknowledged, Premnath appears to also consider these

Displacement

Another issue that may be addressed by Majoub's statement is that of physical displacement. His claim that the wealthy landowners in his community no longer wanted the poor to live near them "because they will ask for things" and their chickens might sneak onto the wealthy landholders' land[29] might help to address questions surrounding the claim in Isa. 5.8 that the Judean latifundialists הושבתם לבדכם בקרב הארץ.[30] Perhaps like Hajj Naouar, and as is common among elites in developing agrarian societies,[31] wealthy Judean landowners wanted to keep poorer farmers away from their property; rather than simply seizing land, they worked to ensure that they were the sole benefactors of the land's productive capabilities. Hajj Naouar's attitude toward living near the poor, in connection with the societal patterns upon which Premnath interprets Isa. 5.8's economic context, could be used to add credence to his theory that the prophetic authors' use of the word מקום refers to the disappearance of landholdings from the Judean countryside in eighth-century Judah.[32] Additionally, whereas Premnath references Hans Wildberger's theory that the words בקרב הארץ indicate that Judean latifundialists lived alone in urban centres,[34] Majoub's modern account highlights the economic reasons as to why latifundialists would want to drive disenfranchised farmers out of the countryside instead.[35]

Hajj Naouar's desire to keep only a few workers could also address John Holladay and William Domeris' claims that large es-

---

wealthy landowners to have been members of Judah's ruing elite (Premnath, *Eighth Century Prophets: A Social Analysis*, 102).

[29] King, *Liberalization Against Democracy*, 87.

[30] "...were made to live alone in the midst of the land."

[31] Lenski, *Power and Privilege*, 220.

[32] Premnath, *Eighth Century Prophets: A Social Analysis*, 101.

[33] "...in the midst of the land."

[34] Wildberger, *Isaiah: A Commentary* (trans. Trapp; 3 vols.; vol. 1; Minneapolis: Fortress Press, 1991), 198. Premnath, *Eighth Century Prophets: A Social Analysis*, 102.

[35] There are several ancient and modern examples of affluent people's desire to live separately from the poor and to drive them out of the land, from the biblical account in Job 31 to modern gated communities.

tates did not develop in Judah until the Persian period, at the earliest, based on an absence of workers' barracks before that time.[36] Domeris argues that if large estates had been created prior to the Persian period, evidence of barracks to house the workers would be expected.[37] However, considering Majoub's claim that wealthy landowners in Tunisia wanted to keep poorer peasants away and the number of employees to a minimum, it appears that barracks are not always required as land is consolidated. Similar attitudes among eighth-century Judean latifundialists would not be implausible, considering that two of Judah's main exportable crops, grapes and olives, demand very little labor. David Hopkins writes that, once established, grape vines and olive orchards "are stable for many years and yield their produce with a minimum of care," and "crop producing tasks can be undertaken fairly leisurely and in an extensive rather than intensive manner."[38] If small estates were consolidated for the creation of wealth, whether for the state or for private individuals, it would not make sense for latifundialists to employ large numbers of workers. Such an analogical hypothesis does not require modern economic paradigms to be forced on the ancient world, as Morris Silver has been accused of,[39] but simply the question "what benefit would latifundialists gain by employing

---

[36] Holladay. "The Kingdoms of Israel and Judah: Political and Economic Centralization in the Iron IIa-b (ca. 1000-750 BCE)," in *The Archaeology of Society in the Holy Land* (ed. Levy; London: Leicester University Press, 1998), 392-93. Domeris, *Touching the Heart of God: The Social Construction of Poverty Among Biblical Peasants* (466; eds. Camp and Mein; London: T&T Clark, 2007), 133-34.

[37] Domeris, *Touching the Heart of God*, 134. Despite the further detail that Domeris gives, this appears to be a rather weak basis from which to argue that there were no large estates prior to the Persian period. Why would barracks be so essential? If farmers had not been physically displaced, could they not have lived in their former homes and worked the fields? Would there be a need to concentrate them in one place at night? Additionally, Domeris appears to negate his argument by claiming that the pressures brought about by Assyrian tribute demands led to the creation of state vineyards (Domeris, *Touching the Heart of God*, 108).

[38] Hopkins, *The Highlands of Canaan: Agricultural Life in the Early Iron Age* (ed. Flanagan; vol. 3; Sheffield: Almond, 1985), 227.

[39] Chaney, "Bitter Bounty," 19.

more workers than necessary," especially if crops are being cultivated for profit? Again, although the Tunisian example cannot offer historical proof as to what happened in eighth-century Judah,
this modern case study provides a base through which to both explore assumptions such as those of Domeris and Holladay, and
develop new interpretations of the prophetic texts. The actions of
Hajj Naouar, as represented through Majoub's account, help to
raise the important points that changing economic conditions can
lead to changes in social relations and that it is not in the interest of
latifundialists to hire a lot of employees and to keep many peasants
on or near their land.

Attitudes toward displacement in Tunisia might also provide a
useful point from which to explore Chaney's claim that "the injustice of [the farmers'] loss of hereditary lands and livelihood was
aggravated by a cruel irony – many now worked land that had been
in their families for generations, but they worked it as landless day
laborers."[40] Not only does the Tunisian experience provide an example of some displaced farmers becoming wage laborers as a consequence of latifundialization, but it also highlights that not all of
those who lose their land find such work. Again, a latifundialist's
desire to increase profits is likely to lead to displacement rather
than employment.

Diminished Sense of Piety Amongst the Elite

Connected to the notion that new economic goals had weakened
what Majoub refers to as a "moral economy" is an apparent change
in religious practice among wealthy individuals. Addressing Hajj
Naouar's almsgiving habits, Majoub claims, in his comparisons between times past and present, that the wealthy farmers only give
the zakat, and although "it's probably the full one-tenth, but that's
it."[41] Majoub's dissatisfaction at the fact that Hajj Naouar *only* gives
the minimum requirement suggests that greater charitable contributions had been expected in the past. Perhaps the gift-giving expectations that Majoub has for the wealthy are unrealistic, but considering his apparent recollection of a time when the affluent gave

---

[40] Chaney, "Whose Sour Grapes?": 109.
[41] King, *Liberalization Against Democracy*, 87.

willingly to the poor, it could be that his dissatisfaction reflects a growing disregard for religious-based charitable giving and a personal sense of religious duty among community leaders, where giving the bare minimum becomes enough. Such a shift would reflect the individualistic attitudes that accompany periods of economic intensification and demonstrate the way religious principles often bend to accommodate a society's economic transformations.[42]

Considering these sorts of changes in piety, the example of Hajj Naouar might provide insight into the righteous anger expressed in Isa. 5.8–10 and Mic. 2.2–4. According to Gottwald, "With the change of political and economic forms [in the eighth century] came the evolving forms of ideology and religion."[43] The Tunisian context might provide a useful analogy through which Gottwald could explore and strengthen this theory, and consider the argument that the prophetic authors who wrote against economic injustice played a conservative role in Judean society rather than offering a radical new approach.

Although voices like Majoub's do not speak for Judean farmers, the voice of this impoverished Tunisian farmer, who witnessed the series of changes that Tunisia experienced since independence, raises important questions and provides a fresh perspective through which to view biblical texts and previous interpretations. In Tunisia, patron-client relations that had once been cordial became soured as emphasis on revenue production became intensified. The portrayal of a two-dimensional situation with wealthy urbanites on one side and poor farmers on the other, as presented in several commentaries on Isa. 5.8–10 and Mic. 2.1–2, is called into question by such a context. Another challenge to the commonly held rich-versus-poor motif in Isa. 5.8–10 and Mic. 2.1–2 comes from the fact that it is not always the poor who suffer from the effects of latifundialization.

---

[42] Bayly. "'Archaic' and 'Modern' Globalization in the Eurasian and African Arena: c. 1750-1850," in *Globalization in World History* (ed. Hopkins; London: Pimlico, 2002), 52-53.

[43] Gottwald, *The Hebrew Bible in Its Social World and in Ours* (Atlanta: Scholars Press, 1993), 182-85.

Observations of an Educated Peasant

Tunisia's poorest citizens were not the only ones who suffered as their country attempted to benefit from corporate globalization. Blaming both the government and Tebourba's economic elite for hardship in his community, an educated peasant named Hadi also suffered from the centralization of Tunisia's agrarian sector and the affiliated latifundialist policies.[44] Rather than fostering the fair and equitable growth that the World Bank had claimed that their SAPs would secure,[45] Hadi argues that government policies continually ensured that all arable lands would become consolidated under the control of local elites. He explained to King that "small farmers are being run out of farming. The government doesn't want to divide the land into small parts. They are distributing it hundreds of hectares at a time, so the poor can't afford it."[46] Hadi's claims do not only address the situation in Tebourba, but what has been occurring across the country as the government worked to place land under the control of the country's ruling and economic elite as the country's small-scale farmers became disfranchised.[47] Hadi's accusations address some of the contextual theories that have been proposed in relation to Isa. 5.8–10 and Mic. 2.1–2.[48]

---

[44] King, *Liberalization Against Democracy*, 87.

[45] World Bank, *Report and Recommendation of the President of the International Bank for Reconstruction and Development to the Executive Directors on a Proposed Loan in an Amount Equivalent to U.S. $150.0 Million to the Republic of Tunisia for an Agricultural Sector Adjustment Loan* (Washington D.C.: World Bank, 1986), 16.

[46] King, *Liberalization Against Democracy*, 87.

[47] Anderson, *The State and Social Transformation in Tunisia and Libya*, 242. Payne. "Economic Crisis and Policy Reform in the 1980s," in *Polity and Society in Contemporary North Africa* (eds. Zartman and Habeeb; Boulder: Westview, 1993), 144. Ashford, "Succession and Social Change in Tunisia," *International Journal of Middle East Studies* 4, no. 1 (1973): 36. King, *Liberalization Against Democracy*, 38.

[48] It is important to reiterate that although Hadi's experience does not directly address the experiences of subsistence farmers in the eighth-century Judah, his insights may provide a useful interpretive tool. Considering that ruling elites tend to concentrate wealth among their supporters, as was common in Assyria, and such activities are especially prevalent during periods of increased trade, the scenario that Hadi describes can

Patronage and Displacement

The scenario that Hadi presents reiterates some of the issues that were addressed by Majoub, such as the physical and economic displacement of peasants. The ruling elites' bid to centralize the productive capabilities of Tunisian agriculture by allocating large plots of farmland to their supporters represents an ancient strategy for solidifying control over land management.[49] This modern example could serve as an analogy for John Hayes, Stuart Irvine, Leslie Hoppe, and Blenkinsopp's theories that the primary actors in Isa. 5.8 were members of the political elite who wanted to gain control over Judah's productive potential.[50] Considering the socio-economic implications of this modern instance of injustice could also help to expand Hoppe's theory that the prophets decried such a system of latifundialization "because of its blatant, state-administered injustice."[51]

The troubles that Hadi refers to in his interview with King are realized in the plight of a fifty-two-year-old peasant named Ibrahim, a second-generation farmer who rents land in Tebourba. King writes that Ibrahim's life "is a constant search for the funds to rent more land and pay for irrigation, but he is continually priced out of the market... In a matter of a few years the rent of his two hectares

---

work as starting point from which to consider the prophetic complaints and commentators' interpretations.

[49] Payne. "Economic Crisis and Policy Reform in the 1980s," 144. Postgate ed. *Neo-Assyrian Royal Grants and Degrees* (ed., *Studia Pohl: Series Maior. Dissertationes Scientificae de Rebus Orientis Antiqui*; Rome: Pontifical Biblical Institute, 1969), 9-16. Lenski, *Power and Privilege*, 220.

[50] Hayes and Irvine. "The Kingdoms of Israel and Judah: Political and Economic Centralization in Iron IIA-B (ca. 1000-750 BCE)," in *The Archaeology of Society in the Holy Land* (ed. Levy; New York: Facts on File, 1995), 103. Hoppe, *There Shall Be No Poor Among You* (Nashville: Abingdon Press, 2004), 11. Blenkinsopp, *Isaiah 1-39* (19; eds. Albright and Freedman; New York: Doubleday, 2000), 211. While Chaney also points to members of Judah's political establishment as the instigators in Isa. 5.8 and Mic. 2.2, he places blame on wealthy individuals as well (Chaney, "Bitter Bounty," 24. Chaney, "Whose Sour Grapes?," 107).

[51] Hoppe, *There Shall Be No Poor Among You*, 11.

has risen from 150 to 500 dinars a year."[52] Such levels of rent inflation make it nearly impossible to survive as a small-scale farmer.
Frustrated with his predicament, Ibrahim told King, "Privatization
is bad for small farmers and the poor because we aren't getting
anything. There are a lot more unemployed people and some people are leaving Tebourba completely. They can't make it here."[53]
Although Ibrahim's lament addresses a twentieth-century economic
context, it provides a key example of one of the by-products of
interregional trade: the economic and physical alienation of the
poor. Due to competition and the favoritism given to large-scale
farmers, latifundialists are able to remain alone in the midst of the
land as others are forced to relocate in urban areas or migrate to
different regions.[54] Ibrahim's predicament could serve as a contextual analogy to Chaney's claim that the fifth chapter of Isaiah addresses a conflict that arose "over a process of agricultural intensification, which enriched the powerful few but dispossessed and
impoverished many peasants."[55] Since scholars like Chaney and
Premnath already use analogy by employing recurring patterns of
exploitation in agrarian societies into their interpretations of prophetic texts, drawing on examples of these patterns, as found in
Ibrahim's story, can provide evidence for the socio-economic contexts behind claims that people joined houses and fields together
until there was room for none but themselves.

Multiple Perpetrators

As mentioned above, many biblical commentaries approach the
targets of the accusations in Isa. 5.8 and Mic. 2.2 as a single group
within Judean society, such as merchants, politicians, or judges.

---

[52] King, *Liberalization Against Democracy*, 84.

[53] King, *Liberalization Against Democracy*, 84.

[54] Radwan Jamal, and Ghose note that between 1962 and 1981 an estimated twenty-nine percent of Tunisia's incremental labor force emi-
grated to foreign contries in search for employment. Many returned from
Europe in the 1980s as a result of the recession (Radwan, et al., *Tunisia:
Rural Labour and Structural Transformation* (London: Routledge, 1991), 23-
25, 92-94).

[55] Chaney, "Whose Sour Grapes?," 117.

Hadi's account of Tunisian latifundialization, in contrast, does not place blame on a single segment of the elite, but finds fault in the actions of both government officials and the wealthy individuals. Hadi found the 'umda[56] responsible for facilitating an abusive system of patronage in which local economic elites were all too happy to participate and perpetuate. Hadi complained that favoritism and corruption allowed members of the economic elite to purchase large latifundia while poor or better-trained Tunisians received nothing. In an interview with King, Hadi claimed,

> Wealthy people – it doesn't matter where they got their money, they can be lawyers, doctors, or whatever – will go to the 'umda and plan on getting the land in one person's hands. Later they will divide the money with the 'umda. I know that they aren't using technical criteria for the land, because people like me who studied agriculture can't get any.[57]

Hadi's complaints against those responsible for land consolidation reflect both a concerted effort among government officials to divide the country's farmlands among wealthy elites and the wealthy Tunisian's eagerness to take the land, even though it would probably be better managed by less affluent, but more qualified, farmers. Hadi's observations on Tunisian latifundialization could provide a useful analogy for scholars like Hoppe, who argue that the authors of Mic. 2.2 castigate "Judah's elite for creating a two-tiered society of wealthy and poor."[58] Peasants like Hadi, who were not born into poverty, have been alienated from the benefits of trade by systems of favoritism. This modern example could also be beneficial for analyzing and strengthening Domeris' theory that poverty was socially constructed in ancient Palestine, rather than a passive outcome.[59] Through employing the principles of cultural-evolutionary

---

[56] The 'umda are Local administrative officials in rural areas who are appointed by the Ministry of the Interior to control the countryside and report back to their state governor. King, *Liberalization Against Democracy*, 51-52.

[57] King, *Liberalization Against Democracy*, 87.

[58] Hoppe, *There Shall Be No Poor Among You*, 76.

[59] Domeris, *Touching the Heart of God*, 95-127.

theory and the current world system as a model, such instances of generated class division could be used to shed light on the past.

The involvement of the *'umda* in the allocation of Tunisian land can provide a useful analogy with which to explore theories on Judean latifundialization. Although the *'umda* were not a part of eighth-century Judean society, a modern example of government-controlled administrators allocating farmland to wealthy elites under similar sociological circumstances may provide new insights for scholars, like Köhler and Dearman, who have considered the phrases באור הבקר יעשׂוה [60] and כי יש־לאל ידם,[61] to refer to the legal involvement of Judean judges.[62] In addition to the accusations made by Hadi and Majoub, evidence of changing social relations and attitudes that lead to abusive activities are found in the accounts of wealthy Tunisians. A wealthy landowner named Hajj Elloumi, for example, holds great disdain for his impoverished neighbors.

Contempt for the Poor Among the Elite

The Tunisian latifundialist Hajj Elloumi was born into a very wealthy family, having inherited 150 hectares of land from his father. After the French were forced out of Tunisia, Elloumi was able to increase his fortunes, allowing him to give his sons his personal holdings of three hundred hectares and the eight-hundred-hectare cooperative lease that he controlled.[63] The wealth that Elloumi was able to accumulate stands in stark contrast to the lives of Majoub and Hadi.

Despite Elloumi's quickness to praise his own generosity whenever possible, King notes that he speaks of the poor with contempt. Elloumi told King that "the lives of the poor are disorganized. They live with nature, not with their heads. The poor are

---

[60] Mic. 2.1 "…in the light of day they do it."

[61] Mic. 2.1 "…for it is in the power of their hand."

[62] Dearman, *Property Rights in the Eighth-Century Prophets: The Conflict and its Background* (eds. Roberts and Talbert; vol. 106; Scholars Press: Atlanta, 1988), 46. Köhler, *Hebrew Man* (trans. Ackroyd; London: SCM Press, 1956), 151.

[63] King, *Liberalization Against Democracy*, 91.

the miserable in spirit. They don't respect laws. They're sneaky and will steal. They do things against religion."[64] Such an outlook reflects the attitudes commonly held by elite members of advanced agrarian societies, who often develop contempt for those who toil. Elloumi's comments about the poor may offer some valuable insights into how members of the elite, like those referred to in Isa. 5.8–10 and Mic. 2.1–2, justify the subjugation of others.

A Positive View of Land Privatization

Unlike Majoub, Hadi, and Ibrahim, Elloumi believes that the privatization scheme that took place in the 1970s was a positive step for Tunisia, but King notes that his interpretation of the events that followed are "outright inaccuracies."[65] For example, despite the massive fifty-percent cut in customary working days that resulted from Elloumi's takeover of a cooperative, which caused massive unemployment problems for local laborers, he insisted that

> The privatization program is designed to help the country: production is improved and it increases work for the people. Production was very low when we took over. Today we are producing at 80 percent of capacity. This means that the workers are happy. You have to remember that workers are selfish. If you're not careful, they won't work.[66]

According to King, Elloumi's sentiment is common among wealthy farmers, with many other latifundialists expressing similar levels of contempt toward their community's impoverished citizens.[67]

The management-based perspective of latifundialization expressed by Elloumi provides a useful analogy through which to consider Chaney's theory on diverging peasant and elite goals in eighth-century Judah.[68] While respecting the significant differences between Judean and Tunisian economics, Elloumi's words provide a modern example of the divergent ambitions that exist between

---

[64] King, *Liberalization Against Democracy*, 91.
[65] King, *Liberalization Against Democracy*, 91.
[66] King, *Liberalization Against Democracy*, 91.
[67] King, *Liberalization Against Democracy*, 97.
[68] Chaney, "Bitter Bounty," 22-23.

latifundialists and mixed-subsistence farmers: the former values productivity and efficiency while the latter values the ability to provide for his or her family. Elloumi's concern with productivity appears to blind him to the plight of his neighboring farmers who lost fifty-percent of their employment, assuming that they should find joy, rather than desperation, in improved efficiency.

Maintaining an Economic Advantage Over the Vulnerable

Beyond ignoring the needs of the impoverished, increased competitiveness has led some wealthy Tunisians to conspire against their small-scale neighbors. For example, when a wealthy farmer named Abdelkader was awarded a cooperative contract that came with a US$280,000 loan, he invested the money in the latest refrigeration technology, giving him a significant advantage over neighboring fruit farmers.[69] In response to Abdelkader's increased refrigeration capacity, a group of small-scale farmers approached the local governing body to propose the creation of a cooperative that would provide refrigeration to its members. While local administrators were considering this cooperative proposal, Abdelkader and his friends went to the local governing body and ensured that it was dropped from the agenda.[70] Without the support of local leaders, these farmers had to struggle to compete with Abdelkader's advanced fruit operation. Such a scenario dovetails with Chaney and Premnath's theory that Judean subsistence farmers were unable to compete with the expenses that specialization agriculture and interregional trade demand, leading to debt and foreclosure on their land.[71] This example could also serve as an analogy through which to contemplate the complaint found in Mic. 2.1 against

הוֹי חֹשְׁבֵי־אָוֶן וּפֹעֲלֵי רָע עַל־מִשְׁכְּבוֹתָם בְּאוֹר הַבֹּקֶר יַעֲשׂוּהָ כִּי יֶשׁ־לְאֵל יָדָם.[72]

---

[69] King, *Liberalization Against Democracy*, 93.
[70] King, *Liberalization Against Democracy*, 93.
[71] Chaney, "Bitter Bounty," 18-19, 26-27. Premnath, *Eighth Century Prophets: A Social Analysis*, 13-14.
[72] "...them who plan wickedness and make evil on their beds; at morning light they do it because the power is in their hands."

Although we cannot know if this is what happened in ancient Judah, the modern example can provide a useful analogical tool through which to consider these issues.

Not all of the impoverished residents of Tebourba share the negative views that many wealthy and poor residents have of each other, and this in and of itself has the potential to provide an important insight into the motivations behind the prophetic authors who addressed landownership abuse.

An Alternative Perspective

The account of a fourteen-year-old girl named Hayat not only provides evidence of changing social relations between the wealthy and the less affluent in Tunisia, but a change in how some poor peasants perceive their own place in Tunisian society. Hayat, born long after the *habous* collectives and subsequent 1960s cooperatives had been dissolved, grew up watching her parents struggle to maintain employment. Her father, displaced when the cooperative he worked on was privatized in the 1970s, took Hadi out of school so that she could help support her parents and six younger siblings.[73] Hayat notices the same lack of empathy that Majoub finds among the wealthy, claiming that some prosperous landowners do not give any charitable donations while others give only a small fraction of what is required: providing two bags of wheat instead of ten.[74] Despite the fact that her life has not been easier than that of other poor laborers, Hayat's views on the wealthy differ from those of her elders.

Converse to Majoub, Hayat does not harbor contempt toward the latifundialists in her community, but expresses immense gratitude toward them. More important to Hayat than a noticeable lack of charitable offerings, she is thankful for the employment that the wealthier members of the community provide for her and her family, even if it is sporadic. Hayat claims, 'I like the rich because I work for them. I can only do well if they are doing well. Sometimes we work less than six months a year. What would we do without

---

[73] King, *Liberalization Against Democracy*, 86.
[74] King, *Liberalization Against Democracy*, 86.

rich people?"[75] Whereas Majoub can recall a time in which the community worked together for the common good,[76] the younger Hayat appears to be unable to envision a life of self-sufficiency and secure employment, free from total dependence upon the wealthier members of her community.

The socio-economic context into which Hayat was born, which makes six-month lulls in unemployment appear inevitable,[77] is converse to a subsistence environment, in which labor efforts are maximized for the benefit of the primary producer rather than the members of a non-productive administrative class.[78] The gratitude and sense of dependence that Hayat's words express appear to be the product of four decades of reforms that made farmers like Majoub, Hadi, and her father dependent upon the economic aspirations of Tunisia's economic and political elite.[79] This favorable attitude toward latifundialists reveals the extent of the cultural impact that Tunisia's post-independence economic reforms have had on this young farm laborer and could help biblical scholars to address the hidden contextual issues lying behind prophetic texts. Perhaps the prophetic authors were not only addressing land seizures and offences against a religious segment of Judean society, but the cultural consequences of losing a way of life that had been relied upon for generations.

Hayat and Majoub's contrasting views of the economic situation in Tebourba can offer a couple of important insights for the exploration of biblical texts. First, Hayat's account serves as a reminder that not all parties act or respond to a single phenomenon in the same way. For example, Hayat duly notes that not all wealthy individuals hold back in giving alms to the poor, which is also evidenced in King's interview with Hadi.[80] It appears that many com-

---

[75] King, *Liberalization Against Democracy*, 86.

[76] Less than fifty years before King conducted this series of interviews

[77] King, *Liberalization Against Democracy*, 86.

[78] Bell. "The Social Relations of Property and Efficiency."

[79] This is an attitude of dependence is one that elites seek to instill. Nolan and Lenski, *Human Societies: An Introduction to Macrosociology*, 227. Johnson and Earle, *The Evolution of Human Societies*, 313-14.

[80] King, *Liberalization Against Democracy*, 87.

mentators easily fall into the trap of blindly taking sides with the biblical authors, as noted by Clines,[81] which can lead to blanketed assumptions about both elites and the poor in Judean society.[82] Second, the sense of dependence that Hayat, Majoub, Ibrahim, and Hadi experience raises another important interpretive point, which may address questions surrounding the motivations behind those who composed and redacted the accusations found in Isa. 5.8–10 and Mic. 2.1–2: shifting structures of dependence.

The degree to which these Tunisian peasants depend upon the wealthy and political elites is reflected in complaints about their inability to access land, working for those who abuse them, and Hadi's appreciation of being given any work at all. However, to suggest that this dependence is the sole product of the effects of corporate globalization in Tunisia would be inaccurate. Many Tunisian peasants were highly dependent upon an elite group within Tunisian society prior to independence in 1956, and even before the advent of French colonialism in the mid-nineteenth century: Tunisia's religious establishment.

C. SHIFTS IN REGIONAL POWER STRUCTURES

Unlike the post-independence hierarchical structure in Tunisia, which was based on the power and influence of the ruling elite, much of pre-independence Tunisia's cultural and economic activity revolved around a hierarchical structure based upon the power and influence of the religious establishment.[83] The profits generated by the *habous* lands that had sustained the religious elite's finances and lifestyle also funded charitable hospitals and schools while providing a reliable source of employment that benefited rural communities.[84] As demonstrated through Hayat's account, Tunisian inde-

---

[81] Clines, *Interested Parties: The Ideology and Readers of the Hebrew Bible* (ed. Exum; Sheffield: Sheffield Academic Press, 1995), 77.

[82] Kaiser, *Isaiah 1-12: A Commentary*, 65. Kissane, *The Book of Isaiah*, 57. Smith, *Micah - Malachi*, 24. Alfaro, *Justice and Loyalty*, 25.

[83] Anderson, *The State and Social Transformation in Tunisia and Libya*, 43.

[84] Anderson, *The State and Social Transformation in Tunisia and Libya*, 234-35. Boulby, "The Islamic Challenge": 592. Powers, "Orientalism, Colonialism, and Legal History," *Comparative Studies in Society and History* 31,

pendence created a major shift in the region's power structures; the small-scale farmers who had worked on the *habous* and had depended upon the religious elites who ran these Muslim endowments, alongside the additional plots of land that they were often granted for their own families' subsistence, became subject to a new ruling class.[85] Unlike their previous patrons, who were beholden to a Muslim ethic that emphasized charity toward the poor, their new patrons were not obligated to fulfill such commitments: in fact, they worked actively to remove or transform this ethic in Tunisian culture. Small-scale farmers were not the only ones to be adversely affected by these changes. As Tunisia achieved independence and struggled to become an active participant in corporate globalization, the religious elite quickly found that their main source of revenue had come into jeopardy.

From the inception of Tunisian independence the newly installed ruling class sought to dismantle the religious hierarchies of the past by undermining their economic power and the influence that they had on Tunisian society. In addition to weakening the religious elite's grasp on the country's farmland and the revenue that it produced, the government worked to marginalize the influence of the *ulema*, or Muslim legal scholars, by closing their schools and removing certain Muslim festivals from the Tunisian calendar.

The Tunisia's ruling elite worked in a variety of ways to weaken traditional links between religion and society. Tozy notes that, in the spirit of modernization and bringing Tunisia into a new economic era, the government suspended the *sharia* courts and "attacked the [conservative] Zeitouna mosque university system,[86] symbol of an 'outmoded' society and locus of reproduction of a

---

no. 3 (1989): 536. Duwaji, "Land Ownership in Tunisia: An Obstacle to Agricultural Development," 44, no. 1 (1968): 129.

[85] Anderson, *The State and Social Transformation in Tunisia and Libya*, 43.

[86] The Zeitouna, or Zaytouna, Universities preserved traditional Muslim traditions. Those who were opposed to the maintenance of the Zeitouna saw them as oppressive institutions that thwarted political progress, oppressed women, and stagnated the development of the arts in Islam. See Robin Ostle, "Mahmud al-Mas'adi and Tunisia's 'Lost Generation,'" *Journal of Arabic Literature* 8, (1977): 165. Ostle, "The Romantic Revolution?," *Journal of Arabic Literature* 26, no. 1/2 (1995): 102-03.

small, competing elite of a few important families (Ben Achour, Djait, and others)."[87] These moves undermined the religious elite's political influence while eroding their ability to control the nature of religious discourse in Tunisian society. Marion Boulby explains,

> ...by the mid-1960s the political and economic demise of the *ulema* was clearly apparent. Deprived of their land, controlled by the state in the classroom and the mosque, the *ulema* had lost much of their ground to the state. Some of the sheikhs at [Zeitouna] decided to leave Tunisia for other parts of the Islamic World.... On the other hand, many of the *ulema* capitulated to Bourguiba's reforms.[88]

The choice given to Tunisia's Muslim leaders to either physically or ideologically abandon the Zeitouna Mosque and its educational system, which was founded in 720 CE to train religious teachers as they prepared to preach to new converts,[89] represented a significant break from over twelve hundred years of Muslim heritage. Beyond weakening the role of Islam in Tunisian life through disenfranchising the religious elite in educational and legal matters, the Tunisian government sought to isolate Islamic sensibilities through eliminating various traditional Muslim practices.

One of the most controversial acts of President Bourguiba was his call for Tunisians to stop observing the fast of Ramadan on the grounds that it decreased the productivity of the state. Beyond making a demand of such cultural significance, which was received by many as an affront against Islam, Bourguiba illustrated his defiance of the sanctity of the fast by drinking a glass of orange juice during Ramadan at a public rally.[90] Although Bourguiba made ef-

---

[87] Tozy. "Islam and the State," in *Polity and Society in Contemporary North Africa* (eds. Zartman and Habeeb; Boulder: Westview Press, 1993), 104–05.

[88] Boulby, "The Islamic Challenge": 593.

[89] Saoud, *The Impact of Islam on Urban Development in North Africa* (Foundation for Science Technology and Civilization, 2004 [March 4, 2010); http://www.muslimheritage.com/uploads/naurban.pdf.

[90] Boulby, "The Islamic Challenge: Tunisia Since Independence": 592. Anderson, "Obligation and Accountability: Islamic Politics in North Africa," *Daedalus* 120, no. 3 (1991): 107.

forts to link his call for an end to the observance of Ramadan to a
new interpretation of Islam, his disregard for Islamic sensibilities
was thinly veiled as he proclaimed, "During Ramadan work stops.
At this moment when we are doing the impossible in order to increase production, how can we resign ourselves to seeing it slump
to a value near zero?"[91] Such a statement exemplifies the prioritization of finance over traditional Muslim sentiment, as is common in
agrarian societies as they adopt a stronger political economy.[92] Not
only did the new ruling elite relieve the religious establishment of
one-fifth of Tunisia's arable lands, which served as a main source
of revenue, but they also weakened their influence and disregarded
norms and teachings that were counterproductive to Bourguiba's
economic goals.[93]

Tunisian Power-Shifts and the Prophetic Texts

So how can the suffering of the Tunisian *ulema* shed light on prophetic texts against landownership abuse? Although there is no
direct data to connect the common loss of revenue and prestige
that Tunisia's religious establishment suffered to the experiences of
YHWHist leaders in eighth-century Judah, a tentative literary link
does exist; Hezekiah's religious reforms. According to the biblical
narrative, Hezekiah called for a centralization of Judean religious
practice in Jerusalem that was achieved by destroying regional al-

---

[91] Boulby, "The Islamic Challenge": 594.

[92] Knapp. "Copper Production and Eastern Mediterranean Trade,"
157. Pomeranz, *The Great Divergence: Europe, China, and the Making of the
Modern World Economy* (Princeton: Princeton University Press, 2000), 119-
20.

[93] The interpretive value of the backlash that came from members of
the religious elite as the *habous* were closed in the 1950s and as rising sentiment against the government's failed policies came to a head in the
1970s and 80s, is an area that I hope to peruse in future research. For
more information on these events and the reactions of the religious elite
see al-Nayfar, "How Can a Muslim Live in this Era?," no. 153 (1988).
Jones, "Portrait of Rashid al-Ghannoushi," *Middle East Report* 153, no. 19-
22 (1988). al-Ghannoushi, "Deficiencies in the Islamic Movement," *Middle
East Report* 153, no. 23-24 (1988).

tars[94] and demanding that the people of Judah send their tithes to Jerusalem.[95] The authors of 2 Chr. 30 also claim that Hezekiah made a decree that all of his subjects, from Beer-sheba to Dan, should resume the Passover pilgrimage to Jerusalem.[96] Each of these activities, purportedly to have been carried out by the king of Judah in the late eighth century, would not only have centralized YHWHist practice in Jerusalem, but much of the religion's revenue.[97] Regardless of whether or not these reforms were actually put into practice in the eight century, they suggest a desire to produce religious reforms that would have brought prosperity to Jerusalem and centralized the cult practices of a Judean religious community.

Considering the economic significance of temples in ancient Palestine, which served as treasuries and centres of trade and land management,[98] such a move by Hezekiah to direct YHWHist income into the capital would have been highly lucrative for a Judean state struggling under the pressures of development and an Assyrian threat. However, while increased economic activity in Jerusalem may have served the *ruling* elite, such reforms would have likely upset the power and economic structures that supported the livelihood and status of many within the *religious* elite – save any provisions to protect the religious establishment. Although a lack

---

[94] 2 Kgs. 18.22, 2 Ch 32.12, Isa. 36.

[95] 2 Ch. 31.4-6, 11.

[96] 2 Chr. 30.5 כי לא לרב עשו ככתוב "...for they have not done it in numbers as prescribed."

[97] Even had Jerusalem not been the capital of Judah at this time, these acts still represent the centralization of YHWHism in one location.

[98] Temples throughout Mesopotamia depended on landlordism for their income. Robert Adams claims that the Eanna in Uruk, for example, was the largest landed economic establishment of its time (Adams, *Heartland of Cities: Surveys of Ancient Settlements and Land Use on the Central Floodplain of the Euphrates* [Chicago: University of Chicago Press, 1981]). Marty Stevens notes that role of landownership in the Jerusalem temple is not as clear. While the verses Lev. 27.14, 16, 21; Num. 35.1-3 indicate that individual houses, fields, and cities were dedicated to YHWH and under the control of the priests, passages like Lev. 27.19 specify that the previous owners had the right to redeem the land (Stevens, *Temples, Tithes, and Taxes: The Temple and the Economic Life of Ancient Israel* [Peabody, Massachusetts: Hendrickson Publishing, 2006], 82-85).

of extra-biblical and archaeological evidence demands that a degree of speculation be employed in any interpretation of these texts, biblical evidence of such religious reforms in combination with the economic changes that were experienced in eighth-century Judah justify considering such a scenario. Since Tunisia presents an example of a recurring pattern of state interference with religious establishments, the Tunisian example may provide insight into the motivations behind prophetic complaints against injustice.

Potential Motivations Behind the Composition of Isa. 5.8–10 and Mic. 2.1–2

Several biblical scholars, including Andersen and Freedman, David Peterson, Dearman, Premnath, and Chaney, have offered theories as to why a group of religious elites would have been so upset about the abuse of Judean farmers' property rights as to publicly denounce these acts and preserve their complaints. These theories include compassion for those who were victimized by land seizures, righteous anger against those who upset YHWH's divine order, or a combination of these motivations.[99] Petersen, for example, proposes that while Isaiah speaks out for the benefit of the "poor," in leveling his accusations against economic injustice the prophet appears "to root those norms in God's covenant with the people, Isaiah understands the nature of the deity as holy as the authorization for these ethical principles."[100] According to this commonly held view, the shift in land ownership referred to in these texts not only victimized those who had lost their land, but went against a long-established YHWHist tradition of land tenure that violated the deity's commands.

Although Hans Kippenberg, Walter Houston, and Blenkinsopp do not suggest that compassion and piety did not play a part in the prophets' motives, they address a potential societal element to land-tenure abuse: the dangers that a sweeping shift in land

---

[99] Petersen, *The Prophetic Literature: An Introduction* (Louisville, KY: Westminster John Knox Press, 1989), 90. Andersen and Freedman, *Micah*, 270-74. Dearman, *Property Rights in the Eighth-Century Prophets*, 52-57. Premnath, *Eighth Century Prophets: A Social Analysis*, 102, 106.

[100] Petersen, *The Prophetic Literature*, 90.

ownership policy could have presented to eighth-century Judean society.[101] Blenkinsopp writes,

> The main threat to social stability and the traditional way of life of the peasantry was undoubtedly the alienation and foreclosure under mortgage of land held in the family units for generations. Hence the violence of prophetic diatribe against those who covet fields and who join house to house, field to field (Mic. 2:2; Isa. 5:8).[102]

Through upsetting an established system of land tenure, leaders would have risked rebellion and potential interruptions in essential food production, as occurred during the privatization of Tunisia's government cooperatives in the 1970s, which could have threatened both the stability and the lives of Judah's inhabitants.[103] The above interpretations of prophetic motivation offer useful theories that have provided a basis for understanding prophetic complaints against economic injustice, and in particular, land ownership abuse. A further understanding of these motivations may be developed through the use of cultural-evolutionary theory in combination with the direct and indirect effects of corporate globalization on Tunisia's mixed-subsistence farmers and religious establishment.

It has been established that as agrarian societies abolish or modify religious practices to facilitate new economic goals, the economic and political advantages enjoyed by members of the religious elite are often disturbed. Some of those within religious establishments, however, will capitulate and accept the tides of change. In line with this pattern, some Muslim leaders within Tuni-

---

[101] Kippenberg, *Religion und Klassenbildung im antiken Judäa* (Göttingen: Vandenhoeck & Ruprecht, 1982), 122. Houston, *Contending for Justice: Ideologies and Theologies of Social Justice in the Old Testament* (London: T&T Clark, 2006), 30. Blenkinsopp, *Sage, Priest, Prophet: Religious and Intellectual Leadership in Ancient Israel* (ed. Knight; Louisville: Westminster John Knox Press, 1995), 161.

[102] Blenkinsopp, *Sage, Priest, Prophet*, 161.

[103] This issue was addressed in Chapter Four. When Tunisian farmlands were centralized under the elite in the 1970s the agrarian cycles were disturbed, leading to food shortages (Ashford, "Succession and Social Change in Tunisia": 36).

sia's religious elite capitulated to President Bourguiba's demands to
reinterpret their doctrines in ways that would facilitate the government's economic agenda and were thus allowed to keep their
posts.[104] Those members of the religious establishment who refused to abandon the traditional Muslim practices of Tunisia became disenfranchised, causing some to enter into exile as their
revenue stream was cut by the closure of the habous endowments.
As a consequence, these members of the religious elite were
stripped of their posts as traditional Muslim practices became seen
as an impediment to economic growth, reflecting the anti-
traditionalist sentiments that were common among many mid-
twentieth century economists.[105] Although the *ulema* did not lose a
significant amount of popularity among the people, per se, their
political influence was seriously undermined. Considering that Isa.
5.8–10 and Mic. 2.1–2 are attributed to a period of great socio-
economic change as Judah entered into a major world system, that
such circumstances often upset traditional religious practices, and
biblical evidence of profitable religious reforms,[106] the Tunisian
scenario offers a few tempting analogies that address long-standing
questions around the prophetic compulsion to both protest land
seizures and to preserve these complaints.

If religious principles did regulate land ownership in eighth-
century Judah, or at the time of the composition of these texts, as
suggested by the curses found in Isa. 8.9–10 and Mic. 2.3–4, an
overturn of such a system would have had adverse effects on the
religious establishment. Granting that this land system had benefited members of the religious elite in YHWHist communities,
which cannot be proven but would not be unexpected considering
the close connection between religious and economic practices in

---

[104] Tozy. "Islam and the State," 110. Boulby, "The Islamic Challenge": 595.

[105] Lerner, *The Passing of Traditional Society* (Glencoe: The Free Press,
1958), 87-89. Shils, "Political Development in the New States," *Comparative Studies in Society and History* 2, no. 3 (1960). Duwaji, "Land Ownership
in Tunisia: An Obstacle to Agricultural Development."

[106] 2 Kgs. 18.22, 2 Ch. 30.5; 31.4-6,11; 32.12, Isa. 36.7.

agrarian societies,[107] such a change could have disrupted their political, economic, and social way of life. Out of the Tunisian material and recurring societal patterns, with all necessary caveats, one can see how the anger expressed toward those who seized land may not have only been directed at the displacement of Judean farmers, but also at the disenfranchisement of a segment of Judah's religious establishment who had depended upon those farmers for support. The notion of large members of the elite losing their status as a result of changing economic conditions is not limited to the Tunisian experience, as members of the economic elite in other cultures have also fallen into the middle or lower classes as a result of increased interregional trade.[108] Even if YHWHist leaders had not previously benefited directly from Judean systems of land management, the issue could have been used to add a sense of piety to their grievances against other consequences of a centralization of the cult.[109] Additionally, it may have been safer for the prophets to protest against the exploitation of farmers than the destruction of their worship sites or a loss of tithe-income to the Jerusalem Temple.

The idea that complaints against Judean landownership abuse had served the authors' self-interests does not devalue their complaints against the suffering of the disadvantaged. The effects of latifundialization on subsistence farmers and the prophets' concerns for these people are not disputed here. Rather, the example of cultural evolution's effects on Tunisia's Muslim leaders, and those of other agrarian societies, offers another possible conse-

---

[107] Knapp. "Copper Production and Eastern Mediterranean Trade," 157. Rappaport, "The Sacred in Human Evolution," 36-37. Hughes, "Sustainable Agriculture in Ancient Egypt," *History of Agriculture and the Environment* 66, no. 2 (1992): 16.

[108] Ghai and Alcántara. "The Crisis of the 1980s in Africa, Latin America, and the Caribbean: An Overview," in *The IMF and the South: The Social Impact of Crisis and Adjustment* (ed. Ghai; London: Zed Books Ltd on Behalf of The United Nations Research Institute for Social Development, 1991), 26, 31, 36.

[109] Such a strategy would not have been unlike the use of land protection decrees by ancient Near Eastern rulers to promote themselves up as just rulers.

quence of Judean landownership abuse that appears to have been overlooked in commentary: that the cultural-evolutionary changes of late eighth-century Judah led to the displacement of religious leaders who had previously been supported by the very Judean farmers for whom their complaints were written. As found in the Tunisian example, it should not be assumed, as it often appears to be, that only the poor are vulnerable to social change. As societies evolve, so do the institutions upon which various groups depend.

D. CONCLUSION

The potential benefits of employing examples of the cultural-evolutionary patterns found in modern agrarian societies, resulting from the transformative effects of corporate globalization, to the field of biblical studies are not limited to issues of land tenure. Using the negative effects of corporate globalization as an interpretive tool can help to provide new avenues through which to approach other prophetic grievances that are attributed to the late eighth-century BCE, or any other period of heightened economic activity.

Although the vast socio-economic differences between modern-day Tunisia and eighth-century Judah must be respected and handled with care, it would be a waste of potential resources to ignore their similarities. The changes that Tunisia and developing countries all over the world have experienced as a result of corporate globalization share a lineage with the kinds of abuses that the prophetic authors addressed, and which cultural evolutionists would expect to have emerged as Judah experienced unprecedented levels of population growth and urban development in the late eighth century . While keeping in mind the value, limits, and hazards that accompany work based on analogy and the use of comparative studies, approaching prophetic complaints against injustice through the lens of corporate globalization can provide a new method for exploring prophetic complaints against economic injustice. While the study of recurring exploitative patterns found in the modern context of corporate globalization cannot provide definite historical contexts for prophetic complaints against land ownership abuse, it can help scholars to approach contextually ambiguous texts from fresh angles and derive new interpretations from a limited body of evidence.

7 CONCLUSION

The recurring patterns of change and exploitation that cultural-evolutionary theorists associate with periods of economic development in agrarian societies has allowed Marvin Chaney, D.N. Premnath, and other biblical scholars to offer fresh perspectives and new interpretations of contextually ambiguous prophetic texts. However, if the use of analogy and cultural evolution are going to be employed in biblical scholarship, it seems that further insights could be gained from considering the effects of these recurring evolutionary patterns on modern-day subsistence communities. The objective of this study has been to determine whether or not cultural-evolutionary theory's interpretive value can be augmented by considering the socio-economic effects of cultural evolution – including the abandonment of subsistence practices and their affiliated socio-religious norms, forced land consolidation and the hoarding of wealth among an elite minority – on a modern, and thus tangible, agrarian society that has been absorbed into the current world system: corporate globalization.

Alongside biblical scholarship, it has been necessary to employ a wide-range of material from the fields of economics, sociology, anthropology, and political science in order to offer an understanding of how twentieth-century CE economic and political practices can provide an interpretive framework through which to consider complaints against injustices that are attributed to eighth century Judah. Such an interdisciplinary endeavor has its natural drawbacks that might turn some away from this approach, such as vast differences between eighth-century Judah and modern-day socio-economic practices, the fact that no one person can be an expert in all pertinent fields, and the inability of this method to produce definitive results. Robert Coote and Keith Whitelam offer a helpful rejoinder to those who would abandon the use of social-scientific models, like cultural-evolutionary theory, on these grounds. Addressing the uncertainty that is inherent in the use of the social sciences in their research on the emergence of early Israel, Coote and Whitelam write,

> ...historical nihilism is not the only choice in the face of this residue of uncertainty. Certainty is not a prerequisite to understanding. It is the will to understand rather than simply the will to know for certain that is the driving force for the inquiry to be undertaken [in their social-scientific approach].[1]

A lack of material evidence for an issue such as landownership abuse should not lead biblical scholars to abandon the topic altogether but search for other means of understanding. The detailed study presented in this book on prophetic texts against landownership abuse and their commentators, the theories that underlie cultural evolutionary theory, the effects of cultural evolution and trade in the ancient Near East, and the history of corporate globalization have produced insights that can contribute to the field of biblical studies by offering a fresh approach to biblical interpretation.

---

[1] Coote and Whitelam, *The Emergence of Early Israel: In Historical Perspective* (SWBA 5; ed. Flanagan; Sheffield: Almond Press, 1987), 20.

A. WHAT HAS BEEN DISCOVERED

The Contextual Problem and the Use of Cultural Evolution

Attempts to uncover the elusive socio-economic contexts behind prophetic complaints against land ownership abuse that are attributed to the eighth-century Judah have been frustrated by a lack of archaeological and literary evidence. Without any actual documents of land transference, deeds of ownership, or royal edicts pertaining to land in Israel or Judah, biblical scholars have had to piece together a socio-economic context for these passages with very little information. Although it might be assumed that such an absence of information would offer a wide range of potential interpretations of passages like Isa. 5.8–10 and Mic. 2.1–2, a common contextual view developed within the field of biblical studies that envisioned a few venal merchants who took land from poor farmers by corrupting the courts of an otherwise healthy and just economic system.[1] Such a scenario *could* have been the context to which the prophetic authors wrote, but there is certainly not enough evidence to attract the sort of consensus status that this interpretation has enjoyed. Furthermore, recent interpretations of the archaeological record cast doubt on the idea that the Judean state would have been advanced enough to foster such a "golden age" to be corrupted in this manner. It is for this reason that scholars like Chaney, Premnath, Hopkins, and Gottwald have looked outside of biblical studies for alternative understandings of these complaints.[2] To this end,

---

[1] Smith, *Micah - Malachi* (eds. Hubbard, Barker, Watts and Martin; 58 vols.; vol. 32; Waco: Word Books, 1984), 24. Köhler, *Hebrew Man* (trans. Ackroyd; London: SCM Press, 1956), 151. Chaney, "Bitter Bounty: The Dynamics of Political Economy Critiqued by the Eighth-Century Prophets," in *Reformed Faith and Economics* (ed. Stivers; Lanham: University Press of America, 1989), 16.

[2] Chaney, "Micah - Models Matter: Political Economy and Micah 6:9-15," in *Ancient Israel: The Old Testament in its Social Context* (ed. Esler; London: SCM Press, 2005). Premnath, *Eighth Century Prophets: A Social Analysis* (St. Louis: Chalice, 2003). Hopkins. "Bare Bones: Putting Flesh on the Economics of Ancient Israel," in *The Origins of the Ancient Israelite States* eds. Clines, Davies and Jarick; vol. 228 of *JSOTSS*; Sheffield: Sheffield Aca-

cultural-evolutionary theory has been a particularly useful approach.

As explained above, cultural-evolutionary theorists find that agrarian societies experience a set of common evolutionary patterns when they are faced with periods of significant economic development, regardless of time or culture.[3] As agrarian efforts that had once been focused on family-centered subsistence strategies become refocused on the production of large surpluses in order to feed expanding populations and export goods, farmers tend to lose their land, their way of life, and the fruits of their labor.[4] Approaching texts like Isa. 5.8–10 and Mic. 2.1–2 through the lens of these recurring cultural-evolutionary patterns has allowed both Chaney and Premnath to offer alternative contextual interpretations and to breathe new life into the conversation on the discussion of economic injustice in the Hebrew Bible. Instead of reiterating a previously held contextual consensus, Chaney and Premnath have each found reason to argue that the prophetic authors were not simply addressing the greed of a corrupt few, but rather the consequences of a fundamental evolutionary leap in Judean political and economic practice that had been brought about by population growth and increased trade as the Neo-Assyrian Empire expanded into the Southern Levant.[5] Such a theory is not unsubstantiated, considering

demic Press, 1996). Gottwald, *The Hebrew Bible in Its Social World and in Ours* (Atlanta: Scholars Press, 1993).

[3] Johnson and Earle, *The Evolution of Human Societies: From Foraging Group to Agrarian State* (Stanford: Stanford University Press, 2001).

[4] Berdan. "Trade and Markets in Precapitalist States," in *Economic Anthropology* (ed. Plattner; Stanford: Stanford University Press, 2002), 79-80. Lenski, *Power and Privilege: A Theory of Social Stratification* (New York: McGraw-Hill Book Company, 1966), 220. Johnson and Earle, *The Evolution of Human Societies: From Foraging Group to Agrarian State*, 29-32.

[5] Premnath, *Eighth Century Prophets: A Social Analysis*, 94. Premnath, "Latifundialization in Isaiah 5.8-10," in *Social-Scientific Old Testament Criticism* (ed. Chalcraft; Sheffield: Sheffield Academic Press, 1997), 302-03. Chaney, "Whose Sour Grapes?: The Addressees of Isaiah 5:1-7 in the Light of Political Economy," in *The Social World of the Hebrew Bible: Twenty-Five Years of the Social Sciences in the Academy* eds. Simkins and Cook; *Semeia*, ed. Brenner; Atlanta: Society of Biblical Literature, 1999), 107.

the period to which these complaints against land ownership abuse are attributed.

Historical and Archaeological Precedence

As has been established, it appears that ancient Palestinian communities moved back and forth along a continuum of greater and lesser dependence on subsistence practices dating back to the Early Bronze Age.[6] Although cycles of population growth may have caused these peripheral communities to move along this continuum without external influence, the degree to which they depended upon subsistence strategies was often determined by the waxing and waning of neighbouring empires.[7] As Egyptian and Mesopotamian Empires grew in strength and economic power, urban centers were established alongside trade routes in the lowlands in order to benefit from interregional trade and prosperity. As these neighbouring empires collapsed and trade became an insufficient means of support, Palestinian communities would migrate back to the safety of the highlands to resume more family-centered subsistence strategies.[8] This cyclical movement along the subsistence continuum continued into the eighth century BCE, when the region was absorbed into the Neo-Assyrian world system.

It is because of the significant societal changes that Judah experienced as it entered into the Assyrian world system that cultural-evolutionary theory can provide a useful interpretive model for exploring the socio-economic contexts behind prophetic com-

---

[6] Edens, "Dynamics of Trade in the Ancient Mesopotamian 'World System,'" *American Anthropologist* 94, no. 1 (1992). Coote and Whitelam, *The Emergence of Early Israel*, 63-64. Harrison, "Shifting Patterns of Settlement in the Highlands of Central Jordan during the Early Bronze Age," *Bulletin of the American Schools of Oriental Research*, no. 306 (1997): 19. Richard, "Toward a Consensus of Opinion on the End of the Early Bronze Age in Palestine-Transjordan," *Bulletin of the American schools of Oriental Research*, no. 237 (1980): 24.

[7] Coote and Whitelam, *The Emergence of Early Israel*, 72-80.

[8] Coote and Whitelam, *The Emergence of Early Israel*, 73. Dever, "Archaeological Sources for the History of Palestine: The Middle Bronze Age: The Zenith or the Urban Canaanite Era," *The Biblical Archaeologist* 50, no. 3 (1987): 159.

plaints against injustice attributed to that time. Evidence of dramatic levels of population growth,[9] increased efforts to cultivate
and process olives and grapes,[10] expansion into previously uninhabited or cultivated rural areas,[11] significant building projects in urban
and rural areas,[12] and the import of luxury goods that are not found
in Judah prior to the late eighth century[13] all point to a societal evolution that would have demanded greater administrative control
and a centralization of production. Evidence of significant economic growth and trade activity in the nearby Philistine cities of
Ekron and Ashkelon further suggest unprecedented trade activity
in the region, which would have placed pressure on the fertile lands
of neighbouring Judah to produce greater quantities of olives and
grapes for oil and wine production.[14] As Judean culture evolved to
meet the organizational challenges of this period of population
growth, increased, trade, and Assyrian vassalage, so too would the
region's approach to agrarian economics.

The societal changes that appear to have taken place in the
late eighth and the early seventh centuries BCE provide a founda-

---

[9] Shiloh, *Excavations at the City of David* (vol. 19; Jerusalem: Institute of
Archaeology, Hebrew University of Jerusalem, 1984), 19. Finkelstein and
Silberman, "Temple and Dynasty: Hezekiah, the Remaking of Judah and
the Rise of the Pan-Israelite Ideology," *JSOT* 30, no. 3 (2006): 265.
Liverani, *Israel's History and the History of Israel* (London: Equinox, 2007),
152.

[10] Fantalkin, "The Final Destruction of Beth Shemesh and the *Pax
Assyriaca* in the Judahite Shephelah: An Alternative View," *Tel Aviv* 31, no.
2 (2004): 255. Finkelstein and Na'aman, "The Judahite Shephelah in the
Late 8th and Early 7th Centuries BCE," *Tel Aviv* 31, no. 1 (2004): 73-75.

[11] Shiloh, *Excavations at the City of David*, 19. Finkelstein and Silberman, "Temple and Dynasty": 265. Liverani, *Israel's History and the History of
Israel*, 152.

[12] Liverani, *Israel's History and the History of Israel*, 152. Finkelstein and
Silberman, "Temple and Dynasty": 265.

[13] Faust and Weiss, "Judah, Philistia, and the Mediterranean World:
Reconstructing the Economic System of the Seventh Century B.C.E.,"
Bulletin of the American Schools of Oriental Research no. 338 (2005): 75.

[14] Fantalkin, "The Final Destruction of Beth Shemesh": 255.
Finkelstein and Na'aman, "The Judahite Shephelah in the Late 8th and
Early 7th Centuries BCE": 73-75.

tion to Chaney's and Premnath's cultural-evolutionary approach to understanding prophetic complaints against economic injustice. Considering that agrarian societies tend to 1) abandon subsistence strategies, 2) consolidate land in a bid to increase the efficient cultivation of exportable goods, and 3) consolidate the benefits among an administrative class during periods of rapid development, the presence of the injustices that the prophetic authors attribute to late eighth-century Judah would not be surprising. Whether or not passages like Isa. 5.8–10 and Mic. 2.1–2 actually originated in the eighth century or were referenced from a later period of significant development, such as the Persian or even the Hellenistic period, the recurring patterns that are addressed through cultural-evolutionary theory offer a new way of looking at these texts and have provided a new interpretive approach for biblical scholars who have had to work with a very limited body of evidence.

The Evolution of World Systems into the Modern Day

It has also been established that the world systems of the Bronze and Iron ages were not phenomena of an ancient era, but have continuously evolved into greater and more efficient world systems that, as Andrew Bosworth notes, "envelope ever-larger regions and ever-larger bodies of water."[15] If social scientists like Bosworth, Rennstich, Modelski, and Thompson are correct in their claim that corporate globalization is not simply a product of the twentieth century, but the culmination of five millennia of world systems evolution, then the modern economic context is not entirely divorced from the world system into which Judah was absorbed.[16] As addressed in Chapter Three, Rennstich claims that despite the vast

---

[15] Bosworth. "The Evolution of the World-City System," in *World System History: The Social Science of Long-Term Change* eds. Denemark, Friedman, Gills and Modelski; London: Routledge, 2000), 276.

[16] Rennstich. "Three Steps in Globalization," in *Globalization and Global History* eds. Gills and Thompson; vol. 2 of *Rethinking Globalizations*, ed. Gills; London: Routledge, 2006), 204-8. Modelski. "World System Evolution," in *World System History: The Social Science of Long-Term Change* eds. Denemark, Friedman, Gills and Moldeski; London: Routledge, 2000), 35-37.

differences between the world systems of the ancient and the modern world, the driving logic behind these systems remains the same.[17] In other words, although corporate globalization has developed into a far more efficient and far-reaching system than its Iron Age ancestor, the driving motivations of power and wealth – and the wounds that the fruits of these motivations inflict upon subsistence farmers – are common. It is this connecting thread and the recurring nature of cultural evolutionary patterns that allow the possibility for corporate globalization to address ancient contextual questions for which archaeological and literary evidence is scarce.

Modern-Day Corporate Globalization and Tunisia

The Failure/Success of Corporate Globalization

Although there are connections between corporate globalization and the world system into which Judah was absorbed, the differences between ancient and modern world systems are as important as their similarities. A key difference between corporate globalization and all previous world systems is the number of precautions that the delegates of the Bretton Woods Conference took to help diminish the negative impacts that increased trade tends to have on peripheral communities and their rural producers. During the formation of corporate globalization at the end of the Second World War, the delegates at Bretton Woods established the International Monetary Fund and the International Bank for Reconstruction and Development to regulate trade between members and ensure equitable growth by promoting exchange-rate stability. This was to be done, in part, by making capital available for developing countries so as to protect them from predatory lenders in the private financial sector.[18] The IMF's website still proclaims its mandate to "fos-

---

[17] Rennstich. "Three Steps in Globalization," 205.

[18] Bernstein, "A Practical International Monetary Policy," *The American Economic Review* 34, no. 4 (1944): 781. Brown, "The International Monetary Fund: A Consideration of Certain Objection," *The Journal of Business of the University of Chicago* 17, no. 4 (1944): 199. Smithies, "The International Bank For Reconstruction and Development," *The American Economic Review* 43, no. 4 (1944): 790-91.

ter global monetary cooperation, secure financial stability, facilitate international trade, promote high employment and sustainable economic growth, and reduce poverty around the world."[19] Although the development of a social conscience is a unique aspect of the current world system, it has been the failure of the IMF and the World Bank to execute their mandates to protect the needs of the vulnerable, as outlined in Chapters Four and Five, that is of significant interest to this thesis.

Due in part to an unbalanced system of governance that gives the greatest amount of decision-making power to the world's wealthiest nations,[20] the policies of the IMF and the World Bank have sparked riots and protests around the world[21] while attracting condemnation from human rights organizations and economic think-tanks like UNCHR, UNICEF, and the Meltzer Commission.[22] The structural adjustment programs that are implemented through IMF and World Bank loan conditions have been denounced by national leaders, economists, and political scientists as far too intrusive and skewed toward benefiting the world's most powerful countries. As a result, developing areas of the world have experienced heightened levels of poverty and suffering while the world's wealthiest nations have profited.[23] The IMF and the World

[19] IMF, *International Monetary Fund Homepage* ([March 5, 2009]); available from http://www.imf.org/external/about.htm.

[20] Buira. "The Governance of the IMF in a Global Economy," in *Challenges to the World Bank and IMF: Developing Country Perspectives* (ed. Buira; London: Anthem Press, 2004), 15.

[21] Walton. "Urban Protest and the Global Political Economy: The IMF Riots," in *The Capitalist City* eds. Smith and Feagin; Oxford: Basil Blackwell, 1987).

[22] Türk, "The Realization of Economic, Social, and Cultural Rights," in *Economic and Social Council, Commission on Human Rights* (New York: United Nations, 1992). United Nations Children's Fund, *The State of the World's Children* (New York: Oxford University Press, 1989). Meltzer Commission, "The Meltzer Report," (Washington D.C.: United States Congress, 1999).

[23] Pérez, "Letter to Michel Camdessus," (1989). Buira. "An Analysis of IMF Conditionality," in *Challenges to the World Bank and IMF: Developing Country Perspectives* (ed. Buira; London: Anthem Press, 2004), 59. Mosley, et al., *Aid and Power: The World Bank & Policy-Based Lending* (2vols.; vol. 1 & 2;

Bank have not only failed to fulfill their mandate to prevent the abuses that cultural-evolutionary theorists associate with rapid economic development in agrarian societies, they have actually become active agents in facilitating such abuses. This is not to suggest that international financial institutions like the IMF and the World Bank or those who work in them are callous and wicked; rather, the failure of these IFIs to curb such abuses attests to the relentless nature of these societal patterns that tend to recur as agrarian societies lessen their dependence on subsistence strategies in favor of a more powerful political economy. Despite attempts made by some of those who worked to design the modern world system in a way that would create equitable development and trade, their attempts were thwarted by the desire for power and wealth among both governmental leaders and IFI members, as found in the Tunisian example. If such abuses occur even when core societies try to protect the interests of peripheral societies, consider the suffering that an Iron Age world system would have inflicted upon rural producers whose wellbeing had not been considered.

The Tunisian Example

As a result of the newly-established Tunisian government's attempts to engage in corporate globalization since the 1950s, small-scale farmers have suffered from the same abusive patterns that cultural-evolutionary theorists associate with agrarian intensification. As Tunisian farmers were pressured to abandon subsistence

London: Routledge, 1991), 68-72. Kahler. "External Influence, Conditionality, and the Politics of Adjustment," in *The Politics of Economics Adjustment* eds. Haggard and Kaufman; Princeton: Princeton University Press, 1992), 131. Bardhan. "Efficiency, Equity and Poverty Alleviation: Policy Issues in Less Developed Countries," in *Poverty, Agrarian Structure, & Political Economy in India: Selected Essays* (ed. Bardhan; New Delhi: Oxford University Press, 2003), 9-11. Woods. "The Challenge to International Institutions," in *The Political Economy of Globalization* (ed. Woods; New York: St. Martin's Press, 2000), 205. Redclift and Sage. "Resources, Environmental Degradation, and Inequality," in *Inequality, Globalization, and World Politics* eds. Hurrell and Woods; Oxford: Oxford University Press, 1999), 127-28. Collier and Quaratiello, *Basta!: Land and the Zapatista Rebellion in Chiapas* (Oakland: Food First Books, 2005), 45-52.

practices and their associated socio-religious norms in order to pave the way for more lucrative farming strategies, lands were seized and consolidated into latifundia as a ruling elite hoarded the benefits amongst themselves and their supporters.[24] As Rhys Payne notes, when the IMF and the World Bank became involved, the benefits of their structural adjustment programs in Tunisia were primarily made available to the country's leaders.[25] Many of the benefits of twentieth-century development would not reach the majority of Tunisians.

Even when the Tunisian government responded to the societal unrest that resulted from its initial reforms in the 1950s by implementing a producer-friendly socialist strategy, its implementation ended up serving the political and economic elite, who eventually became disgruntled and forced the government to reinstate a latifundialist agenda.[26] Attempts to appease the most vulnerable in Tunisian society during this period of agrarian development did not lead to equitable growth but to fatal levels of poverty and oppression, as was experienced through the IMF and World Bank-backed privatization policies of the 1970s and 1980s.[27] Tunisia's rural producers and urban poor did not suffer these cultural-evolutionary changes alone, as the government attacked the religious establishment in a bid to wrest their allegedly outmoded influence and socio-economic norms from Tunisian society.[28] Again, if governmen-

---

[24] Radwan, et al., *Tunisia: Rural Labour and Structural Transformation* (London: Routledge, 1991), 37-38. Payne. "Economic Crisis and Policy Reform in the 1980s," in *Polity and Society in Contemporary North Africa* eds. Zartman and Habeeb; Boulder: Westview, 1993), 143-48. King, *Liberalization Against Democracy: The Local Politics of Economic Reform in Tunisia* (Bloomington: Indiana University Press, 2003), 117.

[25] Payne. "Economic Crisis and Policy Reform in the 1980s," 148.

[26] Radwan, et al., *Tunisia: Rural Labour and Structural Transformation*, 30.

[27] Disney, "The Working Class Revolt in Tunisia," *Middle East Research and Information Project Reports* no. 67 (1978): 12. United Nations Children's Fund, *The State of the World's Children*.

[28] Anderson, *The State and Social Transformation in Tunisia and Libya: 1830-1980* (Princeton: Princeton University Press, 1986), 234-35. Boulby, "The Islamic Challenge: Tunisia Since Independence," *Third World Quarterly* 10, no. 2, Islam & Politics (1988): 592.

tal leaders who rule under a world system that values human and worker rights, at least in writing, it is difficult to imagine that their ancient counterparts would not have been less accommodating to agrarian communities.

What Has Been Discovered

The interdisciplinary approach of this study has demonstrated that the negative effects of corporate globalization can offer a new and valuable lens through which to consider the prophetic texts that condemn economic injustice in eighth-century Judah, and through which to evaluate biblical commentary on such passages. Although the use of modern-day abuses alongside cultural-evolutionary theory cannot provide a definitive picture as to the socio-economic contexts to which these prophetic authors wrote, it can help scholars to read these ambiguous texts in a new light, offer new interpretations, and better assess other scholars' work. Through bringing together evidence of cultural-evolution and word-systems patterns in eighth-century Judah and the Assyrian world system alongside evidence of these same patterns in Tunisia and the modern world system of corporate globalization, Chaney's and Premnath's approach to landownership abuse in prophetic texts attributed to eighth-century Judah can be augmented. Additionally, the interpretive model offered in this book has produced several opportunities for future study.

B. Contributions Offered By This Study

The interpretive model offered here serves to augment the use of cultural-evolutionary theory in biblical studies. Through adding the negative effects of corporate globalization to a social-scientific approach that has been adopted by such biblical scholars as Chaney, Premnath, and Hopkins, tangible agrarian societies can be used to ask new questions of biblical texts. Exploring the negative effects of the current world system on Tunisia's agrarian communities has helped to reveal a variety of key contextual considerations that can be applied to studies on prophetic texts against economic injustice.

The Issue of Perpetrators and Victims

While commentators like Smith and Kissane offer an unsupported, yet commonly held, view of a group of greedy Judean businessmen who schemed to rob poor farmers of their land and livelihood,[1] Chaney's and Premnath's cultural-evolutionary approach presents a sound argument for a Pan-Judean shift in economic strategy which brought about a new system of land management that had oppressed farmers eighth-century Judah.[2] Out of this alternative context Premnath claims that Isa. 5.8–10 and Mic. 2.1–2 addressed a process of latifundialization in which wealthy urban elites took small plots of land that were used by "small peasants" for residence and cultivation.[3] Such a rendering of these passages is very insightful but may neglect other contextual possibilities upon which the modern context can help to shed light.

Insights into the Perpetrators

As found in the context of corporate globalization, although modern urban elites create land-management policies and are often the

---

[1] Smith, *Micah - Malachi*, 24. Kissane, *The Book of Isaiah: Translated from a Critically Revised Hebrew Text with Commentary* (2vols.; vol. 1; Dublin: Browne and Nolan Limited, 1941), xl, 57.

[2] Chaney, "Bitter Bounty: The Dynamics of Political Economy Critiqued by the Eighth-Century Prophets," 16. Premnath, "Latifundialization in Isaiah 5.8-10," 305-06.

[3] Premnath, *Eighth Century Prophets: A Social Analysis*, 100, 105.

ones who are responsible for latifundialization, they do not always act alone. Unlike the removed community of urban merchants that Herbert envisioned in Isa. 5.8,[4] wealthy Tunisian farmers played a significant role in taking land from their neighbors and ensuring that the latter remained in a subservient position. This is demonstrated in the case of Abdelkader's successful attempt to prevent his less affluent neighbors from establishing a refrigeration cooperative so that they could compete with his technically advanced facilities.[5] Perhaps the Judean offenders to which the authors of Isa. 5.8 referred were not as distant as many commentators have assumed, but rather were members of the very rural communities that were affected. Although ruling elites most likely played the largest role in the societal transformation of eighth-century Judah, modern examples of cultural evolution offer a useful reminder that the farmers who lost their land may have had a share in the blame.

The example of Afghan opium-poppy cultivators offers another example of how subsistence farmers can share the responsibility for their own demise. Many of these farmers' refusals to return to subsistence farming, despite governmental incentives and the risk of losing their crops to Coalition forces, reveal that subsistence farmers will sometimes abandon traditional agrarian practices out of their own volition in order to take advantage of lucrative trade opportunities. Perhaps some Judean subsistence farmers, like those of Bronze-Age el-Hayyat,[6] decided to take a chance by abandoning risk-reducing subsistence practices for specialized cultivation in a bid to profit from expanding olive oil and wine markets. While some farmers would have ultimately lost such a gamble to Judah's erratic weather conditions, those who were more successful could have acquired their neighbors' land to further their fortunes. Farmers could also have used the same processes of latifundialization that Chaney and Premnath attribute to Judah's ruling elite,

---

[4] Herbert, *The Book of the Prophet Isaiah: Chapters 1-39* (eds. Ackroyd, Leaney and Packer; Cambridge: Cambridge University Press, 1973), 51.

[5] King, *Liberalization Against Democracy*, 93.

[6] Falconer, "Rural Responses to Early Urbanism: Bronze Age Household and Village Economy at Tell el-Hayyat, Jordan," *Journal of Field Archaeology* 22, no. 4 (1995): 411.

namely debt exploitation. Whether the motivation of the prophetic complaints was a break from a previous agrarian culture or YHWH's divine order, as suggested by several commentators,[7] the victims might have been as guilty as those who acquired their land.

The Tunisian example also highlights a potential context that is not often addressed in commentary: the element of betrayal. Whereas commentaries on landownership abuse in Isaiah and Micah often portray the instigators as a class of people who were inherently wicked and would be expected to oppress their neighbors,[8] the laments of Majoub illuminate that fact that oppression can come from unexpected sources. The change of intra-societal relations that came with a new economic strategy in Tunisia led the same wealthy farmers who had generously supported smaller-scale farmers like Majoub to suddenly shun their less fortunate neighbors and hoard all of the benefits of trade.[9] Such a common outcome of a shift to a trade-based strategy, exemplifying the characteristics of individualism and competitiveness that appear as subsistence strategies give way to a strong political economy,[10] provides a new interpretive angle through which to approach latifundialization in eighth-century Judah. Perhaps the Judean farmers did not only suffer a loss of self-sufficiency and displacement but the betrayal of fellow community members as well.

---

[7] Petersen, *The Prophetic Literature: An Introduction* (Louisville, KY: Westminster John Knox Press, 1989), 90. Andersen and Freedman, *Micah* (24E; eds. Albright and Freedman; New York: Doubleday, 2000), 270-74. Dearman, *Property Rights in the Eighth-Century Prophets: The Conflict and its Background* (eds. Roberts and Talbert; vol. 106; Scholars Press: Atlanta, 1988), 52-57. Premnath, *Eighth Century Prophets: A Social Analysis*, 102, 106.

[8] Alfaro, *Justice and Loyalty: A Commentary on the Book of Micah.* (Grand Rapids: Eerdmans, 1989), 25. Andersen and Freedman, *Micah*, 274. Smith, *Micah - Malachi*, 24. Kaiser, *Isaiah 1-12: A Commentary* (London: SCM Press LTD, 1972), 65.

[9] King, *Liberalization Against Democracy*, 86-87.

[10] Nolan and Lenski, *Human Societies: An Introduction to Macrosociology* (Boulder: Paradigm Publishers, 2004), 149.

Insights into the Victims

Economically and socially vulnerable members of a society are the most obvious victims of cultural-evolutionary change, as has been displayed in the Tunisian example. As economic and ruling elites work to gain from a strengthening political economy, subsistence farmers who are accustomed to working for the benefit of their immediate community lose their self-sufficiency as they are forced to abandon their risk-reducing lifestyle.[11] One of the key problems that these farmers face as their land is absorbed into latifundia is displacement, as was the case in Tunisia.[12]

Instances of displacement in Tunisia have proven useful in addressing previous interpretations of Isa. 5.8–10 and Mic. 2.1–2. The wealthy landowner Naouar's desire to keep his less fortunate neighbors and their chickens off of his land, and to employ only a few farmers to work his fields, may help to support Chaney's claim that Judean subsistence farmers were forced to toil as wage laborers on the same land that they had once farmed for themselves.[13] While there were a few farmers who suffered such a fate on Naouar's land, most lost their access to employment altogether. Naouar's strategy provides an extra-biblical example of how it is in the best interest of a latifundialist to keep only a limited number of workers employed. If Judean latifundialists wanted to increase profits, it would have behooved them to keep as few employees as possible, which would have left many without employment. Even if subsistence farmers had become debt slaves, who would not have received a wage, grape and olive cultivation are relatively low maintenance pursuits, making it difficult to justify the housing and feeding of a large number of such slaves throughout the year.[14] The

---

[11] Johnson and Earle, *The Evolution of Human Societies* (Stanford: Stanford University Press, 1987), 273. As mentioned in above, subsistence farmers are not always forced, but the process does not tend to be entirely voluntary (Lenski, *Power and Privilege*, 220).

[12] Hopkins, "Tunisia: An Open and Shut Case," *Social Problems* 28, no. 4, Development Processes and Problems (1981): 386.

[13] Chaney, "Whose Sour Grapes?," 109.

[14] Hopkins, *The Highlands of Canaan: Agricultural Life in the Early Iron Age* (ed. Flanagan; vol. 3; Sheffield: Almond, 1985), 227.

Tunisian experience serves as an example of how the displacement that is addressed in Isa. 5.8, and referred to in Chaney and Kissane's work, would have been expected in a society that was moving away from subsistence practices in order to benefit from increased trade opportunities.[15]

Examples of landownership abuse and cultural evolution in modern agrarian societies also highlight that the poor and the vulnerable are not the only ones who are susceptible to societal change. Aside from supporting the idea that political elites had instigated the landownership abuses referred to in Isaiah and Micah, the complaints of the educated peasant, Hadi, reveal that middle-class farmers also lost their land and livelihood to Tunisia's twentieth-century cultural evolution. Additionally, the Tunisian example brings attention to the fact that members of various elite classes can also suffer as the economic and social system upon which they depend for status and revenue are overturned; as societies evolve, so do the institutions upon which various groups depend.

The suffering of Tunisia's religious elite raised questions about the motivations of the prophetic authors' complaints against landownership abuse. As world systems alter economic strategies, the religious norms attached to previous agrarian practices also come into question;[16] in the Tunisian case this meant a loss of social status and financial independence for those who enjoyed the benefits of centuries-old Muslim hierarchies. Considering that this is a common pattern as agrarian societies undergo economic development, such a scenario is worth contemplating in the eighth-century Judean context. In light of Hezekiah's religious reforms, which would have channeled YHWHist income into Jerusalem at the same time that a developing Judean state was struggling under the pressures of population growth, increased trade, and an Assyrian threat, the motivations behind prophetic complaints can be read from a new perspective. While the notion of suffering among elite classes does not appear to be considered in biblical commentaries

---

[15] Chaney, "Whose Sour Grapes?," 109. Kissane, *The Book of Isaiah*, xl.

[16] Bayly. "'Archaic' and 'Modern' Globalization in the Eurasian and African Arena: c. 1750-1850," in *Globalization in World History* (ed. Hopkins; London: Pimlico, 2002), 52-53.

that deal with economic injustice, the modern example of corporate globalization can help to highlight its prevalence in times of
economic change.

The perspectives gained from considering modern examples
of injustice due to corporate globalization alongside recurring patterns of landownership abuse do not reveal the identities of the
perpetrators and victims of latifundialization in eighth-century
Judah, but they do offer new ways of looking at these complaints,
which can help to provide more nuanced interpretations. It is in
this way that considering landownership abuse resulting from corporate globalization can help to augment Chaney's and Premnath's
application of ecological and structural aspects of cultural evolution
in approaching contextual ambiguous texts.

C. POTENTIAL FOR FUTURE STUDY

The interpretive model that is presented here opens a wide range of possibilities for future study. Each of the insights listed above can be examined further and elaborated upon with greater detail to both evaluate previous interpretations of landownership abuse in the Hebrew Bible and also to offer fresh interpretations of the texts themselves. The identities of perpetrators and victims, the motivations behind Judean landownership abuse, the motivations behind the prophetic authors' complaints against these perceived injustices, and the potential societal consequences of Judean latifundialization can all be explored further through considering modern examples of how agrarian societies are affected by the expansion of corporate globalization.

Beyond issues of landownership abuse, the Tunisian case study provides a foundation for exploring other prophetic complaints attributed to eighth-century Judah. One question that I would like to explore through the lens of President Bourguiba's religious reforms is the identity of the false נבאים or prophets of Jer. 6.14 and Jer. 14.15. Perhaps the prophetic authors' disdain for these false prophets is akin to the anger that was experienced by pious Tunisian *ulema* who watched many of their colleagues as they turned a blind eye to the injustices created by Bourguiba's economic reforms and capitulated to the government's new interpretations of Islamic doctrine. Considering the societal changes that took place in late eighth-century Judah, it could be that the authors of Jer. 6.14 and 14.15 had referred to those who betrayed older YHWHist norms in order to maintain their status in a changing Judean economic landscape. Additionally, an exploration of the possibility that the religious reforms attributed to late eighth-century Judah had been developed as a scheme to facilitate a changing economic strategy may offer new insights to texts that address this supposed centralization of YHWHist practice or attest to the likelihood of their implementation. Perhaps examples of altered societal relations, such as those experienced in Tunisia's rural communities, can offer greater insight into prophetic texts that decry the callousness of the wealthy toward the poor, as found in Amos 4.1–3.

The interpretive model presented in this book could also provide opportunities to explore the relevance of prophetic complaints in addressing modern injustice. If the recurring nature of cultural-evolutionary patterns can enable modern manifestations of injustice to shed light on ancient examples, it seems logical that the prophetic complaints can find a voice in addressing modern injustice.[1] Such research could be useful to those who use a biblical approach to challenge injustice in the world today, such as faith-based non-governmental organizations (NGOs) that address injustice on an international scale or synagogues and churches that confront injustice at the local level. By reverse-engineering the interpretive model presented in this paper, the connections that appear to exist between prophetic texts and modern injustice could prove useful to both those within and outside of academic circles.

From complaints against landownership abuse and accusations of corruption amongst the religious elite to laments against decadence and callousness toward the poor, various examples of the negative effects of corporate globalization can offer something new to the field of biblical studies by augmenting the interpretive value of cultural-evolutionary theory. Such a practice can offer a wealth of new material and approaches though which to consider texts that are attributed to a time in which Judah underwent a significant period of cultural evolution as it was absorbed into a world system that shares a lineage with its twentieth-century descendant, corporate globalization. Although a great number of discrepancies exist between these modern and ancient contexts, the very important connections that do exist can help to further our understanding of prophetic complaints against landownership abuse and other forms of injustice.

---

[1] For a study on this see topic Coomber. "From Prophets to Profits: Ancient Judah and Corporate Globalization," in *Bible and Justice: Ancient Texts, Modern Challenges* (ed. Coomber; vol. Bible World of, eds. Davies and Crossley; London: Equinox, Forthcoming).

BIBLIOGRAPHY

Acheson, James M. "Management of Common-Property Resources," in *Economic Anthropology*. Edited by Stuart Plattner. Stanford: Stanford University Press, 2002.

Adams, Robert M., *Heartland of Cities: Surveys of Ancient Settlements and Land Use on the Central Floodplain of the Euphrates*. Chicago: University of Chicago Press, 1981.

Ahmad, Eqbal and Stuart Schaar. "Human Rights in Morocco and Tunisia: A Critique of State Department Findings." *Middle East Research and Information Project*, no. 67 (1978): 15-17.

al-Ghannoushi, Rashid. "Deficiencies in the Islamic Movement." *Middle East Report* 153, no. 23-24 (1988).

al-Nayfar, Shaikh Hamid. "How Can a Muslim Live in this Era?" *Middle East Report*, no. 153 (1988): 24-26, 50.

Alfaro, Juan I., *Justice and Loyalty: A Commentary on the Book of Micah*. Grand Rapids: Eerdmans, 1989.

Alport, E.A. "Socialism in Three Countries: The Record in the Maghrib." *International Affairs* 43, no. 4 (1967): 678-92.

Alt, Albrecht. "Meros," Pages 274-77 in *Kleine Schriften Zur Geschichte des Volkes Israel*. Edited by Albrecht Alt. München: C.H. Beck'She Verlagsbuchhandlung, 1953.

Amiran, Ruth, *Early Arad*. Jerusalem: Israel Exploration Society, 1978.

Amuzegar, Jahangir. "The IMF Under Fire." *Foreign Policy*, no. 64 (1986): 98-119.

Andersen, Francis I. and David Noel Freedman, *Micah*. Edited by William Foxwell Albright and David Noel Freedman. AB 24E. New York: Doubleday, 2000.

Anderson, Lisa, *The State and Social Transformation in Tunisia and Libya: 1830-1980*. Princeton: Princeton University Press, 1986.

_____. "Obligation and Accountability: Islamic Politics in North Africa." *Daedalus* 120, no. 3 (1991): 93-112.

Ashbel, D. "Israel, Land of (Geographical Survey): Climate." Pages 181-94 in vol. 9 of *Encyclopaedia Judaica*. Jerusalem: Keter Publishing House, 1971.

Asheri, David. "Laws of Inheritance, Distribution of Land and Political Constitutions in Ancient Greece." *Historia* 12, (1963): 1-21.

Ashford, Douglas E. "Succession and Social Change in Tunisia." *International Journal of Middle East Studies* 4, no. 1 (1973): 23-39.

Avigad, Nahman, *Discovering Jerusalem*. Oxford: Blackwell, 1984.

Ballantyne, Tony. "Empire, Knowledge and Culture: From Proto-Globalization to Modern Globalization," Pages 115-40 in *Globalization in World History*. Edited by A.G. Hopkins. London: Plimco, 2002.

Ballard, Robert D., Lawrence E. Stager, Daniel Master, Dana Yoerger, David Mindell, Louis L. Whitcomb, Hanumant Singh, and Dennis Piechota. "Iron Age Shipwrecks in Deep Water off Ashkelon, Israel." *American Journal of Archaeology* 106, no. 2 (2002): 151-68.

Bardhan, Pranab. "Efficiency, Equity and Poverty Alleviation: Policy Issues in Less Developed Countries," Pages 3-18 in *Poverty, Agrarian Structure, & Political Economy in India: Selected Essays*. Edited by Pranab Bardhan. New Delhi: Oxford University Press, 2003.

Bayly, C.A. "'Archaic' and 'Modern' Globalization in the Eurasian and African Arena: c. 1750-1850," Pages 47-73 in *Globalization in World History*. Edited by A.G. Hopkins. London: Pimlico, 2002.

Beckhart, B.H. "The Bretton Woods Proposal for an International Monetary Fund." *Political Science Quarterly* 59, no. 4 (1944): 489-528.

Bell, Duran. "The Social Relations of Property and Efficiency," Pages 29-45 in *Property in Economic Context*. Edited by Roberto C Hunt and Antonio Gilman. Oxford: University Press of America, Inc., 1998.

Belshaw, Cyril S., *Traditional Exchange and Modern Markets*. Englewood Cliffs, N.J.: Prentice-Hall, 1965.

_____. "Reviewed Work(s): Stone Age Economics by Marshall Sahlins." *American Anthropologist* 75, no. 4 (1973): 958-60.

Ben Zvi, Ehud, *Micah*. Edited by Gene M. Tucker Rolf P. Knierim, and Marvin A. Sweeney. The Forms of the Old Testament Literature XXIB. Grand Rapids: Eerdmans, 2000.

Ben-Tor, Amnon. "New Light on the Relations Between Egypt and Southern Palestine During the Early Bronze Age." *Bulletin of the American Schools of Oriental Research*, no. 281 (1991): 3-10.

Berdan, Frances F. "Trade and Markets in Precapitalist States," Pages 78-107 in *Economic Anthropology*. Edited by Stuart Plattner. Stanford: Stanford University Press, 1989.

_____. "Trade and Markets in Precapitalist States," Pages 78-107 in *Economic Anthropology*. Edited by Stuart Plattner. Stanford: Stanford University Press, 2002.

Bernstein, Edward M. "A Practical International Monetary Policy." *The American Economic Review* 34, no. 4 (1944): 771-84.

_____. "The International Monetary Fund." *International Organization* 22, no. 1 (1968): 97-106.

Biersteker, Thomas. "Globalization as a Mode of Thinking," in *The Political Economy of Globalization*. Edited by Ngaire Woods. New York: St. Martin's Press, 2000.

Bird, Graham. "Introduction," in *Third World Debt: The Search For A Solution*. Edited by Graham Bird. Worchester: Edward Elgar Publishing Limited, 1989.

Blakely, Jeffrey A. and James W. Hardin. "Southwestern Judah in the Late Eighth Century B.C.E." *Bulletin of the American Schools of Oriental Research*, no. 326 (2002): 11-64.

Blenkinsopp, Joseph, *Sage, Priest, Prophet: Religious and Intellectual Leadership in Ancient Israel*. Edited by Douglas A. Knight. Library of Ancient Israel. Louisville: Westminster John Knox Press, 1995.

_____. *A History of Prophecy in Israel: Revised and Enlarged*. Louisville: Westminster John Knox Press, 1996.

_____. *Isaiah 1-39*. Edited by William Foxwell Albright and David Noel Freedman. AB 19. New York: Doubleday, 2000.

Boafo-Arthur, Kwame. "Ghana: Structural Adjustment, Democratization, and the Politics of Continuity." *African Studies Review* 42, no. 2 (1999): 41-72.

Boas, Franz. "Psychological Problems in Anthropology." *The American Journal of Psychology* 21, no. 3 (1910): 371-84.

_____. "History and Science in Anthropology: A Reply." *American Anthropologist* 38, no. 1 (1936): 137-41.

_____. *Race, Language, and Culture*. New York: The Free Press, 1966.

Borowski, Oded, *Agriculture in Iron Age Israel*. Boston: American School of Oriental Research, 2002.

Boserup, Ester, *The Conditions of Agricultural Growth: The Economics of Agrarian Change under Population Pressure*. New York: Aldine Publishing Company, 1965.

Bosworth, Andrew. "The Evolution of the World-City System," Pages 273-83 in *World System History: The Social Science of Long-Term Change*. Edited by Robert A. Denemark, Jonathan Friedman, Barry K. Gills, and George Modelski. London: Routledge, 2000.

Boulby, Marion. "The Islamic Challenge: Tunisia Since Independence." *Third World Quarterly* 10, no. 2, Islam & Politics (1988): 590-614.

Boyd, Robert and Peter J. Richerson, *Culture and the Evolutionary Process*. London: University of Chicago Press, 1985.

Brody, Aaron. "From the Hills of Adonis through the Pillars of Hercules: Recent Advances in the Archaeology of Canaan and Phoenicia." *Near Eastern Archaeology* 65, no. 1 (2002): 69-80.

Broshi, Magen. "The Expansion of Jerusalem in the Reigns of Hezekiah and Manasseh." *Israel Exploration Journal*, no. 24 (1974): 21-26.

Broshi, Magen and Ram Gophna. "The Settlements and Population of Palestine during the Early Bronze Age II-III." *Bulletin of the American Schools of Oriental Research*, no. 253 (1984): 41-53.

Broshi, Magen. and Israel Finkelstein. "The Population of Palestine in Iron Age II." *Bulletin of the American Schools of Oriental Research*, no. 287 (1992): 47-60.

Brown, Edward E. "The International Monetary Fund: A Consideration of Certain Objection." *The Journal of Business of the University of Chicago* 17, no. 4 (1944): 199-208.

Brown, Francis, S.R. Driver, and C.A. Briggs. *The Brown-Driver-Briggs Hebrew and English Lexicon: With an Appendix Containing the Biblical Aramaic: Coded with Strong's Concordance Numbers*. Peabody, Mass: Hendrickson Publishers. 2001.

Buira, Ariel. "An Analysis of IMF Conditionality," in *Challenges to the World Bank and IMF: Developing Country Perspectives*. Edited by Ariel Buira. London: Anthem Press, 2004.

_____. "The Governance of the IMF in a Global Economy," in *Challenges to the World Bank and IMF: Developing Country Perspectives.* Edited by Ariel Buira. London: Anthem Press, 2004.

Bujazan, Michael, Sharon E. Hare, Thomas J. La Belle, and Lisa Stafford. "International Agency Assistance to Education in Latin America and the Caribbean, 1970-1984: Technical and Political Decision-Making." *Comparative Education* 23, no. 2 (1987): 161-71.

Cannon, Byron D. "Administrative and Economic Regionalism in Tunisian Oleiculture: The Idarat al Ghabah Experiment, 1870-1914." *The International Journal of African Historical Studies* 11, no. 4 (1978): 584-628.

Cantor, Norman F., Inventing the Middle Ages: The Lives, Works, and Ideas of the Great Medievalists of the Twentieth Century. Cambridge: Lutterworth Press, 1992.

Carter, Ralph G. "Leadership at Risk: The Perils of Unilateralism." *PS: Political Science and Politics* 36, no. 1 (2003): 17-22.

Castells, Manuel, *End of Millennium.* 3 vols. Vol. 3, The Information Age. Oxford: Blackwell Publishers, 2000.

Castillo, Rosalva Aída Hernández and Ronald Nigh. "Global Processes and Local Identity Among Mayan Coffee Growers in Chiapas, Mexico." *American Anthropologist* 100, no. 1 (1998): 137-47.

Chaney, Marvin L. "Systemic Study of the Israelite Monarchy," Pages 51-76 in *Social Scientific Criticism of the Hebrew Bible and Its Social World: The Israelite Monarchy.* Edited by Norman K. Gottwald. Semeia 37. Decatur, Georgia: The Society of Biblical Literature, 1986.

_____. "Bitter Bounty: The Dynamics of Political Economy Critiqued by the Eighth-Century Prophets," Pages 15-30 in *Reformed Faith and Economics.* Edited by Robert L. Stivers. Lanham: University Press of America, 1989.

_____. "Whose Sour Grapes? The Addressees of Isaiah 5:1-7 in the Light of Political Economy," Pages 105-22 in *The Social World of the Hebrew Bible: Twenty-Five Years of the Social Sciences in the Academy.* Edited by Ronald A. Simkins and Stephen L. Cook. of *Semeia* Edited by Athalya Brenner. Atlanta: Society of Biblical Literature, 1999.

_____. "'Coveting Your Neighbor's House' in Social Context," Pages 302-17 in *The Ten Commandments: The Reciprocity of Faith-*

fulness. Edited by William P. Brown of *Library of Theological Ethics* Edited by Robin W. Lovin, Douglas F. Ottati, and William Schweiker. Louisville, Kentucky: Westminster John Knox Press, 2004.

_____. "Micah - Models Matter: Political Economy and Micah 6:9-15," Pages 145-60 in *Ancient Israel: The Old Testament in its Social Context.* Edited by Philip F. Esler. London: SCM Press, 2005.

Chase-Dunn, Christopher, Daniel Pascitui, Alexis Alverez, and Thomas D. Hall. "Growth/Decline Phases and Semi-Peripheral Development in the Ancient Mesopotamian and Egyptian World-Systems," in *Globalization and Global History.* Edited by Barry K. Gills and William R. Thompson of *Rethinking Globalization.* London: Routledge, 2006.

Chew, Sing C. "Neglecting Nature: World Accumulation and Core-Periphery Relations, 2500 BC to AD 1990," Pages 216-34 in *World System History: The Social Science of Long-Term Change.* Edited by Robert A. Denemark, Jonathan Friedman, Barry K. Gills, and George Modelski. London: Routledge, 2000.

Chick, C.A., Sr. "The West's Changing Attitude Toward Africa." *The Journal of Negro Education* 29, no. 2 (1960): 191-97.

Chirichigno, Gregory C., *Debt-Slavery in Israel and the Ancient Near East.* Edited by David J.A. Clines and Philip R. Davies. Journal for the Study of the Old Testament Supplement Series 141. Sheffield: Sheffield Academic Press, 1993.

Chomsky, Noam. "World Order and Its Rules: Variations on Some Themes." *Journal of Law and Society* 20, no. 2 (1993): 145-65.

_____. *Hegemony or Survival: America's Quest for Global Dominance.* London: Hamish Hamilton, 2003.

_____. *Failed States: The Abuse of Power and the Assault on Democracy.* London: Penguin Books, 2007.

Chossudovsky, Michel, *The Globalization of Poverty.* 2d ed. Pincourt, Québec: Global Research, 2003.

Clines, David J.A., *Interested Parties: The Ideology and Readers of the Hebrew Bible.* Edited by Cheryl Exum. Journal for the Study of the Old Testament Supplement Series 205. Sheffield: Sheffield Academic Press, 1995.

Collett, Nigel, *The Butcher of Amritsar: Brigadier-General Reginald Dyer.* London: Hambledon and London, 2005.

Collier, George A. and Elizabeth Lowery Quaratiello, *Basta!: Land and the Zapatista Rebellion in Chiapas.* 3d ed. Oakland: Food First Books, 2005.

Comte, Auguste, *Introduction to Positive Philosophy.* Edited by Frederick Ferré. Indianapolis: Bobbs-Merrill, 1970.

Conklin, Margaret and Daphne Davidson. "The I.M.F. and Economic and Social Human Rights: A case study of Argentina, 1958-1985." *Human Rights Quarterly* 8, no. 2 (1986): 227-69.

Cook, Scott. "The Obsolete 'Anti-Market' Mentality: A Critique of the Substantive Approach to Economic Anthropology." *American Anthropologist* 68, no. 2 (1966): 323-45.

Coomber, Matthew J.M. "From Prophets to Profits: Ancient Judah and Corporate Globalization," in *Bible and Justice: Ancient Texts, Modern Challenges.* Edited by Matthew J.M. Coomber. Bible-World. London: Equinox, Forthcoming.

Coote, Robert B. and Keith W. Whitelam, *The Emergence of Early Israel: In Historical Perspective.* Edited by James W. Flanagan. The Social World of Biblical Antiquity Series 5. Sheffield: Almond Press, 1987.

Corbo, Vittorio and Jaime de Melo. "Lessons from the Southern Cone Policy Reforms." *World Bank Research Observer* 2 (1985): 111-42.

Cowgill, George L. "On Causes and Consequences of Ancient and Modern Population Changes." *American Anthropologist* 77, no. 3 (1975): 505-25.

Crisp, Brian F. and Michael J. Kelly. "The Socioeconomic Impacts of Structural Adjustment." *International Studies Quarterly* 43, no. 3 (1999): 533-52.

Crist, Raymond E. "Land for the Fellahin, XI: Land Tenure and Land Use in the Near East." *American Journal of Economics and Sociology* 19, no. 3 (1960): 311-322.

Dahl, Raynold P. "Agricultural Development Strategies in a Small Economy: The Case of Tunisia." Pages: Staff Paper, USAID, 1971.

Dalton, George. "Economic Theory and Primitive Society." *American Anthropologist* 63, no. 1 (1961): 1-25.

_____. "Economic Theory and Primitive Society," Pages 143-67 in *Economic Anthropology: Reading in Theory and Analysis.* Edited by Edward E LeClair and Harold K. Schneider. New York: Holt, Rinehart, and Winston, INC., 1968.

Dandamaev, Muhammad A., *Slabery in Babylonia: From Nabopolassar to Alexander the Great (636-331 BC)*. Edited by Marvin A. Powell, David B. Weisberg, Translated by Victoria A. Powell. DeKalb, Illinois: Northern Illinois University Press, 1984.

Davies, Philip R., *In Search of Ancient Israel*. Edited by David J.A. Clines, Philip R. Davies, and John Jarick. Journal for the Study of the Old Testament Supplement Series 148. Sheffield: Sheffield Academic Press, 1995.

Davies, Philip R. and John Rogerson, *The Old Testament World*. 2d ed. Louisville: Westminster John Knox Press, 2005.

Davis, Ellen F., *Scripture, Culture, and Agriculture: An Agrarian Reading of the Bible*. New York: Cambridge University Press, 2009.

Dávila, Francisco Suárez. "The Developing Countries and the International Financial System: 25 Years of Hope, Frustration, and Some Modest Achievements," in *G-24: The Developing Countries in the International Financial System*. Edited by Eduardo Mayobre. Boulder: Lynne Rienner Publishers, 1999.

Deacon, Bob. "Social Policy in a Global Context," Pages 211-47 in *Inequality, Globalization, and World Politics*. Edited by Andrew Hurrell and Ngaire Woods. New York: Oxford University Press, 1999.

Dearman, John Andrew, *Property Rights in the Eighth-Century Prophets: The Conflict and its Background*. Edited by J.J.M. Roberts and Charles Talbert of Society of Biblical Literature Dissertation Series 106. Scholars Press: Atlanta, 1988.

Debbasch, Charles, *La République Tunisienne*. Paris: CNRS, 1962.

Deist, Ferdinand E., *The Material Culture of the Bible: An Introduction*. Edited by Robert P Carroll. The Biblical Seminar 70. Sheffield: Sheffield Academic Press, 2000.

Dever, William G. "Archaeological Sources for the History of Palestine: The Middle Bronze Age: The Zenith or the Urban Canaanite Era." *The Biblical Archaeologist* 50, no. 3 (1987): 149-77.

Dewar, Robert E. "Rainfall Variability and Subsistence Systems in Southeast Asia and the Western Pacific." *Current Anthropology* 44, no. 3 (2003): 369-88.

Diakonoff, Igor M. "Main Features of the Economy in the Monarchies of Ancient Western Asia," Pages 13-32 in *Troisème Conference Internationale D'histoire Économique*. Edited by M.I. Finley. Paris: Mouton, 1969.

Disney, Nigel. "The Working Class Revolt in Tunisia." *Middle East Research and Information Project Reports*, no. 67 (1978): 12-14.

Domeris, William Robert, *Touching the Heart of God: The Social Construction of Poverty Among Biblical Peasants.* Edited by Claudia V. Camp and Andrew Mein. Library of Hebrew Bible/Old Testament Studies 466. London: T&T Clark, 2007.

Dornbusch, Rudiger, Jose Vinals, and Richard Portes. "Mexico: Stabilization, Debt and Growth." *Economic Policy* 3, no. 7 (1988): 231-83.

Dorsey, David A., *The Roads and Highways of Ancient Israel.* Baltimore: Johns Hopkins University, 1991.

Dorsey, Gray. "Free Enterprise vs. The Entrepreneur: Redefining the Entities Subject to the Antitrust Laws." *University of Pennsylvania Law Review* 125, no. 6 (1977): 1244-64.

Drayton, Richard. "The Collaboration of Labour: Slaves, Empires, and Globalizations in the Atlantic World, c. 1600-1850," Pages 98-114 in *Globalization in World History*. Edited by A.G. Hopkins. London: Plimco, 2002.

Driver, G.R., *Canaanite Myths and Legends.* Edinburgh: T&T Clark, 1956.

Durkheim, Émile, *The Elementary Forms of the Religious Life*. Translated by Joseph Ward Swain. London: Allen & Unwin, 1971.

_____. *The Division of Labour in Society*. Translated by W.D. Halls. Basingstoke: Macmillian, 1984.

Duwaji, Ghazi. "Land Ownership in Tunisia: An Obstacle to Agricultural Development." *Land Economics* 44, no. 1 (1968): 129-32.

Economist, The. "Bretton Woods." *The Economist* CXLVII, no. 5266 (1944): 138-39.

Edelman, Diana. "Tyrian Trade in Yehud Under Artaxerxes I: Real or Fictional? Independent or Crown Endorsed?," Pages 207-46 in *Judah and the Judeans in the Persian Period*. Edited by Oded Lipschits and Manfred Oeming. Winona Lake, Indiana: Eisenbrauns, 2006.

Edens, Christopher. "Dynamics of Trade in the Ancient Mesopotamian 'World System.'" *American Anthropologist* 94, no. 1 (1992): 118-139.

Eitam, David. "Tel Miqne-Ekron: Survey of Oil Presses: 1985." *Excavations and Surveys in Israel* 5: 1986 (1987): 72-74.

Ekholm-Friedman, Kajsa. "On the Evolution of Global Systems, Part I: the Mesopotamian Heartland," Pages 152-84 in *World System History: The Social Science of Long-Term Change*. Edited by Robert A. Denemark, Jonathan Friedman, Barry K. Gills, and George Modelski. London: Routledge, 2000.

Elat, Moshe. "The Economic Relations of the Neo-Assyrian Empire with Egypt." *Journal of the American Oriental Society* 98, no. 1 (1978): 20-34.

Entelis, John P. "Reformist Ideology in the Arab World: The Cases of Tunisia and Lebanon." *The Review of Politics* 37, no. 4 (1975): 513-46.

Esler, Philip F. "Social-Scientific Models in Biblical Interpretation," Pages 3-14 in *Ancient Israel: The Old Testament in its Social Context*. Edited by Philip F. Esler. London SCM Press, 2005.

Falconer, Steven E. "Rural Responses to Early Urbanism: Bronze Age Household and Village Economy at Tell el-Hayyat, Jordan." *Journal of Field Archaeology* 22, no. 4 (1995): 399-419.

Falkenmark, Malin. "Rapid Population Growth and Water Scarcity: The Predicament of Tomorrow's Africa." *Population and Development Review*. Supplement: Resources, Environment, and Population: Present Knowledge, Future Options 16 (1990): 81-94.

Fantalkin, Alexander. "The Final Destruction of Beth Shemesh and the *Pax Assyriaca* in the Judahite Shephelah: An Alternative View." *Tel Aviv* 31, no. 2 (2004): 245-61.

Faust, Avraham. "The Rural Community in Ancient Israel During Iron Age II." *Bulletin of the American Schools of Oriental Research* 317, (2000): 17-39.

Faust, Avraham and Ehud Weiss. "Judah, Philistia, and the Mediterranean World: Reconstructing the Economic System of the Seventh Century B.C.E." *Bulletin of the American Schools of Oriental Research*, no. 338 (2005): 71-92.

Fellner, William. "The Commercial Policy Implications of the Fund and Bank." *The American Economic Review* 35, no. 2 (1945): 262-71.

Finkelstein, Israel and Neil Asher Silberman. *The Bible Unearthed: Archaeology's New Vision of Ancient Israel and the Origin of Its Sacred Texts*. New York: Touchstone, 2001.

_____. "Temple and Dynasty: Hezekiah, the Remaking of Judah and the Rise of the Pan-Israelite Ideology." *Journal for the Study of the Old Testament* 30, no. 3 (2006): 259-85.

Finkelstein, Israel and Nadav Na'aman. "The Judahite Shephelah in the Late 8th and Early 7th Centuries BCE." *Tel Aviv* 31, no. 1 (2004): 60-79.

Finley, M.I., *Politics in the Ancient World*. Cambridge: Cambridge University Press, 1984.

_____. *The Ancient Economy*. 2d ed. Sather Classical Lectures 43. Berkeley and Los Angeles: University of California Press.

Fischer, Stanley. "Sharing the Burden of the International Debt Crisis." *The American Economic Review* 77, no. 2 (1987): 165-70.

Flynn, Dennis O. and Arturo Giráldez. "Globalization Began in 1571," Pages 232-47 in *Globalization and Global History*. Edited by Barry K. Gills and William R. Thompson. Rethinking Globalization. London: Routledge, 2006.

Frank, Andre Gunder. "Bronze Age World System Cycles." *Current Anthropology* 34, no. 4 (1993): 383-429.

Fried, Morton H., *The Evolution of Political Society*. New York: Random House, 1967.

Friedman, Jonathan. "Marxism, Structuralism and Vulgar Materialism." *Man* 9, no. 3 (1974): 444-69.

_____. "Marxism, Structuralism and Vulgar Materialism." *Man* 9, no. 3 (1977): 444-69.

Fukuyama, Francis, *The End of History and the Last Man*. London: Penguin, 1992.

Gastel, Scott. *DOT Lays Out Ambitious, Sustainable Vision In New Strategic Plan, "Sustainable Streets."* New York City DOT: New York City Government, Last Updated Date 2008 [cited March 2, 2010]. Available from http://www.nyc.gov/html/dot/html/pr2008/pr08_011.shtml.

George, N. Halm. "The International Monetary Fund." *The Review of Economics and Statistics* 26, no. 4 (1944): 170-75.

Ghai, Dharam and Cynthia Hewitt de Alcántara. "The Crisis of the 1980s in Africa, Latin America, and the Caribbean: An Overview," Pages 13- 42 in *The IMF and the South: The Social Impact of Crisis and Adjustment*. Edited by Dharam Ghai. London: Zed Books Ltd on Behalf of The United Nations Research Institute for Social Development, 1991.

Gilboa, Ayelet. "Iron Age I-IIA Pottery Evolution at Dor-Regional Contexts and the Cypriot Connection," Pages 413-25 in *Mediterranean Peoples in Transition: Thirteenth to Early Tenth Centuries BCE*. Edited by Seymour Gitin, Amihai Mazar, and Ernest Stern. Jerusalem: Israel Exploration Society, 1998.

Gitin, Seymour. "Tel-Miqne-Ekron in the 7th Century B.C.E.: The Impact of Economic Innovation and Foreign Cultural Influences on a Neo-Assyrian Vassal City-State," Pages 61-79 in *Recent Excavations in Israel: A View to the West*. Edited by Seymour Gitin. Dubuque: Kendall/Hunt, 1995.

Gitin, Seymour and William G. Dever. "Recent Excavations in Israel: Studies in Iron Age Archaeology." *The Annual of the American Schools of Oriental Research* 49, Recent Excavations in Israel: Studies in Iron Age Archaeology, (1989): iii-v+vii+ix+xi-xii+1-105+107-131+133-141+143-152.

Gitin, Seymour and Trude Dothan. "The Rise and Fall of Ekron of the Philistines: Recent Excavations at an Urban Border Site." *The Biblical Archaeologist* 50, no. 4 (1987): 197-222.

Godelier, Maruice, *Perspectives in Marxist Anthropology*. Cambridge: Cambridge University Press, 1977.

_____. "Infrastructures, Societies, and History." *Current Anthropology* 19, no. 4 (1978): 763-771.

Gold, Joseph. "Voting and Decisions in the International Monetary Fund." Washington D.C.: IMF, 1972.

Goodfellow, D.M. "The Applicability of Economic Theory to So-Called Primitive Communities," Pages 55-65 in *Economic Anthropology: Readings in Theory and Analysis*. Edited by Edward E. LeClair and Harold K. Schneider. New York: Holt, Rinehart, and Winston, 1968.

Gorringe, Timothy, *Fair Shares: Ethics and the Global Economy*. New York: Thames & Hudson, 1999.

Gottwald, Norman, *The Tribes of Yahweh: A Sociology of the Religion of Liberated Israel 1250-1050 B.C.E.* London: SCM Press, 1979.

_____. The Hebrew Bible in Its Social World and in Ours. Atlanta: Scholars Press, 1993.

Grabbe, Lester L., Ancient Israel: What Do We Know and How Do We Know It? London: T&T Clark, 2007.

Grayson, Albert Kirk, *Assyrian Rulers of the Early First Millennium BC. II, (858-745 BC)*. Royal Inscriptions of Mesopotamia: Assyrian Periods 3. Toronto: University of Toronto Press, 1996.

Grey, Austin. "The Monetary Conference and China." *Far Eastern Survey* 13, no. 18 (1944): 165-67.

Griffiths, J. Gwyn. "Eight Funerary Paintings with Judgement Scenes in Swansea Wellcome Museum." *The Journal of Egyptian Archaeology* 68 (1982): 228-52.

Halpern, Baruch. "Erasing History: The Minimalist Assault on Ancient Israel." *Bible Review*, no. 11 (1995): 26-35,47.

Harber, Charles. "Tunisian Land Tenure in the Early French Protectorate." *Muslim World* 63 (1973): 307-15.

Hardesty, Donald L., *Ecological Anthropology*. New York: Wiley, 1977.

Hardt, Michael and Antonio Negri, *Empire*. Cambridge, MA: Harvard University Press, 2000.

Harik, Iliya. "Privatization: The Issue, the Prospects, and the Fears," in *Privatization and Liberalization in the Middle East*. Edited by Iliya Harik and Danis Sullivan. Bloomington: Indiana University Press, 1992.

Harrison, Timothy P. "Economics with an Entrepreneurial Spirit: Early Bronze Trade with Late Predynastic Egypt." *The Biblical Archaeologist* 56, no. 2 (1993): 81-93.

———. "Shifting Patterns of Settlement in the Highlands of Central Jordan during the Early Bronze Age." *Bulletin of the American Schools of Oriental Research*, no. 306 (1997): 1-37.

Harvey, David, *The New Imperialism.*. Oxford: Oxford University Press, 2003.

Hayes, John H. and Stuart A. Irvine, *Isaiah, the Eighth-Century Prophet: His Times and Preaching*. Nashville: Abingdon, 1987.

———. "The Kingdoms of Israel and Judah: Political and Economic Centralization in Iron IIA-B (ca. 1000-750 BCE)," Pages 368-98 in *The Archaeology of Society in the Holy Land*. Edited by Thomas E. Levy. New York: Facts on File, 1995.

Heimann, Eduard, *History of Economic Doctrines*. New York: Oxford Press, 1945.

Herbert, A.S., *The Book of the Prophet Isaiah: Chapters 1-39*. Edited by P.R. Ackroyd, A.R.C. Leaney, and J.W. Packer. The Cambridge Bible Commentary: New English Bible. Cambridge: Cambridge University Press, 1973.

Hermassi, Elbaki, *Leadership and Development*. Berkeley: University of California Press, 1972.

Herr, Larry G. "Archaeological Sources for the History of Palestine: The Iron Age II Period: Emerging Nations." *The Biblical Archaeologist* 60, no. 3 (1997): 114-83.

Herzog, Ze'ev. "The Fortress Mount at Tel Arad: An Interim Report." *Tel Aviv* 29 (2002): 3-109.

Hill, Kenneth and Anne R. Pebley. "Child Mortality in the Developing World." *Population and Development Review* 15, no. 4 (1989): 657-87.

Hilton, Rodney H. "Peasant Movement In England Before 1381." *The Economic History Review* 2, no. 2 (1931): 117-36.

Holladay, John S., Jr. "The Kingdoms of Israel and Judah: Political and Economic Centralization in the Iron IIA-B (ca. 1000-750 BCE)," Pages 368-98 in *The Archaeology of Society in the Holy Land*. Edited by Thomas E. Levy. London: Leicester University Press, 1998.

_____. "Assyrian Statecraft and the Prophets of Israel." *The Harvard Theological Review* 63, no. 1 (2002): 29-51.

Hopkins, A.G. "Globalization With and Without Empires: From Bali to Labrador," Pages 220-42 in *Globalization in World History*. Edited by A.G. Hopkins. London: Pimlico, 2002.

_____. "The History of Globalization – and the Globalization of History?," Pages 11-46 in *Globalization in World History*. Edited by A.G. Hopkins. London: Pimlico, 2002.

Hopkins, David C. "The Dynamics of Agriculture in Monarchical Israel," Pages 177-202 in *Society of Biblical Literature 1983 Seminar Papers*. Edited by Kent Harold Richards. Chico, California: Scholars Press, 1983.

_____. *The Highlands of Canaan: Agricultural Life in the Early Iron Age*. Edited by James W. Flanagan. The Social World of Biblical Antiquity 3. Sheffield: Almond, 1985.

_____. "Life on the Land: The Subsistence Struggles of Early Israel." *The Biblical Archaeologist* 50, no. 3 (1987): 178-91.

_____. "Bare Bones: Putting Flesh on the Economics of Ancient Israel," in *The Origins of the Ancient Israelite States*. Edited by David J.A. Clines, Philip R. Davies, and John Jarick. Journal for the Study of the Old Testament Supplement Series 228. Sheffield: Sheffield Academic Press, 1996.

Hopkins, Nicholas S. "The Small Urban Center in Rural Development: Kita (Mali) and Testour (Tunisia)." *Africa: Journal of the International African Institute* 49, no. 3 (1979): 316-28.

_____. "Tunisia: An Open and Shut Case." *Social Problems* 28, no. 4, Development Processes and Problems (1981): 385-93.

Hoppe, Leslie J., O.F.M., *There Shall Be No Poor Among You*. Nashville: Abingdon Press, 2004.

Houston, Walter J., *Contending for Justice: Ideologies and Theologies of Social Justice in the Old Testament*. London: T&T Clark, 2006.

Hudson, Michael. "The Dynamics of Privatization: From the Bronze Age to the Present," in *Privatization in the Ancient Near East and Classical World*. Edited by Michael Hudson and Baruch A. Levine. Cambridge, MA: Harvard University, 1996.

_____. "Private Landownership, Debt, and Fiscal Crisis in the Ancient Near East," Pages 139-69 in *Property in Economic Context*. Edited by Robert C. Hunt and Antonio Gilman. Monographs in Economic Anthropology 14. Oxford: University Press of America, 1998.

Hughes, J. Donald. "Sustainable Agriculture in Ancient Egypt." *History of Agriculture and the Environment* 66, no. 2 (1992): 12-22.

Humphries, Frederick S. "U.S. Small Farm Policy Scenarios for the Eighties." *American Journal of Agricultural Economics* 62, no. 5 (1980): 879-88.

Hurrell, Andrew. "Security and Inequality," Pages 248-71 in *Inequality, Globalization, and World Politics*. Edited by Andrew Hurrell and Ngaire Woods. Oxford: Oxford University Press, 1999.

IMF. *International Monetary Fund Homepage*. [cited March 5, 2010]. Available from
  http://www.imf.org/external/about.htm.

IMF, "Board of Governors. Articles of Agreement of the International Monetary Fund: Article XII, Section 5(a)" [cited March 7, 2009]. Available from
  http://www.imf.org/external/pubs/ft/aa/aa12.htm#5.

International Organization, The. "International Bank for Reconstruction and Development." *International Organization* 12, no. 3 (1958): 381-83.

Jamieson-Drake, David W., *Scribes and Schools in Monarchic Judah: A Socio-Archeological Approach*. Edited by David J.A. Clines and Philip R. Davies. Journal for the Study of the Old Testament Supplement Series 109. Sheffield: Almond Press, 1991.

Johnson, Allen. "The Psychology of Dependence Between Landlord and Sharecropper in Northeastern Brazil." *Political Psychology* 18, no. 2 (1997): 411-38.

Johnson, Allen W. and Timothy Earle, *The Evolution of Human Societies: From Foraging Group to Agrarian State.* 1st ed. Stanford: Stanford University Press, 1987.

_____. *The Evolution of Human Societies: From Foraging Group to Agrarian State.* 2d ed. Stanford: Stanford University Press, 2001.

Johnson, D.E., M.N. Ben Ali, and M.M. Borman. "Rangeland and Marginal Cereal Cropland in Central Tunisia." *Rangelands* 11, no. 5 (1989): 222-25.

Johnstone, William. "Old Testament Expressions in Property Holding." *Uraritica* 6 (1969): 308-17.

Jones, Linda G. "Portrait of Rashid al-Ghannoushi." *Middle East Report* 153, no. 19-22 (1988).

Jursa, Paul E. and James E. Winkates. "Tourism as a Mode of Development." *Issue: A Journal of Opinion* 4, no. 1 (1974): 45-49.

Kahler, Miles. "External Influence, Conditionality, and the Politics of Adjustment," Pages 89-136 in *The Politics of Economics Adjustment.* Edited by Stephan Haggard and Robert R. Kaufman. Princeton: Princeton University Press, 1992.

Kaiser, Otto, *Isaiah 1-12: A Commentary.* London: SCM Press LTD, 1972.

Kapur, Devish and John P. Lewis. "Governance-Related Conditionalities of the International Financial Institutions." *G-24 Discussion Paper Series* 6 (2000).

Karmon, Yehuda, *Israel: A Regional Geography.* London: Wiley-Interscience, 1971.

Katz, Hayah. "Commercial Activity in the Kingdoms of Judah and Israel." *Tel Aviv* 31, no. 2 (2004): 268-77.

Kautsky, John H., *The Politics of Aristocratic Empires.* New Brunswick: Transaction Publishers, 1997.

Kempner, Ken and Ana Loureiro Jurema. "The Global Politics of Education: Brazil and the World Bank." *Higher Education* 43, no. 3 (2002): 331-54.

King, Philip J., *Amos, Hosea, Micah: An Archaeological Commentary.* Philadelphia: The Westminster Press, 1988.

_____. "The Eighth, the Greatest of Centuries?." *Journal of Biblical Literature* 108, no. 1 (1989): 3-15.

King, Stephen J., *Liberalization Against Democracy: The Local Politics of Economic Reform in Tunisia.* Bloomington: Indiana University Press, 2003.

Kippenberg, Hans G., *Religion und Klassenbildung im antiken Judäa.* 2d ed. Göttingen: Vandenhoeck & Ruprecht, 1982.

Kissane, Edward J., *The Book of Isaiah: Translated from a Critically Revised Hebrew Text with Commentary.* Dublin: Browne and Nolan Limited, 1941.

Kletter, R., *Economic Keystones: The Weight System of the Kingdom of Judah.* Journal for the Study of the Old Testament Supplement Series 276. Sheffield: Continuum International Publishing Group, 1998.

Kleve, J.G. "The Control of Annual Plans: The Experience of Tunisia." *The Journal of Modern African Studies* 9, no. 2 (1971): 306-10.

Knapp, A. Bernard. "Copper Production and Eastern Mediterranean Trade: The Rise of Complex Society in Cyprus," Pages 149-72 in *Sate and Society: The Emergence and Development of Social Hierarchy and Political Centralization.* Edited by J. Gledhill, B. Bender, and M.T. Larsen. London: Unwin Hyman, 1988.

Köhler, Ludwig, *Hebrew Man.* Translated by Peter R. Ackroyd. London: SCM Press, 1956.

Kramer, Samuel Noah, *The Sumerians: Their History, Culture, and Character.* Chicago: The University of Chicago Press, 1963.

Kroeber, Alfred L., *Anthropology: Culture Patterns & Processes.* New York: Harcourt, Brace, & World, 1963.

Kuhn, Arthur K. "United Nations Monetary Conference and the Immunity of International Agencies." *The American Journal of International Law* 38, no. 4 (1944): 662-67.

Lang, Bernhard. "The Social Organization of Peasant Poverty in Biblical Israel," Pages 83-99 in *Anthropological Approaches to the Old Testament.* Edited by Bernhard Lang. London: Society for Promoting Christian Knowledge, 1985.

Larson, Barbara K. "Local-National Integration in Tunisia." *Middle Eastern Studies* 20, no. 1 (1984): 17-26.

Larson, Daniel O. "Population Growth, Agricultural Intensification, and Cultural Change among the Virgin Branch Anasazi, Nevada." *Journal of Field Archaeology* 23, no. 1 (1996): 55-76.

Lee, Richard B., *The !Kung San: Men, Women, and World in a Foraging Society.* Cambridge: Cambridge University Press, 1979.

Legros, Dominique. "Chance, Necessity, and Mode of Production: A Marxist Critique of Cultural Evolutionism." *American Anthropologist* 79, no. 1 (1977): 26-41.

Lemche, Niels Peter. "From Patronage Society to Patronage Society," Pages 106-20 in *The Origins of the Ancient Israelite States.* Edited by Volkmar Fritz and Philip R. Davies. Sheffield: Sheffield Academic Press, 1996.

Lenski, Gerhard E., *Power and Privilege: A Theory of Social Stratification.* New York: McGraw-Hill Book Company, 1966.

_____. Ecological-Evolutionary Theory: Principles and Applications. Boulder: Paradigm Publishers, 2005.

Lenski, Gerhard E., Jean Lenski, and Patrick Nolan, *Human Societies: An Introduction to Macrosociology.* 6th ed. New York: McGraw-Hill, 1991.

Lernau, Hanan and Omri Lernau. "Fish Remains," Pages 131-48 in *Excavations at the City of David 1978-1985.* Edited by A. de Groot and D.T. Ariel. Jerusalem: Institute of Archaeology, Hebrew University of Jerusalem, 1992.

Lerner, Daniel, *The Passing of Traditional Society.* Glencoe: The Free Press, 1958.

Levine, Baruch A. "Farewell to the Ancient Near East: Evaluating Biblical References of Ownership of Land in Comparative Perspective," Pages 223-52 in *Privatization in the Ancient Near East and Classical World.* Edited by Michael Hudson and Baruch A. Levine. Cambridge: Peabody Museum of Archaeology and Ethnology, 1996.

Liphschitz, Nili and Gideon Biger. "Cedar of Lebanon (Cedrus Libani) in Israel During Antiquity." *Israel Exploration Journal* 41 (1991): 167-75.

Liss, Julia E., W.E.B. Du Bois, and Franz Boas. "Diasporic Identities: The Science and Politics of Race in the Work of Franz Boas and W.E.B. DuBois, 1894-1919." *Cultural Anthropology* 13, no. 2 (1998): 127-66.

Liverani, Mario, *Israel's History and the History of Israel.* Translated by Chiara Peri and Philip Davies. BibleWorld. London: Equinox, 2007.

Lowie, Robert Harry, *Are We Civilized?* New York: Harcourt, Brace, and Company, 1929.

MacGibbon, D.A. "International Monetary Control." *The Canadian Journal of Economics and Political Science* 11, no. 1 (1945): 1-13.

Maine, Henry Sumner, *Ancient Law: Its Connection with Early History of Society and its Relation to Modern Ideas.* London: Murray, 1905.

Malamat, Abraham. "Mari and the Bible: Some Patterns of Tribal Organizations and Institutions." *Journal for the American Oriental Society*, no. 82 (1962): 143-50.

_____. "Mari." *The Biblical Archaeologist* 34, no. 1 (1971): 1-22.

Malina, Bruce J. "The Social Sciences and Biblical Interpretation," in *The Bible and Liberation: Political and Social Hermeneutics*. Edited by Norman K. Gottwald. Maryknoll, New York: Orbis Books, 1983.

Mamdani, Mahmood. "Uganda: Contradictions in the IMF Programme and Perspective," Pages 183-214 in *The IMF and the South: The Social Impact of Crisis and Adjustment*. Edited by Dharam Ghai. London: Zed Books Ltd., 1991.

Marshall, Judith. "Structural Adjustment and Social Policy in Mozambique." *Review of African Political Economy* 47 (1990): 28-43.

Martinez, Osvaldo. "Debt and Foreign Capital: The Origin of the Crisis." *Latin American Perspectives* 20, no. 1 (1993): 64-82.

Master, Daniel M. "Trade and Politics: Ashkelon's Balancing Act in the Seventh Century BCE." *Bulletin of the American Schools of Oriental Research*, no. 330 (2003): 47-64.

Matthews, Victor H. and Don C. Benjamin, *Old Testament Parallels: Laws and Stories from the Ancient Near East*. 2d ed. Mahwah, New Jersey: Paulist Press, 1997.

Mays, James Luther, *Micah: A Commentary*. London: SCM Press LTD, 1976.

McIntyre, Elizabeth. "Weighted Voting in International Organizations." *International Organization* 8, no. 4 (1954): 484-97.

McKay, Donald Vernon. "The French in Tunisia." *Geographical Review* 35, no. 3 (1945): 368-90.

McNutt, Paula, *Reconstructing the Society of Ancient Israel*. Library of Ancient Israel. Louisville: Westminster John Knox Press, 1999.

Mead, Margaret, *Continuities in Cultural Evolution*. New Haven: Yale University Press, 1964.

Meinis, Henk K. "Molluscs," Pages 122-30 in *Excavations at the City of David 1978-1985*. Edited by A. de Groot and D.T. Ariel. Jerusalem: Institute of Archaeology, Hebrew University of Jerusalem, 1992.

Mellars, Paul A. "The Ecological Basis of Social Complexity in the Upper Paleolithic of Southwestern France," Pages 271-97 in *Prehistoric Hunter-Gatherers: The Emergence of Cultural Complexity*.

Edited by Douglas T. Price and James A. Brown. London: Academic Press, 1985.

Meltzer Commission, *The Meltzer Report*. Washington D.C.: United States Congress, 1999.

Mendenhall, George E., *The Tenth Generation: The Origins of the Biblical Tradition*. Baltimore: Johns Hopkins University Press, 1973.

Micaud, Charles A. "Leadership and Development: The Case of Tunisia." *Comparative Politics* 1, no. 4 (1969): 468-484.

Miller, J. Maxwell. "Palestine During the Bronze Age," Pages 363-390 in *The Biblical World*. Edited by John Barton. New York: Routledge, 2002.

Miller, Robert. "Water Use in Syria and Palestine from the Neolithic to the Bronze Age." *World Archaeology* 11, no. 3 (1980): 331-41.

Mkandawire, Thandika. "Crisis and Adjustment in Sub-Saharan Africa," in *The IMF and the South: The Social Impact of Crisis and Adjustment*. Edited by Dharam Ghai. London: Zed Books Ltd on Behalf of The United Nations Research Institute for Social Development, 1991.

Modelski, George. "World System Evolution," Pages 24-53 in *World System History: The Social Science of Long-Term Change*. Edited by R.A. Denemark, J. Friedman, B.K. Gills, and G. Moldeski. London: Routledge, 2000.

Modelski, George and William R. Thompson, *Leading Sectors and World Powers: The Coevolution of Global Politics and Economics*. Columbia, SC: University of South Carolina Press, 1996.

Mohammed, Aziz Ali. "Who Pays for the IMF?," Pages 37-53 in *Challenges to the World Bank and IMF: Developing Country Perspectives*. Edited by Ariel Buira. London: Anthem Press, 2003.

Moore, Clement Henry. "The Neo-Destour Party of Tunisia: A Structure for Democracy?" *World Politics* 14, no. 3 (1962): 461-82.

Morales, Edmundo. "Coca and Cocaine Economy and Social Change in the Andes of Peru." *Economic Development and Cultural Change* 35, no. 1 (1986): 143-61.

Moran, William. "The Conclusion of the Decalogue: Ex 20:17-Dt 5:21." *Catholic Biblical Quarterly* 29, no. 4 (1967): 543-54.

Morgan, Lewis Henry, *Ancient Society: Or, Researches in the Lines of Human Progress from Savagery through Barbarism to Civilization*. New York: H. Holt and Company, 1907.

Mosley, Paul, Jane Harrigan, and John Toye, *Aid and Power: The World Bank & Policy-Based Lending*. 2 Aid and Power 2. London: Routledge, 1991.

Murphy, Robert F. "Basin Ethnography and Ecological Theory," in *Languages and Cultures of Western North America*. Edited by E.H. Swanson. Pocatello: Idaho State University Press, 1970.

Na'aman, Nadav. "Population Changes in Palestine Following Assyrian Deportations." *Tel Aviv* 20 (1993): 104-24.

_____. "The Abandonment of Cult Places in the Kingdoms of Israel and Judah as Acts of Cult Reform." *Ugarit Forschungen* 34 (2002): 585-602.

_____. "The Distribution of Messages in the Kingdom of Judah in Light of the Lachish Ostraca." *Vetus Testamentum* 53, no. 2 (2003): 169-80.

_____. "Ekron Under the Assyrian and Egyptian Empires." *Bulletin of the American Schools of Oriental Research*, no. 332 (2003): 81-91.

Neale, Walter C. "Reciprocity and Redistribution in the Indian Village: Sequel to Some Notable Discussions," Pages 218-36 in *Trade and Market in the Early Empires*. Edited by Conrad M. Arensberg Karl Polanyi, Harry W. Pearson. Chicago: Henry Regnery Company, 1957.

Negueruela, I., J. Pinedo, M. Gómez, A. Miñano, I. Arellano, and J.S. Barba. "Seventh-century BC Phoenician Vessel Discovered at Playa de la Isla, Mazarron, Spain." *The International Journal of Nautical Archaeology* 24, no. 3 (1995): 189-97.

Netting, Robert McC., *Hill Farmers of Nigeria: Cultural Ecology of the Kofyar of the Jos Plateau*. Seattle: University of Washington Press, 1968.

_____. *Cultural Ecology*. Menlo Park, CA: Cummings, 1977.

New York City, Department of City Planning. *New York City Department of City Planning*. New York City Department of City Planning, Last Updated Date 2007 [cited February 24, 2010]. Available from http://www.nyc.gov/html/dcp/html/census/popdiv.shtml.

New York Times, The. "France Suspends Aid to Tunis, Retaliating on Seizure of Land." *The New York Times*, 13 May 1964.

_____. The. "Tunisian Harvests Cut by Seizures." *The New York Times*, July 26 1964.

_____. The. "World Bank Loans of $81.1-Million to 3 Nations." *The New York Times*, June 14 1974.

Nicolaï, André. "Approche structurelle et effet de domination Une application: la Tunisie." *Revue économique* 7, no. 5 (1956): 738-76.

Niemann, Hermann Michael. "Royal Samaria: Capital or Residence? or: The Fondation of the City of Samaria by Sargon II," Pages 184-207 in *Ahab Agonistes: The Rise and Fall of the Omri Dynasty.* Edited by Lester L. Grabbe. London: T&T Clark International, 2007.

Nolan, Patrick and Gerhard Lenski, *Human Societies: An Introduction to Macrosociology.* 9th ed. Boulder: Paradigm Publishers, 2004.

O'Brian, Patrick Karl. "Colonies in a Globalizing Economy, 1815-1948," Pages 248-91 in *Globalization and Global History.* Edited by Barry K. Gills and William R. Thompson of *Rethinking* Edited by Barry K. Gills. London: Routledge, 2006.

Ofer, Avi. "The Monarchic Period in the Judean Highland: A Spatial Overview," Pages 14-37 in *Studies in the Archaeology of the Iron Age in Israel and Jordan.* Edited by Amihai Mazar. Sheffield: Sheffield Academic Press, 2001.

Officer, Lawrence H. "The International Monetary Fund." Proceedings of the Academy of Political Science: International Trade: The Changing Role of the United States 37, no. 4 (1990): 28-36.

Ohmae, Kenichi, *The End of the Nation State: The Rise of Regional Economies.* London: HarperCollins, 1996.

Olson, Mancur, *The Logic of Collective Action: Public Goods and the Theory of Groups.* Cambridge, Mass: Harvard University Press, 1965.

Oppenheim, A.L. "Babylonian and Assyrian Historical Texts," Pages 265-317 in *Ancient Near Eastern Texts Relating to the Old Testament.* Edited by J.B. Pritchard. Princeton: Princeton University Press, 1969.

Osieke, Ebere. "Majority Voting Systems in the International Labour Organization and the International Monetary Fund." *The International and Comparative Law Quarterly* 33, no. 2 (1984): 381-408.

Ostle, R.C. "Mahmud al-Mas'adi and Tunisia's 'Lost Generation.'" *Journal of Arabic Literature* 8 (1977): 153-66.

_____. "The Romantic Revolution?." *Journal of Arabic Literature* 26, no. 1/2 (1995): 93-104.

Overholt, Thomas W. "Prophecy: The Problem of Cross-Cultural Comparison," Pages 55-78 in *Anthropological Perspective on Old Testament Prophecy*. Edited by Robert C. Culley and Thomas W. Overholt. Chico, CA: Society of Biblical Literature, 1982.

Özerdem, Alpaslan. "Disarmament, Demobilisation, and Reintegration of Former Combatants in Afghanistan: Lessons Learned from a Cross-Cultural Perspective." *Third World Quarterly* 23, no. 5 (2002): 961-75.

Parkinson, F. "The International Monetary Fund in Economic Development: Equality and Discrimination." *Journal of African Law* 26, no. 1 (1982): 21-48.

Parsons, Kenneth H. "The Tunisian Program for Cooperative Farming." *Land Economics* 41, no. 4 (1965): 303-16.

Pastor, Manuel, Jr. and Gary Dymski. "Debt Crisis and Class Conflict in Latin America." *Review of Radical Political Economics* 22, no. 1 (1990): 155-78.

Pastor, Manuel, Jr. and Carol Wise. "State Policy, Distribution and Neoliberal Reform in Mexico." *Journal of Latin American Studies* 29, no. 2 (1997): 419-56.

Payer, Cheryl, *The World Bank: A Critical Analysis*. New York: Monthly Review Press, 1982.

Payne, Rhys. "Economic Crisis and Policy Reform in the 1980s," in *Polity and Society in Contemporary North Africa*. Edited by I. William Zartman and William Mark Habeeb. Boulder: Westview, 1993.

Pérez, Carlos Andrés. "Letter to Michel Camdessus." *IMF Survey*, (1989): 82-83.

Petersen, David L., *The Prophetic Literature: An Introduction*. Louisville, KY: Westminster John Knox Press, 1989.

Petras, James and Howard Brill. "The IMF, Austerity and the State in Latin America." *Third World Quarterly* 8, no. 2 (1986): 425-48.

Pfeiffer, Karen. "How Tunisia, Morocco, Jordan and Even Egypt Became IMF 'Success Stories' in the 1990s." *Middle East Report*, no. 210 (1999): 23-27.

Plattner, Stuart. "Introduction," Pages 1-20 in *Economic Anthropology*. Edited by Stuart Plattner. Stanford: Stanford University Press, 2002.

_____. "Markets and Marketplaces," Pages 171-208 in *Economic Anthropology*. Edited by Stuart Plattner. Stanford: Stanford University Press, 2002.

Polanyi, Karl. "The Economy as an Instituted Process," Pages 243-70 in *Trade & Market in the Early Empires*. Edited by Conrad M. Arensberg Polanyi, Harry W. Pearson. Chicago: Henery Regnery Company, 1957.

_____. "The Economy as Instituted Process," Pages 122-43 in *Economic Anthropology: Reading in Theory and Analysis*. Edited by Edward E LeClair and Harold K. Schneider. New York: Holt, Rinehart, and Winston, INC., 1968.

_____. *The Livelihood of Man*. Edited by Harry W. Pearson. Studies in Social Discontinuity. London: Academic Press, 1977.

Pomeranz, Kenneth, *The Great Divergence: Europe, China, and the Making of the Modern World Economy*. The Princeton Economic History of the Western World. Princeton: Princeton University Press, 2000.

Postgate, J.N. ed. *Neo-Assyrian Royal Grants and Degrees*. Scientificae de Rebus Orientis Antiqui; Rome: Pontifical Biblical Institute, 1969.

Powers, David S. "Orientalism, Colonialism, and Legal History." *Comparative Studies in Society and History* 31, no. 3 (1989): 535-71.

Premnath, D.N. "Latifundialization in Isaiah 5.8–10," Pages 301-12 in *Social-Scientific Old Testament Criticism*. Edited by David J. Chalcraft. Sheffield: Sheffield Academic Press, 1997.

_____. *Eighth Century Prophets: A Social Analysis*. St. Louis: Chalice, 2003.

_____. "Loan Practices in the Hebrew Bible," Pages 173-85 in *To Break Every Yoke: Essays in Honour of Marvin L. Chaney*. Edited by Robert B. Coote and Norman K. Gottwald. Sheffield: Sheffield Phoenix Press, 2007.

Pritchard, J.B., *Ancient Near Eastern Texts Relating to the Old Testament*. Edited by J.B. Pritchard. 3d ed. Princeton: Princeton University Press, 1969.

Purves, Pierre M. "Commentary on Nuzi Real Property in the Light of Recent Studies." *Journal of Near Eastern Studies* 4, no. 2 (1945): 68-86.

Radwan, Samir, Vali Jamal, and Ajit Ghose, *Tunisia: Rural Labour and Structural Transformation*. London: Routledge, 1991.

Rappaport, Roy A., *Pigs for the Ancestors*. New Haven: Yale University Press, 1967.

_____. "The Sacred in Human Evolution." *Annual Review of Ecology and Systematics* 2 (1971): 23-44.

Redclift, Michael and Colin Sage. "Resources, Environmental Degradation, and Inequality," Pages 122-49 in *Inequality, Globalization, and World Politics*. Edited by Andrew Hurrell and Ngaire Woods. Oxford: Oxford University Press, 1999.

Rennstich, Joachim Karl. "Three Steps in Globalization: Global Networks from 1000 BCE to 2050 CE," Pages 203-31 in *Globalization and Global History*. Edited by Barry K. Gills and William R. Thompson. Rethinking Globalizations 2. London: Routledge, 2006.

Richard, Suzanne. "Toward a Consensus of Opinion on the End of the Early Bronze Age in Palestine-Transjordan." *Bulletin of the American Schools of Oriental Research*, no. 237 (1980): 5-34.

_____. "The Early Bonze Age: The Rise and Collapse of Urbanism." *The Biblical Archaeologist* 50, no. 1 (1987): 22-43.

Richards, Paul. "Local Strategies for Coping with Hunger: Central Sierra Leone and Northern Nigeria Compared." *African Affairs* 89, no. 355 (1990): 265-75.

Rodríguez-Garavito, César A. and Luis Carlos Arenas. "Indigenous Rights, Transnational Activism, and Legal Mobilization: The Struggle of the U'wa People in Columbia," Pages 241-66 in *Law and Globalization from Below*. Edited by Boaventura de Sousa Santos and César A. Rodriguez-Garavito. Cambridge: Cambridge University Press, 2005.

Rogerson, John and Philip R. Davies. "Was the Siloam Tunnel Built by Hezekiah?." *The Biblical Archaeologist* 59, no. 3 (1996): 138-49.

Roussier, Jules. "L'application du chra' au Maghrib en 1959." *Die Welt des Islams*, New Ser. 6, no. 1/2 (1959): 25-55.

Rudebeck, Lars. "Developmental Pressure and Political Limits: A Tunisian Example." *The Journal of Modern African Studies* 8, no. 2 (1970): 173-98.

Sahlins, Marshall David, *Stone Age Economics*. Chicago: Aldine-Atherton, 1972.

Sanabria, Harry. "Consolidating States, Restructuring Economies, and Confronting Workers and Peasants: The Antinomies of

Bolivian Neoliberalism." *Comparative Studies in Society and History* 41, no. 3 (1999): 535-62.

Sanderson, Stephen K., *The Evolution of Human Sociality: A Darwinian Conflict Perspective.* Lanham, Maryland: Rowman & Littlefield Publishers, 2001.

Saoud, R. *The Impact of Islam on Urban Development in North Africa.* Foundation for Science Technology and Civilization, Last Updated Date 2004 [cited March 4, 2010. Available from http://www.muslimheritage.com/uploads/naurban.pdf.

Schloen, J. David, *The House of the Father as Fact and Symbol: Patrimonialism in Ugarit and the Ancient Near East.* Edited by J. David Schloen. Studies in the Archaeology and History of the Levant 2. Winona Lake, IN: Eisenbrauns, 2001.

Schvarzer, Jorge. "Economic Crisis and the Commonwealth Caribbean: Impact and Response," Pages 43-68 in *The IMF and the South: The Social Impact of Crisis and Adjustment.* Edited by Dharam Ghai. London: Zed Books Ltd on Behalf of The United Nations Research Institute for Social Development, 1991.

Sherratt, Susan and Andrew Sherratt. "The Growth of the Mediterranean Economy in the Early First Millennium BC." *World Archaeology* 24, no. 3 (1993): 361-78.

Sherratt, Susan. "'Sea Peoples' and the Economic Structure of the Late Second Millennium in teh Eastern Mediterranean," Pages 292-313 in *Mediterranean Peoples in Transition: Thirteenth to Early Tenth Centuries BCE.* Edited by Seymour Gitin, Amihai Mazar, and Ernest Stern. Jerusalem: Israel Exploration Society, 1998.

Shiloh, Yigal, *Excavations at the City of David.* 19, Qedem. Jerusalem: Institute of Archaeology, Hebrew University of Jerusalem, 1984.

Shils, Edward. "Political Development in the New States." *Comparative Studies in Society and History* 2, no. 3 (1960): 265-92.

Silver, Morris, *Prophets and Markets: The Political Economy of Ancient Israel.* Boston: Klwer-Nijhoff Publishing, 1983.

Skogly, Sigrun I. "Structural Adjustment and Development: Human Rights – An Agenda for Change." *Human Rights Quarterly* 15, no. 4 (1993): 751-78.

Smith, Ralph L., *Micah–Malachi.* Edited by David A. Hubbard, Glenn W. Barker, John D.W. Watts, and Ralph P. Martin. Word Biblical Commentary 32. Waco: Word Books, 1984.

Smithies, Arthur. "The International Bank For Reconstruction and Development." *The American Economic Review* 43, no. 4 (1944): 785-97.

Sombart, Werner, *A History of the Economic Institutions of Modern Europe.* New York: F.S. Crofts and Co., 1933.

Sparks, Kenton L., *Ancient Texts for the Study of the Hebrew Bible: A Guide to the Background Literature.* Peabody: Hendrickson Publishers, 2005.

Stager, Lawrence E. "The Periodization of Palestine from Neolithic through Early Bronze Times," Pages 22-41 in *Chronologies in Old World Archaeology.* Edited by R. Ehrich. Chicago: University of Chicago, 1992.

_____. "Ashkelon and the Archaeology of Destruction: Kislev 604 BCE." *Eretz-Israel* 25 (Joseph Aviram Volume), no. 61*-74* (1996).

Stallings, Barbara. "International Influence on Economic Policy: Debt, Stabilization, and Structural Reform," Pages 41-88 in *The Politics of Economic Adjustment.* Edited by Stephen Haggard and Robert R. Kaufman. Princeton: Princeton University Press, 1992.

Stern, Ephraim, *Archaeology of the Land of the Bible.* The Assyrian, Babylonian, and Persian Periods 2. New York: Random House, 2001.

Stern, Ernest H. "The Agreements of Bretton Woods." *Economica, New Series* 11, no. 44 (1944): 165-79.

Stevens, Marty E., *Temples, Tithes, and Taxes: The Temple and the Economic Life of Ancient Israel.* Peabody, Massachusetts: Hendrickson Publishing, 2006.

Steward, Julian H., *Theory of Culture Change: The Methodology of Multilinear Evolution.* London: University of Illinois Press, 1955.

_____. "Problems of Cultural Evolution." *Evolution* 12, no. 2 (1958): 206-10.

Strange, Susan, *The Retreat of the State: The Diffusion of Power in the World Economy.* Cambridge, 1996.

Tadmore, Hayim, *The Inscriptions of Tiglath-Pileser III, King of Assyria.* Jerusalem: Israel Academy of Sciences and Humanities, 1994.

Thompson, Carol B. "Regional Economic Policy Under Crisis Conditions: The Case of Agriculture within SADCC." *Journal of Southern African Studies* 13, no. 1 (1986): 82-100.

Thurow, Lester C., *The Future of Capitalism: How Today's Economic Forces Shape Tomorrow's World*. New York: William Morrow and Company, Inc., 1996.

Tozy, Mohammed. "Islam and the State," Pages 102-22 in *Polity and Society in Contemporary North Africa*. Boulder: Westview Press, 1993.

Türk, Danilo. *The Realization of Economic, Social, and Cultural Rights*. United Nations, Last Updated Date 1992 [cited March 2, 2010]. Available from http://www.unhchr.ch/huridocda/huridoca.nsf/(Symbol)/E.CN.4.SUB.2.1992.16.En?Opendocument.

Tuteja, K. L. "Jallianwala Bagh: A Critical Juncture in the Indian National Movement." *Social Scientist* 25, no. 1/2 (1997): 25-61.

United Nations, The. "Organization, Food and Agriculture," in *World Food Report*. Rome: United Nations, 1984.

United Nations Children's Fund, The, *The State of the World's Children*. New York: Oxford University Press, 1989.

van Seters, John, *In Search of History: Historiography in the Ancient World*. New Haven: Yale University Press, 1983.

von Rad, Gerhard, *Old Testament Theology*. Edited by James L. Mays, Carol A. Newsom, and David L. Petersen. Translated by D.M.G. Stalker. 2 vols. Vol. 2. Louisville: Westminster John Knox Press, 1962.

Vreeland, James Raymond. "Why Do Governments and the IMF Enter Into Agreements? Statistically Selected Cases." *International Political Science Review* 24, no. 3 (2003): 321-43.

Walton, John. "Urban Protest and the Global Political Economy: The IMF Riots," in *The Capitalist City*. Edited by Michael Peter Smith and Joe R. Feagin. Oxford: Basil Blackwell, 1987.

Waltz, Susan E. "Antidotes for Social Malaise: Alienation, Efficacy, and Participation in Tunisia." *Comparative Politics* 14, no. 2 (1982): 127-47.

Ward, William A. "Early Contacts Between Egypt, Canaan, and Sinai: Remarks on the Paper by Amon Ben-Tor." *Bulletin of the American Schools of Oriental Research*, no. 281 (1991): 11-26.

Weber, Max, *Ancient Judaism*. Translated by Hans H. Gerth and Don Martindale. London: The Free Press, 1952.

_____. *The Theory of Social and Economic Organization*. Edited by Talcott Parsons. Translated by A.M. Henderson and Talcott Parsons. New York: The Free Press and Collier Macmillian Publishers, 1964.

White, Leslie A., *The Evolution of Culture: The Development of Civilization to the Fall of Rome*. New York: McGraw-Hill, 1959.

Whitelam, Keith W., *The Invention of Ancient Israel: The Silencing of Palestinian History*. London: Routledge, 2001.

_____. "Constructing Jerusalem," in *Flowing with Milk and Honey: Visions of Israel from Biblical to Modern Times*. Edited by Leonard J. Greenspoon and Ronald A. Simkins. Durham, North Carolina: Duke University Press, 2002.

Wildberger, Hans, *Isaiah: A Commentary*. Edited by. Translated by Thomas H. Trapp. 3 vols. Vol. 1, Continental Commentaries. Minneapolis: Fortress Press, 1991.

Williamson, John. "On Seeking to Improve IMF Conditionality." *The American Economic Review* 73, no. 2 (1983): 354-58.

Woods, Ngaire. "The Challenge to International Institutions," Pages 202-20 in *The Political Economy of Globalization*. Edited by Ngaire Woods. New York: St. Martin's Press, 2000.

World Bank, The, *Report and Recommendation of the President of the International Bank for Reconstruction and Development to the Executive Directors on a Proposed Loan in an Amount Equivalent to U.S. $150.0 Million to the Republic of Tunisia for an Agricultural Sector Adjustment Loan*. Washington D.C.: World Bank, 1986.

_____. *Republic of Tunisia, Agricultural Sector Adjustment Loan: Medium-Term Agricultural Sector Adjustment Program*. Washington, D.C.: World Bank, 1986.

_____. *World Development Report 1988*. [cited March 2, 2010]. Available from http://econ.worldbank.org/external/default/main?pagePK=64165259&theSitePK=469372&piPK=64165421&menuPK=64166322&entityID=000178830_98101912131965.

Wright, Robert, *The Moral Animal: Evolutionary Psychology and Everyday Life*. London: Abacus, 1996.

Yaron, Reuven. "Social Problems and Policies in the Ancient Near East," Pages 19-41 in *Law, Politics, and Society in the Ancient Mediterranean World*. Edited by Baruch Halpern and Deborah W. Hobson. Sheffield: Sheffield Academic Press, 1993.

Younker, Randall W. "The Iron Age in the Southern Levant," Pages 367-82 in *Near Eastern Archaeology: A Reader*. Edited by Suzanne Richard. Winona Lake, IN: Eisenbrauns, 2003.

Zaccagnini, Carlo. "The Price of Fields at Nuzi." *Journal of the Economic and Social History of the Orient* 22, no. 1 (1979): 1-32.

Zaibet, Lokman T. and Elizabeth G. Dunn. "Land Tenure, Farm Size, and Rural Market Participation in Developing Countries: The Case of the Tunisian Olive Sector." *Economic Development and Cultural Change* 46, no. 4 (1998): 831-48.

Ziadeh, Nicola A., *Origins of Nationalism in Tunisia.* Beirut: Librarie du Liban, 1969.

INDEX

Made in United States
North Haven, CT
21 September 2022

24384561R00221